The Five Stages
of the Soul

Charting the
Spiritual Passages That
Shape Our Lives

Harry R. Moody, Ph.D.
and David L. Carroll

The Five Stages of the Soul

ANCHOR BOOKS

A Division of Random House, Inc.

New York

First Anchor Books Trade Paperback Edition, August 1998

Copyright © 1997 by Harry R. Moody, Ph.D., and David L. Carroll

*Note: In some cases characters in this book are composites drawn from
interviews and classroom experiences with several individuals. Names were
changed, when requested, to protect confidentiality.*

The Library of Congress has cataloged the Anchor hardcover
edition of this book as follows:
Moody, Harry R.
    The five stages of the soul : charting the spiritual passages that
shape our lives / Harry R. Moody with David Carroll. — 1st Anchor
Books ed.
        p.   cm.
Includes bibliographical references.
1. Spiritual life.   2. Moody, Harry R.   I. Carroll, David, 1942–
II. Title.
BL624.M6623   1997
291.4'4—dc21   97-2070
                                                               CIP

ISBN: 0-385-48677-4

www.anchorbooks.com

Printed in the United States of America

12   11   10   9   8   7   6

Acknowledgments

The foremost acknowledgment here is to one person and one person above all: to David L. Carroll, my co-author, who helped find the words and the voice to tell the story of the five stages of the soul in these pages. A word like "collaboration" cannot begin to describe the mysterious process whereby two minds become one, nor does the word gratitude begin to express my feelings to David.

I want to thank those who read parts of the manuscript in progress: Bob Atchley; Hannah Carroll; Joe and Jaird deRaismes; David S. Hobler; Marilyn Howard; Esther and Patrick Quinlan; Andy and Melanie Rock; and most of all to my wife, Elizabeth.

This book would not have been possible without the early and continuing confidence of Madeleine Morel and Barbara Lowenstein of Lowenstein-Morel Associates. Special thanks also go to Roger Scholl, editor at Doubleday, whose helpful suggestions, insightful criticisms, and tireless support were invaluable for making a better book. Thanks, too, to Monsignor Charles Fahey, former director of the Third Age Center at Fordham University.

I owe an enormous debt to those who have been so supportive to me over many years: above all, to Rose Dobrof, Brookdale Professor of Gerontology at Hunter College and Founder of the Brookdale Center on Aging, as well as to key staff at the Brookdale Center, especially Sam Sadin, Pat Gilberto, and Mollie Muller. The Brookdale Foundation has supported the work of the Brookdale Center at Hunter for more than two decades, and I remain profoundly grateful for their generosity.

I have learned so much from colleagues with whom I have worked over many years on humanistic aspects of lifespan development, including Dr. Robert Kastenbaum; Dr. Robert Butler; Dr. Allen Chinen; Marc Kaminsky and the late Barbara Myerhoff; Dr. Seyyed Abdullah; Mel Kimble; Eugene Thomas; Robert Disch; and my friend Ronald Manheimer, with whom I taught philosophical autobiography many years ago. Two other companions on the journey deserve special note: Andy Achenbaum and Thomas Cole, my co-editor of the "Aging and the Human Spirit" newsletter.

There are many others who have contributed directly or indirectly to the evolution of this book, including Ram Dass; Rabbi Zalman Schachter; Ali Rodell; Brynn and Jesse Shutter; Dr. Jon Dudley Dorman; Tom and Andrea Boggs; Betsy Davis; Bryanne Nanfito; Ken Stuart; Jon Carroll; Dan Collier; Dr. Robert Solod; Layla Carroll; Charles and Vivian Campbell; Lydia Bronte; Eric Levesque; Mark Endelman; Louise and Dr. William Welch; the Rev. William Teska and Gregory Johnson, companions on my trip to Mount Athos; Brother Forbis and Brother Robert of Holy Cross Monastery; and the late Lawrence Morris, who taught me so much about the meaning of age and about why the last years may matter most. I am grateful to friend and journalist Connie Goldman for permission to reprint parts of an interview with my friend Carol Segrave; and to Hugh Downs, long-time board member of the Brookdale Center on Aging.

This book owes a great deal to countless students, seminar participants, interviewees, friends, and colleagues whom space does not allow to name directly in these acknowledgments. In particular I am grateful to those enrolled in my midlife workshops at the Brookdale Center and the Omega Institute. I thank Gloria Cavanaugh of the American Society on Aging for sponsoring workshops on "Conscious Aging" and the search for meaning in the second half of life. I have long appreciated the support of the national Elderhostel organization, above all its president, William Berkeley; senior vice president, Michael Zoob; program director, Judy Goggin; and Dan Dowd, New York State Elderhostel coordinator.

Research assistance in preparing this book was provided by Fatimah Johnson of Swarthmore; the staff of the Hunter College library; the C. G. Jung Foundation Library of New York; and the Palisades, New York, library.

Finally, thanks to Maryam and Habib for their patience.

—*Harry R. Moody*

Contents

part one

The Call
and the Search

We are shaken by secret shudders and dark forebodings; but we know no way out, and very few persons indeed draw the conclusion that this time the issue is the long-since-forgotten soul of man.

CARL JUNG

chapter 1

Stages of the Soul

In everyone's heart stirs a great homesickness.

RABBI SEYMOUR SIEGEL

But the Unnameable was not in the wind. And after the wind, an
earthquake; but the Unnameable was not in the earthquake. And
after the earthquake, a fire; but the Unnameable was not in the fire.
And after the fire, a still, small voice.

I KINGS 19:11–12

THAT LITTLE VOICE AGAIN

Standing at the Crossroads

"Time is running out," the little voice whispers.

It's a sunny July morning on vacation. Or maybe midafternoon on a
lazy weekend. Everyone is out of the house. There are no calls to return, no
people to see. The day is yours.

You pick up that novel you've been dying to read. But soon you put it
down again—reading makes you restless. So you try going for a walk, but
that's not satisfying either. Something is eating at you inside, and none of the
usual diversions seem to help.

Back in the living room, the view out the window is the same as it was yesterday, and the day before. You chat with a friend on the phone for a few minutes and this passes the time. But when you hang up there's the silence again.

There's nothing wrong, really. Nothing's pressing. You look forward to these moments of peace and quiet all year long. Why then is it so difficult to let go and enjoy?

Finally you realize what's troubling you. It's that little voice again, the one that keeps piping up during the silences and raising the same litany of disturbing questions.

"Is this all there is?" it asks. "This home? This mate? This job? This life?"

"Time is running out," it whispers. "A portion of my life is already over. Shouldn't things be better? Or at least *different?*"

But better than what? Different from what?

We're not sure. All we know is that one morning each of us, rich or poor, successful or not so successful, wakes up in the midst of life to find ourself in the same troubling place: the woman who always wanted a baby but one day finds herself past childbearing age; the doting parents whose children have all grown up and left the nest; the set-the-world-on-fire career-ist trapped in a no-exit job—or no job at all; the suddenly graying wunderkinds who always thought themselves "younger than others"; the wildly successful professionals who've made a small fortune, but who can't seem to enjoy their success; the artists and writers and poets whose youthful hopes lie buried beneath a pile of rejection slips; the tired lovers and par-amours, the twice-married and thrice-married, all coming to suspect that romantic relationships are not, after all, the best way to fill that deep, lonely place in the heart.

Many of us, it turns out, in one way or another come to this same sober realization, that life does not seem to be giving us what we want. But what it *is* we really want, we can't exactly say.

There's one thing we do know for sure, however: this little voice has a way of provoking rebellious thoughts.

Wasn't life supposed to get better and better as the years pass? we ask. Didn't I do what I was supposed to: go to school, join the team, work hard, pay my dues?

Now we're thirty-four years old. Or forty-four years old. Or fifty-nine. And the years have given us neither the pleasures we assumed we'd get nor the big payoffs we always dreamed about. Rewards and laurels may come from time to time, it's true, but the happiness they bring doesn't last very long. There are the peak moments, of course, and the stretches of sunshine. But why do they always seem overshadowed by the gnawing sense of un-fulfillment, the sameness of days? George Orwell said it as well as anyone: "Most people get a fair amount of fun out of their lives, but on balance life is suffering and only the very young or the very foolish imagine otherwise."

"I have reigned more than fifty years in victory and peace," the great caliph Abdul Rahim once remarked. "During this time I have been beloved by my people, dreaded by my enemies, and respected by my allies. Riches and honors, power and pleasure have all been at my beck and call, nor has any earthly pleasure been missing to complete my sense of perfect bliss. In this situation I have diligently numbered the days of pure and genuine happiness that have fallen to my lot. They number fourteen."

And so here we stand, together at the crossroads in the midst of life with the artists, wunderkinds, and kings, gazing Janus-like forward and back, trying to figure out what the rest of our days on earth will bring. Trying to formulate a strategy. Trying to discover where the gold of happiness and fulfillment lies hidden. Trying to find out if there really *is* any gold.

And then that little voice comes again: *Time is running out. Is this really all there is?*

Escape Routes to Nowhere

"It's like we're all passengers on the same big boat," a thirty-eight-year-old English teacher said to me recently at a workshop on midlife. "The boat is heading upriver, following its own unfathomable course. When I was younger I thought I was steering the ship. You know: captain of my soul, master of my fate, that sort of heroic thing. Now I know I'm just another passenger. And what's more scary, I realize I have a lot less control over where the boat's heading than I thought I did. It's even starting to look as if one day the whole crew of us is going to, well, God knows what. Sail off the end of the earth. Or just quietly sink."

I thought of a remark made once by the Zen master Suzuki Roshi: life, he said, is like setting sail on a boat that we all know is someday going to sink.

Such thoughts are troubling. But what can we do except live as fully as possible, and enjoy the things we've been told will make us happy?

So we have a love affair. We buy a new car—or at least a new dress. We look for a better job, or work harder at the one we have. ("Work is less boring than pleasure," remarked Baudelaire.) We visit the gym. We monitor our diet. We rent videos. On Sundays we peruse the travel section of the paper, looking for an escape that will whisk us away from this stale reality and make us feel like we're really alive. Or knowing that it can never be so, we use drugs and alcohol to fill the void.

Yet no matter what diversions we turn to, that little voice keeps returning. *"Is this it?"* it asks again and again. *"This home, this job, this life?"*

"And if it is, why do I feel so unfulfilled at a time in life when I'm supposed to be enjoying the greatest rewards? If these are the best years of my life, why do I feel so empty?"

Charting the Stages of Life

When I was a child, I was certain that I would live to be at least a hundred years old. Probably two hundred. Other people died in their seventies and eighties, I knew. But I would be the exception.

For hours at a time I stared at photographs of exotic tribe dwellers in *Life* magazine and *National Geographic,* noting the older faces in particular: the Hopi Indian great-grandmother with a full-sized sheep over her shoulders and a great-grandchild under her arm; the Tibetan monk reputed to be a hundred and ten years old with his kind, almost supernaturally detached eyes sparkling into mine; the Caucasian farmers with their hands wrinkled into parchment and their bushy Stalin mustaches only a touch grayed. I read how these gnarled children of time played volleyball when they were a hundred and six and spawned healthy children at ninety-three. And about the hundred and fourteen-year-old French laborer who informed an interviewer through a cloud of cigar smoke that the secret of reaching a ripe old age was "cognac, hard work, and love of Jesus."

What seemed most intriguing about these images was the process of aging itself. What made it happen? How did it work? Why is it that our minds and bodies change so much during a lifetime, but something in us remains essentially ourselves? And why do we get old and die in the first place?

These cosmic puzzlements, which even as a child seemed to me to be at the heart of the matter, were, I soon discovered, questions that were hastily passed over in the social sciences.

Later, as an adult, I learned that the study of the human life course had attracted a great deal of attention in the intervening years and that it had now come into its own as a field of psychological study. By the late 1970s, Professor Daniel Levinson had worked out his soon to be famous theory of adult life span transitions, an idea that was later popularized by Gail Sheehy's account of "passages." Levinson's theory claimed that psychological change occurs according to a schedule of chronological phases and "trigger points"—the early adult phase, the adult phase, midlife transition, the middle adult years—that are common in all our lives. Following Levinson's work, a large body of professional and popular literature poured forth.

And yet, the notion of passages was not a new one. The image of age-related milestones can be traced back to antiquity, where doctors in ancient Greece were already staging the phases of physical growth and human disease. In our own era, the practice of dividing life into discrete juncture points evolved principally through the study of child development.

In the mid-1940s, for example, Dr. Benjamin Spock navigated a generation of Americans through the voyage of parenthood by suggesting that children mature via a series of predictable and age-related psychobiological periods. Drawing on a pioneering body of developmental research by Piaget, and taking a lead from Freud, Dr. Spock informed the world that these periods are programmed into the developmental calendar of all children. While each child acts them out in different ways, he maintained, every child passes through them.

Carrying the notion of stages several steps further in the next decade, Harvard professor Erik Erikson argued that the formation of personality does not halt abruptly at the end of childhood or adolescence, as Freud believed, but that human beings continue to evolve psychologically throughout the course of their lives. Erikson maintained that this evolution takes place in a series of age-related stages that follow one another in a predictable progression through infancy, youth, midlife, and old age. All of these stages, Erikson claimed, have their own conflicts, their own trials and compensations. And each offers a unique opportunity for greater self-confidence and maturity.

While Western literary and religious tradition had long spoken of the "Ages of Man," the notion that human development passes through a lifetime of transitional phases was initially a novel concept in psychology. With the coming of Erikson, Levinson, and others, this new way of looking at human behavior was avidly endorsed by a sizable segment of the social sciences. Hereafter it was taken for granted that, while climbing the ladder of life, every human being advances step by step along a bridgework of age-related rungs, and that these rungs can be measured, inventoried, tested, and observed. This vivid perspective on human development provided psycholog-

ical professionals with a new chart of the psyche, and a highly useful therapeutic tool.

And yet, and yet . . . while this new way of thinking about life's
journey enlarged our picture of human behavior, and allowed us to evaluate
psychological maturation in terms of the entire life course, something was
missing from the picture. The Eriksonian model remained persuasive, but it
was somehow incomplete.

What Erikson and his colleagues had omitted, I realized, is an element
of the human condition that has always been at the heart and soul of every
human culture from primordial times—*the spiritual element*. If we are to have
an inclusive picture of our human potential, it seemed to me, especially as
this potential unfolds in the adult periods of our lives, a map is required that
includes the sacred as well as the secular. Without this vitally essential component, no theory of human development can be authentic or complete.

During the time I began to have these realizations, I had already been in
the field of aging and life course development for more than twenty years and
had amassed a sizable amount of documentation on every aspect of the
human journey. Having collected case studies and listened to hundreds, if not
thousands of people who were searching for contentment in their lives, I also
realized that mainstream psychological theories of development, complete as
they were in some areas, simply did not address a certain perennial yearning
for meaning that exists in all our lives.

To satisfy this yearning a different approach seemed necessary.

For each of us to make sense of this search for meaning in the proper
way, I concluded, we need a new account of the human journey that (1) is
framed in clear and well-organized terms, (2) integrates the spiritual elements
of life with the worldly, and (3) serves as a clear map that we can use to find
the fulfillment and sense of meaning that is missing from our lives. The great
medieval mystic Meister Eckhart wrote that each human soul is the "foot-
print of God." In this sense we are all on the same journey; yet each of our
personal signatures is also unique. In devising a paradigm of adult human
development, I knew I had to find a theoretical framework that takes account
of these individual differences and at the same time places them in the
context of a universal journey of discovery.

Over the years, as I looked deeper into the relationship between the life
cycle and spiritual growth, it gradually became clear that there is indeed a
correlation between the two: just as there are age-related stages of maturity in
each of our lives, I discovered, so there are sequential stages of spiritual
opportunity—*spiritual* passages, as well as social and psychological ones.

These stages are not precise, and cannot be measured with clockwork precision. Matters of the soul are never so predictable. Nonetheless, from the many observations I have made over the years it is clear to me that these stages—Stages of the Soul, as I have chosen to call them—can, in fact, be charted, and do, in fact, play a part in people's lives with such remarkable frequency that they approach the norm.

Finally, I realized that the existence of mappable spiritual markers within the context of the life course is by no means a new idea. Looking to the past, to tales of medieval quests, to Dante's *Divine Comedy,* to Bunyan's *Pilgrim's Progress* with its multifold allegorical stages of inner development, even to sacred dances and rites of passage in which spiritual stations are acted out or portrayed, it is clear that such methods express for us a sense of the soul unfolding through time in the human heart.

In the famous Zen Buddhist sequence of paintings known as "The Ox Herding Series," we find a classic example of staged spiritual chronology. In the first of its ten images (there are sometimes twelve) we see a seeker yearning for the ox, symbol of his soul or primal nature. But alas, he does not know where to find it. In the next several paintings the seeker catches sight of the tracks of the ox and begins to search for them over the hills and plains of this world. Finally he sees the ox, and after a struggle, tames it. In the next stage both ox and seeker lie down together in harmony beneath a willow tree, and in the following picture both disappear into a moment of ego death, and breakthrough to higher realms of consciousness. In the last of the stages the seeker is resurrected and returns to the marketplace of the world, where he helps others find their own spiritual way.

The structure of the great religions of the world—Christianity, Judaism, Taoism, Islam, Buddhism, Hinduism—are all likewise rooted in ideas of progressive developmental passages, as are many of the most profound myths and teachings of antiquity. The notion of stages of the soul, in short, is a universal one; and hence the question: How do we take this universal approach to human development and apply it in a practical way to our own lives?

The more I pondered this question, the more I realized that indeed a clear pattern of spiritual stages does exist. This pattern is always new, but old as well. It is modern, yet utterly ancient. And while the need to discover this pattern runs deep in our blood, the social stimulus to do so has largely been lost in our own culture. It is only now, at the end of the tumultuous twentieth century, that we are beginning to rediscover it.

Where do we start?

Jack Benny's Little Joke

In most societies the official beginning of the second half of life is more symbolic than statistical. In Buddhist countries, and in Thailand in particular, midlife begins at thirty-five if you're married, thirty if you're not (marriage, both actuarial tables and tradition tell us, increases life expectancy). Among certain Indonesian rain-forest tribes the second half of life starts the day you have your first child. For tribes along the Sepik River area of New Guinea you became a full-blown adult male after taking your first human head. Still other cultures have no notion of chronological age at all.

Up to the time of Shakespeare people viewed their age strictly in terms of social role or season of life. "And one man in his time plays many parts," the Bard wrote, "his acts being seven ages." In Elizabethan days you viewed yourself as a schoolchild, say, or a maiden, a bearded middle-aged soldier, an elder. You defined your age not by the number of years lived but by the rite of passage you had most recently celebrated—confirmation, marriage, parenthood, grandparenthood. Official birth records were not kept in the West until modern times, and few people ever knew precisely how old they were. Birthdays, we learn, are a modern invention.

What about longevity? These figures have been dismally low for the past several thousand years, probably around twenty-five to thirty years of age on the average. Statistically speaking, from birth the average Greek citizen or Roman nobleman had less than an even chance of seeing his third decade. The average monk or farm wife in thirteenth-century England enjoyed only slightly better odds.

Even at the beginning of the twentieth century life expectancy was still below age fifty for men and women alike. Such figures were weighted by infant and childhood mortality, however, and tend to be deceptive. If you wander through an old cemetery in Europe or America today you will notice a strikingly wide range of dates on the headstones—many deaths before twelve, certainly, but a surprising number after seventy and eighty as well.

In our own era, longevity measurements are now as carefully recorded as the time of day. According to the U.S. Census Bureau, life expectancy at birth is presently seventy-five years for men, eighty for women; which means that, statistically speaking, the second half of life begins for a man at age thirty-seven and for a woman at forty.

The mid to upper thirties are thus a dividing age marker along life's road, a symbolic halfway point on the way to our biblical "threescore years and ten."

"We see in this phase of life between thirty-five and forty," Carl Jung writes in his famous essay "The Stages of Life," "that a significant change in the human psyche is in preparation. At first it is not a conscious and striking change; it is rather a matter of indirect signs of a change which seems to take its rise from the unconscious. Often it is something like a slow change in a person's character; in another case certain traits may come to light which have disappeared in childhood; or again, inclinations and interests begin to weaken and others arise to take their place."

While Jung's is as good a description as we have of the onset of the mid-adult years, it is only one way out of many for measuring this elusive milestone. In America, for instance, tongue-in-cheek convention assures us that as long as we remain on this side of the dividing line between age thirty-nine and age forty, we can justifiably think of ourselves as young.

When I was a boy I listened to the Jack Benny show on the radio every Sunday night. At this time the great comedian was clearly past the halfway marker himself, a fact that he made great sport of by regularly claiming to be "thirty-nine." Variations on this joke were sounded at least once every program.

"You know you're not thirty-nine anymore," Benny quipped, "when it takes you more time to recover than it does to tire you out."

"I'll be thirty-nine this year," Benny tells a friend. "And I never lie about my age."

"Jack," the friend shoots back. "You lie about your *dog's* age."

And so forth.

As a six-year-old listener I had a difficult time understanding why Benny made such a big fuss about his age, and why the audience greeted these "thirty-nine" jokes with such guffaws.

Even after my parents explained the premise it didn't make much sense to me. From my childish point of view all birthdays after age twelve were pretty much the same. Or more to the point, they all blended into an unfathomably and ridiculously remote condition known as "being grown up."

Today I understand very well why Jack Benny joked about being thirty-nine, and why the audience laughed so loudly—perhaps too loudly—at this jolly reminder of their mortality. No doubt many of them were "thirty-nine" themselves. And no doubt many were experiencing the same subtle changes of body and mind that Benny had undergone when he rounded the bend of midlife, reminding him, and all of us, that the time had come to say farewell to the first half of life and welcome in the second.

Forever Young

Of course, none of us ever really believes we are getting older.

"Middle age is always ten years older than you are," is a sentiment Jack Benny would endorse, along with a majority of baby boomers. For the fact is that deep inside ourselves most of us feel twenty-five no matter what the date on our personal calendar tells us.

This sense of being outside our own aging process, I tell students in my midlife seminars, is not necessarily the result of vanity or denial. Its cause is more commonly found in the fact that we perceive physical aging in a different way than we perceive psychological aging.

Physical aging, we all know well, progresses relentlessly from birth to old age, and its evidence in the mirror is difficult to deny. Psychological aging, on the other hand, is a far more subtle form of self-perception that follows its own mysterious rhythms and tides and pays little attention to body change or even to the linear passage of time. I have talked with a great many elderly people through the years about how it feels to be old. While responses vary, there is one point they invariably come back to: young people may look at them as feeble white-haired elders, they tell me, but inside they think of themselves as being the same person they were when they were young. "Your body grows old," a ninety-three-year-old woman said to me, "but in your mind you stay timeless."

Of course, if your life work happens to place you in the field of aging, as it does for me, people automatically assume that you *of all people* are comfortable with the idea of the passage of time. Just as funeral directors are supposed to be at ease with the notion of death, so those in the field of aging are assumed to take their own aging in stride.

But aging comes as a surprise to *everyone*.

I still remember the seismic shock I experienced the day members of my office gave me a surprise fiftieth birthday party. One of my closest colleagues, long past retirement age herself, came up to me at the party, pecked my cheek, and said cheerily, "Well, how does it feel to realize that you have fewer years ahead of you than behind you?"

My Own Awakenings

"You have your whole life *ahead of you,*" the silver-hair speaker on the podium informed us. It was graduation day, Calhoun High School, June 1963.

All of us heard and believed that day. Because the speaker was right—we did have our whole lives ahead of us. In the photograph on my bureau I still see my class standing there in rank and file in our ill-fitting graduation gowns, waiting for the speaker, whose name I can't remember, to finish up so we could turn the tassels around on our graduation caps and get on with our lives.

Today my graduation photograph has yellowed in a way I never suspected photographs of myself would yellow. As I stare at it, I can't help but notice how dated people's clothes look. The occasional Beatles haircuts, so rebellious in their time, are laughably conventional now, and out of style. Even the women's purses and the handkerchief in my father's pocket give the photo an eerie air of lost memory. This photograph proves that, yes, I was there all right. But my mind resists the fact that the event happened *so long ago.* The span between who I was then and who I am now seems an infinite distance. Or no distance at all.

And yet, for all of this, the whole span from then till now seems more than anything else to be a voyage, an odyssey, a stage-by-stage journey of the soul.

On my frequent trips to Washington, D.C., I often find time to stop by the National Gallery of Art. Here I visit one of my favorite series of paintings, *The Voyage of Life,* by the nineteenth-century American artist Thomas Cole.

The first painting in the series, *Childhood,* depicts an infant seated in a gilded boat. The boat is just emerging from a womblike cavern and floats serenely along the River of Life, bearing the child to his destiny.

In the second canvas, *Youth,* the child has grown to early manhood. He stands in the stern of the same gilded boat, one hand firmly on the tiller, the other pointing toward a Taj Mahal-like pleasure dome shimmering in the sky ahead of him, symbol of youthful dreams. The River of Life he navigates on flows across a placid countryside. All the youth must do to reach this vision is continue steering his course straight ahead.

What the young pilot does not see from his perspective in the boat is that a mile or so downstream the river makes a hairpin turn *away* from this utopian castle in the clouds. It then flows through a grove of dense, tangled trees, reminiscent of Dante's "dark wood," and finally emerges out the other side into a roaring rapids.

Here we pick up the third painting in the series, *Manhood.* The figure is now middle-aged. He is no longer standing proudly at the helm, but crouches in the bottom of the boat in a posture of prayer. The tiller he gripped so assuredly in the previous picture has snapped off somewhere in the churning waters, and his boat zigzags wildly through a maze of rapids, rocks, and whirlpools.

The man in this painting, we realize, has been transported from the dream-lined highway of youth to the labyrinthine currents of real life, where he finds events spinning out of control. If we were to replace Cole's heroic imagery with updated versions of this universal predicament, we could as easily situate our man revolving in one of Jackson Pollock's chaotic whorls. We might see his tiny figure crawling around on the complex, interlocking machinery of a Piet Mondrian painting or inching his way along the grid of a Minimalist sculpture. He could be locked into a matrix of Andy Warhol's Campbell's soup cans, or lost among the shiny chrome fenders and display window reflections of the Photorealists. We might even meet him on the assembly line with Charlie Chaplin in *Modern Times.*

I think of these *Voyage of Life* paintings when I remember that once upon a time I was that youth in the gilded boat, pointing to the vision ahead of me in the sky. How differently life has turned out than I thought it would. Like so many other members of the war and postwar generations, I was brought up to believe that the human journey takes us steadily across untroubled waters from cradle to grave; or better, escorts us along a single straight and well-paved highway that extends across the landscape of the years to the horizon, where a contented future awaits us just on the other side. Walt Whitman put it into verses that were once an anthem for roaming youth:

> *Afoot and light-hearted I take to the open road,*
> *Healthy, free, the world before me,*
> *The long brown path before me leading wherever I choose.*

This long brown path first appeared to me at an early age—my first day of school, to be exact, when I was five, the same year, 1950, that Polaroid film made its appearance on the shelves, Minute Rice revolutionized cooking, and North Korea invaded South Korea.

Here in kindergarten I immediately began assimilating the hidden curriculum of modern life. The fine print reads something like this: Be a good leader or a good follower, adopt your culture's values, work hard, and don't make waves. If you stick to your end of the bargain and keep moving straight ahead on ambition's highway, your rewards will be waiting. These rewards will multiply as you get older, until one day you'll have everything you want and be happy. As narrator Ronald Reagan assured me every week on TV's *General Electric Theater:* "Progress is our most important product."

So I kept to the road. I worked diligently in school and college, did my part, and for a while the promises came through on schedule.

Then things started going wrong.

The first jolt for me came in the late 1960s. I had studied hard to earn my Ph.D. in philosophy. But when I set out to find a job in my field I discovered that the market for college teachers had collapsed. I was forced to work in a low-level position at a bank.

For other people, the shocks came a little later. By the time many people had reached their forties, grim realities that Walt Whitman never anticipated were common topics when friends got together to talk: soul-shattering divorces, chronic illness, job loss, addiction, depression. Values and institutions that once made people's course in life seem so streamlined and predictable—education, marriage, the work ethic, team play, company loyalty, promotion, retirement—were being recalibrated, if not abolished entirely. And in the shakedown many began to think the unthinkable, that the future might not be better than the past; it might even be worse.

"I was brought up to believe that things were just going to get better and better forever," said Florence, a thirty-eight-year-old health-care professional. "Then the years moved along. Each year I realized I was less free than I'd thought. My financial position and my enthusiasm, my relationships, were all getting harder to maintain, not easier. One day I kind of lost it. I remember looking at myself in the mirror, just crying. 'Nobody ever told me how hard it was going to be,' I kept yelling at my reflection."

"When I graduated from business school in the sixties I believed I could get any job I wanted," a businessman named Ted told me, echoing Florence's words. "Grow up and become any kind of person I liked. An entrepreneur. Explorer. President of the United States. All that rah-rah stuff. Today I work at a job I don't like very much to keep my kid in college. I don't have the heart to tell my kid that he's going to be trapped in the same way."

"It was a jolting realization," a career counselor told me, "to reach my fortieth birthday and find myself to be none of the following: rich, beautiful, successful, famous, thin, and happy."

Through the years I have heard hundreds more stories of "jolting realizations" from people confronting the passage of time. Most of these stories converge on a central theme: life is harder than they told us it would be.

Such revelations are not a new discovery, of course, but they always come as a shock when we first experience them. They make us realize that life runs straight for only a mile or so outside of town. Then it begins to swerve and detour, taking us to places we never intended to visit—never, in fact, knew existed. Indeed, our lives often seem more like a labyrinth than a long brown road.

Beginning the Quest

As a child I was brought up in the Lutheran Church, where I was raised on a diet of conventional Protestantism. Even at an early age, however, I managed now and then to catch glimpses of a deeper spirituality below the surface, a teaching that philosopher Jacob Needleman refers to as "Lost Christianity."

Intimations of this buried wisdom could be found, I discovered, in many places, including the Bible itself: St. Paul's injunction to "pray unceasingly"; Jesus's reply, when urged by his disciples to partake of food: "I have meat to eat that ye know not of." When asked by his disciples why he speaks to the people in parables, Jesus told them, "Because it is given unto you to know the mysteries of the kingdom of heaven, but to them it is not given."

Both Jesus and St. Paul suggested that human beings are "asleep." Were they, I wondered, hinting at some hidden dimension of human consciousness? Was something flawed in the way we normally perceive the world? "Arise," the New Testament tells us over and over again, and "awake."

But arise from what? Awake to what? I was especially struck by a passage I read from the pen of Origen, an early Church father, in his work *De Principiis* (IV.i). "What do we find when we come to the Gospels?" he asks. "Is there not hidden there an inner, also a divine sense?"

As I grew older I became acquainted with a wider selection of Christian literature, some of which hinted at a catacomb of meaning hidden below the conventional Christian surface. The luminous teaching tales of the Desert Fathers still remain emblazoned in my mind. In one story, a desert hermit known as Abbot Lot visits his elderly teacher, Abbot Joseph, informing him with great passion that "to the best of my ability, Father, I have kept the rule of our order and performed the fast. I pray regularly. I meditate and practice contemplative silence. I strive to purify my heart of wicked and extraneous thoughts. What more can I do?"

Hearing this, Abbot Joseph stands up, stretches out his arms, and causes his fingers to burst into ten lamps of flame. "Why not become totally changed into fire?" the old abbot exclaims, displaying in one supernatural gesture the difference between ordinary religious teaching and the explosive miracle of true divine knowledge.

Later still, in the middle 1960s, like thousands of other college students, I read J. D. Salinger's *Franny and Zooey*. Like others, I was baffled when Franny, the lovely, metaphysically minded heroine who comes to Yale on a college weekend, faints at the end of the first story. What could have caused such odd behavior?

Rereading the narrative several times and searching for clues, it became apparent that Franny's blackout was self-induced. She had, the story told, been reading a classic of Eastern Orthodox Christianity entitled *The Way of the Pilgrim*. From this nineteenth-century masterpiece of spirituality she learned a secret prayer technique used for centuries by Russian and Greek monks. It was known as the Jesus Prayer. This ancient, potentially dangerous technique involved the constant repetition of an invocation to Jesus accompanied by concentration on one's heartbeat and a rhythmic control of breath. Franny, it seems, had practiced this prayer too enthusiastically and had hyperventilated.

But awareness of one's heartbeat? Control of the breath? This didn't sound much like the Christianity I'd been weaned on in Lutheran Sunday school.

Reading more about it, I discovered that there were indeed esoteric elements in the Eastern Orthodox Church that had long been forgotten in Western Christianity. There were so many, in fact, that some theologians referred to this tradition as "Christian Yoga."

My next question was an obvious one: Was this Christian yoga still alive in the twentieth century?

Climbing Mount Athos

In the summer of 1968 I traveled across Europe with the Yale Russian Chorus on an international singing tour. Events were politically topsy-turvy that summer, and everywhere we went confusion followed. At the beginning of the tour we arrived in France just days after student riots had turned the streets of Paris into a barricade and toppled Charles de Gaulle from power. At the end of the tour we left Czechoslovakia days before divisions of Russian soldiers rolled across the border, sent in, as the Russian Foreign Minister explained it, "to restore the peace."

It was an electrifying time. But for me the significance of the tour ultimately had little to do with riots, or the Cold War, or even music. It had more to do with this notion of "Lost Christianity," and with the answers I had felt might be lurking in the monasteries of Eastern Europe. The high point of the trip turned out to be a voyage outside of time, to the thousand-year-old Greek city of churches and monasteries known as Mount Athos.

Shrouded in fog along the Aegean coast, the theocratic republic of Mount Athos, with its Byzantine towers and miracle-working icons, has been a powerhouse of monastic tradition in the Eastern Orthodox Church for more than ten centuries. Here, it seemed, one might find traces of Needleman's "Lost Christianity." Here one might find hints concerning what Abbot Joseph meant when he invited his disciple to become "changed into fire."

But while I had heard a great deal about this mystical society of monks, I was unprepared for the intense, even alarming piety of the men I met there. This was especially true of a monk named Father Pyotr. This saintly ascetic, old beyond counting, lived alone in a cliffside cave high above one of Mount Athos's many monasteries. Here, for forty years, I was told, he had spent his days and nights in perpetual prayer, just as St. Paul recommended.

Determined to visit him, I found a local translator, then set off one morning before sunrise to visit the old monk's lair. The climb up the trail was dauntingly steep, and by the time my translator and I reached the cave Father Pyotr had already finished his noon devotions.

The first thing I noticed when we arrived was the lack of access to food or water. I asked Father Pyotr how he survived. His English was limited, and my translator came to the rescue.

"Every morning," the good father said, "I lower a bucket over the side of the cliff. Every evening I haul it back up. The bucket is full of cheese and bread to fill my belly, thanks be to God, and to the generous monks below."

I asked what he would do if the bucket ever came up empty.

He smiled and said that he had been living in this cave for more than half his life. Every day he prayed to God to send him food and drink, and every day the food and drink arrived. "Do you think I should start worrying about that now?" he asked with a twinkle.

Like Father Zosima in *The Brothers Karamazov,* Father Pyotr belonged to a spiritual tradition stranger than anything we know of in Western Christianity, a mystical system dating back to the Desert Fathers and involving complex, Oriental-like techniques in its worship such as breathing exercises, prostration, chanting, and prolonged fasts. Though much of this teaching has been lost, a portion remains, encapsulated here, it seemed to me, in this wise old hermit.

Though my conversation with Father Pyotr was brief and filled with many charged silences, the effect of our exchange lasted a lifetime. The old monk talked about prayer and the life of a solitary recluse. But it was what he said to me at the end of the visit that made the deepest impression. As my guide and I were preparing to start down the trail, I mentioned that we were headed next to a church on the other side of the mountain. Father Pyotr looked at me with blazing eyes and asked in his broken English, "Do you know where you are going?"

My guide quickly answered on my behalf, saying we had a map.

"Do you know where you are going?" Father Pyotr said again.

"Of course," the guide replied, a trifle irritated at having his navigating skills questioned.

But I understood very clearly what the old monk was asking me.

And I understood that I did not have an answer: I did not know where my life was going, or what its meaning and purpose might ultimately be.

I also knew that this ancient sage from another time and a distant teaching was telling me that it was my task as a human being to find out.

Beginning a Journey of a Thousand Miles

As time passed, the old monk's words returned to me at regular intervals, almost as if he had slipped a spiritual timed-release capsule into my consciousness. Our meeting made me realize that whatever I might do in life, I would never escape the need to answer the question he had planted in my soul: Where am I going? Where are *any of us* going?

One must, of course, begin a journey of a thousand miles with the first step. And so my initial response to the old monk's challenge was to delve more deeply into subjects I was already studying, which in this case meant philosophy.

Five years of graduate school later, it was apparent that I would not find the answers in the Philosophy Department at Columbia University, any more than Thomas Merton could find them here a generation before me. The French philosopher Jacques Maritain had zeroed in on the problem of academic philosophy with devastating accuracy: "Truly, philosophers play a strange game," Maritain wrote. "They know very well that one thing alone counts, and that all their medley of subtle discussion relates to that one single question: why are we born on this earth? And they also know that they will never be able to answer it. Nevertheless, they continue sedately to amuse themselves. Do they not see that people come to them from all parts of the compass, not with a desire to partake of their subtlety, but because they hope to receive from them *one word of life?* If they have no such words, why do they not cry them from the housetops? . . . And if they do not have such words, why do they allow people to believe they will receive from them something which they cannot give?"

Still, the study of philosophy was not a total loss. It was during these years that I discovered a much neglected "underground philosophy" that ran like a golden thread through Western philosophy in the writings of the Christian mystics, the Gnostics, the Neoplatonists, and a select group of others. In a single utterance, for example, the great Christian mystic Meister Eckhart changed my picture of reality forever. "The eye with which I see God," he exclaimed, "is the eye with which God sees me." God was not a titanic being staring down at me from a distant heaven, this statement helped me understand. He was inside me, I was inside Him. His eye was my eye, my eye His. Everything was One.

Plato likewise hinted at a mystical wisdom far different from anything I'd ever studied before. In a letter written during the last years of his life, the great Greek philosopher made the remarkable statement that he had never once revealed the secret side of his teachings. I have not written the true philosophy, he admitted. It must always be hidden, passed like a spark from teacher to pupil but never divulged in writing.

Could this "true philosophy" also be the meat "that ye know not of" that Jesus spoke of? Was it not also a key to the parables in the Gospels?

If this was the case, no wonder it is so difficult to find the inner kernel of truth in philosophy class. Perhaps the real truths cannot be understood through words. Perhaps they can be known only by a living transmission from teacher to student, and by direct experience within the soul.

The Summer of Love

Like thousands of others in 1967, the Summer of Love, I made the journey cross-country to San Francisco, where at the meeting of Haight Street and Ashbury Street the Peace-Love revolution was building to a hallucinogenic crescendo. Everywhere I looked in this fantastic dreamscape I saw head shops, students dancing half naked to Indian music, long-haired youths in front of laundromats meditating in the lotus position. A remarkable utopian enterprise seemed to be birthing itself here, a collective religious experiment, the outcome of which might very well change the world and usher in a new age.

But these hopes were short-lived. The event that made the futility of this dream clear to me took place one rainy summer afternoon in a cafeteria in the heart of the Haight-Ashbury district. As I entered the café and glanced around, my eyes fell on a group of young people in the back of the room dressed in Hindu-style robes and chanting quietly. Among them was one of the most beautiful young women I'd ever seen, singing away like a choirgirl, her eyes turned upward as if in ecstasy. The girl's beauty was so striking and otherworldly that I found myself thinking about her all that afternoon.

Six months later I was walking in the same area of Haight-Ashbury when I noticed an emaciated-looking young woman coming toward me with an unsteady gait. Her forehead was pocked with scabs and her skin was tinted a sallow yellow. As we passed, our eyes met. The shock of recognition almost knocked me over: it was the same young woman I had seen chanting piously in the coffee shop; but a kind of Dorian Gray version, as if her whole being had aged and withered in less than half a year.

I realized at that moment that this beautiful young woman, ravaged by God knows what physical and chemical abuses in the name of peace and love, was emblematic not only of the frailties of the Peace-Love movement; she symbolized how easily spirituality can be confused with imitations of spirituality—with robes and drug highs and summer fun. This young woman was a walking warning that the spiritual journey is not a game for children; that it is an adult undertaking fraught with cautions, one that involves an ongoing series of stages, each bringing its own demands, its own rewards, and its own dangers. Without expert guidance along the route, I understood, and without a degree of wisdom and maturity to lead us, a person can easily run aground.

The Bible tells us, "Many are called but few are chosen." If I was going to become seriously involved in a spiritual search, I knew, I'd have to be prepared and well versed in the rules. Without proper knowledge and discretion, anyone can find themselves a burned-out case, like the beautiful girl from the cafeteria.

And yet the aspirations that so many people partook of in the 1960s did not entirely disappear when the Peace-Love experiment collapsed. In retrospect, these aspirations went below ground for many people, plowed under by social change and the need to survive in increasingly difficult times.

As the decades passed, I heard friends asking with growing frequency:

Why don't I feel better about my life? Why does time seem to be going by so quickly? What makes me feel so restless and discontented? Why don't my love relationships give me the fulfillment I thought they would? Why aren't my children turning out the way I'd hoped? Why don't these new hobbies and classes and second careers—these attempts to become more "authentic"—give me the satisfaction I'd expected? Why is it that nothing seems to last? What does it all mean?

Most of us were unprepared to deal with such stark quandaries. "The worst of it all," wrote Jung, "is that intelligent and cultivated people live their lives without even knowing the possibility of transformation. . . . Wholly unprepared, they embark on the second half of life."

The philosopher Immanuel Kant once wrote that the philosophy of life can be boiled down to three basic questions: What do I know? What should I do? What may I hope?

I began to wonder: Could any of us say what we really hoped for? Did any of us know where we were going?

Brookdale and the Dark Wood

As director of the Brookdale Center on Aging, a university-centered institution devoted to research and education in the field of aging, I hear of doctors every day going about their business prolonging lives. Almost never do I hear them asking why they're making such heroic efforts. Matters of the soul are rarely discussed in the social and medical sciences.

What could we do at Brookdale, I slowly came to wonder, to help people return to these essential questions? The questions about meaning that so many of us ask ourselves as life progresses.

My first response was to establish a branch at the Center where people could deal with real issues of purpose through the medium of reminiscence and life review. By retrieving past memories and looking at these memories reflectively, Brookdale staff members have consistently found, participants are able to work through unresolved conflicts of regret, grief, guilt, and unfulfilled dreams.

Working with the talented poet Marc Kaminsky, Brookdale brought together people from all walks of life—poets, psychotherapists, educators, businesspeople—in hopes that they would find buried meaning in their past, and spread the message that life can be something more than a tale of sound and fury.

Yet over time, and despite the powerful insights that people gained from these encounters, it became increasingly apparent that something vital was missing from the curriculum, something essential that goes beyond sheer memory and reminiscence. Even the light of self-reflection, it seemed, could not erase certain chronic feelings that even the most successful people talked to me about—feelings of incompleteness, of discontent and futility, of quiet desperation. "I've learned a lot about myself in this program," one thirty-nine-year-old woman said to me. "But none of what I've learned changes the fact that life seems like one long day's journey into night."

Then around the time of my thirty-fifth birthday something strange happened.

A month or so before the actual day I began to wake up every morning at five o'clock feeling vaguely disoriented—feeling both as if something had died and something was trying to be born. What was going on?

Then it struck me. Thirty-five, I realized, is a special age. It's the age that many cultures designate as the halfway point in life. It is the age at which Dante conceived the *Divine Comedy,* that greatest of all midlife spiritual journeys. "Midway through this mortal life," the great Italian poet wrote, "I found myself astray, in a dark wood. Ah, who can say how terrible it was!"

In the years leading up to my halfway anniversary, I now realized, I too had wandered into a dark wood. But a wood of my own making—dark not because it was evil, but because my own preoccupation with worldly matters had kept me so far from the light. Dark because I had been so deluded as to think that my life would one day afford me an opportunity to stop what I was doing, breathe easily, and enjoy what I had worked so hard and long to attain.

But the truth of the matter was quite different. The truth was that I had *less time* now to enjoy my life; less time to be the fulfilled person I thought I should be by this point in my life. Like a swollen river, the momentum of life was pulling me along faster and faster, leaving me little to grab on to as I was washed downstream. Time was not only running out. It was running away.

But time for what? More career advances? A bigger house? A better marriage? Having it all?

And then there was always that little voice: "Is this all there is? Is there really nothing more?"

Confused by these emotions, and wondering if others my age were going through the same bouts of self-questioning, I talked about these matters to colleagues and friends.

Many of them, I learned, were undergoing similar moments of disorientation and a longing for something more. A surprisingly large number were drawn to questions of spirituality and religion. For some this experience was new and novel. For others it was a return to the ideals of their youth. All agreed that these feelings were changing their lives.

I was fascinated to discover, for instance, that Robert Atchley, the author of a highly respected and best-selling textbook in the field of aging, had become seriously involved in the practice of yoga and meditation and was regularly visiting a spiritual master in India. My colleague Lydia Bronte, consultant to leading foundations, had, to my surprise, been pursuing a passionate search for higher consciousness for many years. An old friend, Connie Goldman, author and radio journalist on *All Things Considered,* was shifting her interest from the arts to spiritual growth. Historian and editor of *The Oxford Book of Aging,* Tom Cole one day informed me that he was seriously drawn to the idea of becoming a rabbi. My colleague Andrew Achenbaum, who had made his mark as a historian of Social Security, was now deeply engrossed in the study of Christian traditions.

The more colleagues and contemporaries I compared notes with, the more it became evident that the new spiritual hunger they spoke of was similar to that expressed by scores of people I had worked with in seminars and classes around the country. Each of their stories was different, of course. Yet there was a sequence to them, a chronological unfolding from one stage of awareness to another.

I began to realize what ingredient had been missing from our attempts at Brookdale to help people find meaning and direction in their lives. It was the same ingredient that was left out in various theories of life course development.

The spiritual element was once again missing.

"I Never Believed in Anything Much"

Intrigued, I widened the circle of my inquiries and began talking to adults from many sectors of life. As it happened, I was already working with Elderhostel, a national organization devoted to bringing liberal education to retired people, and soon I turned the search for meaning into the centerpiece of my Elderhostel classes. In these classes and in my midlife workshops I now heard stories from people old and young who had been leading ordinary lives and who suddenly found their worlds disrupted by a spiritual call.

A nurse in one of my Atlanta seminars told me, "I've gotten this inner calling to investigate what's at the bottom of life. Under everything. Have you ever seen a little child take a toy apart? They're not just being destructive.

They're looking for something. They're trying to get to the heart of what makes the universe tick. That's what I'm about right now. I've got the urge to understand the world inside me."

"Around the time my third child was born," a social worker in Chicago told me, "I stopped wanting to live. Just stopped. Postpartum depression —it lasted for over a year. When it passed, something unusual started happening to me. I got this inkling to read the Bible. Just read. So I did it—cover to cover a couple of times. It was like the Bible was calling to me, trying to get a message across. Which is strange, because I was never a religious person."

"I never believed in anything much," a middle-aged medical technician named Sven told the group. "Until the day my son fell off his motorcycle and was crushed under a truck. It was near-fatal, and he was in the hospital for a year. During the time of his rehabilitation I started to get the call inside that I should pray. My son got better, and you bet I kept on praying."

Not everyone in my workshops was so forthcoming with their experiences, and many would discuss them only in private. For one older man, the quest for meaning had become a protracted and somewhat frustrating ordeal. "I've been struggling for more than thirty years," he told me after class one day, almost in hushed tones. "I search. I pray. Sometimes I talk to God as if He was standing there listening to me. It's exasperating, but I can't go back anymore. I'm hooked, you could say: I've got the bug to discover who I am."

Occasionally the people I came into contact with talked about miraculous moments of compassion and bliss.

Anna, a longtime practitioner of Transcendental Meditation, described how several years ago she had been hiking in the White Mountains of New Hampshire. Coming to a trail stop, she took out her lunch and began to eat. Suddenly she noticed two small deer watching her nearby. She studied these animals with admiration for several moments, then noticed that both seemed to be emitting a kind of shimmering glow. The longer she stared at them, the brighter the glow became, and the more she felt herself slipping into an excited, disoriented state of mind. Finally she entered a kind of ecstasy.

"I was in this state for God knows how long," Anna told one of my spellbound workshop groups. "Maybe five minutes. Maybe fifty. I've never been sure. When I came to, the deer were gone, and there was this just unbelievable sense of peace. I've never been the same person since it happened."

These, of course, were the positive experiences. During seminar sessions I also heard tales of exploitation by charlatans and pseudoreligious cults, of searches that ended in despair. While participants were ostensibly in my workshop to discover more about the relationship between their inner and outer lives, some of them had no genuine wish to explore this relationship except in the most superficial ways.

In class, for example, I often give my students parables and myths to meditate on—Sufi and Christian teaching stories, poems, scriptural verses, fairy stories, firsthand accounts. Some members of the class, I've found, read these stories and a lightbulb goes on. They become animated and are sometimes moved to tears. They say things like "Something in this story speaks to me!" or "I never heard anything like this before!"

For another portion of the class, however, the same excerpts leave them baffled or indifferent. "Seems like your typical fairy tale," is a common response. Or: "I'm not sure I get the point."

Are these two groups speaking the same language? I often wonder. Have they read the same material? Are they talking about the same passages?

Finally, what I began to realize from this wide range of reactions was that each person has his or her own inner timetable for self-discovery and that the search for meaning cannot be forced. One doesn't make the grass grow, as the Chinese saying goes, by pulling it. Some people are brought up in a religious atmosphere and end up spending their lives pursuing devotional activities. Others are raised with religion and flee it like the plague.

A majority of us are somewhere in between. We grow up touched in one way or another by spiritual idealism, and then, frequently, this influence fades during our twenties and thirties when we are making our way in the world. Then one day somewhere in the early, middle, or later part of adult life this contemplative impulse reemerges.

Precisely when it comes and what forms it takes depends on a variety of cultural and environmental factors. From the literally thousands of people I had spoken with by now at Brookdale, Elderhostel, and midlife workshops across the country, as well as from the extensive research material available, it was clear to me that when it's time for ideas of meaning and spirituality to take root in a person's life, they will. If the time is not yet ripe, they won't.

Of the many intense encounters that took place in my teaching, a single moment stands out in my memory above the rest. One morning after class was over I was walking in the corridor and was accosted by a student named Rita Cole, a chicly dressed woman of a certain age, with large hoop earrings and eyes that radiated a bit of agitation and a hint of despair.

"Can I speak to you for a minute, Dr. Moody?" she asked.

I stopped and waited.

"I feel like I'm on a treadmill," she said, talking with a haunted urgency. "I go to these Elderhostel programs. I volunteer for charity work. I attend every adult education course I can find. I'm in therapy. I'm busy all the time, you know, but—nothing helps. I keep feeling so empty.

"What is it I'm not getting?" she asked, more to herself, I thought, than to me. "What am I supposed to do?"

I looked at Rita and wanted to tell her that the pain she was feeling was not there simply to torment her. These feelings of depression and emptiness were symptoms of something far more fundamental. They stemmed from a kind of primal pain of separation that we all feel—a separation from something deep in our hearts and souls. We're all in a state of mourning for something we've lost, I wanted to tell her, though we may not identify it this way. And all of us are desperate to get it back again.

But I didn't say any of this. Because I knew these words wouldn't take away her pain. Instead, I did what I'd done before when students spoke to me of emptiness and separation. I quoted several verses from the great Sufi poet Rumi—verses that tell the story of a reed plucked from its reed bed in a lake and fashioned into a flute; how to this day whenever the flute is played its melancholy song tells of its yearning for the home it was separated from so long ago.

"We've all been plucked from that same reed bed," I said to Rita. "And our pain is going to continue as long as we remain separated from what we've lost.

"We may or may not someday find our way back to that place," I told her. "But even if we simply realize what's important in life and begin to start searching, that effort alone will go a long way towards relieving us of this primal pain."

THE SOUL'S STAGES

Realizing What's Important

Since the dawn of civilization human beings have recognized a structure to the life course from infancy through old age. Traditional societies have expressed this idea of life stages through symbol, myth, and ritual, while contemporary societies have relied on the social sciences to discover a map of life. But the stages of life, we now come to understand, are not simply "discovered," anymore than lines of latitude or longitude are found painted on the earth. From my interviews and historical research, it gradually became clear to me that redrawing the map of life depends in crucial ways on how we conceive the role of purpose and meaning in life. This search for meaning must be recognized as the driving force in the construction of new paradigms for growth and development over the life course.

The urge to find deeper purpose in life, if heeded and encouraged, unfolds in a sequence of stages that exerts a slow but sure metamorphic effect on the adult personality. In the end, one who has passed through these stages emerges as a more fulfilled and self-realized individual. These stages of the soul are the foundation for a new map of life.

Among the world's religious beliefs, the middle adult years have long been considered *the* critical time for addressing questions of the Spirit. Among Hindus the life course is divided into four stages. During youth a child learns and studies, usually under the watchful eye of an aged guru. In early adulthood he or she raises a family, works at a trade, and lives the life of a householder. In the third stage, during the middle adult years, after one's children are older and the second half of life begins, a married couple leaves their home and spends their life together in prayer and contemplation. In old age they complete the circle of spiritual life by returning to their community and teaching young people what they've learned.

Another version of the stages of life comes from William Butler Yeats, who compares the monthly thirty-day cycle of the moon with the human life course in his strange, mystical book *A Vision.* Within this lunar cycle, Yeats tells us, the halfway mark is reached on the fifteenth day, which in the human life course corresponds to the thirty-fifth year. "This is a moment of great mystical importance," writes Joseph Campbell about Yeats's prophetic map of life. "Here your consciousness, your body and its consciousness, are at their prime, and you are in a position to ask yourself, Who or what am I? Am I the consciousness, or am I the vehicle of consciousness? Am I this body which is the vehicle of light, solar light, or am I the light."

Contemporary research supports the notion that the middle years are the time when an interest in spiritual life increases most intensely. A recent Gallup survey designed to measure commitment to religion in America tells us that between the ages of twenty-five and thirty-five a total of 23 percent of Americans attend worship services "at least weekly." This figure increases with age until at ages forty-five to fifty-five the proportion of Americans attending religious services weekly rises to nearly 30 percent.

Frequency of prayer shows a similar upswing. For persons aged twenty-five to thirty-five the proportion of Americans who pray "several times a day" is 17 percent. This number climbs to 24 percent by age forty-five. Among sixty-year-old Americans more than 33 percent acknowledge performing regular prayer.

There are several other studies that reach approximately the same conclusions as the survey above. Yet despite this recognized tendency to turn toward matters of the Spirit as life matures, a majority of clinical psychologists still avoid discussing this subject in any context, and notions of developmental spirituality remain rare in the literature of human development. Within the psychotherapeutic community only a few convincing exceptions stand against the rule.

One of the most conspicuous of these is found in the work of Carl Jung, whose famous essay "The Stages of Life" represents the first serious attempt among psychotherapists to describe a spiritual sequence in the life course. Jung points out how an "inexorable inner process" begins in people almost automatically when they reach thirty-five or forty. Youthful illusions are shed. Repressed childhood ideals resurface. Early interests and ambitions lose their fascination, and more mature ones take their place. A person gropes toward wisdom, and a search for enduring personal values begins. Either we begin a quest for meaning at midlife, Jung warns, or we become simply "an applauder of the past, an eternal adolescent—all lamentable substitutes for the illumination of the self."

"Whoever carries over into the afternoon [of life] the law of the morning," writes Jung, "must pay for so doing with damage to his soul . . ."

Another early giant of psychotherapy, the Italian Roberto Assagioli, made spirituality in the life course a dominant part of his therapeutic method. Like Jung, Assagioli believes that the search for life's purpose can begin only after a person has lived long enough and made enough mistakes to recognize that an unexamined life goes nowhere. A "normal" man, Assagioli insists in his famous essay "Self-realization and Psychological Disturbances," "takes life as it comes and never questions its meaning or purpose; he devotes himself to the satisfaction of his personal desires; he seeks enjoyment of the senses, emotional pleasures, material security, or achievement of personal ambition." He is, in short, spiritually asleep. Then time passes. This normal man marries, has children, tastes of life's vicissitudes, and moves into his middle years where one day he is surprised and alarmed by the changes that start to take place in his psychological world. These changes often come after a major disappointment or an emotional shock. But not always. The Call, as I term it, can also come without any apparent reason. "The change begins often with a growing sense of dissatisfaction," writes Assagioli, "of lack, of something missing. But this something missing is nothing material or definite; it is something vague and elusive, that he is unable to describe." Eventually, Assagioli tells us, this disquieting inner pressure sends us on a search for the soul.

Among mental health professionals, models of the spiritual journey frequently turn up in studies by transpersonal psychologists. Roger Walsh and Frances Vaughan, for example, have defined six common elements of the spiritual process. These include (1) ethical training, (2) attentional training, (3) emotional transformation, (4) motivation, (5) refining awareness, and finally (6) attainment of wisdom. These aspects of the spiritual journey are interdependent, claim Walsh and Vaughan, yet they do not come about all at once but tend to unfold in organic sequence like the growth of an embryo in the womb.

A few other seminal thinkers talk of the middle adult years in similar terms: as a time when people begin to instinctively detach themselves from the activities of youth and start the search for lasting values.

Erik Erikson, the great pioneer of human life course psychology, speaks of mature adulthood as a moment of choice. On the one hand, we can opt for what he terms "generativity"—passing down to others the wisdom and knowledge we have acquired in the first half of life. Or we can take the lesser course, choosing rut-bound psychological "stagnation."

Aging serves as a spiritual alarm clock, adds writer and therapist Thomas Moore. Aging, says Moore, is "one of the ways the soul nudges itself into attention to the spiritual aspect of life." According to Moore, as we enter the second half of life and our bodies begin to slow down, this reminder of mortality compels us to ponder the larger realities. "Aging," he writes, "forces us to decide what is important in life."

From these examples and many others that I have come across in research and interviews, it has become clear that the attraction to spirituality is a fundamental part of human existence, and that an impulse in this direction will make itself known in some form, and at some time, in the lives of a great number of people.

At the same time, it is also clear that this vital element of human existence has been ignored by a majority of psychologists, and has been consistently left off the maps of the life cycle by the very professionals who are telling us how to live and age successfully.

There is something dangerous in this omission, I believe, something that needs to be brought to people's attention before it is too late; something that our culture must know about and address, especially now that the disquiet in people's hearts is so evident, and when so many are seeking to regain that indefinable quality in themselves that Thomas Moore calls "a sense of soul."

"What Are We to Have?"

One middle-aged music therapist in my Philadelphia seminar asked, "Why should I change my world around at this point in life and drop everything for something I'm not even sure exists?"

This is a proper question to ask. A wonderful question, really, and one that should—must—be asked by all of us. It is this very question, I tell my students when the question comes up, that is raised in the New Testament—in Matthew 19:27. Here the disciple Peter rather boldly approaches Jesus after the Master has announced that it is more difficult for a rich man to enter heaven than it is for a camel to pass through the eye of a needle.

A strange time to raise such a question, it would seem, but Peter presses the issue: "We have given up all things to follow you," he says. "What now are we to have?" What does the spiritual way put into our hands and into our pockets? Peter wants to know. Why should we make such strenuous efforts? What do we stand to gain?

When I'm asked this question I answer it in two ways, through people's hearts and through their minds.

First, through the heart. Life course psychology research shows that as people age they become increasingly risk-averse—less willing to go out on a limb, to change, to take a chance. The older we get, the less time we have to repair our mistakes. Suppose I make a disastrous investment at age forty-nine. Suppose I choose the wrong job at fifty-six, the wrong mate, the wrong road. By the time I discover my mistake I may not have enough time to set things straight or to start over again, the way I could when I was twenty-three years old.

Practically speaking, therefore, I tell the class that it's perfectly realistic to be wary of taking risks during the middle years.

On the other hand, I say that if we feel our lives are not giving us what we want, and if we suspect we're headed down a dead-end street, then we have to ask ourselves what we can do to make things better.

Two options are open.

The first is to do nothing—to go on living the way we've always lived, and accept the consequences.

The second is to take a chance, and seek a way out of our dissatisfaction.

Which of these two choices would you prefer to take? I ask my students.

Most of them choose the second.

Next I answer the question "What are we to have?" in a more formal, intellectual way—through the head.

I supply the answer to this question by handing out a typed sheet to every student in the class. This sheet contains a list of steps and definitions that characterize the spiritual quest. I tell my students that whatever questions may arise concerning the whys and hows of the spiritual journey will probably be addressed somewhere on this sheet.

The list reads as follows:

1. *From a spiritual perspective, the purpose of life is to achieve soul realization.* There is a transcendent spiritual quality within the heart of every man and woman, a potential known and sought after from time immemorial. If fully awakened, this spiritual quality removes seekers from the ordinary sorrows and confusions of life, and provides heightened states of aliveness, joy, and certainty. The meaning and purpose of life is therefore not hidden but clear. It is to find and awaken this higher part of ourselves. We call this higher part *the soul.*

2. *The importance of spirituality is largely ignored in modern society.* All of us are born with a degree of spiritual potential. But due to the immeasurable and intangible nature of spirituality, and because we live in a materialistic age, the existence of this invisible potential remains largely speculative and unacknowledged. It has not always been this way. Up to the last century the greatest philosophers, scientists, and artists believed in a Divine Intelligence, and sought to integrate it into their teachings. It is only our present scientifically oriented age that ignores the importance of religio-spiritual values in a person's life, and that denies the universality—and in many cases the possibility—of transcendent states of consciousness.

3. *Spirituality completes us.* The idea of a search for the soul presumes that the ordinary man and the ordinary woman are, in a manner of speaking, "unfinished." In this sense, we are all incomplete beings, with many secret and hitherto unexplored parts of ourselves that lie fallow all our lives unless they are awakened and cultivated. Human beings, this idea insists, have the possibility of achieving a state of being that far surpasses anything we ordinarily know, and that far exceeds both the emotional and intellectual boundaries set by our ordinary, everyday consciousness. We can be different people than we are; it is possible. Some would even insist that this transfiguration

from the ordinary to the extraordinary is the very quintessence of all spiritual undertaking.

4. *Spiritual awakening is most likely to happen in the adult years.* Though a person's spiritual potential can express itself at any point in the life cycle, even in early youth, it tends to become most active during the adult years. Expressions of spiritual interest are especially likely to appear after people have lived through a certain number of life experiences—the birth of children, the death of parents and other loved ones—and begin to question whether their present life gives them the gratification they're seeking. Yet while there is no question that deep psychospiritual changes typically occur during midlife and beyond, there are also individuals who go through all the stages of awakening during the first half of life. According to tradition, Jesus died at age thirty-three. Shankara, the greatest exponent of the Hindu Vedanta, lived only thirty-two years. The spiritual journey, in other words, while it is most likely to unfold in the middle or later years, cannot be ultimately tied to a specific age. In fact, when all is said and done this journey should be understood not so much as a time-bound system but as a *story,* a metaphoric model that portrays the higher life in all its mysterious and manifold possibilities.

5. *Spirituality unfolds in a series of steps and stages.* I call these steps the Stages of the Soul. All of us are invited to participate in this drama of self-transformation at some point in our lives. There is no guarantee, however, that we will take advantage of the chance when it comes. Some people choose not to. While the invitation to the spiritual journey is a birthright, it is entirely our own choice whether or not we embark on the journey once we are called.

6. *Spiritual awakening requires struggle and effort.* Unlike physical aging, the spiritual function within a person does not unfold and progress automatically according to a biologically preprogrammed schedule. Our spiritual capacity exists *as a possibility only.* If it is to unfold in all its five stages, it must be intentionally and consistently encouraged over a period of time via struggle, commitment, and effort.

7. *Not everyone passes through all the stages.* Though the Stages of the Soul tend to follow one another in sequence (as I discuss below and in the chapters to follow), this sequence is not written in stone. There is no way of predicting whether a person will pass through all the stages from beginning to end. A person may, for instance, experience the first stage but go no further. Unlike our inner biological clocks, the development of the soul unfolds ac-

cording to a schedule of its own that is independent of both manipulation and desire. As with the growth of a plant, spiritual potential can be watered and nurtured; but it cannot be coerced into flowering.

8. *Each person's experience of the Stages of the Soul is different.* Every person experiences the Stages of the Soul in a different way. Each person's spiritual journey is unique. At the same time, enough similarities exist between individual journeys to allow us to speak in terms of patterns and to identify a common chronology. The unfolding of the spiritual stages can be observed in other people, and can be experienced with undeniable certitude within ourselves.

9. *The Stages of the Soul are "spiritual" stages.* By "spiritual" I mean that the experience of the Five Stages: (a) shifts our center of being away from the external world and toward the inner life of the soul, (b) encourages a sense of disengagement from the ordinary problems of daily living, (c) increases our commitment to virtuous behavior—kindness, generosity, unselfishness, love, (d) raises our normal state of consciousness to a higher "transpersonal" level that awakens new and extraordinary faculties within us, (e) creates a desire to give back to the world what we have gained spiritually and to devote ourselves in service to others.

Finally, in my research into human spiritual development I have come to identify five Stages of the Soul. Each one of these stages leads naturally to the next, and at the same time is a logical extension of the one that comes before. Taken as a group the Five Stages comprise the complete cycle of the spiritual quest.

The Five Stages of the Soul are:

1. The Call
2. The Search
3. The Struggle
4. The Breakthrough
5. The Return

What follows is an overview of what we can expect to encounter in these five stages. In the rest of the book, we will discuss how these stages unfold in people's lives, and the ways in which they can change our lives, and our destinies.

THE FIVE STAGES OF THE SOUL

Stage One: The Call

Recognized by sacred traditions everywhere as the first step in the pursuit of spiritual wisdom, the Call is known by many names—conversion, summons, change of heart. This turning is, as one writer describes it, "from the circumference to the center, from appearance to reality, from the sensible to the intelligible, time to eternity . . ." Phrased another way, as the great Hindu saint Sri Ramakrishna tells us: "You hear the roar of the ocean from a distance. By following the roar you can reach the ocean. As long as there is a roar, there must also be the ocean."

Ibrahim ibn Adham, mighty king of Balkh, was one day sitting on his throne when he heard a noise above him on the roof. "Who's there?" he called out.

"It's my camel that's making all the noise," came the reply.

"How is it possible for a camel to be on a roof?" asked the king.

"How is it possible for a man who wishes to know God to sit on a throne?" the answer came back. The next day Ibrahim ibn Adham renounced his kingdom and set out to pursue the Call.

For most of us, the Call comes in less dramatic ways.

Brother Lawrence, a seventeenth-century Carmelite monk whose book *The Practice of the Presence of God* is seminal reading for Christians, heard the Call quietly one winter day. The sight of a barren tree, he told his biographer, made him realize that its leaves would return in the spring, and that soon after this flowers and fruit would follow.

This simple thought, Brother Lawrence's biographer writes, "set him loose from the world, and kindled in him such a love for God that he could not tell whether it had increased during the more than forty years he had lived since."

Brother Lawrence's biographer adds to these observations that "there are all too many of us now past middle age who feel soiled and weary—the bloom rubbed off from our aspirations—our hopes scaled down to the living of a life more mediocre every day. To such it comes like second wind to consort with a man of fifty who takes hold of himself and finds heaven on earth among the pots and pans of an institution's kitchen. We may demur that he is of finer stuff than we; but no, he pleads, I did nothing but let God have His own way with me."

Stage Two: The Search

We respond to the Call with a Search. For most of us the Search begins with the quest for guidance.

The number of choices here is extraordinary: the Kabbalah and dream workshops, Zen Buddhism and AA, mythology and parapsychology, Christian mysticism and Christian Science. There is a universe of compelling paths to choose from. But as we shall see, one must explore with discretion. "It took me a year just to weed out the groups I *didn't* want to visit," a disgruntled man in one of my classes told me.

Once the search for a teaching is completed, a second type of search then begins: seeking after the place within us where our spiritual impulse lives and grows. "The seeking after God," remarks the Sufi writer Yacub ibn Said, "is an endless process, even for the saint. We must try to rediscover the Friend in our hearts every moment. Our Search is an attempt to keep remembering what we already know."

On a conscious level the Search is a quest for a spiritual practice that seems right for us. On a deeper level what we are really looking for is a secret "something" not easily put into words but that we sense is out there somewhere, someplace, waiting for us, *calling* to us—the "secret God behind the gods" as Emerson calls it. "Turn ye unto me," says Zechariah, "the Lord of hosts, and I will turn unto you."

Stage Three: The Struggle

Once guidance is found, whether through a church, a spiritual guide, or a more contemporary way, the soul's true passage begins. This passage partakes of a cosmic dimension as well as a human one. Those who set out on this passage become spiritual kin to the heroes and heroines of scripture and myth.

Like any seeker on a quest, spiritual heroes and heroines must endure trials, pass tests, and be challenged along the way. These challenges may not look to us today like the devils and dragons depicted in myth. But they surely behave like them. They haunt us in thoroughly modern garb, and in the body of thoroughly modern problems: disillusionment, depression, regret, impatience, a sense of futility and cynicism, a tendency to become habit-bound and set in our ways. They appear as insensitive bosses, faithless lovers, ungrateful children, bouts with chronic disease. They fall upon us from the realm of the inanimate in the shape of mounting bills, accidents and acts of God, rejection slips, tax audits, all the large and small woes that beset the modern pilgrim.

Though these enemies seem familiar and even trivial at times, their arrows burn in our sides as deeply as the arrows burn in the sides of mythological heroes, diverting us from our spiritual efforts. To reach our goal we must meet these obstacles head-on.

In this sense, the Struggle *is* the way.

Stage Four: The Breakthrough

"I went into the yard to the pump," describes a thirty-five-year-old man, speaking about his spiritual Breakthrough experience. "And just as I got there it came—a shock, a flood of light, and along with, or immediately following, the shock and the subjective glow—like a great internal blaze—came the feeling of absolute harmony with the power that made all things and is in all things. All striving stopped—there was nothing to stive for—I was at peace."

Making this quantum leap into a state of at-oneness with something beyond ourselves, spiritual traditions tell us, is the reason why we are born on earth, and why we struggle. Not to propagate our species. Not to satisfy nature. Not even to learn, or create, or love. But to discover those parts of ourselves that are connected to the Supreme Principle of the universe. "To know the sweetness of the Infinite within us," remarked the fifteenth-century Christian mystic Nicholas of Cusa. "That is the cause, the reason, the purpose, the *only* purpose of our being."

A Breakthrough comes at a moment when the spiritual forces collecting inside us can no longer be held in check. A sudden surge of energy pushes things to the limit; then follows a burst of vision, and the hidden forces of the world pour into consciousness. Something is changed in us, and we are never the same.

This inner awakening, as Assagioli describes it, "is characterized by a sense of joy and mental illumination that brings with it an insight into the meaning and purpose of life; it dispels many doubts, offers the solution of many problems, and gives an inner source of security . . . a new loving and lovable individual now smiles at us and the whole world, eager to be kind, to serve, and to share his newly acquired spiritual riches."

Although inevitably illuminating, there are many levels of Breakthrough experiences, some small, some great, some lasting, some temporary. In the Breakthrough chapter, we will meet men and women who have lived through these experiences, and discover the different ways in which their encounters have changed them.

Stage Five: The Return

Experiencing a spiritual Breakthrough leaves its mark on a person forever. The Sufis refer to such people as "the Changed Ones." Yet, as the Zen proverb tells us: "Before enlightenment you chop wood and carry water. After enlightenment you chop wood and carry water."

Life goes on as before, and we go on with it in the ordinariness of everyday life. There's still work to do, families to raise, money to earn, and further spiritual progress to be made. At the same time, we now have special knowledge and experience to give back to the world, and we accomplish this task in a hundred different ways. This is the stage of Return.

Some people, for example, emerge from a Breakthrough experience as kinder and better individuals. Others become deeply committed to service and humanitarian projects. Still others, particularly those who have undergone repeated Breakthrough experiences over a long period of time, take their place as guides and mentors. One of these special people may be the storekeeper down the block or the neighbor across the street. These people speak to us of eternity in the silent language of the ordinary: in the way they eat a meal or sit in a chair; in a chance remark, an offhanded nod, a glance on the bus. With enough effort, we too can be among them.

Let Us Now Begin

And they *are* among us. Once, for example, in a seminar on midlife spirituality I was leading a discussion on the *Odyssey,* and attempting to tie it into a discussion of the Five Stages of the Soul. Most students in the class were familiar with this timeless Greek myth, so I inquired if anyone had thoughts concerning what its inner spiritual themes might be. I asked how its themes could be applied to the problems that we face in the midst of our ordinary lives.

The notion that ancient myths could provide guidance for our present life seemed to surprise the class. A sea of blank faces stared back at me. Finally one woman who hadn't spoken much in previous classes raised her hand and began to deliver a remarkable analysis.

Odysseus, she said, though a king, has fallen into exile because of a long separation from his true home. In the interim his kingdom has been overrun by raucous young suitors. These suitors, she explained, represent the misdeeds of our youth that keep our soul—represented here as Odysseus's wife, Penelope—prisoner in its own house. Penelope, the woman said, can only be set free after her husband, symbol of the ego, has passed through the appropriate trials and tribulations, then undergone the final ego-reducing indignity of returning to his own kingdom a beggar. "In this way," the woman said, "we are all kings in exile. We are all suffering trials and tribulations in order to get our spiritual kingdoms back."

When the woman stopped speaking, the rest of the class was stunned. At first no one said a word.

For my part, I was surprised and delighted that a student had penetrated so deeply into the inner meaning of an ancient myth. Every experienced teacher lives for an event like this: a moment when someone in your class "gets it," and you feel that all the effort of teaching has been worthwhile.

This student, it turned out, was an ex-nun who had spent her years since leaving the nunnery studying comparative religion and mythology as part of her own personal journey, and who had experienced several intensive Breakthroughs. Her comments that night sparked an extraordinary class discussion that was centered on the idea of the Five Stages of the Soul. I pointed out to them how this sequence of Call, Search, Struggle, Breakthrough, and Return appears in many fairy tales and myths. Someone in the class added that a similar sequence occurs in the lives of many great people. Someone else suggested that the five-stage sequence appears in certain movies.

By the end of the evening nearly everyone in the class had participated in the discussion, and we had talked about a multitude of ways in which the Five Stages show up in our lives and culture. We also spoke about related issues, about how we've all lost something precious from childhood, and how we all want to get it back again—just as the ancient stories like the *Odyssey* tell us we can. About how the traditional teachings of myth, religion, and the Spirit are not old at all, but timeless—and thus always new.

It was a message I've tried to convey in a hundred different ways, sometimes successfully, sometimes not. But the message got through most clearly that night when, glancing at the faces in the classroom, I said simply,

"Each of you knows in your heart that time is running out. We all know that we've all got fewer years ahead of us than behind us, and that the real questions are: Why am I here? What will I do with the rest of my life? What does it all mean?"

I went on to point out that these aren't exactly new questions. They're old questions, the oldest in the world, and also the most important questions we can ask, even if the answers to them are so hidden and elusive. They're the questions people have been asking themselves for untold thousands of years, and that they're still asking themselves today—now more than ever.

I glanced at the clock and realized that time was short. But it didn't matter. I had said what I wanted to say, and what I thought they needed to hear. I could tell from the faces around the room that my message had gotten through. But just as I was beginning to celebrate the good feelings, far in the back of the room I noticed a gray-haired, balding man who seemed disgruntled. I wanted to pretend I hadn't seen him. But I knew I couldn't do that.

"Professor Moody," he began hesitatingly. "You say these are the questions people have been asking themselves for five thousand years. But I haven't *got* five thousand years. I don't know how many years I do have. What can these Stages of the Soul do for someone like me?"

Other heads nodded in agreement.

It was the end of the evening. More words seemed superfluous. So instead I told the class a story.

I told them about a trip I'd made to the western steppes of Turkey some years ago. I explained how some friends had taken me to a windswept, desolate part of the countryside where the marble tomb of a Sufi saint sits looking out on a thousand miles of wilderness. Above the gateway, I told them, inlaid in stone, is a row of verses written by the saint himself; verses that have inspired visitors to this tomb for seven hundred years. And that inspired me in the same way.

"Well?" several people in the class asked. "What do they say?"

For a split second there flashed into my mind the thought of Rita, standing outside the Elderhostel classroom with that sad, desperate look on her face. Then I saw the blazing eyes of Father Pyotr.

"The verses read like this," I said, glancing from face to face across the room: " 'Come back, O you who still have breath to read these words, come back! There is still time!' "

And there is.

chapter 2

Hearing the Call

The day you were born a ladder was set up
to help you escape from this world.

RUMI

HEARING THE CALL

The Call

For many years psychologists have recognized that in each person's life a moment arrives when he or she discovers a central life task, a calling or "vocation." We experience this moment as a rite of passage advancing us from one stage of maturity to another. Psychologist Daniel Levinson identifies this moment of transition as "entering the adult world."

The spiritual Call has parallels to the vocational call, but at the same time it is different. Like other transitory life passages, the spiritual Call ushers us into new psychological territory with ourselves. And like other passages, it changes the way we look at ourselves and others. This, however, is where the similarity ends. The stages spelled out by Levinson, Erikson, and others are specifically age-related, marking a shift in the way we relate to our job, our family, our ambitions, and to other people—that is, to the external world. The spiritual Call, on the other hand, is not necessarily age-related—it can come at any point in our adult life—and it is an entirely personal and interior experience that may not even be noticeable to those around us.

In what form or circumstance does the Call enter a person's life? There are a thousand possibilities, depending on who we are, where we are, and what we need.

Sometimes, for example, people hear the Call when they have everything they want from life and then discover it's not enough. Conversely, the Call can be triggered by a sickness or a setback, by an episode of suffering so intolerable a person is forced to seek refuge in something stronger than the ordinary mechanisms of the ego. It may arise as a slow-growing realization, born of the passing days and years. Or it may come from a recognition that the things of ordinary life are leaving us hungry and incomplete, and that some deeper part of ourselves is yearning for a higher form of nourishment.

Sometimes the Call reveals itself in dreams. At other times people are drawn to it through a special book, a profound philosophy or idea. In certain cases the inner summons is brought, as Joseph Campbell explains, by a "herald"—a teacher, a mentor, a magical stranger we meet on the road of life. For still others, the Call explodes in a single flash of recognition: yes, we say, this is what's missing in my life! This is what I've been looking for all along!

There are as many Calls as there are human souls. Yet despite the different ways the Call comes to us, its message is always the same—the same voice spoken in a thousand different tongues: Come back! Come back! it says. There is still time.

The Great Secret

As I walked onstage at the first National Conference on Conscious Aging that afternoon I could feel my heart beating in my chest. Onstage sat a panel of distinguished guests in the field, including Ram Dass and Marion Woodman. The moderator had just introduced me to an audience of a thousand people, with glowing remarks.

There was just one problem. My host had introduced me as *the wrong person*. He'd confused me with Dr. Raymond Moody, the celebrated author of *Life After Life*.

"I'm not the person you think I am!" I wanted to shout to the audience as I mounted the stage. But more importantly, what I really should have said to them that day was: *"You're* not the person you think you are!"

This, I wanted to tell them, is the great secret we all hide from each other—and from ourselves.

Of course, on one level we all know perfectly well who we are. We know our names, our birthdays, our family tree. We know what our favorite books are, and how much money we have in the bank. We know what we like and what we hate.

But is what we do in life, and what we want from life, the whole story? Does the sum of our tastes and desires really define who we are? Isn't there more to us than this?

Yes, say the world's great spiritual traditions, there is.

Below the threshold of ordinary consciousness, they insist, lies a different self entirely, a luminous, pristine identity that represents our true nature, but that is buried under layer upon layer of false individuality. This nugget of soulhood is what we bring with us at birth, and it is what we take with us when we leave the world. In the interim, people pass from birth to death without knowing that this deeper identity exists. It is sealed off from our daily awareness by a thousand mental walls and emotional barriers. No matter how diligently we search throughout the world or within the corridors of ordinary philosophy and introspection, we will never find it.

In an engraving titled *Everyman* by the great Flemish artist Peter Bruegel, we see several cantankerous looking merchants rummaging through a mound of sixteenth-century consumer goods. Comprising the pile are barrels of foodstuffs, gambling paraphernalia, sacks of money, kitchen utensils, books, linens, tools, toiletries, all representative of the human inventory. The grave intensity with which the men ferret through this mountain of merchandise shows that they have not found what they are looking for. They are, what's more, bearded and old, bitter-looking and absorbed, a sign that they have been combing through the mound for a lifetime. Behind them on the wall hangs a picture showing a jester figure sitting among shards, staring at himself in the mirror. The legend below it reads: "No one knows himself." A poem at the foot of the engraving sums up the futility of this farcical treasure hunt—of trying to find one's true identity in the material world! "And no man knows himself despite such seeking; no light will help him in this lonely place. Strange! Though he looks with eyes forever open, he never sees at last his own true face."

This sensation that we are more than the sum of our parts, and that we are somehow cut off from a mysterious "other" self inside, is one reason why people tend to feel so disconnected and incomplete as the years pass. Although we may be thirty or forty or fifty years old, somehow it feels as if we've only half lived up till now, or not lived at all.

"It's as if I've drifted through the decades, one after the other, in a kind of a dream," a friend of mine told me. "Or that I've lived, yeah, but always on the edge of things. Always on the outside. I've never been able to find the source, if you know what I mean.

"It's out there somewhere, I know," my friend said. "That sweet spot, that sense of gratification I'm looking for. Trouble is, it always seems one step away. It's always just down the block, you know, just beyond your reach. Do other people feel that way? Maybe they've found it, I say to myself. But never me."

How, then, *can* the soul be found? Where is it hiding?

Or *is* it hiding? According to sacred tradition, the soul is always within reach, always waiting for us and calling to us. In the Koran, God says, "I am closer to you than your own jugular vein." In the Gospels, Jesus says, "The Kingdom of God is within you." The problem is not that the soul is absent; it's that our faculties of inner sight are not functioning well enough to see it. We have not yet, as Blake advises, cleansed the doors of our perceptions. What is in front of our very eyes remains veiled.

Rabbi Moshe Hayyin Efraim tells the story of how a village fiddler once played his instrument with such electrifying brilliance that everyone who heard the music immediately leaped up and began dancing. Whoever happened to walk by at that moment recognized the magic of the sounds and joined in. Then a deaf man came strolling by. The deaf man had never heard music, so the spectacle before him seemed like the frantic behavior of madmen—senseless leaping and jumping. Without ears to hear, eyes to see, the story implies, the magic that is before our very eyes escapes us.

The belief that there are many hidden parts within us, and that these parts play a strange but very real role in our lives, is fascinatingly illustrated in a passage from the famous book by the philosopher and mystic P. D. Ouspensky, *In Search of the Miraculous.*

In this saga of his years spent as a student of the Greco-Armenian mystic George Gurdjieff, Ouspensky insists that deep within every human psyche there exists higher mental and emotional centers capable of *unimaginably* sublime states of consciousness. But due to the hypnotic power of worldly influences, these centers remain inactive in most people—"asleep" in Gurdjieff's terminology. Unless their potential is awakened by proper guidance and spiritual practice, people spend their entire lives living at a level of awareness that is far lower than it could be, and *should be*. As a result, most of us end up experiencing the world through a tiny slit in our perceptions, living, as an ancient allegory has it, in the basement of a thousand-room palace. We are not who we think we are.

How does one find evidence of these hidden parts within oneself and others? The human psyche is like an onion, with layer upon layer surrounding the golden core of the soul. Though only a chosen few saints have constant access to this core, under certain conditions layers of the onion can be peeled away.

One day, Ouspensky tells us, a group of disciples gathered in Gurdjieff's apartment to discuss his ideas. In the middle of the meeting Gurdjieff placed two of the group members in a trance. In their absorbed state, the first subject of this "experiment," a frivolous young man suddenly became serious and astute, and all traces of his superficiality vanished. The second, a prominent middle-aged intellectual ordinarily full of topical opinions and brilliant conversation fell strangely silent.

Ask him what he is thinking about, said Gurdjieff, pointing to the older man. The man replied that he was thinking about nothing at all. Ask him what he wants, Gurdjieff continued. The man looked wistfully around the room and seemed to be thinking deeply on the question. Then he replied in a profoundly serious voice, "I think I should like some raspberry jam."

"Neither of them remembered anything the next day," Ouspensky goes on to say. Gurdjieff "explained to us that with the first [middle-aged] man everything that constituted the subject of his ordinary conversation, of his alarms and agitation, was in personality. And when his personality was asleep practically nothing remained. In the personality of the other there was also a great deal of undue talkativeness, but behind the personality there was an essence which knew as much as the personality and knew it better, and when personality went to sleep essence took its place to which it had a much greater right."

What's going on here? we are certainly entitled to ask. What point is Gurdjieff making with these dark enchantments? Is it true that if certain conditions are created within us we become entirely different people than we appear to ourselves and to the world? Is it true that most of what we really are is hidden, even from ourselves, and that these hidden parts cover parts that are deeper still, all the way down to a silent, immutable core? And how might this fact address the question of our own hidden potential?

You Are Not Who You Think You Are

According to the philosophy of virtually all the world's great religions, we all come to this world bearing traits of character that are innately *our own*. These qualities belong to what is cosmic and eternal within us, and as such they are the internal anchor points at which our spiritual evolution can begin. They are elements of our soul, if you will, or, as both transpersonal psychology and the Hindus term it, *the self*.

This self or soul is buried deep inside our psyche, where it remains untouched either by sorrow or by joy and where it contains both the center of our being and the point at which we connect to the Infinite.

On a day-to-day level, our minds have no direct contact with this deeper point of consciousness. We can't speak to it with words or thoughts. We can't control it with our will or imagination. In fact, we can't get in touch with our soul at all.

Yet our soul can get in touch with us, and sometimes *through* us. At such moments its voice is the voice of the spiritual Call.

What vehicle does the self use to speak to our conscious minds?

First and most familiarly, it speaks through dreams. Here the soul takes the form of archetypal symbols—a mentor figure, a golden flower, a shining city, a noble animal. These images convey advice and messages to us while we sleep, appealing to our deeper need for both guidance and transcendence.

"I've had several real spiritual dreams in my life," a man in his sixties told me. "The most powerful one was also the most simple and brief. It came in my mid-forties. All it consisted of was a silver ball rolling along, making a kind of celestial music. I would imagine that this music sounded like the songs that the Sirens sang, or the music that Orpheus played to tame the animals. Just hearing it made me realize that something deeply fundamental was missing from my approach to things. What was it? I didn't know, but somehow it was summed up in this strange music that the silver ball made. That's why this dream, just *this one dream,* got me interested in religion and self-realization."

"God," says the Book of Job, "gives us songs in our sleep."

A second way the soul transmits its wisdom is through the media of sacred art, myth, scripture, and music: Gothic cathedrals, Indian ragas, Chinese landscape paintings, Gregorian chants, passages from the Bible and other sacred books. These sublime sounds, words, and images are intentionally designed to speak to the deepest sectors of our consciousness and to arouse a response, like a celestial echo, from our deepest parts.

The third way in which the soul can speak to us, and a risky one certainly, is by means of physical austerities. In such instances the soul is forced into unveiling itself by means of physical self-punishment—starvation, fire walking, self-flagellation, puncturing the body with needles. These and a multitude of similar methods are still practiced in many parts of the world as a means of putting the ordinary consciousness into suspension and waking up some deeper, more visionary part of the psyche. In the Philippines, for instance, members of an extreme Christian cult allow themselves to be crucified on a wooden cross with iron spikes on Good Friday, like Jesus. Among India's wandering tribe of fakirs there are ascetics who stand on one leg for twenty years, or who travel a thousand miles to a holy shrine by walking the entire length of the journey backward or by rolling the entire way.

Lastly, and most profoundly, the soul calls to us through actual spiritual practice: meditation, prayer, visualization, breath control, ritual, chanting, sacred dance, invocation, and vision quests. These techniques, practiced by all of the world's great religious traditions, are designed to suspend ordinary discursive thought processes and to put us in direct touch with the voice of our higher faculties.

In the past, austerities, dream interpretation, sacred art, and devotional exercises were all part of humankind's experience, and people's lives intertwined with these practices in familiar ways. Today we are not as fortunate. Most of us grow up without benefit of such supports, and as a result we are molded by the profane influences of environment and education at a particularly early age. By the time we reach our teens these worldly influences have crystallized into a kind of fixed mask that we continue to wear for the rest of our lives. Dubbed the "persona" by Jung, this false sense of self ingratiates its way into our mental household at an early age like a sly intruder. It then proceeds to infiltrate every corner of our conscious minds until it becomes the undisputed governor over all we think, say, and do. It is like the German folk tale of Harmless Hans, the court jester who begins as the king's buffoon and ends up running the court and controlling the king's very soul.

Soul and Persona

Where do these worldly influences come from that mold and shape our personalities? From our parents primarily, but also from our family, teachers, friends; and in a more peripheral way from books, films, politics, and popular culture in general. These forces of ordinary life impact on us from all directions at once, until one day we enter the world of adulthood as little more than a bundle of ideas, attitudes, likes and dislikes that have been borrowed from other people—ideas and attitudes that have little, and sometimes nothing, to do with who we are deep inside. To the world, and to ourselves, we appear to be Dina or Jerry, Marsha or Fred. Deep inside we are a mysterious and unknown other. To the world we appear to be forty-three years old. Deep inside a part of us is still only six years old, and wants nothing more than a little raspberry jam.

"Oh my God," Louise Cummins, a colleague from a midwestern university told me last year. "I'm forty-seven and have everything I want. But I keep feeling there's a little unfed orphan inside me that needs something completely different from the things I've spent my life working for. I can't believe where the years have gone. What I have is not really what I want anymore. But I don't know what it is I *do* want now. I don't know how to feed that little orphan!"

Louise Cummins's statement cuts to the heart of the matter. Our soul wants one thing, our mask of personality quite another. This push-me, pull-you struggle between polar opposites creates a tremendous state of inner tension throughout the adult years.

"When I was growing up," said Lisa Hills, a forty-eight-year-old geriatric nurse, "my mother wanted me to be a nurse. Not a doctor, mind you. In those days girls didn't even *think* about becoming doctors. But my real interest wasn't medicine anyway, it was nature and the land; planting, growing things. I was raised in a small town in Ohio. My mother and I kept a garden in our backyard. The hours I spent in that patch walking barefoot on the warm soil, talking to the little vegetable shoots as they poked their adorable heads out of the ground, was as close as anything I've ever had to a religious experience. I decided as a kid that I wanted to buy some land someday and spend my time taking care of it. But my mom was insistent. I had talent for science. She pushed me in that direction. I ended up going to nursing school and settling in a big city.

"I've worked as a nurse now for twenty-some years, but more dutifully than happily, you could say. There's so much to do when you're on the floor. It swallows up everything in your life. I kept feeling that as a person I was getting narrow and out of touch, but there was nothing I could do about it. I'd put all my plans for getting back to nature on the shelf somewhere. I was so busy being a nurse I never thought about anything else.

"Then my son got to be seven or eight and we moved to a suburb of

Columbus. My husband dug a garden and it was like magic: my son loved that little patch of land the same way I did as a kid. He was out there every day hoeing, talking to the plants. Soon I was sharing all the gardening lore with him. It was a rebirth for me, a recontacting of something I thought had withered in me. What fun! What a blast! God, I'd forgotten how much I loved it! If I could have my way, that's what I'd do: farm the earth. But of course, I can't. I'm too immersed in my profession."

Over and over again, both at the Brookdale Center and around the country, I have listened to stories from people that hark back to the tension between the mask of persona and the buried self: between the person we are elementally and the person the world has turned us into. People in their forties and fifties quickly understand what I'm getting at when I mention these ideas in class. The recognition factor is almost instantaneous. There is something deeply evocative about the idea of a secret self struggling to be heard inside us. But there is also something troubling about it as well.

"I just *loved* art and drawing as a kid," a catering consultant named Ann told me. "I did it all the time. It was part of me. Then my art teacher in fourth grade told me I couldn't draw at all. I had no talent. Her remark on my report card that term was: 'Ann continues to whistle in art class.' After that I stopped liking art and rarely drew again."

Diane's story had a similar theme with a different twist. As a young girl she remembers hearing two voices speaking inside her. One wanted to be a nurse, go to Africa, and help Albert Schweitzer save the lives of starving natives. This motif often showed up in her dreams. The other wanted to make a lot of money and marry a millionaire. "As time passed," Diane said, "and everyone talked so much about 'getting rich' and what kind of sports car they'd buy if they had a lot of money, all that stuff, the second part of me won out. So I've spent my life running after the almighty dollar. Still, when I think of Albert Schweitzer and that childhood part of me that wanted to do unselfish things for the world I get sad."

"I remember a moment when I was in camp near Wingdale, Connecticut," David told a class one evening in Philadelphia. "I was watching a colorful sunset. I thought to myself at that moment: something is setting in me too. I was eight years old, in third grade. That's exactly the way I phrased it: something is going down, sinking in me. And something new is rising. Afterward I felt incredibly melancholy."

Another major contributor to our false sense of self is the *imitation factor*. As we grow up, and especially during our teenage years, we fancy ourselves to be uniquely individual when, in fact, we are simply following the herd. Then maturity sets in. With a bit of well-considered self-analysis it becomes apparent that many of the character traits we thought had flowered spontaneously from our innate originality have actually been borrowed from others. Our personalities, we may discover, are a veritable patchwork quilt of bits and pieces picked up along the superhighway of life from friends, relatives, even magazines and movies, then sewn together into a single artificial cloak we wear each day and call "I." When this realization begins to dawn we start to ask, "Where's the real me?"

"I remember talking to my friends as a kid and trying to sound like John Wayne," a psychology professor named Stephen admitted to me one day in my office. "I consciously tried to imitate him. I'd ask myself what would the big guy do in front of a girl, or if someone started to push him around. I remember picturing him in my mind as I talked. I remember striking attitudes like a cowboy. It was as if I was intentionally trying to be somebody else. Once in a while today I catch myself assuming what I think of as my John Wayne swagger."

Sidney's story puts a similar, if somewhat darker emphasis on the power of imitation. Even the unwanted or unintended things we learn as children become a part of us. "When my father was doing chores around the house he'd always scream 'Goddamnit!' in this bloodcurdlingly angry tone whenever the nail went in cockeyed or something. I remember wondering what 'goddamnit' meant. Then after a while I started doing the same thing whenever something went wrong: yelling 'Goddamnit!' At first I didn't feel any anger when I yelled it. It was even kind of fun. But I also remember instinctively realizing it wasn't a good thing I was doing, imitating my father in this way; that there was danger in it; that if I kept shouting 'Goddamnit!' like him every time I messed up I'd start becoming like him. I really remember that. I was about five or six. And sure enough, today whenever anything goes wrong I yell 'Goddamnit!' with the same anger in my voice. Sometimes it's as if I hear my father screaming *through* me. Though he's dead now a decade."

The concept of soul versus persona provides a compelling and instructive perspective on the human condition. The question is, how are we to put such an abstract idea to work on our own life's journey?

Many spiritual traditions answer this question by directing us back to the notion of levels of consciousness. While delving into the unconscious and shining light on our repressed and traumatic past is important, they say, it's only part of the struggle, the psychological part. It's also necessary to move *upwards* as well as downwards; to activate not only our *un*conscious faculties but our *super*conscious ones as well, the higher centers in our heart and mind that many schools of psychology ignore, but which have been the cornerstone of spiritual doctrine from time immemorial. And to do so by using the contemplative techniques that traditional teachings have employed for centuries. Such methods not only broaden our lives. They give us new lives. They help us, in Christian terms, to be born again.

Is it too late to develop these higher potentials in ourselves as we get older? Quite the contrary. During the medieval era certain religious orders only accepted members who were well into their middle years. In Judaism the first half of life is traditionally spent studying the outer teachings of the religion, law and theology mainly. It is only in the second half, when one turns forty years old and has acquired, as they say, "a bellyful of Talmud," that a person is allowed to study the deeper mystical traditions. Islam, too, recognizes the fortieth year as the pivotal age at which a person begins the serious pursuit of religious study. "When [a person] is fully grown, and reaches forty years," says the Koran, "this person says: My Lord, arouse me that I may give thanks for the favors which you have bestowed on me . . . and that I may now do right."

According to many spiritual philosophies, our task throughout life, and *especially* during the middle years, is to rediscover the soul locked inside us and return it to its rightful place at the center of our identity. This is one meaning of the biblical injunction "Ye must become as little children." It is not our task to become childish, the Bible tells us, but to become *childlike;* to recover our untarnished self from beneath the layer upon layer of ego that covers it; and to use this pristine center as a platform for spiritual growth.

Our essential self, in this sense, embodies the evolving point of our soul. It is what we were before the world had its way with us. And even more importantly, it is what we may become as we move toward the second part of our lives.

The Golden Self

I first read the story of Gurdjieff and his entranced disciples nearly thirty years ago, and at the time it made a vivid impression on me. Like the subjects of this experiment, I felt then, as I do now, that I also am not one person inside but two.

The first of these persons is a highly social being who sits in an office in Manhattan all day, talks on the phone to colleagues around the country, writes scholarly papers, delivers lectures, directs workshops, jokes, argues, gives orders and advice, and at home kicks the soccer ball around with his son. A pillar of the community. That's the visible Harry Moody in the external world.

Beneath this outer mask, however, lives an entirely different being with his roots deeply sunk into the invisible. This second person is a rather gentle, passive soul, a good deal quieter than the erudite professor who goes to the office every day, and a good deal closer to the center of reality. I have caught phantom glimpses of him through the years, sometimes in the midst of ordinary activities, most often during meditation. If asked what he really wants, this hidden self might not ask for raspberry jam exactly. He might tell you instead that what he likes best are sledding, egg creams, and staring at the patterns in clouds. He would certainly say he prefers the serenity of the rose garden and the hermitage to power struggles in the office.

Yet despite its benevolence, this second self of mine remains so remote and silent that at times I wonder why it's there at all. If the soul doesn't play a part in everyday life, what part *does* it play? Surely this soul has important lessons to contribute. Perhaps it can point the way to peace and contentment. Why then does it sit so passively in the shadows of our consciousness, unheard and unacknowledged throughout our lives?

The answer is that it is *not* sitting there passively. It is actually calling to us all the time, sending us message after message. It is talking to us. Perhaps even pleading with us. But it is doing so in its own secret language, the language of spiritual communication—symbol, contemplation, art, ceremony, and especially our dreams.

Contemporary author Andrew Harvey describes one such spiritual dream: he is sitting alone on a deserted beach when he sees a beautiful golden figure in the distance walking toward him. It is unclear whether the figure is a man or woman, but he soon sees that its face is glowing with love. This dream person, shining with a golden aura, sits down next to him and embraces him.

"Who are you?" Harvey asks after a long moment of ecstatic communion.

The mysterious figure smiles and replies, "I am you." In the next instant Harvey wakes up, knowing with utter certainty that he has met his hidden self.

Such radiant figures, when they appear at all, come to us mostly at night, it is true. Yet the fact is that *all of us* have a version of this golden person inside us, and that the search for this being—this self or soul—can become our foremost goal during the middle and later parts of life.

Why is it that spiritual seeking is so favored at this particular stage of life development? Because before we can understand the light and shadow of our own personal history, a certain number of years must first be credited to our experience bank. If and when we hear the Call in youth it can easily fire us with impossible expectations and hopeless idealism for a journey we are not yet experienced enough to understand. If, on the other hand, we first hear the Call in old age, we may feel that too little time is left. The great advantage of being receptive to the Call during the middle years is that we are old enough to know its necessity, young enough to carry it through.

Once we reach a certain point in the life cycle, moreover, the distance that separates us from our early years permits a panoramic view of where we have been and where we can still go. From these heights we begin to discern a purposeful pattern to our past and a meaningful goal for the future. "We live life forward," the philosopher Sören Kierkegaard once remarked, "but only understand it backward." At this point in our lives we understand that there are deceptions and dangers to be wary of. We know enough when to be skeptical and how to gauge our powers and strengths. At the same time, we now realize that our time on earth is limited, and that if we are going to move toward something genuine, we must do it soon.

Spiritual awakening is a process, not an event, as we had imagined it to be when we were younger. It is a journey of stages, not a one-shot awakening on a mountaintop. Our inner self is not revealed in a colossal burst of revelation. It is glimpsed in moments, flashes, in what James Joyce called "epiphanies." For these moments to reveal themselves experience is necessary, and the passing of years. Something must ripen in us and mature like a fruit before we begin to spiritually awake. We do not find our soul on demand. The soul finds us and calls us; and only when the time is right.

This stepwise unveiling of the hidden self has echoes in nature and the world around us, even in the cosmic process of evolution itself. Harvard biologist Stephen Jay Gould, for example, suggests a view of evolution that he terms "punctuated equilibrium." Through careful study of the fossil records, Gould points out, we learn that for aeons of time no record can be found of evolutionary advance. Then suddenly eruptions of dramatic change "punctuate" this equilibrium: older species quickly die out, new ones come into existence to fill the biological niche. After this surge of activity exhausts itself, equilibrium returns and another long period of stability follows.

Paralleling this theory in human terms, life course psychologists now recognize that individual lives also follow their own path of punctuated equilibrium: they advance not in an orderly series of sequential changes, but in sudden spurts of growth and creativity sandwiched in between long stretches of stability.

This, moreover, is the main theme developed by Yale psychologist Dr. Daniel Levinson, in his pathbreaking work, *The Seasons of a Man's Life*. Levinson found that every human life is segmented into intervals of relative constancy, which in turn is pierced sporadically by short, intense bursts of identity reevaluation and a resulting emotional transformation. These moments occur at age-related crossover points or "passages" such as at the end of adolescence or during the approach of middle age. If we can successfully work our way through these upheaval periods we often find ourselves stronger, more well-rounded people on the other side.

What Levinson and other life course psychologists *do not* dwell on, it should be added, is that after passing several of the most significant milestones on the aging chart and realizing we are drawing closer to life's end, many of us begin to undergo a troubling cluster of existential whisperings that are different in kind and mood from anything we have experienced before. This recognition of our own mortality works wonders for focusing the mind and for setting us on the spiritual path. Awareness of death, as it were, is spirituality's greatest friend. It brings to mind an incident in one of Carlos Castaneda's Don Juan books in which Castaneda and his Indian shaman teacher Don Juan are driving along a remote desert road in Mexico late one night. Lulled by the passing hours, Castaneda glances into his rearview mirror and sees a pair of headlights, an unusual sight in this deserted stretch of wasteland.

The lights proceed to follow the car for hours, never drawing closer and never falling back. As the night wears on, Castaneda becomes increasingly uneasy. There is something deeply disturbing about these lights. Finally he tells Don Juan about them.

Don't concern yourself, says the old shaman offhandedly. It's just your death stalking you.

Castaneda, needless to say, finds this assurance cold comfort, and continues driving in a silent sweat. More time passes without change. Then suddenly the lights vanish.

Profoundly relieved, Castaneda announces that Death or whatever it is that has been trailing them has disappeared. Not at all, replies Don Juan. He's just turned off his lights.

In a similar fashion, most of us at times feel tracked by our mortality, especially when we catch a glimpse of its headlights in our own mirror. Such glimpses occur with increasing frequency as we age. They happen when friends die, when parents pass away, when we endure a medical scare. "Don't look back," baseball great Satchel Paige liked to tell the fans. "They might be gaining on you."

Yet an awareness of our mortality need not be a morbid indulgence. It can be a natural and healthy response to an awareness of our place in the life cycle and of our spiritual unfolding.

Psychologists explain, for example, that in the years of early adulthood, in one's twenties and early thirties, the ego-centered parts of a person predominate. During these years, the driving motivation in life is to get ahead and establish an adult identity. At this stage, concerns about the end of life or its transitoriness, and thus with spiritual growth, remain in a state of suspended animation.

In our thirties this need to accumulate and succeed continues and even intensifies. We fine-tune our self-image. We strengthen or sever personal commitments. We sharpen our wits and skills. The emphasis now is on outwardness, mastery, engagement. Beneath it all, though, a silent current of spiritual restlessness runs beneath the surface of our daily affairs.

As we reach our later thirties and early forties, we finally stand at the pinnacle of our aptitude and creativity. No longer are we youthful greenhorns trying frantically to achieve adult status in a grown-up universe. We've learned to play the game by now, and most of us play it well—we are competent, effective, seasoned citizens of the world. As social psychologist Bernice Neugarten observes, forty or fifty years of living give us a treasure that can only be won by experience: acute and well-tempered judgment.

The problem for many people at this stage of maturity is that the prime of life is not always so prime, and success not always so successful. For a colleague of mine, Robert Atchley, success in fact proved more of a burden than a boon. At age thirty-five Atchley had already been appointed a full professor of sociology and written a best-selling book in his field. "The elevator had gone to the top and just kept going," he told me as we sat together one afternoon at a national conference and talked about his personal journey.

"I'd followed the whole program, just like the Little Engine That Could. I'd made the climb up the mountain and reached the top. But now I was also at the end of the line. I could have taken on another mountain, I suppose, chugged up to the top again: 'I think I can, I think I can!' But no—

enough is enough. I didn't want to do that again. Why? Because at that point in my life I'd had all the success anybody could ever want *and it wasn't enough*. I decided there had to be a better way. I wanted to find some kind of reflective, inner-looking element to my life."

In sociological terms, Robert Atchley had "plateaued out." Having reached the summit of his profession early, he had won the big prizes, then decided that the big prizes weren't what he really wanted at all.

"Did this feeling of wanting to turn to a reflective lifestyle come in a kind of blinding flash?" I asked him.

"No," he replied. "It was more like sinking into quicksand. It just started to dawn on me as I went through a series of successes: Well, where do I go from here? What now? I'm where I thought I always wanted to be. I've gotten all the jollies. So what? I felt a sense of letdown. An inner void. It's how you feel when you finish a big project like your Ph.D. You expect that the weight of the world is going to lift from your shoulders. But it doesn't. You don't get lasting satisfaction from achievement-oriented kinds of things, I decided. The only real things are things of the heart and spirit. So I started following that part of myself."

Robert Atchley's experience of effort, reward, and letdown is a common phenomenon among many successful people at midlife. A public opinion poll taken in 1994 by the National Opinion Research Center shows that over half of all adults in their twenties find their lives "exciting." By the time people reach their forties this proportion dips to 46 percent, then down to 34 percent for those over sixty. Unless adults find new and deeper sources of meaning in life, the second half of life can become a period of diminishing emotional returns.

For Priscilla Brager, a student in one of my midlife workshops, early success came in a variety of forms, leaving her wealthy and well positioned. Then a few months before turning fifty Brager left her glamorous job at an advertising firm on Madison Avenue; just as she had walked out on a budding career as an opera singer, and before that as an international marketing consultant living all over the world in romantic settings. None of these dazzling careers seemed to satisfy her.

"I was very much into the show of the world, into being somebody," Brager told me over coffee one evening after class. "Around fifty I began thinking: now that I don't have to work for a living anymore, how do I want to spend the rest of my days? I decided to find a new direction. Madison Avenue wasn't it. Music was no longer the way. I didn't really know what to do.

"So I started to indulge myself in everything that you shouldn't do. You know, just lying around all day watching television, listening to music, eating, reading best-sellers, doing what you think you'd want to do if you were rich and free. I traveled to a lot of great places, sometimes on a whim. It was just like, you know, snap your fingers: Why don't I go to Egypt today to see the pyramids! And off I'd go.

"Gradually all this wore off and I found myself more and more drawn to reading books on philosophy and religion, mostly Hindu and Buddhist. I felt there was a good deal in what I read but still, I said to myself, who knows? Maybe it's all speculation. Is there some underlying reality? Or is all this just fantasy to make life more interesting?

"I can't explain what happened after that. All I can say is that in the course of these explorations I found myself in a church one day. Then, at one moment, the grace of God descended upon me.

"There is nothing else I can say about the experience. It was a glimpse of a certainty, just a small moment. But very clear. Not particularly that Jesus Christ is the Son of God, or that Christianity is the way to happiness. Nothing like that. Just that there is a Reality more meaningful than everything we see around us, and that the purpose of life is to find that Reality. I knew in that single moment that this certainty is the only thing that counts, and that I wanted to spend my life finding it."

When the spiritual muse called Robert Atchley, he found himself sitting in, as he called it, the "quicksand" of a slow, painful spiritual unfolding. Priscilla Brager, on the other hand, found herself sitting in church. Both had been given too much of what they thought they wanted, and both had turned to some higher strength within themselves for renewal. What they were experiencing was the very thing the Chinese book of wisdom, the *I Ching*, describes when it says, "A time of abundance is usually brief. Therefore a sage might well feel sad in view of the decline that must follow."

Though we are at the summit of our strength and authority as we mature, something in many of us seems less certain of who we are than ever before. The goals of achievement that were so clear to us the day we graduated from high school or applied for our first job are now blurred and uncertain. Our health, our finances, our political system, our means of employment, the dependability of friends, all turn out to be less under control than we'd supposed. Indeed, life itself has become more layered and imponderable than it appeared from the vantage point of age twenty-one. Brought up in the 1940s, 1950s, and 1960s, when business was booming and optimism for the future had reached manic proportions, perhaps no other generations in American history have been weaned on such rosy expectations. But now that the piper is being paid in the 1990s and many of us are simultaneously entering midlife, confidence and idealism have given way to perplexity and disorientation. "I often find confusion in conclusions I concluded long ago," sings the middle-aged Siamese emperor in *The King and I*. And meanwhile, our precious time is running out. "The crisis of middle age," writes poet May Sarton, "has to do as much as anything with a catastrophic anxiety about time itself. How has one managed to come to the meridian and still be so far from the real achievement one had dreamed possible at twenty? And I mean achievement as a human being as well as within a career."

Carl Jung once wrote that the great question in the second half of life is whether we human beings are "related to something infinite or not." If we decide that we are not, or if we have no heartfelt need to answer this question, if we are steadfastly committed to pursuing a materialistic existence, this commitment provokes a sadness, and we feel lost among the aging crowd. In Christian terms, we are self-condemned to wander in Dante's dark wood, prisoners of the cosmic dream. "The care of this world," the Gospels warn, "and the deceitfulness of riches, and the lusts of other things entering in, choke the word and it becometh unfruitful." "But such sadness," the *I Ching* tells us, "does not befit [the sage]. Only [a person] who is inwardly free of sorrow and care can lead in a time of abundance. He must be like the sun at midday, illuminating and gladdening everything under heaven."

As we stand in the strong, bright midday sun of our human voyage, an opportunity awaits us now that will not come again, a "time of abundance" as the *I Ching* calls it. This opportunity is speaking to us in a voice we have not heard before. It is telling us to awaken from the ego-bound dreams that have kept us separated from our soul's birthright for the first half of our lives, and to follow, as Wallace Stevens calls it, "the poem in the heart of things." It is telling us that we are not who we think we are, and that our time is running out. But also that there is a great brightness ahead of us, and much hope, if we will just turn our gaze to the light. The golden Self within us can still be discovered and set free, it says. It is there. It is waiting for us. It is calling to us.

There is still time.

The Second Journey of Life:
Hearing the Call

As the first of the five spiritual stages—Call, Search, Struggle, Breakthrough, Return—the Call is like the gate of a Buddhist shrine or the portal of a Gothic cathedral, a celestial doorway inviting us to enter consecrated ground, and partake of the sacred. It is akin to what the Lakota Indians term "hearing with the ear of the heart, returning home like the flight of the jay." Or to the Christian concept of mutual turning: "Do thou think of Me," wrote St. Catherine of Siena, "and I will ever think of thee." Just as the first journey of life takes us from childhood to adulthood, so the Call that comes in the midst of our life invites us on what Gerald Collins has named "the second journey," a journey of the soul leading to a joy and wisdom far greater than anything we ever imagined in the journey of youth.

The Call motif is common in both religious allegory and folk epic. Joseph Campbell speaks of it in mythological terms as "the call to adventure," telling us how it summons the hero, moving his spiritual center of gravity away from society and toward an unknown land outside of time. "This fateful region of both treasure and danger," writes Campbell, "may be variously represented: as a distant land, a forest, a kingdom, underground, beneath the waves, or above the sky, a secret island, lofty mountaintop, or profound dream state; but it is always a place of strangely fluid and polymorphous beings, unimaginable torments, superhuman deeds, and impossible delight."

Of all the many stories I use in my classes to explain the basics of the spiritual Call, none is more evocative and instructive than a Gnostic tale known as "The Hymn of the Pearl." This ancient story, which has several forms but one abiding theme, speaks both to the heart and to the head in a way few others do.

Here's how it goes:

Once upon a time the great King of Heaven decides to send his beloved son on a sacred mission to earth to find and bring back the "Pearl that resides in the sea."

Anxious to take on this sacred mission and prove his loyalty, the prince leaves his father's kingdom with great determination. The moment he arrives in this world, however—that is, the moment he is born—he forgets both his mission and his royal origins. Drawn to the world's attractions, our hero becomes accustomed to this alien land and finally comes to believe it is the only home he has ever known. One version of the myth tells that while in the womb the prince repeats to himself over and over that when he is born he will not forget who he is and why he has come to earth. But then at the moment of birth, as the world's sights and sounds engulf him, he cries out in sorrow, "Alas! Alas! I have forgotten!" According to legend, this is the secret meaning behind every newborn infant's cry.

Time passes. The prince marries, has children, and indulges in the age-old labors and pleasures of human existence, all the while remaining in a state of spiritual forgetfulness.

Decades go by. Then in his fortieth year, a milestone age for spiritual awakening, the King of Heaven sends his son a message: remember, seek, struggle, accomplish, return.

But the prince pays no attention. He is too immersed in life.

So the King sends the message again, this time in a different form.

Again it is ignored.

Message after message is sent down over a period of years—Eastern religions would say over many lifetimes. Gradually the prince begins to comprehend the meaning of these heavenly dispatches and to recognize their urgency. In the end, after much hesitation and many slips and falls, he answers his father's Call, finds the Pearl of Great Price—his spiritual nature—and returns home from exile.

Like a plait of silver threads, several critical motifs run through this tale, all of them highlighting its underlying theme of the Call, and all designed not simply to entertain us but to rouse some sleeping part of our psyche as well. In this sense "The Hymn of the Pearl" is not simply an allegory of the Call at midlife; it is *a form of the Call itself,* a sacred teaching story designed to wake up the dormant spiritual strength in those to whom it is recounted.

Many years ago while in college I first read the books of the great Zen teacher D. T. Suzuki. Zen was already in vogue on the university circuit at the time, and I wanted to introduce myself to Suzuki's writings and add some knowledge of Japanese culture to my academic background.

Just a few pages into the first of the master's books, however, I realized there was something unusual, even uncanny about what I was reading. All the volumes on my college reading lists that year were full of the usual scholarly facts and theories. But here was something unexpected and unique. This author wasn't writing academic philosophy. He wasn't interested in propounding a brilliant new theory or winning scholarly accolades. What was he interested in? He was interested in *me,* and in my spiritual progress. With a compassion that leaped off the pages, this Buddhist scholar from another country and another time wanted me—and every person who read his books—to question the substance of their personal reality, to remember why they had come to the world, and to live their lives as if these questions were matters of life and death. There is, in short, something in Suzuki's writings, as well as in "The Hymn of the Pearl," that, as a psychoanalyst friend of mine puts it, "speaks to the back of our head"—that reminds us of something we once knew with crystalline clarity and have since forgotten.

But what? What is it that "The Hymn of the Pearl" is reminding us of? Here are some principal themes.

The Call comes to us in undramatic and unrecognized ways. For some people the idea of a spiritual Call seems like a hackneyed bit of romanticism, almost Hollywood in its theatricality. "It's like something out of a Cecil B. De Mille movie," a friend said to me. "Like when De Mille does the voice of God on Mount Sinai in *The Ten Commandments:* Moses! Come forth, O Moses!"

In his enthusiasm to dismiss all "rhetorical devices," as he calls them, my friend missed the point. For most of us the distinguishing feature of the Call is not its theatricality; it is quite the opposite: it is its very *lack* of drama. For a majority of us the Call is so undramatic, so *un-Hollywood,* that the first few times it comes to us we usually miss it entirely. Like the prince, we are so preoccupied with the obligations of "getting and spending" that we fail to recognize our own heavenly messages. They are drowned out by the TV; by phone solicitations, by arguments at the office, by the demands of spouses and lovers, children and accounts overdue.

Minnie Purl, a teacher who attended several of my classes at Brookdale, told me that it took ten or twelve years for her to hear the ache in her own heart. "The fact that there was a hole in my life and that I could fill it only with devotion was staring me in the face. I could feel it all the time. But somehow I didn't put two and two together. It's really weird, but you can have a craving for a long time and not know it's there."

"My mother raised me religious," said Donald Howard, another teacher in our classes, "but it never took. I didn't think it took. Even though I said my prayers regularly and even had conversations with God inside my head, it took till I was in my forties to realize that God was this really central thing in my life. I had been talking to Him and bargaining with Him for years. But in some way—it's hard to explain—I didn't give myself to Him until my second divorce gave me some time alone to think and realize my real situation."

"I started feeling the need for something metaphysical in my life around the time I had my third child," Janet Richards told a group of us one night at a seminar for retired people. "I was thirty-eight at the time. I started doing yoga to get back in shape after the birth. I did it for a year and got gradually more and more fascinated. Then I started reading yoga philosophy. After that I tried meditating, stopped for a while, went back to it a couple of years later. The bug never left me. But it took a lot of time to just sort of gestate in me before I realized how hooked I was on yoga and yogic philosophy. Finally, by the time I was in my fifties, I was meditating on a regular basis."

Brother Robert, a monk who resides at the Holy Cross monastery in the lower Hudson Valley, gave me his own view of this subject one autumn day in his refectory: "We often carry around an image in our minds that a spiritual Call is a dramatic event—like Paul on the road to Damascus. There's this expectation that a blinding light will come and give us certainty about what we must do. But the Call we're talking about is something more subtle. It's a calling but it's also something that says yes, and something that says 'I'm not sure.' We have to listen carefully to the message, live with it, try it on for size, look at ourselves in the mirror with it on for a while before we get its full meaning and significance."

To complicate things further, the Call may come in unlikely and seemingly unspiritual voices. We hear it speaking to us on the day our last child leaves home for college; or by the bedside of an ailing parent; or in the obituary of a distant acquaintance accidentally glimpsed in the newspaper.

In a little-known Grimm's fairy tale called "Death Messengers," the issue of recognition is tackled directly. In this story, the spirit of Death accosts a giant along the highway and starts to lead him away to the Kingdom of the Dead. The giant proclaims he is not ready to die, and the two titanic beings come to blows. In the showdown Death gets the worst of it and the giant ambles off, leaving Death by the side of the road beaten and bloodied.

Soon a young man happens by. Spying the beaten victim lying in a ditch, he revives him with kind words and a sip of whiskey from his flask.

"Do you know who I am?" Death asks when he is recovered.

The youth shakes his head.

"I am Death. I spare no one. Some day I will call for you as I do for all living beings. But to show how grateful I am for your help I will send my messengers to warn you before I come for your soul. This way you will have time to prepare."

Being something of a wastrel, the young man is delighted at his good fortune and goes happily on his way, knowing now that he can carry on to his heart's delight until the messengers arrive.

Soon he comes to a town, heads to the tavern, and gambles away his money. By and by he is reduced to poverty. But he knows he will not starve. Death has promised to send his messengers first.

Before long the young man is on his feet again and continues his merry ways. After some time a string of sorrows arrive to plague him. Yet he is confident that none of these sorrows will lead to his demise. The messengers have not appeared.

Finally the young man falls seriously ill and his friends are sure he will die. But the youth cheers them up. Death had promised, after all. And sure enough, he soon recovers.

One day this carefree youth is cavorting as usual with his comrades when a knock is heard at the door. The young man opens it and finds Death waiting at the doorstep. "Follow me," says the hideous presence, "your hour of departure has arrived."

"But that can't be!" cries the boy. "None of your messengers came!"

"Indeed they did," answers Death. "One after the next. First I sent poverty. Then a string of sorrows. Then sickness. And besides all these, did not my brother Sleep visit you every night and make you lie in your bed still and silent as a corpse? All these beings were my messengers. You simply did not recognize them."

The Call comes in many forms. In "The Hymn of the Pearl," a number of messages must be sent to the busy prince before he begins to notice them.

This is a wonderfully consoling idea when we think about it. The Divine King in this story is not a cruel, thunderbolt-flinging despot, nor is he a remote deity seated on a far mountaintop. He is rather a compassionate parent who patiently coaxes his forgetful children in a dozen different ways, some of them kindly, some stern, all of them necessary; until one day the children have ears to hear and begin their Return. The same is true of the Call.

"This idea of the spiritual Call," Brother Robert said to me at his monastery. "You find it mentioned in a lot of Christian literature. It's like being invited to a very rich banquet. God welcomes all of us with His glorious hospitality. He says, you know: try the liver pâté, I think you'll like it. And suppose you say no. Well, He's not going to be insulted. There are many other foods on His table to keep you interested and coming back for more. The smoked turkey. The stuffed mushrooms. He offers them to you one at a time."

"So God is not offended if we fail to respond to His Call right away?" I asked.

"The only way you're going to insult God," Brother Robert replied, "is by refusing to eat at His table at all. By turning your back on his hospitality. But don't worry. God is richer and more generous to us in His Call than we are in our hearing. So I often tell people: you need to choose. God holds this opportunity out for you. If you don't take it today He holds out a different opportunity for you tomorrow. Wait until the time is right. Then enjoy the banquet."

As I sat there that fall day in the Hudson Valley and listened to Brother Robert, my mind went back over the years to the many people in my classes who had heard the Call in such different ways. I thought of the woman abruptly divorced in midlife who discovered, to her surprise, that she preferred aloneness to marriage, and that she now had time at last to give to her search for self-transcendence. I thought of the man who left one job for another, lost this second job, considered suicide, and was saved only when his old pastor invited him back to church. I thought of the ballet dancer who retired early and in the stretches of boredom and inactivity that followed began for the first time to hear the voice of her inner self. Brother Robert said that there are many different foods on God's banquet table, perhaps even a different food for each of us; God is rich and generous in his Call.

The exiled prince is you and me. The prince's story is your story and my story. Like him, we have come to this world from a place beyond the stars. And like him, knowingly or unknowingly, we are strangers in a strange land.

"I feel so far away from where I really belong," is a phrase I often hear from the people I talk to, along with the comment: "I'm not really sure who I am anymore." We all feel like this to a greater or lesser degree.

In the 1970s a writer friend of mine named Richard told me his experience appearing on a TV quiz show called *To Tell the Truth*. The premise of this famous program was that three guests claim to be the same person. Two of these guests are impostors, one is real. A panel of celebrities has to decide between them.

"I was the real person," Richard told me, "surrounded by two pretenders. The pretenders had to sound like they knew what they were talking about, and they did it with great skill, making up these amazing on-the-spot improvisations to stump the panel. By the time I got through taping the show that day and listening to all the lies, I felt like I'd spent my day in a hall of mirrors. When I got home that night I wasn't exactly sure who I was anymore either. I felt like asking, 'Will the real me please stand up.' "

What Richard experienced that day is an amusing magnification of what we all feel from time to time in our daily lives—will the real me please stand up!

A forty-four-year-old social worker spoke in one of my midlife workshops about how as a child she experienced a peculiar sensation of "homesickness." "I couldn't have been more than five years old," she told the class. "But I had this sense that I didn't belong to the people I was living with—my family, the house where I lived, the other kids in kindergarten. I felt like I had come from another world. I felt that somehow I'd been plunked down in the midst of these strangers as a test or trial. The feeling was like being homesick, and was so real it frightened me. As I grew older, I forgot it. I didn't want to think of myself as 'weird' or 'different.' But a tiny part of the feeling has always stayed with me and never gone away."

Many of us experience variations on this same theme, and not just as little children. I recall, for instance, walking down a hallway at Hunter College one day and seeing a sign that caught my eye:

This is a test! It is *only* a test. This is *not* your real life.
If it were your real life you would have been given
better operating instructions.

The part of us that feels homesick recognizes the painful truth: this is *not* our real life. At the moment we hear the Call, we begin to realize that life *is* a test, and that if we are not living our real life, then we are failing the test and running out of time. The problem is to find those "better operating instructions" that will enable us to be the person we were meant to be.

A phrase I also hear frequently from those I've talked with is: "I feel so far away from where I really belong." One woman described a recurring daydream in which she is wandering through a huge metropolis, lost and surrounded by anonymous people who pass her by on all sides as if she's invisible. All the time she keeps saying to herself, "I've got to get home, got to get home!" A middle-aged physician told me of a dream he had on his thirty-fifth birthday. As the dream begins, he is riding in a chariot with a group of angelic beings. The chariot hits a rut and he tumbles out. The beings in the vehicle look back and gesture for him to keep following. The countryside the man is traveling through is barren and lunar, and populated with unfriendly people who look on disdainfully. "The irony of it is," the doctor told the class, "that these unfriendly people are just like you and me: humans, not aliens. They don't represent some other world. They are my own world! My people! Us! Me!"

When people relate these stories of exile and homesickness they often speak in an embarrassed voice, as if there is something eccentric about having such thoughts. I assure them that *many* people have such feelings, and that on an unconscious level this sense of exile refers not only to our social fears but to our spiritual needs as well. "We're all homesick," one person I encountered said to me, "for our souls."

The Call comes both from outside us and within us. We cannot answer the Call unless we have the capacity to hear it. One person may be invited on the spiritual search and become intoxicated with a wish to know more. Another indifferently dismisses such ideas for many years, perhaps even a lifetime. We've all met people of this kind, individuals who pride themselves on a staunch materialism, a stony agnosticism, who busy themselves in the tasks and duties of everyday life without any apparent wish to penetrate the deeper secrets of life. "When the worst person hears about the Tao," says the *Tao Te Ching*, "he laughs out loud. If this person did not laugh at the Tao, it would be unworthy of being called the Tao." One thinks of the character of Papageno, the Bird Catcher, in Mozart's opera *The Magic Flute,* the "natural man" content with eating, sleeping, and sex, uninterested, repelled even, by the thought of spiritual adventure. "As for the unbelievers," says the Koran, "it is all the same whether you have warned them or not—they do not believe. God has therefore set a seal on their hearts and on their hearing, and on their eyes is a covering."

Here then is a cosmic mystery: why does one person receive the Call, recognize it as something profound and personal and necessary, while another ignores the inner yearning entirely?

While there are innumerable explanations for this puzzling phenomenon, one of the most compelling ways of seeing this question is through Gurdjieff's notion of "Magnetic Center," a concept that corresponds roughly to what we call intellectual curiosity—but with a metaphysical twist.

From childhood, this theory tells us, we are exposed to a wide range of influences. Though these influences appear to be numerous, they can be divided into two basic categories: "A" influences and "B" influences.

"A" influences are those we encounter in the raw elements of everyday life—business, family, politics, sex, food, money, health, education, entertainment, the whole passing parade of conventional existence. "A" influences, Gurdjieff asserts, set the wheels of life spinning and put humanity on the move. They are the forces that "keep people going round and round," as psychiatrist Maurice Nicoll explains it, "always thinking they are going somewhere, toward some goal. . . . We do not see we are living in a Hall of Mirrors and are going in no direction whatever. . . . The mirrors are so arranged that it seems as though one were going straight ahead. Actually one is going nowhere; just round and round."

This feeling of going in circles is one I encounter with great frequency in my lectures and work. A woman in her late thirties once told me that "I dreamed one night that I was trapped on a circus carousel and couldn't get off. Every time I tried to climb off the platform the thing went faster and faster. When I woke up I felt the dream was telling me my life is going in circles and I can't get off."

Now enter "B" influences, the preliminary corrective to this sense of turning in circles.

"B" influences include all the inspirational and elevated impressions that have entered our consciousness over the years. They reach us from a number of sources: from religion, art and metaphysics, certainly, as well as philosophy and psychology, literature and poetry. They come to us in fairy tales, myth, nature, even magic and the supernatural; from the things we learn at the hands of wise parents, mentors, fellow seekers—from anything that ignites our sense of wonder and a nostalgia for the Infinite. "Most of us can remember the strangely moving power of passages in certain poems read when we were young," writes psychologist William James, "irrational doorways as they were through which the mysteries of fact, the wildness and the pang of life, stole into our hearts and thrilled them . . . we are alive or dead to the eternal inner message of the arts according as we have kept or lost this mystical susceptibility."

Time passes, and these influences leave subtle impressions on our unconscious minds. Gradually they coalesce into a kind of spiritual lodestone which, being "magnetic," attracts similar influences, all of which resonate to things harmonious, ideal, and sacred.

"If the Magnetic Center receives sufficient nourishment," writes Ouspensky, "and if there is no strong resistance on the part of the other sides of a man's personality . . . the Magnetic Center begins to influence a man's orientation, obliging him to turn round and even to move in a certain direction. When the Magnetic Center attains sufficient force and development, a man already understands the idea of the [spiritual] way and he begins to look for the way."

Eventually, the Magnetic Center or whatever we wish to call it—the conscience, the inner voice, the scent of the soul—grows strong enough to influence our behavior and to incline us more and more in a spiritual direction. Finally the spiritual force inside us reaches a psychological critical mass and begins sending out SOS signals. "Help me," these messages say. "I'm lost, I'm frightened, I'm alone, I need a light to guide me—to show me the way back home."

The answer that comes back out of the deepest depths of the universe—and out of our own soul—is the Call.

The Call comes in stages.

Suppose the prince in "The Hymn of the Pearl" came to earth today and we decided to pay him a visit. What would we find?

Physically he probably looks like you or me. Chances are he has a job, a house, a family. He has prejudices and principles. If someone told him he was on earth to accomplish a divine mission he would laugh it off as a joke in slightly bad taste.

The prince has an idealistic side, and is well-meaning at heart. He's kind to his wife or significant other. He gives to charity, drives the disabled gentleman across the street to church on Sunday. He's a good fellow, a sensible householder. Nonetheless, he seems to perform these kindnesses mechanically, not really understanding the spirit behind them or the place inside himself where they originate. Perhaps he even believes in a Higher Power. At certain moments a vague remembrance tugs at his heart. But he is unable to incorporate this feeling into his daily life, and he rarely thinks about spiritual matters of any kind. All in all, the prince's attitude toward reality amounts to something like this: what I can see and feel, taste and touch is all that really interests me in this world. The rest is for the philosophers to figure out.

As the years pass, and as the prince grows older, something begins to change. Perhaps these changes are triggered by a crisis or loss: a death, the breakup of a marriage, the loss of a job, anything that shatters confidence in life's predictability.

Or the change may start as a small but gnawing dissatisfaction that is not necessarily connected with any particular event, a longing or agitation that cannot be put into words but that will not go away. After a while, the pleasures that once made the prince happy turn stale: children grow up, elderly parents die, old friends fall out of touch, life goals are attained, only to reveal themselves as unsatisfying or incomplete.

Soon the prince starts asking himself disturbing questions about the meaning of life, and is unable to answer them. Though he cannot quite say why, he feels cut off and incomplete. A desire for deeper answers builds up within him in increments, almost without his knowing it. Soon it becomes impossible to return to his old way of thinking. He is anxious to make a leap in the dark toward something different now, but he is also afraid to let go of the familiar.

In the end our prince reexamines his attitudes toward life to their very roots, and he concludes that what is bothering him has nothing to do with his family. It has nothing to do with the job or even with other people. The real problem, he now believes, is not that he has earned too little or loved too much. It is that he has been deaf to the Call of his father, the King.

When at last the Call is heard it makes us wonder what it finally took to make our prince remember his royal birthright and to realize he was being summoned to return. Did he fumble his way toward this moment of recognition like the rest of us? Possibly. Perhaps he was taking a walk one summer evening and happened to glance up at the sky. "How long has it been" he asked himself at this moment, "since I've looked at the stars? What's happened to me? Who have I become? How can I get back to that place I left so long ago? How can I find my way home?"

Like the prince, we do not think of ourselves as special. The reason some people do not respond to the Call is that they find it impossible to think of themselves as special enough to receive a spiritual summons. It's not always easy to think of ourselves as a prince or a princess. "I'm plain people," we hear ourselves saying.

Many of us, I have observed, have a tendency to deny the very thing in us that is most noble. Meanwhile everything in our personal environment gladly conspires. "Keep your place in line!" the world shouts like an angry fifth-grade teacher, scolding us into anonymity. "What makes you think you're so special!"

And soon we're forced to agree: my boss, my unfriendly neighbor, the bureaucracy are all correct: I am no one special.

On the whole, spiritual traditions teach us exactly the opposite lesson. You *are* someone special, they tell us, because you possess a spark of the divine. You do have Christ within. "We have the mind of Christ," says St. Paul, celebrating his newfound freedom of the spirit. You *are* a prince or a princess, say spiritual traditions: a duckling waiting to become a swan, a Buddha in disguise from yourself, God's vicar on earth. You just don't know it yet.

How? Why?

Return to the Bible and look at certain passages you've heard all your life, I tell people in my seminars. Phrases like "The kingdom of God is within you" or "my peace I give unto you." The "you" referred to in these utterances is not spoken to some abstract person. It is spoken to *you*. They are speaking to *you*. When Moses guides his people out of Pharaoh's wicked country, it is *you* he is leading from ordinary life to the Promised Land of the Spirit. When Jesus invites onlookers to be his followers, he's inviting *you, today, this very moment* to sit at his table and partake of the holy bread and wine.

We not only find these secret messages in scripture, we can hear them too with our own soul and in dreams that have a prophetic meaning.

In preparation for those nights when special dreams come, I suggest to my students that they keep a notebook by their bedside. Dreams communicate urgent inner messages that cannot be conceived or imagined by the ordinary mind, I tell them. To help remember, you may want to write them down when they occur. At certain times their message can convey a life-changing Call: *Come. Now. It's time.*

If you have not been spiritually active up to this point, I tell them, perhaps you should get to know your dreams better. Since time out of mind humankind has understood that nocturnal images convey psychological and spiritual messages inaccessible to our waking state. "A dream not considered," says a Gnostic proverb, "is like a letter from God left unopened." Many people through the years have been guided through difficult periods of life by such dreams, or shepherded back to the spiritual fold. Shelly, a forty-nine-year-old student in one of my midlife seminars, described a set of significant dreams that exerted a profound effect on his future.

In the first dream he found himself floundering helplessly in a pit of mud and muck. A beautiful horse walked by. Although it was streaked with mud and dirt, he could see it was a superb animal. He grabbed the horse's tail, and it pulled him out of the mire. "That pretty much summed up the kind of life I was living at the time," Shelly confessed. "The mire was my life. The horse was my inner spirit pulling me out."

The second dream came less than a month later. This time Shelly was holding a horse by the reins—he couldn't tell if it was the same animal as before—leading it across a medieval battlefield. Shattered corpses were strewn around him. There were pools of blood, broken lances, acrid smoke everywhere. Clearly a titanic battle had been fought here, but he paid no attention. A tower in the distance was drawing him irresistibly on. It glowed with a weird phosphorescence. He could see some type of bustling activity going on inside one of the tower windows but couldn't tell what all the activity was.

The last dream in this sequence occurred a week later. This time Shelly was *riding* a horse rather than walking or being pulled. Next to him was a macabre-looking man riding a black mule. The man wore a bucket on his head like a character out of a Hieronymus Bosch depiction of hell and was covered with slime and dirt. The terrifying man tried to grab Shelly's reins but Shelly held them tight. Shelly's horse then broke into a gallop and Shelly became frightened. Finally the horse lifted off the ground and soared into the sky, making graceful turns and loop-the-loops as it climbed. Shelly's fear fell away. He looked down and saw New York Harbor and the Statue of Liberty below him. This symbol of freedom made him deeply happy. Shelly woke up feeling invigorated and full of peace. "It was as if I had gone on a pilgrimage," he said. "Or had a catharsis. Around this time in my life a lot of other spiritual things were happening. I started getting into self-development. How could I keep turning my back on such obvious pleas from my own soul?"

Set aside ten to fifteen minutes for yourself every day, I tell my students. Find a congenial environment where you can be comfortable—a darkened room, a quiet park bench. Think about the feelings you're experiencing, about whether a Call is coming to you and what it means for you. What is the Call telling you to do? Do you feel you can do it?

Listen to the voices that arise in you. Quiet your mind and concentrate on a single point or image: the sounds going on around you right now, or the deep, in-out rhythm of your breath. Practicing this kind of internal "listening" each day will help you understand the new feelings you are experiencing.

Another useful step is to seek out people who seem to be going through the same emotional or spiritual passages as yourself. It's true that some people in your circle may find you strange for going off on this new track. They won't understand why you're attending those odd meetings, going back to church, sitting zazen, reading the Scriptures or *The Diamond Sutra,* attending prayer groups. But others *will* understand, more people, perhaps, than you think. It amazes me how many individuals I meet across the country who have had spiritual experiences of some kind but are too embarrassed to share them.

A study of religious and mystical encounters among the American population conducted by the National Data Program for the Social Sciences in 1988 and 1989 shows that almost *a third of Americans* have had a mystical or numinous experience in their lives, while *65 percent* have undergone paranormal experiences. A majority of these respondents have witnessed unusual encounters—ESP, clairvoyance, numinous experience, spiritualism—at least several times in their lives. Only a small percentage of respondents reported *never* having had a paranormal or mystical experience. What's more, based on information from previous surveys, the number of people undergoing such experiences has increased appreciably over the past twenty years. There is, it turns out, a vast underground of people who have experienced a Call and yet are hiding their mystical lights.

We live our lives in a state of sleep. When the Call comes it reminds us of many things. Most essential perhaps is that we have been asleep; not allegorically asleep, but literally asleep—that is, in a condition of lesser consciousness. Just as we go to sleep at night, dream our dreams, then wake in the morning and know that we have slept, so the great religious traditions tell us that spiritual awakening produces this same transformation from a lower state of consciousness to a higher. We think we are fully cognizant and aware. But in truth we are wandering about in a waking daydream characterized by an endless stream of thoughts, images, and imaginings that fill our head during the day. This waking dream serves as a kind of veil to keep us separated from contact with our soul. "Even though apparently awake," says a Hindu scripture, "one is still asleep if one sees multiplicity. Wake up from the dream of ignorance and see the one Self. The Self alone is real."

Themes of spiritual sleep, enchantment, and hypnotic imprisonment have fascinated humankind for millennia. A medieval tale is told of a cruel master who owns a great many slaves. The slaves continually escape, so one day the master devises an ingenious method for keeping them under control. He transports the slaves to a small island in the middle of the ocean and here he hypnotizes them, telling them that the island is the entire world, that there is nothing beyond this tiny piece of land, and that to even think of trying to leave the island is utter folly. There is, after all, no place else to go.

Deeply entranced, the slaves work dutifully under their master's command from this time on and never give a thought to escape.

Then one day a boat arrives bearing a visitor from far away.

The visitor warns the slaves that they have been hypnotized by a cruel master who wishes to use them for his own selfish ends. The visitor promises that if the islanders listen to his instructions he will teach them how to unhypnotize themselves and make their escape.

But not everyone is interested in this message or pleased by it. Many of the island dwellers conclude that the visitor is a lunatic or a charlatan, and some try to drive him away. Nonetheless, a small group of followers understand the visitor's message and come to trust him. Over time the visitor teaches them the secrets of building boats, weaving sails, reading maps, and navigating ocean currents. He shows them methods for unhypnotizing themselves, and tells them all about the great continent beyond the sea where he has come from, and of the wonders awaiting them there.

Eventually, after much work and struggle, a group of followers succeed in escaping to the faraway continent, where they are welcomed with great fanfare and joy. Most of the other prisoners, however, remain behind on the island, where to this day you can hear them jeering at anyone who suggests that their tiny plot of land in the middle of the ocean is not the entire world.

The island in this story is our normal state of consciousness. The prisoners are you and I, while the identity of the evil master depends on one's perspective. From a psychological standpoint he is the human ego. In older traditions the master is a malevolent god or demiurge. For those theologically inclined, he is the hypnotic presence of evil, the "spirit that denies," the devil.

The visitor, on the other hand, represents the spiritual teacher. The negative reaction the islanders have to this message is typical of the reaction of doubters everywhere. The continent beyond the sea stands for higher states of consciousness, and the group of followers who escape are those who pursue the spiritual path.

This theme of imprisonment and spiritual escape is a favorite motif not only of storytellers but of philosophers as well. The most eloquent and disturbing example, perhaps, is Plato's famous allegory of the cave from his masterpiece, *The Republic*.

Plato begins by telling us about a cavern deep in a mountainside where human beings have been chained to a wall since early childhood and where their heads are restrained in such a way that they can only stare straight ahead. Never once have these prisoners looked to the side or turned around. Naturally, they assume that what they see on the wall in front of them is all there is of reality; just as we humans come to believe that our universe is limited to what we perceive with our five senses.

In reality, however, the cave is brimming with interesting activities just beyond the prisoners' line of vision.

Near the mouth of the cave, for example, a fire is kept continually burning. In front of the blaze mysterious beings walk back and forth carrying various objects that cast their shadows on the wall. Since the chained captives only see the wall, they think these reflections are solid objects in a real world. Some prisoners even devote their lives to studying the flat shapes that dance by them, and to writing learned dissertations on their size and movements. Prizes are awarded to those who present the most accurate descriptions.

Although the prisoners are able to converse, they do so only with each other's two-dimensional shadows, thinking that these reflections are complete people. Any suggestion that an entire world exists beyond the wall, that there is a fire that casts the silhouettes, that stars, a moon, even a great blazing sun exists outside the cave—such talk invites ridicule and even hostility from the chained slaves. Just as it did among the hypnotized slaves on the island.

Now what if by some miracle of effort or good fortune, Plato asks, several prisoners should break free of their chains and turn around to look at the flame?

If this were to happen, he says—and we can almost hear his laughter thundering down at us through the centuries as he contemplates the prospect—the glare from the fire would make the wretched escapees tremble with fear; their familiar domain, their shadow universe, now vanishes before their eyes. In its place stands a vista of stereoscopic vividness, a swirling universe of forms and spheres, of light and color, of massive three-dimensional designs.

At first the prisoners are stunned. After a lifetime of shadows, the light is unbearable. Their anguish is intensified when they are ushered out of the cave into the sunlight, where the landscape is so alien, so unlike the familiar cave world, that the prisoners think they are hallucinating or going mad.

Time passes. The escapees accustom themselves to this new reality. Gradually it becomes apparent that this new world does indeed have three dimensions, and that the shadow land they left behind is the illusory one. Slowly, over time, our refugees from the cave become accustomed to the light, and finally learn to live joyously in this vast new domain. Still, it will be many, many years before they are capable of looking directly at the sun.

Do all the escaped prisoners adapt to their new home outside the cave?

Alas, no. For some, Plato tells us, the light is simply too strong. After struggling to accustom themselves to this strange world they finally abandon their efforts and return to the cave, where they find their old seats waiting for them in front of the wall. Settling back into their habitual places, they refasten the chains and do their best to forget what they have seen, eventually coming to believe that it was all a dream. For these returning prisoners the comfortable bondage of shadow and illusion is preferable to the blinding radiance of the real world. "The self is in the dark," writes St. John of the Cross, "because it is blinded by thy light greater than it can bear." It is much like the sentiment expressed in Stephen Crane's poem from *The Black Riders:*

> *I was in darkness;*
> *I could not see my words*
> *Nor the wishes of my heart.*
> *Then suddenly there was a great light—*
> *"Let me into the darkness again."*

In practically every spiritual tradition, humankind is believed to pass through life in a kind of quasi-somnambulant awareness. This dreamlike condition we call our ordinary consciousness. While young we are often too immersed in the adventure of life to notice how mechanically and predictably this form of consciousness makes us behave. Like the slaves on the island or the prisoners in the cave, we are programmed to obey a regimen of behavior that as teenagers and young adults we accept without question: get educated, get married, get a job, get ahead, get, get, get.

"When I was a kid," an older woman named Kate told me, "I plowed through life doing this, doing that, like a robot. When I finally landed in AA from having almost drunk myself to death in response to all this doing, I learned that I'm responsible for my actions. I realized much of my life had been lived under a spell like a good little automaton. I was walking through life obeying these inner commands about 'I should be this' and 'I should be that.' AA helped me realize that none of this was really me, and that whatever alive, awake part I have inside me hadn't been operating properly for years."

"People are asleep," the Prophet Muhammad said, "and when they die they wake." The great Chinese Taoist Chuang-tse tells the story of the butterfly's dream:

"Once upon a time, I dreamed I was a butterfly fluttering over the flowers, to all intents and purposes a true butterfly. I was conscious only of following my fancies as a butterfly, and was unconscious of my individuality as a man. Suddenly, I awakened, and there I lay, myself again. As I lay there in bed, I did not know whether I was a man dreaming I was a butterfly—or a butterfly dreaming I was a man."

Just after I turned forty, I won a national fellowship and went on sabbatical at the University of Southern California where I experienced my own version of Chuang-tse's dilemma. In a dream I find myself ushering people through a beautiful new house that I'm currently living in. As we walk from room to room, I announce to the visitors that if this house were not so far away from my friends on the spiritual path I would live here forever. Then a man appears at the door with a huge catapult and starts to smash down the walls. I tell the visitors that my wonderful house is indestructible, as solid as "a nuclear power plant." Then I stand watching as the house crumbles and burns.

At this point I "wake up" and tell myself that none of these events are really happening. In actual fact, I'm still sound asleep and dreaming deeply.

Still immersed in the dream, I turn to my wife and ask, "Is what's happening right now a dream too?"

"No," she assures me, "you're awake, it's not a dream."

But I know she's wrong. I force myself to wake up, this time for real. I open my eyes and sit up in bed. The California morning has dawned blue and balmy outside my window, but the world seems strangely out of joint, and I struggle, like Chuang-tse, to figure out: am I sleeping, am I awake, am I dreaming—who am I?

This dream, it turns out, took place at a time in my life when many of my worldly goals were being fulfilled. Yet strangely, the dream teems with menace and anxiety about the future. The beautiful new house seems to represent the attainment of long-anticipated career goals: what Daniel Levinson calls "the dream of youth." But clearly I feel lonely and distant from my friends and fellow seekers, and from the golden person inside me. I have expended too much energy pursuing these goals in the first part of my life, the dream is reminding me, and not enough pursuing the Spirit.

Finally I imagine I've been awakened. In this dream within a dream I believe I can distinguish illusion from reality. But be careful, the dream warns me. At any moment your beautiful house may be destroyed. What seems like awakeness may also be an illusion.

Such experiences are referred to in psychology as "lucid dreaming"—

knowing you are dreaming *while* you are dreaming. This phenomenon has recently become a subject of study among psychologists. Some investigators, such as Jayne Backenbach and Harry Hunt believe that lucid dreams and meditation involve similar processes in the brain, and that both have physiological parallels such as depth of somatic arousal and variations of alpha waves registered in the brain.

Sleep, dreams, hypnotic imprisonment of the soul: these shadowy phantoms must all be dealt with while en route through the five spiritual stages. There is an Eastern tale of a poor man who is discouraged by life. He lives in a tumbledown cottage and scratches out a meager living on the land surrounding it. One day a mysterious stranger arrives at his door.

"You live in a vast mansion," the man tells him. "You just do not realize it yet."

The man laughs. Anyone can see his house is small. But the stranger is insistent.

Slowly, with the guidance of his new friend, the man begins to discover hidden parts of his dwelling. First he finds one forgotten room, then another and another, until entire lavish suites are revealed. In the end the man becomes proprietor of a thousand-room palace, the same that he had once mistaken for a single dilapidated room.

The story of hidden riches in one's own backyard turns up time and again in folktales and myth. In Judaic lore, Rabbi Isaac hunts for certain sacred books for many years across the countryside, returning empty-handed and in despair. Once at home, his wife shows him that the precious writings were stored under his bed the entire time.

This theme also weaves itself into our dreams. Many of us have dreamed of finding a lost room in our house or of discovering something precious in a familiar or neglected place. Carl Jung, in his autobiography, *Memories, Dreams, Reflections,* ascribes his theory of the structure of the psyche to such a nocturnal vision. Jung describes a dream in which he is standing in the upper story of a strange house. The rooms are furnished pleasantly but he feels the urge—the Call—to look downstairs.

Here everything is older, dating back to the Middle Ages. He goes from room to room thinking: Now I must really explore this whole house. Before long he discovers a stone stairway that winds down to a still lower level. Descending, he finds himself in a beautifully vaulted room exceedingly ancient. Carefully studying the stone floor, he notices a slab with a ring protruding. He pulls it and the slab comes up, revealing yet another staircase. At the bottom a dark cave is cut into the rock. Thick dust is everywhere. Scattered bones and pottery shards litter the dirt floor. He discovers two human skulls, very old and half disintegrated.

Then he wakes up.

The next day Jung goes to his friend and colleague Sigmund Freud for an analysis of this strange vision. But the Viennese master's interpretation is relentlessly sexual and somehow inadequate.

"It was plain to me," Jung writes, "that the house represented a kind of image of the psyche. That is to say, of my then state of consciousness, with hitherto unconscious additions." The multileveled house, in short, represented the hidden parts of our own psyche, separated from us by the veil of ordinary consciousness.

"In my Father's house are many mansions," says John 14:1, "if it were not so I would have told you. I go to prepare a place for you."

Like the prince, we have forgotten our mission. When the film *Star Wars* opens—a long time ago in a galaxy far, far away—young Luke Skywalker is living with his aunt and uncle on an obscure windswept planet. An apparently ordinary young man, Luke has no special sense of destiny or calling. Except for one small whim. Through the years he has heard rumors of a reclusive friend of his long-dead father, a stranger named Obewan Kenobe. For reasons he does not understand, the thought of this stranger intrigues him.

"A crazy old man," Luke's uncle assures him. "I don't think he exists anymore."

"Did Obewan know my father?" Luke asks.

His uncle's answer is evasive, and Luke begins to sense that his destiny is somehow intertwined with this phantom presence. He yearns to meet him. At the same time, Luke has no reason to think he has any type of destiny at all. He is, after all, just a normal young man. Like the prince. No one special.

"Looks like I'm going nowhere," Luke tells himself, agreeing to stay at home as his uncle insists, feeling the same overburdening sense of stagnation that many of us do as our lives turn in circles.

Symbolically speaking, Luke's aunt and uncle represent our own prosaic inner voices that urge us to follow the safe and easy road, and that discourage all thought of a spiritual destiny: "I need you here," his uncle tells him; just as the world tells us we have an obligation to our civic responsibilities; and that we are, after all, too busy running the company or taking care of the children to search beyond life's established perimeters. As with all great myths, *Star Wars* speaks on several levels at once and to several generations, both as a tale of youthful idealism *and* as an allegory of lifelong spiritual evolution.

Time passes. Then comes the miracle, a Call from heaven in the form of a satellite plunging to the ground from outer space. On this heavenly missile ride R2D2 and C3PO, two mechanical angels bearing a coded message from Princess Lea, who is imprisoned, like our own souls, by alien powers on a distant planet.

The situation is grave and time is running out. But like many of us, Luke does not fully comprehend the message at first. Its meaning is garbled and he needs help to decipher it. So he leaves home in search of the mysterious Obewan, instinctively sensing that his father's old friend can help.

"Obewan?" the stranger says quizzically when Luke tracks him down. "That's a name I haven't heard in a long time."

Ironically, the old man has almost forgotten his warrior's name and his life's mission, just as young Luke is searching for his. Both champions need each other, just as we need our youthful dreams *and* our grown-up wisdom before we are complete enough to hear the Call. What *Star Wars* evokes so vividly in this meeting is the reciprocal relationship between youthful vision and mature experience; between the adventurous dreams within us that remain forever young and the surefooted acumen that develops with age and self-mastery.

And so Obewan helps Luke decipher the heavenly message, and in the process launches him on his fate. At the same time, Luke's arrival rouses Obewan to his destiny, not only as a Jedi Knight but as a teacher and guide to successive generations. Thus, Obewan evokes the Call in Luke; but just as importantly, Luke rekindles the Call in his mentor, and allows him to close the circle of his own fate.

"You must learn the ways of the Force," the old Jedi tells his young pupil after they have become friends. But Luke shrinks back. Like the hero in "The Hymn of the Pearl," he ignores the Call, replying, "I can't get involved. I've got work to do."

So he returns home to his familiar world, only to find his house a smoking ruin, like the beautiful house in my own dream.

Luke's old life is over now, just as the first half of our lives is inexorably separated from the second. He has no choice but to go forward, to embark on the hero's journey under the guidance of Ancient Wisdom. "There's nothing for me here now," he declares. "I want to learn the ways of the Force."

Luke's challenge, the *Star Wars* myth seems to be saying, is our challenge too. Can we summon the vision and warrior's spirit to answer our own Call? Will we have the fearlessness to leave what is familiar and secure? Will we finally set out on a venture of the heart that will change us to our very roots? Will we, like Luke—and like the prince—remember the mission entrusted to us so far away and long ago?

We Shall Be with All the World

And where does this mission finally take us? Where does the story of the prince with its false starts, blunders, and final triumph ultimately lead? What does this story, and all other stories of the Call like it, ultimately tell us?

Simply this: that you, I, all of us, are a great deal more than we think we are.

It tells us that a deep-seated inertia and doubt is holding us back from following this Call; but that at the same time something within us is urging us on.

Also that a wonderful treasure trove of possibilities awaits us once we set out on this journey. These treasures include peace of mind, deeper understanding of ourselves and others, higher consciousness at times, and a return to the spiritual land from which we have so long been exiled.

Finally, it tells us that in answering the Call and following the golden thread of spirituality, we fulfill a mission that we may not fully understand at first; but that we are inexplicably drawn toward, and that we know in our hearts is necessary; a mission that our ancestors have followed before, and that human beings will continue to follow until the end of time.

"We have not even to risk the adventure alone," writes Joseph Campbell, "for the heroes of all time have gone before us; the labyrinth is thoroughly known; we have only to follow the thread of the hero-path. And where we had thought to find an abomination, we shall find a god; where we had thought to slay another, we shall slay ourselves; where we had thought to travel outwards, we shall come to the center of our own existence; where we had thought to be alone, we shall be with all the world."

chapter 3

Answering the Call

"If you bring forth what is inside you,
what you bring forth will save you.
If you do not bring forth what is inside you,
what you do not bring forth will destroy you."

THE GOSPEL OF THOMAS

ANSWERING THE CALL

The Current of Life and Death

In the past several decades there has been much argument over whether the middle adult years are a period of fulfillment or of crisis.

Daniel Levinson's rather gloomy depiction of midlife as the death of the dream and Gail Sheehy's upbeat version of the same as a time of crisis and resolution have both been challenged, most recently by the work at the John D. and Catherine T. MacArthur Foundation Research Network on Successful Midlife Development, known as MIDMAC.

Gilbert Brim, leader of the MacArthur national network, tells us, "The time has come to get rid of these obsolete ideas." There may be a series of many small crises at midlife, Brim tells us. Or there may be none at all. And when a crisis does happen to come, it does not necessarily bring either growth or resolution in its wake. In short, Brim believes there is no greater number of crises during midlife than at any other time in the life course.

Robert McCrae and Paul Costa, Jr., supporting Brim's assertion, devised a crisis scale engineered to index behavior patterns among the middle-aged. Their studies also failed to find a predictable pattern of midlife crisis or distress. Suicide, admission to a mental health facility, alcoholism—none of these episodes, they found, are higher at midlife—or lower—than at any other time.

Gilbert Brim's own outlook is well expressed in his 1992 book *Ambition,* in which he characterizes the process of adult development as one in which people are constantly reassessing their goals and reorienting their ambitions. The aim of midlife, Brim believes, is to find new challenges that are stimulating without being overwhelming. Ronald Kessler, another leading investigator in the MacArthur MIDMAC network, depicts the years from forty to sixty as a period when long-sought goals of career and relationships are finally fulfilled. In Kessler's sanguine view, people in middle age are mainly healthy and productive. "Midlife is the 'it' you've been working toward," he writes. "You can turn your attention to being rather than becoming."

These views sound authoritative, if a trifle oversimplified, and mostly come down on the side of midlife as an era of fulfillment and achievement. Indeed, Brim presents a typically American notion, picturing existence as a competitive sport in which activity and accomplishment are everything: "What people really want out of life are action and challenge," he writes, "to be in the ball game." Gerontologist Bernice Neugarten agrees, describing positive mental health in the middle adult years as "complexity"—that is, being capable of handling an assortment of life challenges at the same time.

Thus we have it: challenge and response; no predictable crisis during the middle years; happiness as a result of activity and involvement; keep on truckin'. These are the bottom lines offered by the latest findings of empirical researchers.

What sort of guidance can we take from these ideas?

If we had to draw a blueprint of the journey of life as expressed by the MacArthur investigators, it would look something like the pre-Copernican map of the world, with midlife at the center of the universe. The message, somewhat revised since crisis theory was fashionable in the 1970s and 1980s, is that no absolute chart or graph exists for the second half of life at all, but that, all things considered, these years are probably as good as it's likely to get.

Now, there is no doubt that for many people the middle years are indeed the high point of life. There is also no doubt that for many people these years are the low point. And for some of us, the truth lies in between: existence in the middle years is business as usual, with its usual ups and downs.

Yet whether we are happy or sad, productive or burned out, the findings in these surveys tell us the truth about our lives *only* insofar as the external facts are concerned. Deep below the daily cycles of work and love, of winning the game or losing the game, a current of a different order is flowing and swelling, the current of life and death.

Looked at in this way, social science statistics do not, and cannot, address the one true crisis of our existence: *that we are someday going to die, and that there is a debt we owe to our soul that we have not yet started to pay off.* "What matter," asks the Gospels, "if a man gain the whole world but loseth his soul?"

One day a fashionably dressed woman with a worried look approached the great Catholic saint Padre Pia. "Today I turn sixty, Father," she said. "Say something nice to me."

With a mischievous smile the padre leaned over and whispered in her ear, "Death is near!"

And so the questions: Are we ready to say that our time is running out, but that there is still time to do what is necessary? Will we answer the Call when it comes? Will we meet the debt we owe our soul, and start down the road to the mysteries of a new life?

To help us identify these moments of inner summons in our own lives, let's look at the types of Calls experienced by a variety of people, at the ways they respond, and at the animating and often profound things that happen when they answer the Call.

Returned from the Dead

"They woke us up around midnight," John Graham told me in a long and illuminating interview. " 'There's been a small fire in the engine room,' the steward announced through my cabin door. 'But don't worry, it's out now. Hope you don't mind going topside a few minutes to let things air out down here. There'll be free drinks in the lounge.'

"By my estimation our cruise ship was somewhere near the Bering Sea off the Alaskan coast. I peered out the porthole. The night was moonless and still. I had an impulse to turn over in bed and go back to sleep, but my thirteen-year-old daughter was up and around in the next cabin, so I decided I'd better get with the program.

"Throwing on the first clothes I could find, I met my daughter in the corridor and we staggered upstairs bleary-eyed. The crew, meanwhile, was traipsing through the bowels of the ship with blowers getting rid of the fumes. As we walked up the stairs, the air was filled with a black, acrid smoke.

" 'Nothing to get alarmed about,' an officer assured us in the lounge. As a member of the crew myself—I had signed on the cruise as guest lecturer and had brought my daughter along for the ride—I was expected to maintain an air of dignified calm along with the staff. But something inside me was uneasy. The steward had said the fire was extinguished. Why then was so much smoke still billowing up from below?"

At the time this incident took place John Graham was approaching his fortieth birthday and was at a vital juncture in his turbulent life. After returning from Vietnam more than a decade earlier with his share of post-traumatic stress syndrome ("I found myself walking on the shady side of the streets in Palo Alto to avoid sniper fire," he told me), the years that followed led him down many strange and contradictory roads. These included a high position in the State Department, a stint with NATO, and, in his spare time, a deep involvement in psychic healing.

"I did the most amazing things during this period in my life," he reports. "I could make people better just by laying my hands on them. I spent hours outside my body in trance states. Every other Saturday I would conduct seminars at Holiday Inns around northern Virginia, teaching people how to be their own psychics and do trance healing. But at the same time— and this shows you how conflicted I was about my moral direction in life—I was also helping map out war strategies as part of the nuclear planning team at NATO. I was, you could say, confused about my priorities."

None of these experiences seemed to satisfy some restless craving, so John Graham left the Foreign Service and founded his own consulting firm. A year later the firm failed, taking with it his life's savings. When he was down to his last few dollars, a friend offered him a job as a lecturer on a cruise ship bound from Vancouver to Tokyo. He seized the opportunity.

"Around two o'clock in the morning," Graham continues, "after the crew had run around like madmen trying to put out the fire that wasn't supposed to exist, it became apparent that we were in big trouble. This was confirmed when they ordered all crew and passengers onto the stern, where the lifeboats were stowed.

"Out in the open night the sky was breathtakingly clear the way it gets on the ocean in winter. I could see a huge green band of aurora borealis stretching across the horizon. I could also see tongues of fire darting out from several portholes. The firefighters were running around on deck in their gas masks, lit a ghostly orange by the flames. The smoke seemed to be getting thicker and blacker. Every once in a while a plane flew over us dropping CO_2 canisters. The night air was frosty, and most of us hadn't had time to grab warm clothes from our cabins. Several passengers were wrapping themselves up in tablecloths and curtains they'd taken from the lounge. And believe it or not—shades of the *Titanic*—the orchestra filed out onto the deck in their tuxedos and started playing tunes from *Oklahoma!*

"We stood there by the lifeboat stations, not knowing exactly what to expect, when suddenly there was an earsplitting crash. I looked up: the fire had broken through the last of the retaining walls, causing the entire center of the ship to implode and torch into a mountain of flame. At this point the captain gave the order to abandon ship!

"Miraculously, all the passengers and crew made it into the lifeboats without a casualty. We drifted until dawn, when several helicopters arrived like the U.S. Cavalry, and started rescue operations. When I saw those choppers circling overhead, I knew we were going to make it."

But as it turned out, the helicopters could only carry seven or eight passengers each trip, and the rescue process was maddeningly slow. Meanwhile, a winter storm was blowing in.

Graham continues:

"By about three-thirty in the afternoon most of the passengers had been evacuated, including my daughter. Only eight of us remained in the lifeboat, all men. By now the storm was unbelievably severe with torrents of rain and gigantic swells beating at us, some of them thirty feet high. The helicopters tried to pick us up several times but the winds were at gale force. One of the pilots made a last swooping attempt, failed, then flew by and saluted. I knew what he was saying. We all knew: 'Sorry, fellows—good luck—and goodbye.'

"Now we were alone in a raging winter storm at the Arctic Circle, our boat rocking and pitching and feeling like it was going to flip over at any moment. There was, as far as I could see, only one chance for survival. Coast Guard cutters were cruising the area, we'd been told, and one of them might still find us. Our boat was tiny, of course, and our radio dead. There was approximately an hour of daylight left, and we had no flashlights or flares. Once the darkness came, we all knew, our chances of survival would be nonexistent.

"At this point I prayed. The words poured out of my mouth almost involuntarily: 'O God,' I said, 'I've been through a lot of things in my life. Now I'm finally old enough and ready enough to do Your work. I can be a peacemaker. I know how to communicate. I have skills. And now You're going to snuff me out? It's crazy! I don't get it! If Your universe is so damn well organized, why are You killing me just at the moment when I'm ready to do something useful for You?'

"The answer to my question came back almost immediately, and in a clearly audible voice. It was like I was standing in front of the Burning Bush. I wondered if others on the boat could hear it. The voice told me in no uncertain terms that I'd better stop kidding myself, that all my experience wasn't worth a damn unless I did something constructive with it. It told me I'd been given opportunities already and had muffed them. We all have a choice to make concerning which side we're on, it said. And you have to make that choice too.

"Stunned and frightened, I buried my head in my hands and tried to make sense of what I'd just heard. By now I'd been in the lifeboat more than twelve hours. The wind had torn my face to a watery pulp and my eyes were almost swollen shut. I was retching from seasickness, and frostbite was moving up my legs. In situations like this parts of your body start to hurt you never ordinarily think about. The inside of your thighs gets itchy and hot; your nostrils burn from the caked salt. Parts of me, I felt, were already starting to die.

"The storm, meanwhile, was becoming increasingly ferocious and I crouched in my seat totally spent, crumpled up, no ego left in me, waiting for the end. Then suddenly a light went on in my head. Something rose up in me. 'Hey!' I said to myself, almost cheerfully. 'Hey! I get it now! I know what the voice is telling me!'

"At that instant—I mean at *that very instant*—I looked up and saw a Coast Guard cutter plowing through the waves in our direction. Within twenty minutes we were out of the lifeboat and safely on board ship, warm and bundled and dry."

Today, fifteen years later, John Graham still lives in the benign shadow of this eleventh-hour rescue and has adjusted his life accordingly. An internationally known foreign affairs consultant specializing in peace mediation—he recently spent several months in Cambodia overseeing negotiations between the Cambodian government and the Khmer Rouge—he also helps run the Giraffe Project, a Washington State-based organization dedicated to encouraging people to "stick their necks out" to help others.

"I mulled over the experience on the lifeboat for several months after I got home," he told me, "and the more I thought about what happened, the more I realized I'd literally been returned from the dead; I owed everything to God. So naturally I did what the voice told me: I tried to dedicate my life to spiritual causes and helping people. I started holding seminars on peacemaking. I worked at peace mediation. Then I got involved in the Giraffe Project. From that time on I've tried to take spiritual ideals and use them in a practical way—for the environment, say, for education, for public policy. Since that day in the lifeboat I've never had any regrets. And I've never looked back."

But What About the Rest of Us?

It would be difficult to think of a more dramatic spiritual summons than the one that thundered into John Graham's life that day on the frozen seas. What must it be like to live through such a hurricane-force turn, to be rescued in the eleventh hour and given a life renewed?

Still, was it really the voice of God speaking through the raging storm? Perhaps. Or perhaps it was John Graham's own unconscious. It's difficult to know. Most of us, no doubt, have heard similar miracle stories. We read them in magazines, see episodes dramatized on the Discovery Channel—stories of people touched by angels or saved by the light. It all seems very dramatic, very inspirational. Then reality sets in: What about me? we ask. What about you? How many of the rest of us have had such miraculous deliveries?

And the answer is: not many. Indeed, the problem a majority of us face as our lives go by is not dealing with miraculous episodes, but coping with the fact that nothing much is happening at all. Only the old workaday, singalong routines. While we may not come face to face with imminent death very often, neither do we usually undergo sudden, dramatic turning points that reshape our lives.

Here the shadowy side of living rears its many heads: the creeping boredom, the bondage of habit, the worry over lost opportunities and a diminishing future. This claustrophobic network of dullness makes us feel "cut off," in Wordsworth's phrase, "from the creative forces of the world." It's fine, we think, when someone like John Graham is given a clear spiritual message from on high. But a majority of us still find heaven silent and remote, and our lives decidedly unmagical.

In the Gospels, Jesus tells us that if we knock the door will be open to us, that if we seek we shall find.

But *where is this door?* people want to know. Where is the entrance that leads to the road that takes us to heaven's gate? Where is this promised Call? In a way it's almost as if William Butler Yeats's grim prophecy has already proven itself to be true. "Life," says Yeats, "is a preparation for something that never happens."

Finding the Door

I thought of Jesus's statements in the Gospels when I first met with Natasha Noor, an American meditation teacher who has lived on the outskirts of New Delhi for the past fifteen years and who has studied at the feet of Vedantic masters throughout India. A ruddy-cheeked, salt-and-pepper-haired woman of sixty-something, one easily imagines her chanting in foreign temples or trekking through Sherpa country. On her periodic returns to the United States she holds small meditation classes in cities throughout the country.

"The doorway to the mysteries is there—everyone's room is filled with doors," Natasha Noor told me as we sat by a fire one winter evening at my home outside New York City. "There are dozens of doors on the walls that surround us. But the walls are all painted the same drab color. That's why you can't see them. They're camouflaged."

I had heard this idea before, I thought to myself—that if we look hard enough, a way out of the existential dilemma will come. This idea seemed to me to be a bit simplistic.

"So how do you recognize these doors?" I asked.

"The first step is to believe the doors are there in the first place," she replied. "That's the essential thing—to trust in the possibility of something higher, at least to give it the benefit of the doubt. Then the second step is to look for the doorknobs. You have to use your lotus mind for this—see in the dark without eyes, as the Zen masters say. These knobs aren't all that small either. They're really pretty big once you get the knack of finding them. Have you seen those optical illusions that you stare at for a while and suddenly you see a three-dimensional picture in an ordinary design? It's like that. Like the Hindu story where you see a snake in the middle of the road. Then you look again and you see it's not a snake at all. It's a piece of rope. You were fooled. The world is not what you think it is at first glance. It's an illusion; it's something else. One picture of reality has been superimposed over another. You have to refocus your inner eyes."

Phrases like "lotus mind" and "seeing in the dark" somehow seemed too easy, too glib. They presuppose faculties in us that take many years to develop. What most people need, I thought, are basic lessons on how to turn their everyday lives into something meaningful and resonant.

"What if *nothing* seems to be happening?" I asked.

"The fact that nothing is happening is the beacon light you've been searching for," Natasha replied. "Boredom and depression are like neon signs saying, your old games aren't working anymore. No matter how hard you try to squeeze and prod them, you've grown beyond them at this stage of your life. They're children's games. I remember once I was with my teacher in a restaurant in Delhi. There were a couple of wealthy-looking Indian businessmen sitting at a table near us making big money deals. Their voices were booming through the restaurant. My teacher turned to me and said with a little laugh, 'Children playing with their toys.' "

"In other words," I suggested, "we need a different kind of nourishment for our soul at different stages of life?"

"I'd say rather a different game," Natasha replied. "A better game. One that's of another world. You need to listen to find out which game is right for you. If you listen you'll start to hear."

When Nothing Is Happening

Haven't we all had a fantasy about what it would take to make us supremely happy? To fulfill our every dream? To find not only a better game but the best game imaginable?

What if in your own life you could wave a magic wand and have whatever it is you wished? What would you ask for?

Does your dream involve fame? Would you like to be so celebrated that people cross entire oceans to sit at your feet and seek your advice?

Or would money bring the supreme happiness and freedom you seek? Suppose that you have a treasure house full of it—enough to maintain a glittering mansion and a thousand-acre estate with dozens of servants who cater to your every whim.

Is family bliss one of your aspirations? Then envision yourself surrounded by a passel of brilliant, adoring sons and daughters, plus a spouse who devotes her entire waking day to fulfilling your concerns and demands.

Do you want even more? Suppose then that you are thought of in many intellectual circles as the greatest writer who ever lived and that your very name is a watchword for genius and profundity. The literary toast of several continents, you enjoy friendship with the world's greatest thinkers, artists, and statesmen. For many people, in fact, you are considered the wisest, most saintly human being alive on the planet. Practically every word you say is quoted in the capitals of the world, from Moscow to Paris to New York.

Suppose that you had *all* of these gifts at once. Would they be enough to give you permanent happiness and peace?

Perhaps. But these gifts were not enough to make Count Leo Tolstoy happy. In fact, the great Russian novelist, besieged by acclaim in the midst of his rich life, was so dissatisfied with it all that he told anyone who would listen that nothing significant was happening to him anymore, nothing at all. Why? Because all these seemingly compelling events were taking place on the surface of life. Deep inside, his soul was starving, Tolstoy insisted—dying even; and no ordinary medicine could cure him. Thus at age fifty, he tells us, he began to experience a strange new feeling, a grim perplexity that made him believe, as he puts it in his great spiritual testament, *A Confession,* that "I did not know how to live."

At the time this book was published, in 1882, Tolstoy was already a world-famous author, and his masterpiece, *War and Peace,* was being heralded as the greatest novel ever written. Tolstoy was rich, titled, in good health, father of a happy family, lord over a vast estate that included several thriving peasant villages. He had fulfilled more dreams than most of us dare to wish for in a lifetime. He "had it all." But as he entered his fifties "all" began to seem like nothing. "I felt that something had broken within me" he writes, "on which my life had always rested, that I had nothing left to hold on to, and that morally my life had stopped."

Tolstoy began to look on life as a meanspirited trick. This trick is played on us, he insisted, by our own fantasies, and by life's endless rounds of activity. "I could give no reasonable meaning to any actions of my life," he wrote. "And I was surprised that I had not understood this from the very beginning. My state of mind was as if some wicked and stupid joke was being played upon me by someone. One can live only so long as one is intoxicated, drunk with life; but when one grows sober one cannot fail to see that this is all a stupid trick."

Tolstoy began to contemplate suicide. But soon he realized it was not death or oblivion he was seeking. Quite the opposite: what he craved was to discover a wellspring of purpose in the empty world that surrounded him.

Tolstoy retells an ancient Eastern tale that he believes sums up his—and the human—condition: A traveler is running across a field pursued by a ferocious beast. Coming to an empty well, the traveler starts to climb down the well to safety. Halfway toward the bottom, he realizes that a hungry dragon is waiting for him below with open mouth. To save himself he grabs a small branch protruding from a crack in the wall.

Dangling helplessly, the traveler begins to feel his strength ebb away. To make matters worse, a mouse appears above him and starts to gnaw through the branch. As the poor traveler hangs between these two oblivions he glances up and sees a cluster of berries growing nearby. Reaching out, he picks several and swallows them with gusto. How sweet they taste!

This, Tolstoy tells us in his melancholy parable, is the picture of the human condition as he sees it from the hilltop of nearly half a century. Hanging in the well of existence in between the monsters of birth and death, we await annihilation. While dangling, we pass the time gobbling up the small pleasures that fall to our lot. Then the branch snaps and we plunge into nothingness.

We've persevered a certain number of years, Tolstoy tells us. And by now, if we're lucky, we've seen through the charade of society's values and rewards. The next step is to face these monsters of life and death and pose ourselves certain questions. In his words: "What will be the outcome of all my life? Why should I live? Why should I do anything? Is there in life any purpose which the inevitable death which awaits me does not undo and destroy?"

For some time Tolstoy remained stranded between two worlds: his successful but unfulfilled past, and his hope for renewal.

In the end he discovered that these two worlds were not as separate as he had imagined, and that it was the very emptiness, the terrible sense of "nothing happening," that restored his faith in divine providence. Tolstoy came to the conclusion that the apparent emptiness of our lives is a kind of mercy sent to us from the depths of our own being. Its purpose is to shake us loose from overinvolvement in superficial concerns and to call us back to our spiritual roots. "I can refer to this by no other name than that of a thirst for God," he writes. "This craving for God had nothing to do with the movement of my ideas—in fact, it was the direct contrary of that movement—it came from my heart."

For Tolstoy the sense of futility experienced in the midst of a rich life was ultimately recognized for what it really is, *a spiritual vacuum waiting to be filled.* What appeared to be a beast chasing him across a field turned out to be a divine emissary bringing good news: your sacred center awaits your return. Now it is time to begin the second journey of life, the journey of the soul.

In the decades that followed, Tolstoy answered this summons with a passionate Search. Ignoring the honors that were showered on him from across the world, he began to dress and live in the simple manner of a peasant. He grew his own food, provided money and spiritual guidance to all who asked, and lived out his days in service and meditation.

Tolstoy's midlife conversion is not unique. To the contrary, an enormous number of the people I have talked with experience a similar sense of "nothing happening" at the midst of life and a yearning for something more. While none of these people rank as world-class authors or own a villa in the Russian countryside, they are just as well positioned as Tolstoy to look into the heart of their own pain and to see it for what it is—an emptiness that can be filled only, as Tolstoy puts it, with "the thirst for God."

At first, of course, when these pains weigh too heavily they seem like versions of Tolstoy's dragons. Our first reaction may be to deny these feelings or to numb them with a frenzy of work and a frenzy of play; with sports, TV, vacations; or with tranquilizers, alcohol, drugs.

But running away is not the best way to escape the beast. In attempting to sneak out the back door we are often brought face to face with another beast, this one closer to us than the first. At times there even seems to be a beast waiting at every turn of the road and around every corner.

Better, we finally decide, to take our stand. Better not to run; better to meet the creature straight-on, to understand it, even to accept it.

Then, as the days go by and as we stare into the beast's eyes every morning at breakfast and every night on the bus coming home from work, we begin to suspect that this creature is not as malignant as we had supposed; that, in fact, the beast has been sent to us during this critical time of our lives to set us on a better road. Gradually we come to realize that these feelings of futility are playing a catalytic role in our emotional and spiritual development. They are forcing us to give up unprofitable dreams and behavior patterns. They are moving us more in the direction of the soul.

Finally we come to think that these feelings, these so-called beasts, are in truth not an oppression at all but a godsend, the first rungs of a ladder that has been set up for us by an unseen hand to aid in our escape.

All we must do now is start to climb it. And by so doing we answer the Call.

Lessons from the Master

Tolstoy's saga clearly suggests that getting what we want does not always make us happy. This is a tale as old as time, and a resounding cliché perhaps as well. But the truth behind it is incredibly, almost *impossibly* difficult to accept. Why? Because everything in us has been programmed to believe that success and contentment are synonymous. We learned this lesson with our mother's milk: that if we spend our time and talents struggling toward fortune and prosperity, once we have them in our grasp all will be well.

But having it all, Tolstoy realized, isn't enough. The way to happiness, he discovered, lies in a different place.

But where?

This is the second revealing lesson we learn from the Russian master's life: that not all psychological pain is necessarily destructive, and that the way to happiness is often *through* our pain.

The depression and angst so many of us feel toward the middle of our lives does not necessarily come from a neurotic or injured place inside us. It may not be a sickness at all; it can even be a sign of mental health. Certainly it is reasonably clear that Tolstoy was not struggling with a psychotic mood disorder or with guilt feelings about being a "bad" person. Nor was he despondent over unfinished life goals. Quite the opposite: his pain came as a result of having attained these goals, then realizing how stale and unprofitable they were. Tolstoy's problem was not a "problem" at all. It was a solution waiting to be discovered and put to use.

Though the dejection that Tolstoy experienced in the midst of life might be diagnosed today as "clinical depression," there are, I believe, other ways of looking at his condition. In a recent article in *Archives of Psychology, Neurology and Psychiatry,* Drs. Carlo Maggini and Riccardo D. Luche argue that in certain cases the term "depression" should be replaced by the medieval word "acedia." Acedia describes a complex affective disorder subtly different from depression. Originally used to describe one of the Seven Deadly Sins—sloth—the term has been translated at different times through the centuries as "melancholy," "spiritual lethargy," and "psychological malaise." An up-to-date version, and one that I believe characterizes Tolstoy's condition more accurately than any other, is "existential crisis of meaning."

The biblical lamentations of Job, Wolfgang Hofmann suggests in the medical journal *Psychologie Medicale,* reveal this same existential apprehension with all its accompanying symptomatology. In his self-questioning and complaints, Job eventually goes beyond depression, confronting God with fundamental questions concerning the meaning of suffering. God does not answer these questions directly, but listens, then turns all of Job's assumptions about the meaning of life upside down. Finally, after finishing his cycle of suffering, Job, like Tolstoy, is a man reborn, akin in spirit to his biblical counterpart, Jonah, who emerges from his suffering in the belly of the whale spiritually transformed. Indeed, the "monster" of existential anxiety represents the voice that eventually leads Job, Jonah, and Tolstoy to a new and deeper understanding of existence.

What the stories of Tolstoy and Job tell us is that at times we must allow an illness, even one as profound as depression, to run its natural course, revealing in the process the urgent wisdom that has caused it in the first place. This wisdom often turns out to be a need for deeper purpose and meaning. Studies of clinical psychopathology suggest that if we do not come to grips with such questions, pathological symptoms may arise and persist despite intense clinical treatment. Significantly, professional psychiatric organizations have recently revised their diagnostic categories in order to take better account of the religious and spiritual problems that prompt patients to seek help. These changes in the DSM-IV diagnostic system now offer a more sensitive response to such complex and sometimes painful spiritual encounters as conversion, guilt, and depression.

Certainly for those of us raised in a culture of instant gratification, it comes as a refreshing assurance to realize that for some problems the answer is not to "do something," but to wait and watch and experience. Tolstoy's anxiety at midlife lasted for several years. During this time he did not run from his anguish or attempt to deaden it. He faced it, and let it take him where it wanted him to go.

A colleague of mine once told me of a nightmare he'd been having for many years. In this dream a menacing figure is chasing him in a dozen different settings and is always closing in. In one dream the figure takes the form of a dark, sinister man in a raincoat, something out of a film noir. In another it is a rhinoceros or a killer robot à la *The Terminator.* Usually my friend wakes up screaming.

Finally, he told me, his subconscious took action. Trapped by a lion-headed monster one night in his own hallway, my friend's dream spirit assumed a John L. Lewis boxing stance. "All right, you bastard," his dream self yelled, "let's settle this argument right now!" The dream self taunted the creature: "Come on, you creep! What the hell can you do to me anyway!"

The moment these words were out, the monster began to shrink back. For a moment it became rather diffident, almost embarrassed. Then it sat down in front of my friend, deposited a large golden egg at his feet, and disappeared. My friend reached down and picked up the egg. It sparkled in his hands. Then he woke up. From this time on, the dream never returned.

In the case of Tolstoy, the desire to face his suffering squarely became a driving force. Like many of us, his impulse was to grow by simplifying and confronting the obvious. He began by eliminating the distractions and ambitions that were eating into his life. Eventually, three decades later, after many more trials and dark nights of the soul, he was finally to die while making a pilgrimage to the monasteries of Tibet, the legendary home of mystical teachings. Within the depths of his own inner turmoil the Russian master had recognized the beast of midlife desperation for what it is, and for what it can be in all our lives: the "thirst for God," the little voice, calling us to return. He seized the opportunity set before him by destiny, and in his own words "never regretted for a moment this time in my life when I am privileged to pursue my inner spirit."

Our Adversary Is Our Helper

Such techniques—facing our pain, seeing the enemy as a potential ally, learning to wait, giving inner events time to ripen and mature—are methods we too can use, not only for answering the Call but for self-transformation in general. Difficult experiences, we learn, give us a window into rooms within ourselves we are normally unaware of. When we undergo a harsh setback, a crisis, a severe loss, even a prolonged period of sadness or depression, the psychological check valves that keep certain emotions locked inside us are sprung and powerful new feelings come flooding out.

In the fury that follows, we find ourselves caught up in the confusion and distress. We endure these bouts of anguish as best we can and hope for the best. There's not always a great deal we can do for ourselves while they're taking place.

But afterward, when the smoke clears and the trauma is past, we discover that certain rock-hard insights have crystallized from these encounters. We find that age-old psychic debris is purged from us now, and that we are different and better people for having passed through the needle's eye. Certain notions begin to make sense for the first time, such as the Jewish saying: "God is closest to those with broken hearts"; or the quote from the Midrash: "Not to know suffering means not to be human." Something that once held us back, that obscured our vision, has been removed; and the suffering is what removed it.

Among Christian traditions, the concept of pain as a catalyst of self-transformation is a common motif. Early Christian schools illustrated this process with the mysterious metaphor of chemical distillation and refinement, calling it the "alchemy of the soul."

Suffering, this tradition tells us, is like the flame that is used to heat a chemical in a flask. Just as this flame melts away the chemical's impurities and alters its internal structure, so the heat of suffering burns away the psychic impurities that form in our hearts and that veil us from what is higher in ourselves. "In alchemy, nothing bears fruit without having first been mortified," writes Henry Madathanas, eighteenth-century German Christian scholar and mystic. "Light cannot shine through matter if the matter has not become subtle enough to let the rays pass through."

Without the heat generated by suffering, alchemists of the soul insist, the lead of our personas, our outer masks, can never be transmuted into gold. "Pain offers us a kind of crash course in life lessons," one of my students wrote in a class paper. "Without the pain it might take me thirty years to learn something that suffering teaches me in five minutes."

Remember back to moments in your life when you were particularly unhappy or distressed. A moment such as saying goodbye for the last time to someone you love. Being in an accident. Failing miserably in front of others. Such experiences, though unbearably painful, are also exceedingly *real*. You probably remember them more clearly than you remember the good times. Perhaps they taught you lessons you might never have realized if they had never occurred. Perhaps they helped you overcome problems that introspection or the therapeutic process could never address. Perhaps they made you aware of hidden strengths inside you and of an inner voice of guidance.

Looking back on the hard times, it's often apparent that while these experiences hurt us, they also open deep recesses inside our being and make us aware that without the pain of birth nothing new can ever be born. Without such encounters, we realize, we would be less mature today, less aware of who we are and where we wish to go.

Sometimes I ask my students to compose a checklist of the major problems that face them in life. I ask them to prioritize these problems in order of severity, then to reread the list out loud, asking themselves certain questions as they go down the list. For example:

- Is this problem really as dire as I imagine it to be? What are its potential good points? What is the worst that can happen to me? What is the best?
- How can I use this problem, these feelings of dejection or loss or futility, to understand myself better? What are these feelings really telling me? Suppose I were to think of this problem as a messenger standing at my front door with a letter. What does the letter tell me about my life, my needs, my possible course of action?
- Think back to previous similar problems. Now that the pain and suffering associated with them is past, would you avoid the suffering that they brought if you knew you would be deprived of the insights such experiences provide? If so, why? Or why not?
- What hidden messages are there in this for me to learn from? How can I take the suffering that life has handed me and use it as a tool for spiritual growth? If God has given me lemons, how do I now make lemonade?

Through the years many people have recounted stories to me about how an apparent obstacle in their lives turned out to be a catalyst of spiritual growth. One of the most revealing and instructive of these stories was told to me by a middle-aged businesswoman named Wendy Klein.

Wendy graduated from Vassar College in the apocalyptic 1960s. During her years in school she sang earnest folk songs on the steps of the college library, traveled hundreds of miles to hear Joan Baez in concert, and dutifully attended every sit-in and be-in she could find. She also read widely in mystical literature, East and West, and for a while thought seriously about taking up the study of religion. At the same time, Wendy was deeply influenced by the values of the society around her. Even as she was attending morning prayer services at the school chapel and reading St. Teresa and St. John of the Cross, she was taking economics courses and planning a career in finance.

I first made Wendy's acquaintance in a class I taught at New York University titled "Mysticism East and West." The carefully tailored woman who showed up for the first session that night still had hints of these contrasting sides: outwardly successful and conventional, inwardly tuned to a different, mystical drummer.

As I learned in several conversations, Wendy and two of her classmates from Vassar had founded a small advertising agency in New York City. Discovering that the business world of the early 1970s was ambivalent toward ambitious women, she and her partners took the bull by the horns. One of the partners was an heiress. They borrowed money against her bank account, capitalized their Madison Avenue office, and went to work. The firm was one of the few women-owned companies in the advertising business at the time, and it did surprisingly well.

Then in 1978 the partners sold their company for several million dollars. Wendy Klein invested wisely, and soon she was an extremely rich woman. Trying the life of leisure for a short time, her aggressive spirit soon drove her back to the workplace, this time in a high-level job with a public relations firm. In the early 1980s she married a professor of neurology at New York University, and they had two daughters. Living in an eleven-room penthouse in the exclusive Turtle Bay area of Manhattan, Wendy seemingly had everything a person could want. But the more life gave her, she told me, the more jaded and hollow she felt.

"Right now I'm struggling with depression," she told me after class one night. "You know, I never knew what depression was before. It's funny to admit, but whenever I'd heard people say they were depressed I didn't know what they were talking about. I was too busy getting things done. Privately I'd kind of dismiss their complaints—you know, it's all in your head, that kind of thing.

"But when I got into my late forties all that changed. I started feeling a sense of disinterest and barrenness. It was like a seesaw—the more my outer life went up, the more my inner life went down. The more money I made, the more stimulating life got, the more my family and I traveled and did great things—the more bereft I felt. I began to understand the meaning of the word 'depression.' It's frightening, really."

I asked Wendy how the spiritual interests she had taken so to heart during her college years influenced her present life.

"I dropped that part of myself in the frenzy to get the agency off the ground," she said. "Stuff like medieval mysticism had appealed to me in my idealistic days. But I put it aside. I thought about theology and so forth now and then, but, you know, I was just too busy."

Wendy also told me she had started to get back into prayer. "Not that seriously, you know," she said, "but something's stirring."

The course at New York University came to an end, and Wendy Klein and I did not cross paths again until we met at a fund-raising dinner three years later. I was eager to get an update and to learn how she was doing.

As it turned out, Wendy was no longer working at the public relations firm but was attending graduate school at Columbia studying comparative religion. She had made enough money for ten women by now, she informed me, and her husband was supportive of her new venture in life. She still had several arduous years to go before getting her Ph.D., but she felt like a new woman doing what she loved and getting more and more into the spiritual side of herself.

"Was it difficult to give up the glamour?" I asked.

"Sure," Wendy replied. Then, sounding startlingly reminiscent of Tolstoy, she added, "But as I grow older I see that life fools you when you're young."

I asked her what she meant.

"It's like riding a bicycle," she said. "You have to keep pedaling so you don't fall off. As long as you go on rotating those wheels you sail right along. But wow, after a while I started asking myself: Why am I pedaling so hard? What's the big deal about keeping the bike going? Who told me I have to ride a bicycle all my life? Who said I had to ride one at all? Why can't I get off and sit under a tree in the lotus position for a while instead? I'm in my fifties now. Why should I work so hard? What's driving me to keep producing? What kind of illusion am I living under? Who pulled the wool over my eyes?"

"Who do you think did?" I asked, echoing her question.

"We create our illusions with our desires," she answered, "just like my partners and I created the agency twenty-five years ago. When I was younger I had this unquestioning belief in the importance of achievement. That idea became the illusion that drove my life. Now when I look back I see it was all a kind of con job I did on myself. That's the strange thing: I totally believed that the meaning of life was nothing more than getting the job done well and earning other people's approval. I once heard a public-speaking coach say that the greatest thing in speechmaking is sincerity: *if you can fake that, he said, then you've really got it made.* It's a funny way to put it, but I think that's what I did in my thirties and forties. I was faking it. But in complete sincerity."

"Are you still depressed?" I asked.

"I was depressed at the time for a good reason, but I didn't know the reason. I kept thinking it was because I wasn't getting enough done or wasn't fulfilling my talents. Several years ago I started reading the Christian mystics again. One day I came across a line that blew my mind: 'Your adversary is your helper.'

"That's it! I thought. This depression is my helper. It became clear:

God gives us problems so we'll turn to Him for answers. It's His way of getting our attention. Since we don't hear His subtle calls, He has to hit us over the head with a two-by-four. This was the reason why I was suffering so much during that time in my life."

Wendy had fastened on to the very paradox that Tolstoy had also wrestled with: the feelings that imprison and torment us as we grow older are also the very feelings that can lead us to something better. Our adversary is our enemy and our helper at the same time. Our suffering can destroy us, yes. But it can also make us whole. It all depends on how we choose to see it.

The tiny seed lives in the tree and clings to it like a child to a mother, an old fable tells us. Then one day the wind comes along, as the wind must, and blows the seed into the air, where it floats about in the nothingness thinking it is lost. "If only the wind had not blown just then," the seed says to itself. "If only I had been a little stronger and held on to the tree a moment longer. If only the wind were not so cruel." Little does the seed understand that it will soon be dropped into the warm earth, where it will germinate, grow, and become transformed into a majestic tree. When this happens it will look back, understand the entire pattern of its own suffering and fulfillment, and say, "The wind was my helper, the wind was my ally, the wind was my friend."

"Your adversary is your helper." This phrase has stayed with me ever since my conversation with Wendy. It is a kind of beacon, a kind of call. It comes to mind in my personal life as well. I remembered it one day years later as I stood at the reception desk of the Disneyland Hotel in Anaheim, California. Several weeks earlier I had made reservations for my trip to a conference in Anaheim. That morning I'd traveled five hours on a plane across the country, made my way through traffic on the freeway, and arrived at the hotel exhausted, eager to take off my shoes and lie down.

As I was waiting to fill out my registration form at the desk, a clerk looked at me with cheerful brown eyes and said, "I'm terribly sorry, Dr. Moody, but we have no reservation in your name."

I felt the anger rise. It was high season here at Disneyland, and the hotel, I knew, was booked full, along with every other hotel in Anaheim. But I had a reservation here!

I steeled my eyes and threatened to speak to the young lady's supervisor if nothing was done. Indignant thoughts raced through my mind: How can they treat me like this! What kind of idiots do they hire here! It felt as if all the frustrations of a lifetime were concentrated into a single moment—all the feelings of helplessness and of being treated like a nonperson rolled up into one.

The clerk patiently read through the reservation records again. "Sorry, sir, I just don't see your name here."

My anger reached the boiling point. Then something miraculous happened. The late afternoon sun was just streaming through the windows of the lobby, lighting the floors and walls with a radiant amber glow. As I gazed at this glorious burst of light, I suddenly felt light-headed and strangely elated. In a single moment all my anger melted away, and I saw the clerk standing before me as a clean, benevolent being and not simply as an instrument to expedite my travel plans. She was scrambling to do the best she could for an angry stranger, while I was responding to her kindness with the petulance of a spoiled child. I didn't feel ashamed or angry. I simply felt the coming of love, as if a great sheet of ice had melted between me and the world, and I was plunged into the sheer act of *seeing*—of perceiving the fineness and splendor and mystery of a fellow human being.

The hotel staff eventually tracked down my reservation. It wasn't a big deal. What was the big deal was that I had been given a close-up glimpse of my own adversary: impatience. I realized that this adversary had been stalking me for years, sneaking up on me as I wolfed down fast food, whispering angry words when someone else got the parking space, egging me to go faster, do more, get it right! My adversary, I realized, is like an invisible virus that hides itself from my immune system and lies in wait for opportunities to transform me into someone else.

That day at Disneyland I finally got a snapshot of my adversary up close, like one of those secret photos banks take of unsuspecting robbers. In the end, my adversary showed me the way to a higher love. A change in seeing, I realized at that moment, requires a change of feeling as well. Moments of sudden compassion like the one I experienced in the Disneyland Hotel lobby, I now understood, are not achieved by efforts of learning or of will. They come only when the quality of our emotions opens to the essential goodness of all things. A Sufi aphorism says it well:

> *Oh, you who are ignorant of burning and being burned,*
> *know that the coming of love is not learned.*

Without the help of my adversary that day, without the help of my anger and impatience, I would never have received the grace of a special moment of insight—I would never have known the feeling of burning, and being burned.

The Fisherman's Dilemma:
The Story of Our Lives

Let me tell you a tale that in many ways illuminates the essence of answering the Call. Once upon a time in the kingdom of Arabia a fisherman and his family lived by the edge of the sea. Every morning the fisherman walked to the shore and cast his net into the waves, always with success.

One day the winds of fortune changed and the fisherman pulled up nothing but the carcass of a dead ass, a vase filled with sand, and a pile of broken potsherds. In despair, he prayed to God for better luck, and the next day cast his line again. This time he fared no better, hauling in nothing more than an old bottle covered with strange, ancient markings.

As he was about to fling the bottle back into the sea, something checked his hand. He uncorked the bottle and peered inside. In an instant a tower of smoke spiraled up, and a gargantuan genie took shape before his eyes. The giant bowed. "Mighty King Solomon, who imprisoned me in this bottle long ago, I salute you."

The fisherman protested that he was not King Solomon, to which the genie replied that if this be the case, then the fisherman should prepare to die!

Even in his terror the fisherman became irate. "But I freed you!" he cried. "How could you be so ungrateful!?"

The genie explained how at first he intended to reward the person who freed him. But after a thousand years he grew angry, and vowed to slay his rescuer instead.

"I was *kind to you!*" the fisherman cried indignantly. "How can you requite good with evil?"

These pleas fell on deaf ears, and the genie prepared to stomp his rescuer into the dust. But before the giant could act, the fisherman thought with the quick wits of a man who has nothing to lose. "Listen, monster," he shouted up at the genie, "I will go to my grave knowing you to be a liar—one as huge as yourself could never fit into a container so small."

Rankled at having his honor questioned, the genie poured himself back into the bottle by way of demonstration. Instantly the fisherman seized the stopper and stuffed it into the flask.

By now, of course, you recognize the famous tale of the genie in the bottle from *The Arabian Nights*. Or at least a version of it. As with many

favorite narratives, there are several variants of this complex story. It continues:

"Let me out!" shouted the genie, "and I will reward you with wisdom
and riches beyond your wildest dreams."

"What kind of a fool do you take me for?" the fisherman said, pretend
ing not to care.

But he did care. Though he had no wisdom of his own, the fisherman
wanted to be wise.

Should the fisherman trust the ungrateful genie? After much soul-
searching he took a chance and opened the bottle. The genie spiraled out
and, true to his word, led the fisherman on an adventure that would one day
bring him great wisdom and riches.

Now, while "The Fisherman and the Genie" is a childhood classic, in
essence it is also a classic of our own life predicament. As the story opens, the
middle-aged hero's source of livelihood, once so predictable, has mysteriously
failed him. Living on the seashore between water and land, a symbol of the
boundary between the conscious mind and the unconscious, the fisherman
finds that ordinary life no longer satisfies his needs. Everything he pulls up
from the water is dead and broken: the corpse of a jackass, a load of sand,
some broken pottery. The habits and routines that have sustained him for
years are now ineffective. "The old games are no longer working," Natasha
Noor might say.

The fisherman prays for help, and his prayers are immediately answered, though not in the way he anticipates. His net does not magically fill
with fish. The humble piece of jetsam that has washed into the fisherman's
net reveals itself to be a blazing conflagration of supernatural energy, symbol-
izing an encounter with the instinctive forces, both positive and negative, that
have been bottled up inside us "for a thousand years"—or at least since the
timeless time of our own childhood. As we see in folk stories and Scripture,
the angels and demons of our nature appear to us as beggars and genies as
well as fountains of darkness or light; little things can be enormous things;
the world is not what it seems.

Up till now the fisherman has been trolling on the surface of life,
content with hauling in his daily catch, but never wondering what lurks in
the deeper watery depths that surround him. He clings to what he can see,
and sell, and have for dinner. Meanwhile, the superordinary parts of his
psyche remain bottled up inside him. When this awesome power for good or
evil is set loose, a mass of repressed energy erupts.

Now, what is curious about this encounter between the little man and the latent power within him is that the fisherman is indignant at the genie's ingratitude once he is released. "But I freed you!" the fisherman cries out, dumbfounded that anyone could be so ungrateful, baffled that this strange creature is not playing by the rules of the game, that the genie is intent on killing him rather than thanking him. How can life be so unfair?

Here an interesting issue arises. Since this feeling of unfairness is indeed so common in human dealings, and since it threatens the stability of society, society answers back by offering several ingenious strategies to make us feel that justice ultimately prevails.

First among these countermeasures is the promise society makes us of *reciprocity*. Put forth your best efforts, we're told in a thousand liminal and subliminal ways, and life will return the equivalent benefits. Scratch the world's back and the world will scratch yours.

Second is the promise of *entitlement*. You have *the right* to get what you want from life, society tells us. You deserve it. It is your privilege.

Third comes the promise of *reward:* If you behave yourself, work hard, keep your nose clean, and do what society asks, you'll be fairly compensated.

Now, being an ordinary fellow, the first thing the fisherman expects for his kindly deed is that the reciprocity-entitlement-reward expectation will give him the appropriate payback.

This, the fisherman and the rest of us believe, is the way things ought to work in this best of possible worlds. We lend money to our friends. We bend over backward to be fair to our co-workers. We deprive ourselves to put our children through school. We make silent sacrifices to please our mate. For these troubles and for a thousand others we expect to be paid back in kind.

But then several decades into our lives, we discover that other people are not as cooperative as we'd been led to believe. The more we do for them, it turns out, the less they appreciate it. When gratitude comes our way at all— and it rarely does—it often arrives mixed with resentment and hostility. "You know," Gurdjieff once remarked, "when you give something to a man, or do something for him, the first time he will kneel and kiss your hand; second time, he takes his hat off; third time, he bows; fourth time, he fawns; fifth time, he nods; sixth time, he insults you; and seventh time, he sues you for not giving him enough." My colleague Sam Sadin has a pet saying that he trots out at the office in such situations: "No good deed," he says, "goes unpunished."

Our bargain with life, it finally becomes clear to us after a number of years, is really no bargain at all. Bad things do happen to good people. And even the good people are not always so good.

So what do we do now? Become angry at life's unsportsmanlike conduct? Stop being nice?

Not necessarily. For what the wise fishermen among us understand is that we do not always get what we deserve from life, not because we are bad people or because the laws of the cosmos are unfair. Life disappoints us simply because life does not work the way we think it does. That is, life does not operate according to the tit-for-tat rules we have been taught to expect; it works, rather, according to an unfathomably vast cosmic design that operates on a universal as well as a personal level and whose causes and effects extend far into the past and far ahead into the future.

Does this mean that we do not get what we deserve?

Not necessarily. We do get what we deserve. We just don't always get it right away. The good deeds we do today—and the bad deeds—may not pay off till tomorrow, or even a decade from now. And when the reward or punishment finally reaches us, as it must, so much time may have elapsed between the deed and the payoff that we don't recognize a connection between the two events. "Know that acts are not the same color as their retribution," Rumi warns. "No service is colored like the payment. The laborer's wage does not resemble his work. . . . No origin resembles its effect, so you do not know the root of pain and torment."

In the fisherman's case his helpfulness and willingness to take a chance earn him a relationship with the wise but dangerous genie—that is, with his highest potential. This union launches a spiritual adventure that one day gains the fisherman riches and happiness. But this reward does not come as the result of the ordinary push-button laws of human expectations. Things rarely work out that easily or quickly.

The notion that we cannot manipulate our fate so easily flies in the face of conventional wisdom, of course, especially in a society like our own where control is so touted and prized. At the same time, believing that aspects of our life are in higher hands than our own, and that a superior Intelligence watches over all things, frees us from the insufferable burden of thinking we are alone in the universe, and that we have only ourselves to depend on. The world, many of us come to believe as we grow older, works according to a hidden ethic that, mercifully, is not our job to oversee, but that in the end recompenses us for all our efforts, even down to the utmost farthing.

Recently I was attending a surprise party for a childhood friend of mine who just turned fifty. My friend's sister and I had grown up together, and during the evening she told me a memorable story. This woman has had a particularly difficult life. Her husband abandoned her a week after their twin daughters were born. One of the twins almost died several times from asthma. She was betrayed by a string of lovers and double-crossed by several corporate partners. The money her parents left her was embezzled by a business manager and never repaid. On and on. These wounds embittered my friend's sister. She is a person who often dwells on life's unfairness. One of her favorite phrases is: "You can never win."

But at this party she told me about something remarkable that had happened to her recently and that had changed her entire life's perspective. "Several weeks ago," she said, "I was driving to work on the Grand Central Parkway. A couple of miles from the tunnel I hit a miserable traffic tie-up. I was sitting there in the car feeling helpless and anxious the way you do in traffic jams. I was thinking how shitty life is, and how much it's cheated me. Then I happened to notice a little baby tucked into a toddler's seat in a nearby car. Seeing it made me think of my own twin daughters. I started going back, back in time, remembering my girls when they were this size. I remembered how helpless they were, how small and light in my arms. I remembered the smells in their room—talcum powder, formula, baby oil. I could almost hear the crinkling sound of their Pampers. I pictured their little legs and arms wiggling around as I slid them into the pajamas. I saw my hands buttoning buttons and pulling up blankets; blankets that smelled of shampoo and Similac. I remembered how slippery their little bodies were in the bathtub—their goofy giggling when I splashed water on them.

"These memories started to open up like a floodgate inside me right there in Queens traffic. I'm not kidding. It was as if a million memories rushed in at once, as if someone were flicking hundreds of photographs past my eyes in a single second, each one more charming and beautiful than the next.

"And then a really weird thing happened. As I was sitting there literally swimming in these memories, the sound of the car motors around me started to sound very sweet and precious, like music. The sky looked almost purple in its intensity and beauty. The people in the cars around me all looked shining and wonderful. Everything that had happened in my life, both good and bad, seemed okay at that instant, like it was just as it should be. It was as if I suddenly recognized the joy my life surrounded me with. I'd been distancing myself from all this beauty by worry and feeling sorry for myself.

"Finally the feelings got so intense that I put my head down on the steering wheel and started sobbing from sheer joy. Even in the middle of my tears, blubbering like a baby, I remember sitting there thinking that I should even be grateful for the fact that I was in a traffic jam. Without it, I thought, this experience would not be happening."

The Call: Male and Female

Up till now we have assumed that the Call comes to men and women with more or less the same constancy and that spiritual growth is an equal opportunity affair. While there is no reason to doubt this assumption, a critical question introduces us to yet another aspect of the Call: do men and women experience the Call in the same way?

The answer, based on established findings in life course development psychology, as well as many personal interviews done with spiritual seekers, suggests that, in fact, the Call often takes a *different* form for men and women. While the journey's goal is similar for both men and women, the actual process by which people are called can and often does differ according to each sex's psychological needs and biological imperatives.

At the heart of these differences lie several features of life development itself. One of these features, known as "gender crossover," became known from findings suggested by the Kansas City Studies of Adult Life, a landmark study of adult life span development launched in the 1950s. The theory of gender crossover attracted the interest of many researchers, including anthropologist David Gutmann, whose important book *Reclaimed Powers* explores this fascinating phenomenon in full.

The crossover phenomenon takes place when men and women reach midlife and begin to reclaim the powers and prerogatives that up till this age have been stereotypically assigned to the opposite sex. Gutmann, for instance, argues that as men grow older they reclaim their suppressed "feminine" sides by becoming more emotional and receptive. Women, meanwhile, move deeper into the "masculine" zone, becoming increasingly assertive, venturesome, and independent.

Gutmann points to the case of the Druze, a highland Lebanese religious group. As the Druze men grow older, he tells us, they typically relinquish their aggressive, warlike behavior, turning to the more passive activities of community service and religious contemplation. The same shift is noted in cultures across the world, from Kenya to Australia to Native Americans. Among the Comanche and Hopi, for instance, warriors and men of the world sometime dress like women in their later years and assume domestic chores in the community.

Many of us, certainly, have witnessed instances of crossover in our own circle of acquaintances. We see it in men who once prided themselves on being hard-nosed and street-smart but who now display a mellow, relational side after middle age. Perhaps they volunteer for community service. Or they spend more time with their children or grandchildren, take up cooking, become more involved in quiet backyard pleasures.

Most strikingly, middle-aged men find it easier to display the caring feelings that seemed "weak" in their younger days when they were battling other young warriors for market share. As they grow older, we see these same men gravitating toward a new set of emotional standards, loving rather than ruling, cooperating rather than dominating. My own father, a New York City banker and tough-minded businessman in his working years, moved to Florida in his retirement, where he promptly took a low-paying job at Disney World. He took this job not for the money, but for the pleasure of watching so many children have so much fun. Once this nurturant side of a man's nature is uncovered, the step to spiritual involvement can be a short one.

Women, meanwhile, as they mature often become more interested than ever before in leadership, autonomy, and risk taking.

Betty Friedan, in her book *The Fountain of Age,* takes special note of women's tendency to move into the more "masculine" domains of competition and worldly success during the mid-adult years. From the feminist perspective, Friedan finds it heartening that after the parenting duties are completed (with their strongly defined gender roles), men and women are able to get in touch with their suppressed male and female sides. Still, Friedan is not ready to declare victory. The male-female crossover should not simply make us more "masculine" or "feminine," she warns. It should stretch us to untapped levels of maturity and character growth as well.

When do these untapped levels of growth begin? Where do we find them in our own society? One of the points that Friedan has made to me in our own conversations, as well as in her writings, is that our culture provides almost no paradigms of maturity for people in the second half of life. Rites of passage, Friedan maintains, tribal elders, role models, all are conspicuously missing, and their absence leaves us without direction. Where then do we turn?

Here the concepts of answering the Call and the crossover phenomenon begin to merge. As we age and mature, the need to explore unfulfilled zones of the heart and mind—including gender-opposite roles—grows stronger in many people. This is especially true for those who embark on the spiritual path.

"For a while," an ex-airline pilot told me, "just reading the Bible and going to church was enough. But after retirement I got this funny feeling that I wanted to be more a part of things. I felt my heart opening to others as I got increasingly involved in church activities. All this love and closeness was a new thing for me. I had always been suspicious of close involvements."

Women, it seems, as they answer the Call, often feel the need to disentangle from overidentification with family, friends, loved ones, becoming more autonomous, more vocal about where they stand and who they are.

"One of the reasons I got interested in Zen," a female member of a dojo in California told me, "was because the other women at the Institute seemed to have such a wonderful sense of themselves. An older woman who was very advanced in her practice said to me when I was beginning—I'll never forget it—she said, 'When you enter the gate of Zen you're a woman. After you do zazen for a while you're a man. Later you become a child. After that, you're nothing. Still later you go beyond nothing. Finally you become a woman again. If you know all that you know the whole story.'"

The process of answering the Call not only compels us to open new rooms in ourselves. It inspires us to take both the masculine and the feminine qualities we find in our once sealed gender chambers and use them to become more integrated individuals. What we are pursuing at the deepest level when we respond to the Call is a sense of our own completion. This sense of wholeness, it may seem to us when we are young, comes naturally through sex, marriage, and relationships. But experience shows that this is not always the case. No matter how happily married or mated we may be, there is often a nagging sensation of something missing. Eventually, after much trial and error, we discover the great secret: that the "something" we are searching for in members of the opposite sex is really *in ourselves*. If we are going to take advantage of our hidden potential, we now understand, the masculine and feminine sides of our psyche must be united.

Plato, in his dialogue *Symposium*, speaks metaphorically of how male and female are actually the divided halves of one primordial being. Each half, Plato tells us, is looking to the other for its completeness.

Once upon a time, says Plato, Hephaestus, the blacksmith of the gods, asked two people who were madly in love if he should transform them into a single person. "There is not a being among them," remarks Plato, "who when he heard this proposal would deny that this meeting and melting into one another, this becoming one instead of two, was the very expression of an ancient need. And the reason is that human nature was originally one, and we were a whole, and the desire and pursuit of the whole is called *love*."

In the best of all possible worlds, Plato suggests, lovers would be literally fused—androgynous. But reality being what it is, our completion must be built with spiritual struggle and a harmonious fusion of the male and female forces within us. The Call is the plea of the two halves of our own psyche begging to be made whole.

The Lute Player

Like all basic symptoms of the human condition, the crossover phenomenon and its application to spiritual growth shows up in story and myth throughout the world. Several fine examples are provided by psychiatrist Allan Chinen in his delightfully thought-provoking book *Once Upon a Midlife*. One of the few mental health professionals to study folk stories pertaining specifically to spiritual and psychological themes in the middle stretches of life, Chinen points out that the motif of balancing the masculine and feminine is a critical ingredient in many, as he terms them, "middle tales."

"A large body of research demonstrates that psychological androgyny increases at midlife," Chinen writes. "More important, this androgyny correlates with successful aging and greater happiness. Married couples who are satisfied with their marriage have less traditional gender roles compared with younger individuals or with unhappy couples. When middle-aged men and women are given the Rorschach inkblot test, they respond with unique, individualized answers that do not conform to gender stereotypes. Young adults, by contrast, gravitate toward strict, conventional male and female roles."

Among the several folk stories Chinen uses to demonstrate the spiritual side of the crossover phenomenon, the one that most eloquently elucidates the motif of the Call is the wonderful Russian tale "The Lute Player."

"The Lute Player" begins in a peaceful land where a King and Queen rule happily together over a prosperous people. By all rights the King should be contented with his many blessings. But as the years pass he grows restless and one day decides to wage war on a neighboring heathen ruler.

Rallying his armies, the King leads his troops into glorious battle. His Queen is anxious to accompany him, but the King assures her that adventure is man's business and that she should remain at home.

At first the King subdues his adversary and revels in his victories. But soon the tides of fortune change. His armies are routed, and he is thrown into a dungeon by the heathen ruler. Forced into slave labor, the King manages to smuggle a letter out to the Queen, ordering her to sell the royal treasure and send ransom to free him.

The Queen's first impulse is to obey. But then she reconsiders: none of her counselors can be trusted to deliver such a large ransom. And if she makes the journey herself she may be taken prisoner. Finally she decides to set her own course. Shearing off her beautiful long hair, costuming herself in a minstrel suit, shouldering a lute, she travels in male disguise until she arrives at the gate of the heathen ruler's palace. Here she sings a beautiful ballad. The heathen ruler listens, is charmed, and sends for the balladeer.

"Boy," he says. "Your music is magnificent. Stay with me for three days and serenade me. Then I shall grant you your heart's desire."

For three days and three nights the Queen sings her songs and recites poems. At the end of this time the ruler is well pleased and asks the minstrel what he wishes in reward. The Queen replies that while traveling through the countryside a rugged bodyguard is often needed. Perhaps the king can spare such a ruffian from his dungeons?

The ruler readily agrees and the minstrel is escorted to the prison and given the pick of the lot. The Queen quickly recognizes her husband, weakened and humbled, but very much alive.

Now at this point in the story the plot takes a surprising turn. Though the King goes willingly with the minstrel, he fails to recognize that his rescuer is also his wife. The Queen, in turn, keeps her identity secret. The King, it seems, still has lessons to learn.

Together they travel many miles, and along the way the mysterious minstrel nurses the King back to health. Finally they reach their homeland, where the King attempts to reward his rescuer. But the balladeer refuses any reward. And so they part ways.

The Queen now races back to the palace, puts on her royal gown, and walks out grandly to greet the King.

"Why didn't you gather the ransom and free me as I commanded?" the King shouts at her when they meet.

The Queen makes no reply.

"And where did you go?" he asks suspiciously, having learned that his wife has been missing from the palace for several months.

The King then stomps off and the Queen returns to her room. Here she puts on her minstrel clothes, takes up her lute, and approaches the King's chamber, singing a beautiful ballad.

"It is the boy who freed me!" the King cries in delight, hearing the wondrous music. "At least *he* has been faithful!" The King invites the minstrel to enter his chambers. "You have come for your reward at last, O brave singer. What is your wish?"

At this the Queen removes the minstrel hat and cloak to reveal her true identity. Realizing that the Queen has been his benefactor all along, that her subtle wisdom has succeeded where his heroic bravura has failed, the King is overcome with remorse and gratitude. He begs his wife to forgive him, which she gladly does, and together they celebrate their reunion.

The story of "The Lute Player," as we see, develops both the notion of gender crossover and the spiritual Call in much the way that a symphony develops variations on several themes.

As the story opens, the King is marching off with great pomp to play the manly game of war, attempting, perhaps, to revive a lost spirit of youthful adventure and to make his mark before all opportunities for glory fade. He is following a call; but it is the wrong call, the call of the ego rather than the soul. Not until the entire cycle of his folly, fall, awakening, and rebirth have run their course will he realize that his feminine side was both his Call and his salvation.

Despite his initial success—in the beginning we sometimes fool ourselves when we attempt to relive our past—the King learns that recapturing the glories of youth is a foolish dream. Conquest eludes him, and his attempts to recapture these fragments of time gone by bring humiliation and imprisonment. The King is then rescued by the force of the feminine, which up till now he has denied. Intelligence and subtle wisdom are personified in the form of the Queen, who comes to help him in his darkest hour, offering a second Call, this time to true freedom.

For the Queen, on the other hand, the King's defeat serves as a wake-up Call. Resisting the stereotypes of helplessness and passivity, our heroine responds by ignoring her husband's orders and adopting the masculine role of rescuer and champion. She even wears masculine clothes and cuts her hair. (In many traditional stories the act of cutting one's hair is a sign of emasculation for men—think of Samson—while it is an act of defiance and independence for women.)

When the Queen finally confronts her husband's captor, she does not attempt to beat him into surrender as a younger champion might do. Instead she calls on the more mature power of cunning—just like the fisherman. She then proceeds to make friends with her dangerous adversary through the hypnotic power of story and song, outsmarting the same mighty enemy that her husband was unable to subdue with all his manly powers.

The brave Queen, what's more, though a man in outward appearance, accomplishes these deeds by womanly means: song, intuition, gentleness, all of which prove far more potent weapons than brute strength. Though the Queen wears a manly costume and walks the warrior's way, she remains true to her feminine self and to the wisdom of maturity, so different in its style from the heroic gestures of youth.

The rescued King, meanwhile, does not yet have the insight to recognize the true identity of his deliverer, or to see that she is bearing him the Call to freedom. In the fires of defeat he has been purified but not enlightened. For this further enlightenment his wife, symbol of his anima or soul, is necessary.

Like Dante's Beatrice, the Queen leads her husband out of his inferno-like dungeon back to his homeland, his balance point, his center. Here the King at last comes to know the truth: in a flash of self-insight he realizes it was his Queen, his own feminine half, who has been calling him all this time. While in prison and even after his return, the King believed that he had been deserted by his feminine counterpart; that he was alone in his struggle. Now he learns the truth. His soul has always been at his side the entire time, he discovers, guiding him through the wilderness, nursing him back to health, leading him from hell to heaven. This shock of recognition causes the King to experience a Breakthrough and to undergo a moment of enlightenment. Seeing into his illusions and into himself, he is changed forever. Understanding the extent of his blindness, he begs his wife's forgiveness. Together they then merge into completeness, raised to a higher place than before by each answering their own Call, and by enlisting in equal measure the male and female energies within them. In this way both King and Queen, masculine and feminine, the two sides of our own consciousness, are united, completed—and redeemed.

The Sibyl of the Rhine

The Christian church has long been familiar with the intricacies of the Call and of the adaptations the Call must at times make to suit male and female needs.

In the war-torn, plague-ridden years of the late Middle Ages, for example, it was common for women in their forties and fifties to be widowed and deprived of familiar social roles. Large numbers took themselves to nunneries, and there spent the remainder of their days in service and devotion. So many women entered monastic settings at this time, in fact, that in the fourteenth century an entire feminine-based mystical movement arose known as Rhineland (or Rhenish) mysticism, so named for the areas of lower Germany where it prospered.

In the years when Rhenish mysticism was setting down its roots, a group of lay female seekers known as the Beguines gathered together and formed a social support network for middle-aged women who had experienced the Call and gone into monastic seclusion. Out of this merging a century later came the movement known as *devotio moderna*—"modern devotion"—a belief which held that the inner life of the spirit was more important than adherence to ritual or ecclesiastical law. As a result of these and other female-based religious activities, a widespread renewal of spiritual life swept across Western Europe.

One of the greatest of these female mystics, Mechtilde of Magdeburg, concealed her deep spiritual experiences until she was in her forties and no longer able to hide her devotional fires. At this point, following the suggestion of her confessor, Mechtilde began writing about her remarkable mystical experiences in detail. These writings eventually resulted in a book, *The Flowing Light of the Godhead,* one of the classics of medieval spirituality.

An even more extraordinary example of the Call galvanizing latent spiritual leadership is found in the life of Teresa of Avila (1515–82).

A Carmelite nun, for many years Teresa performed her religious duties with lukewarm enthusiasm. Up to her middle years, she writes, "on the one side God was calling me; on the other, I was following the spirit of the world." Teresa's true Call, or what commentators have referred to as her "second conversion," came literally out of the blue in her fortieth year.

One day Teresa was walking down a hallway near an image of Christ Crucified, as she did every day at this hour. Glancing up at the figure, her heart suddenly felt as if it had been "split open." The next moment she was on her knees, dissolved in tears, overcome with remorse for having ignored God so blatantly.

Not long after this remarkable Breakthrough, Teresa began reading St. Augustine's *Confessions,* perhaps the classic midlife conversion narrative. Augustine was also one of those who didn't "get it" until later in life. Augustine's famous prayer, "Lord, give me chastity—but not yet," has remained the watchword for spiritual procrastination down through the ages.

After this "second conversion," St. Teresa turned to constant prayer and began experiencing intense states of what she called "delights and favors of God." She described these states in her *Autobiography,* as well as in *The Way of Perfection.* At this point in her life she stepped fully into the world, helping pioneer a larger spiritual role for women in the church. In 1562, with the authorization of Pope Pius IV, Teresa opened the first female convent of the Carmelite Reform. She then spent the next five years battling ecclesiastical authorities who objected to women forming religious orders. Undaunted, Teresa met a young Carmelite priest named Juan de Yepes, later to be canonized as St. John of the Cross. Working hand in hand with de Yepes, an outlandish thing for a nun to do at the time, she helped him found a Carmelite Reform for men. Before St. Teresa died, with the help of King Philip II of Spain and a coterie of dominant worldly figures, she would become single-handedly responsible for founding twelve monasteries across the nation of Spain.

Now, a point to bear in mind about this upsurge of piety among female mystics in the Middle Ages is that it usually takes many years to reconcile the complementary sides of ourselves and to achieve psychic wholeness. Often this process is accomplished through marriage or in a long-term love relationship. But not always. Some of us are self-initiated, as it were, changing roles naturally as the circumstances of life demand. A fascinating example reveals itself in the life of one of the greatest of all Christian mystics, the medieval seer and saint Hildegard of Bingen.

Hildegard of Bingen was born in 1098 in the Rhineland. As a young woman she had strong religious yearnings, and like many young girls of the time, entered a Benedictine nunnery.

Hildegard spent the first half of her life serving the other nuns, leading a self-effacing, obedient life, and keeping in check the powerful creative forces that brooded inside her. Showing skill as an administrator, she was made prioress of her nunnery in her late thirties and settled into a life of quiet devotion.

Then at age forty-three everything changed.

It was in this year that Hildegard began to have prophetic visions, first one, then another, then so many that, like other great visionaries, she started to think she was going insane. Searching for a religious authority to assess the validity of her experiences, she made contact with the greatest churchman of the day, St. Bernard of Clairvaux, who quickly testified to their authenticity.

From this time on Hildegard shed her deferential persona and assumed an aggressive, sometimes pugnacious stance toward a world that she now believed was her sacred mission to save.

This mission, it turned out, branched out in many directions. Not only did Hildegard introduce new rules and reforms to monastic life. She also began an intensive study of philosophy, medicine, and musical composition. Soon she was writing papers on scientific and medical subjects, including a remarkable text on the human body, and composing sacred music that would be played for centuries after her death. In her spare time she invented her own private language, a mixture of German and Latin written in a surreal alphabet of her own invention. She also undertook ambitious overland missionary journeys, traveling by herself at night, crossing dangerous stretches of the Rhineland, walking through robber-infested forests, all unimaginable feats for a woman of her day.

Determined to fight corruption in the church, Hildegard carried on correspondences with four popes, King Henry II of England, and many worldly notables, whom she bombarded with elaborate manifestos on behalf of both civic and religious reform. By the time she turned fifty the "Sibyl of the Rhine" had become a model of the fighting nun, a woman warrior battling with the male establishment's highest-ranking churchmen of the day, and struggling to found a convent of her own. This she finally did in 1147, moving her flock of nuns to the town of Rupertsberg near Bingen, where she helped design, then build one of the most impressive nunneries in Germany.

And so Hildegard's life continued in this vein until in her eighties she had become a kind of medieval Maggie Kuhn, founder of the Gray Panthers, an advocate of the poor and disenfranchised, a fighter of powermongers in the government and church, a specialist in scolding faithless emperors and making apocalyptic prophesies that are still read today. "I had a marvelous and mystical vision," she wrote in one of her poems. "All my inner organs were upset, and the sensations of my body were no longer felt. For my consciousness had been transformed, as if I no longer knew myself, as if raindrops were falling from the Hand of God upon my soul."

Menopause as Spiritual Call

The theme of raindrops bringing rebirth to arid spiritual soil is one that appears many times in the verses of Hildegard, for whom sin itself is a drying-up of the human spirit. If Hildegard were writing today she might tell us that the only real sin of aging is allowing ourselves to become cold and sapless, cynical and dry. Relevant to her notion of spiritual aridity is the central issue of menopause.

If there is one landmark event to herald the coming of a woman's middle age it is the cessation of menses, a life-changing, sometimes mind-changing episode around which swirls a galaxy of contrasting attitudes, theories, and beliefs. Historically speaking, women's postmenopausal years have been viewed as a dry, sterile period in the female life course, as if removal

from the reproductive cycle somehow robbed women of an essential feminin-
ity. For centuries any public discussion of menopause was unthinkable. The
subject was a closed one, and taboo as well.

By the middle part of the twentieth century, of course, discussions on
sexuality had become a good deal more open, and people began to speak of
menopause in both an open and questioning way. Indeed, since the 1960s,
the issue of whether menopause is a medical challenge that must be treated
with hormone therapy, or a simple act of nature that should be allowed to
take its course, has created a good deal of comment and controversy. While
there is clearly a wealth of helpful advice and good sense to be gained from
these discussions, most overlook another alternative: menopause as a sacred
rite of passage, a new road leading to a deeper and more prevailing sense of
soul.

In the early stages of writing this book I had a number of conversations
with my wife on this subject of spirituality and menopause. Shortly thereafter
she handed me a letter from her friend Esther in Arizona.

My wife and I have always considered Esther to be a person of considerable spiritual savvy. Her viewpoint—and the viewpoint I was to run across in
other women at midlife—is that under certain circumstances menopause can
put women in touch with deeper issues of purpose and existence, and can set
the tone for what may turn out to be a profound and fulfilling time of life.

An English professor at a state university, Esther set down her thoughts
on menopause just after completing her own change. With her permission, I
reproduce excerpts from her letter below:

"I've been thinking about what exactly it is that makes menopause so
significant. A woman doesn't appreciate the grip that sexuality and the reproductive drive have on her soul until these drives subside. It's one of those
things where you can't see its true proportions while you're still inside it.

"For example, a woman at this point in life understands she can't
negotiate the world anymore by being attractive or seductive; that she's past
the time when superficial things like appearance or flirtation can get her what
she wants. This brings up a new kind of honesty and forthrightness that
possibly wasn't there before. She has to be herself now in front of the world,
for better or worse.

"Another thing too: once the body no longer has to prepare a nest every
month, its workload is lightened. What a woman chooses to do with this
extra energy varies according to her inclinations, but I do think menopause is
an *opportunity* to wake up from the hormonal dream we entered at puberty.
It's a reminder of death. And death initiates life on another level. What that

level will be depends on what we've made of our life so far. And because it brings some degree of suffering and disorientation it humbles and purifies, leaving a woman feeling reborn and reoriented, the way one feels after recovering from an illness.

"These are all fleeting insights, of course. The daily battle goes on . . ."

The more my wife and I discussed this issue, the more fascinated I became by the relationship between spirituality and menopause. Offering to assist me in writing on this important subject, my wife began gathering interview material from female friends and colleagues.

As it turned out, the women she talked with had much to say about menopause as a Call to spirituality, so much, in fact, that there is space here only to include the most relevant responses. The results of these conversations made me acutely aware of how our society has demythologized menopause and relegated it to the status of pure biological event, robbing women of a powerful spiritual ally.

In many traditional cultures, for example, various transformative events in a woman's life—the first menstruation, marriage, childbirth, menopause— are observed with rituals that consecrate these transitions, honoring them as sacred rites of passage as well as physiological events, and assuring the women who experience them that their lives are linked to the great cycle of all human life.

"It is in realizing and in living this sacredness," writes the religious historian Mircea Eliade, "that a woman finds the spiritual meaning of her own existence, she feels that life is both *real* and *sanctified,* that it is not merely an endless series of blind, psycho-physiological automatisms, useless and in the last reckoning absurd. For the women too, initiation is equivalent to a change of level, to the passing out of one mode of being into another."

Christine Downing, professor of comparative religion and an eloquent observer of the relationship between menopause and women's spiritual search, describes how when she began her own change of life she "felt alone, uninformed, somewhat afraid—and yet also curious and expectant. I was at the brink of a centrally important life-change and had no knowledge of the myths or rituals that had helped women throughout history live this transition with hope, dignity and depth."

Rites of passage, says Downing, integrate the personal and the transpersonal, the social and the sacred. In this sense veneration is accorded to moments of transition that otherwise—as in our own culture—would be viewed as bothersome "crises" to be dealt with in the psychotherapist's office or through the mouth of a medicine bottle. "Through participation in such rites," Downing writes, "one discovers that one's suffering and confusion are not unique and isolating. The pain one endures in giving up and leaving behind a familiar and cherished life form is simply the pain of being human, what Freud calls 'common unhappiness.' "

Most important, as both Downing and many of the women my wife interviewed insist, if women honor menopause as a sacred transition rather than the loss of womanhood, they can allow themselves to experience change of life in its truest sense—as a passage into a new life: a rebirth.

One of the women my wife spoke with, Brynn, put it this way: "I had preconceptions about menopause. I'd read a lot about it, mostly warnings. Be careful, all the articles say, your hormones are about to go nuts. You won't be yourself. You'll drive yourself and everyone else crazy. You'll get depressed. You'll have hot flashes. Headaches. Disorientation. Yow! When my menopause came there were a lot of unpleasant moments, but, all in all, when it was over I felt like I'd passed through some purifying ring of fire, and that I was a new woman now with a new life in front of me. It was like being biblically reborn."

A point made over and over by women is that freedom from childbearing and being looked on as a sex object allows them to become more involved in matters of the spirit.

One woman named Sarah told us: "Menopause is a gradual process but scary. A contradiction in terms. Slow electric shock therapy. As you move through it you're aware that you're modifying, physically and mentally, and that you'll never be quite the same person when it's over. You realize your body is showing you some big lesson about the ending of things. It's making you aware on a cellular level that you're mortal. Yes, mortal after all.

"Is that bad? No, it's good. Because it's the truth. The truth is always good. It tells you that if you were ever going to do such and such in your life you'd better do it now. Time to get on with raising the flag of conscious living. Time to get with it. Menopause is a middle-age wake-up call."

For Diane, a woman in her forties, menopause came early. Today she sees the changes a woman goes through as a kind of escape from the grip of nature. "Many spiritual traditions talk about the fact that women are more connected to the earth than men," she told my wife. "Much as I hated to admit that this was true, at times in my life it seemed undeniable. I often felt that being a woman, especially an earth mother type, kept me closer to the physical world than I would have liked. Things like giving birth, breast feeding, changing diapers all keep you pretty close to the material world.

Then menopause came along and broke this connection or loosened it. In a sense this gave me a mandate to seek and find spirituality. 'You've done your job,' Nature said. 'You've made your payment to me—kept the human race going and peopled the world. Now go out and discover some of the deeper secrets.'"

An interesting sociological finding, and one that is tied to women's increased spirituality after menopause, is the fact that women often tend to become physically healthier in their postmenopausal years. The evidence for this finding is confirmed by several studies of women at midlife carried out at a West Coast women's college. Data for the studies centered on a cross-sectional sample of 700 female alumnae between the ages of twenty-six and eighty. The first group of alumnae studied included 60 women in their early fifties. The second group included a longitudinal sample of 118 women who were first studied at age forty-three, then again at fifty-two. Subjects in these studies were asked to rate important elements in their lives such as relationships, career, happiness quota, health, and general quality of life.

The results showed that the middle-aged subjects considered their life to be "first-rate" far more frequently than young subjects and old subjects. Most of the women at this age were pursuing careers (78 percent) and enjoying a stable couple relationship (68 percent). They considered their health to be better than average (89 percent), and on a four-point scale 83 percent rated their quality of life as first-rate or at least good. In the longitudinal sample women rated their early fifties very favorably. Menopausal and postmenopausal women noted a decreased incidence of dependency and self-criticism, an increased incidence of self-confidence and decisiveness. In both middle-aged samples, women in their early fifties rated their quality of life, health, and personal happiness higher than those in any other age group.

Mary, a writer and poet, explained that "since I've gotten older and my childbearing apparatus is closed down, my mind feels clear. I feel like I get more accomplished. There's a gentle modification of spirit that's taken place—mostly, I'd say, in my ability to feel joy and compassion, and my willingness to assert myself. It's an energy thing."

A massage therapist named Naomi sees the coming of menopause as both a giving and a getting: "You can no longer give birth now. You give up a privilege. But you get other privileges in return. You no longer feel that same need to please others, to say the right thing, to look the right way. You start feeling more daring, more your own person, more energetic, more in high gear. No one owns you anymore. You want to walk the high wire. You want to run barefoot over glowing coals. You want to solve the riddle of the

Sphinx. In a way some of your youthful ideals and energy return, but in a raised, a sublimated way. It's great!"

Another critical point that was made—and several women made it—is that the end of menopause allows a woman to take her place in the community as mentor and wisdom giver—a "tribal elder," in one woman's words.

According to Priscilla, a college professor: "Menopause is a dividing line in life. It marks the boundaries from being a mother and a wife to being a counselor and a teacher. It gave me permission to think of myself in this new way. I'm now a human being who's lived long enough and hard enough to give guidance to others. It's okay to be an advice giver now."

Carrie, a wife, mother, and woman of the world at forty-seven, says, "After menopause you go from serving your body to serving yourself, to serving your community and God. From small to large. You become the archetypical wise woman—you run with the wolves."

"I'm just generally more aware since my menopause," says Lorette, a woman in her fifties who is currently studying to become a minister. "Of the universality of things. I can see a child run down the aisle of a supermarket and my whole heart leaps up. Because there's such wondrous hope in that little person. There's a kind of heightened emotionality in my life now. Something in me feels physically different. More acute, more tuned in. Stronger. Stranger."

Menopause, in sum, continues to be a complex and controversial issue. Yet clearly for some women the experience of change of life, while perhaps problematic and at times painful, is also cleansing and renewing—"the difficult start," as one woman phrased it, "of a wonderful second life."

"Since finishing menopause," says Hannah Carroll, a social worker and longtime spiritual seeker, "I'm poignantly sensitive to the life cycle now and young people and children. I feel more centered, more awake. Change of life helped me understand life's preciousness, and made me want to get reacquainted with the flowering of all the good and profound things that are around me all the time, but which I don't always notice. My eyes seem more widely opened now since it happened. And when you see more you understand more, and you realize how important having a spiritual belief is. I see a lot of things now that I didn't see when I was young. Middle age is a golden age. You've got it all now, the energy, the understanding. Also the will, plus enough time to do something with it all."

The Teacher and the Call

There is a basic theme that runs through many of the stories and interviews we have looked at so far in this chapter: that the Call erupts in our lives unbidden, often unexpectedly—whether as a near-death experience, as a change in body chemistry, or simply as an urge to find relevancy and deeper purpose. This notion that the Call can come out of the blue and disrupt our familiar routines reminds me of a strange incident I learned of many years ago while I was a graduate student in philosophy. The events surrounding this incident contrast with, but also amplify, the tales we have heard so far.

The story involved a prominent philosophy professor, holder of an endowed chair at one of the most prestigious universities in the world. This remarkably gifted man had attained everything I or any other student of philosophy might ever dream of: erudition, academic honors, and the almost reverent respect of his colleagues. Students from foreign countries flocked to sit at his feet. His writings were read widely, even by nonacademics. Noted for the devastatingly powerful thrust of his logic and his skeptical, probing intellect, no one could stand up to his brilliant arguments in public debate.

And as if all this was not enough, this remarkable man had risen to these heights of greatness at the age of thirty-seven!

Then, as it sometimes does for those overblessed by fate, disaster struck. One day following his normal routine, this professor stood up in front of a lecture hall crowded with eager, worshipful students, and prepared to give his usual brilliant address. He opened his mouth to speak. But not a sound came out. His voice was paralyzed.

The professor tried again, but without success. And again.

Mortified, he stepped down from the podium and slipped out of the lecture hall. The next day he left the university, and shortly afterward disappeared from public view entirely.

Following this distressing performance there was, naturally, an uproar at the university and scandal everywhere the news traveled. The upshot was that within weeks one of the finest academic careers in a generation was in ruins, and a name universally honored in academia had fallen into disgrace.

But that was only the beginning. Several months later even stranger whisperings began to circulate. Apparently the professor had liquidated his affairs, abandoned his family entirely, and taken off into the deserts of the Middle East searching for spiritual guidance to heal himself.

A remarkable story, isn't it? But there's a detail I haven't mentioned. The events in this case did not take place in 1967, when I entered graduate school, but 900 years earlier, in Baghdad. The professor was Abu Hamid al-Ghazzali, one of the greatest philosophers and theologians of the Middle Ages, and a major influence on many great Western thinkers, including St. Thomas Aquinas, who quotes him frequently.

Al-Ghazzali's autobiography, *The Deliverance from Error,* helps us fill in the missing pieces.

After this temporary episode with speechlessness, al-Ghazzali tells us, he suffered a complete mental and physical breakdown, and finally went into seclusion. Here he agonized for months over the fact that the academic philosophy he had spent his life preaching had done *nothing* to answer his own spiritual questions. Indeed, his philosophy had literally ended up choking him.

After much soul-searching, al-Ghazzali made arrangements for his family to be looked after, sold all his personal belongings, and set out alone on foot into the Syrian desert dressed as a wandering dervish or holy man.

For the next twelve years the great scholar lived in Sufi centers across the Near East. Here he studied, fasted, meditated, and sat at the feet of the spiritual masters who had, he tells us, summoned him through a mysterious inner voice. After attaining a degree of spiritual understanding, al-Ghazzali then began to write treatises on divine compassion, reconciling mystical doctrine with religious orthodoxy. Gone was his hard-edged rationalism. In its place came a credo of pure love. So great an impact did his works eventually have on the world that al-Ghazzali's writings are still read today, both in the mosques of the Middle East and in Western universities.

Looking back on al-Ghazzali's serpentine path to illumination, it is fascinating to see the contrast between his response to the Call and that of Hildegard of Bingen. After his shattering experience in Baghdad, al-Ghazzali was driven to forsake the pursuit of pure reason and to turn his gaze toward the power of divine love. Like the King in "The Lute Player," he discovered that youthful weapons for dominating the world, whether they be the tools of logic or the implements of war, are worthless when a person is faced with problems of meaning and existence.

In "The Lute Player," the King's attempt to recapture his youth gained him a prison cell. For al-Ghazzali, the relentless pursuit of philosophical reason led him to a private dungeon of self-satisfaction and rigidity. Like a prisoner in a labyrinth, al-Ghazzali found himself caught in a maze of contradictions that literally left him speechless.

For Hildegard of Bingen, by contrast, the spiritual quest in the second half of life drew her away from the world of the cloister into the arena of male-dominated power and politics. Like the Queen in "The Lute Player," she disguised herself in male costume to better fulfill her destiny as a woman.

A strange symmetry clearly exists between the lives of these two great divines; and yet there is a fundamental difference between them. Hildegard's Call came, as it were, from heaven direct, turning her from a meek novitiate into a tour de force of combined male and female energy. For al-Ghazzali it was his own body—and his own preoccupation with ordinary logic—that set him searching for something closer to the music of the soul.

Two roads, or a thousand roads—but always the same goal.

When I first heard both these stories I remember wondering if the miraculous quality of the Call that comes to towering spiritual personalities like al-Ghazzali and Hildegard is a privilege only of the saints. I might have thought so once, but my attitude was challenged when I heard the story of how another powerful intellectual, this one very much of our own time, experienced the Call.

I had known Charles Campbell for years as CEO of the New York Heart Association. Once a member of the research team on the Manhattan Project, Campbell joined a spiritual group in his late twenties and devoted himself to its activities for more than twenty years.

At the end of this time, Campbell concluded that his group—and his own spiritual progress—was going nowhere. Worse, he was being groomed to take over as one of the leaders. How, he asked himself, can I take a spiritual organization seriously if they ask me, a person without any real spiritual understanding, to guide them? Campbell decided to look for a more authentic link to the ancient wisdom teachings.

Eventually his Search led him and his wife to Iran, in the days when Americans were still welcome. After many twists and turns, he and his wife were introduced to an aged Sufi master and allowed to spend several weeks in his presence. Impressed with the teacher, though not entirely convinced of his philosophy, Campbell returned to New York City, where in the months that followed he thought frequently about the venerable master, but remained dubious about his doctrines.

Two years passed. Then early one morning while sitting in meditation Campbell heard a voice speaking distinctly inside his chest. "Come!" the voice said.

An hour later he heard this same voice on his way to work. Then again at lunch. And if this was not enough, later that day his wife told him that she too was hearing the same voice in her chest. Neither had any doubts who was speaking to them. Five days later Campbell and his wife were on a plane to Teheran.

"I heard you calling me," Campbell announced as he entered the Sufi master's chambers, secretly proud of himself for having displayed such acute spiritual listening.

"Did you now?" the master said with a bemused smile.

"Here—right here in my chest."

"I see," said the master. "And what did I say to you?"

"You were calling me, telling me to come."

A long silence ensued. The master broke it with a barely audible chuckle. "Mr. Campbell, my dear Mr. Campbell. Don't you realize? I've been calling you every day now for two years. It's taken you all this time to finally hear me."

Answering the Call

Throughout this chapter and the ones before, we have witnessed a wide variety of Calls, ranging from lofty celestial visitations to mundane revolts against boredom.

For some people, as we have seen, the Call arrives under the cover of darkness, bringing with it feelings of emptiness, disillusionment, physical disorders, encounters with death. For others it flies in on the wings of luminous dreams and revelations, evoking the lost world of childhood or the exhilarating freedom that comes after dropping old games we no longer need to play. " 'Tis a gift to be simple, 'tis a gift to be free," go the words of an old Shaker tune. " 'Tis a gift to come down where we ought to be."

Then again, the spiritual summons may reach us from a casual contact, a serendipitous meeting out of time: at the burning ghats along the river Ganges, in front of an ancient cathedral, or in a friend's living room.

The gift of the Call is sometimes triggered by a biological rhythm like menopause; or inspired by parables like "The Hymn of the Pearl." Or again, the Call may ripen gradually within us with the passage of time, as dripping water wears down the stone—a natural by-product of the insights gained by the slow, sure process of growing older.

Like the gods and goddesses of Oriental religions who appear in both wrathful and angelic incarnations, the Call takes whatever form is necessary to rouse us from our private dreams. And so in the final analysis, the Call is always uniquely our own.

Whatever form the Call happens to take, however, it is always driven by the same purpose, whispering in our depths that the life we are leading is not our own, not the life we were meant to live. At the end of his long life the Hasidic rabbi Zusia was moved to say, "In the world to come no one will ask me why was I not Moses. I shall be asked, 'Why were you not Zusia?'"

Why indeed? Why is each of us not the person we were meant to be? To ask this question is to hear the Call. And to respond to it is to begin the Search for answers.

chapter 4

Beginning the Search

I imagine that God speaks to me, saying simply, "I kept calling to you, and you did not come." And I answer quite naturally, "I couldn't until I knew there was nowhere else to go."

FLORIDA SCOTT MAXWELL,
The Measure of My Days

BEGINNING THE SEARCH

We Are Always on the Search

Many years ago when I was a young man living on the West Coast I spent several days at a Catholic retreat in Northern California. It was an odd place for me to visit. Growing up in the Lutheran Church, I never had a very positive picture of Catholicism. Though my views became somewhat more open and appreciative after I studied medieval philosophy, I continued to harbor ill-formed preconceptions long into my adult years.

During the second day of my visit I happened to make the acquaintance of a nun, Sister Ann-Marie, an elderly woman whose wisdom and presence made a deep impression on me at the time. That morning we sat together in the monastery herb garden drinking tea and talking about her life and mine. Sister Ann-Marie had entered a nunnery, she told me, when she was thirty-four years old, a year after her husband and son were killed in a boating accident. Since that time she had devoted her life to prayer and good works. When I told her of my own interest in philosophy, and the ups and downs I'd experienced in my serach for guidance, she replied that, as far as she was concerned, every one of us is *always* on a search, saint and sinner alike.

I was curious to know what she meant by this.

"Well," she replied with a soft smile, "when I was a child I searched for my parents' love and approval. Later I searched for good marks in school and for people to like me. When I grew up I searched for a career and then a husband. I wanted a nice place to live after that. When we couldn't have children I searched for a child to adopt. I'm sixty-eight years old now and I'm still searching. It's just that at some point I decided I'd never find what I was looking for in the material world where everything is passing away. I decided that instead I'd search for the one permanent thing in life: God."

Sister Ann-Marie leaned forward in her chair and a twinkle came into her eye. "You know," she continued, "in the end we always find the thing we're searching for if we try hard enough. We have the Lord's personal guarantee on it. He says, 'Seek and ye shall find.' "

The moment I heard Sister Ann-Marie's words I knew in my heart that what she was saying was true, that she had given me a glimpse into a world that was far more constant and genuine than my own. Her story felt very old in some ancient, untapped part of me. It made me realize how so much of my own life had been spent searching for things that give nothing more than momentary satisfaction. And how in the final count I was never satisfied with *anything* for very long. It reminded me of the myth of the Greek king Tantalus, who sits forever in hell surrounded by grapes, fruits, and pools of sparkling water. Every time he reaches out to slake his eternal appetite, the food and drink recede just a few inches beyond his reach. The American writer Stephen Crane puts it this way:

> *I saw a man pursuing the horizon*
> *Round and round they sped.*
> *I was disturbed at this;*
> *I accosted the man.*
> *"It is futile," I said,*
> *"You can never—"*
>
> *"You lie," he cried,*
> *And ran on.*

Had I become this man? Pursuing one horizon after another, one experience after the next, never finding anything of lasting value? Was the world, as the Hindus insisted, really made of *maya*—illusion? Phantom food and phantom water, as in the Greek underworld, a tissue of dreams with nothing behind it but more desires, more enticements, more reaching for something that can never be grasped?

I returned to my room that morning, my head spinning. Sister Ann-Marie's words had touched something distant inside me, yet strangely familiar. The light in her eyes that morning was far more of a testament to truth than anything I'd read in a book.

Suddenly a realization swept over me: the blessed ones in life, I understood in a flash, are not the rich and famous, the geniuses and billionaires and film celebrities—they are those like Sister Ann-Marie, the silent, anonymous spiritual seekers who use their precious time on earth in devotion to something real and permanent within the flux of worldly affairs. The rest of us are horizon chasers, I thought; until the day arrives when our plans are blasted by sickness, age, and finally death.

If what Sister says is true, I thought—and I firmly believed it was—isn't it time to start taking steps toward my own spiritual search? But how do I begin? Enter a monastery? Renounce it all? Sister Ann-Marie's sense of peace and commitment brought back memories of my own childhood religious longings. For a time I'd even considered becoming a clergyman, until I realized the clergy and professional religious people suffer from the same shortcomings as the rest of us. Somehow the shoe didn't fit my foot or, I thought, the feet of many other people.

Of course, as we grow and mature it's common for many of us to reexperience certain longings and emotions we assumed had died inside us long ago. Freud speaks of this encounter as a "return of the repressed," meaning that we never entirely escape certain profound childhood experiences; we simply push them out of our consciousness for a while until they return at a later age. Psychotherapists describe this process primarily in terms of sexual and aggressive urges. Yet there is another aspect to it as well that's overlooked: the return of the spiritual feelings that once nourished us so profoundly as children—the deep emotions of security and belongingness that faith in the magic nature of the universe once brought us. We are all born with these feelings: a capacity for wonder, delight, and an inherent sense of the sacredness of the world around us. They are part of our human inheritance.

Then time passes. We grow older, and our memories of this blithe awareness, at one time so vivid and assuring, are slowly driven underground by a thousand worldly demands. To adapt successfully children must, in the words of the French poet Mallarmé, "abdicate their ecstasy."

Finally we drift into a kind of hibernation of the soul through the autumn of our adolescence and the winter of early adulthood. "At first a childhood, without limits and without goals," muses Rilke. "Ah, sublime unconsciousness! Then comes a sudden terror: schoolrooms, slavery, the fall into temptation and unaccountable loss." Yet even while our soul hibernates, its voice speaks silently to us in a disturbing, nostalgic language we do not understand but sense, as if in a dream. These memories *call to us,* like the biblical voice in the wilderness. "Now in the huge, frigid, empty space inside us," Rilke continues, "alone, yet hidden deep within the adult heart, is a yearning for our first world, the ancient one." It is as if in reaching adulthood we have become divided into two people, one childlike and full of love but buried, the other seated firmly at the throttle, running the show with a grown-up need to survive in a difficult world. Until one day at last we recognize this lost person inside us—this Call—and respond. "As dangerous as repressed sexuality can be," write psychologists Janice Brewi and Anne Brennan, "a repressed spirituality is no less dangerous to the fullness of human life."

Joan Lamming, a sculptor from Chicago, told me her version of this midlife "return of the repressed" with a poignancy that many of us can relate to. Now in her middle fifties, Joan became a convert to the Pentecostal Church more than a decade ago.

"One of the greatest sorrows of my early life," Joan related, "and I'm talking *profound sorrow* here, was the day my father told me there was no Santa Claus.

"Sounds funny—but I was crushed, really crushed. Not just because I couldn't leave carrots out on Christmas Eve anymore and that kind of thing. Let's face it, for most kids Santa Claus is a *version of God;* and the fact that he exists means that God exists too. Santa Claus stands for everything that's magical in childhood, all the miraculous things we never actually see but that as children we trust in our hearts are true. Then one day along comes my father, and thinking he's doing the sensible thing, he sets me straight about reality: we were just kidding you, just playing a trick! Ha, ha! And with that my life begins to slide from the miraculous to the blah. I still remember my response. I said to him, 'But at least there's an Easter Bunny, right, Daddy?'

"He shook his head no.

" 'What about the Sandman?'

"Same shake of the head.

"Then came the last clinging hope.

" 'And . . . there are no . . . Tooth Fairies either?'

"Long pause, then: 'I'm sorry, sweetie . . .'

"With this last bullet between the eyes all the enchanted images that had nurtured me through early childhood withered away instantly. From that day on my faith in God began to decline. For the next twenty or thirty years, through high school and college and into my first marriage, I became an agnostic. It was only in my late thirties that I became interested in religion again and finally joined the church. It was around that time, talking to a lot of people and getting inspired by one of the ministers in particular, that I realized God and Jesus are real. That they are living presences here with us all the time. In one fell swoop the belief was brought back and I began to experience the wonderful feelings I'd had as a kid: a faith in miracles, prayer, a joy in the stories of the Bible and Gospel, all the things that had ended that day when Santa Claus died. 'Yes,' I said to myself. 'There really is magic. There really is a God.' "

This reawakening of spiritual hunger as we age and mature represents a powerful encounter with long-covered-over emotions and lost childhood intuitions. For some people this reawakening comes slowly. Others are called suddenly, even violently, like Paul on his way to Damascus. In either case, our task is to keep the spiritual Call alive once it is sounded, and to use it to our greatest benefit.

But how do we do this in our brave new secular world?

Sister Ann Marie, like Mother Teresa and the few other saintly figures I've encountered, are worthy of immense admiration. They have given themselves fully to spiritual service. This, however, does not mean their path is appropriate for everyone. The majority of us are searching for a different kind of relationship to the sacred, one that allows us to remain working, playing, and loving in the world; a path that helps us to find spirituality in the kitchen and office as well as in a cloister, but that also opens the doors to those deeper levels of living that Sister Ann-Marie so fully embraced.

Such a path is based on the premise that, although we remain in the familiar world, we have no need to reinvent ourselves spiritually from the ground up to compensate. The means of our liberation are already firmly in our hands, we come to learn. We have simply forgotten them rather than lost them. They are camouflaged from us by the seductions of materialism, commercialism, skepticism—the modern "ism" factory that has so many faces. Just as we can never really lose the reality of our deepest being, we can never lose the urge to return to it as well.

In short, what many of us are searching for is a way that leads us to the sacredness of experience in the midst of our ordinary lives and within our own daily state of being—to what Thomas Moore has termed "the natural religion in all things."

Why should it be so difficult to find and adopt this sense of natural religion? Principally because so many of us have been raised to think of spiritual commitment as an all-or-nothing choice. Either we enter a monastery, the myth goes, or live an entirely secular life. Be a nun or be a householder, a saint or a secularist. Nothing in between.

But must the approach to a spiritual life be viewed in such self-excluding terms? Surely there are paths in between these extremes, paths that encourage us to remain in the world, yet allow us to participate in the joys of renewal and reintegration on a daily basis.

And indeed there are. Many of them. We simply have to start searching for these paths in the right places—and in the right ways.

What Are We Really Searching For?

One of the most disconcerting things about hearing the Call and beginning the Search is that we feel so utterly by ourselves, as if no one has ever walked this way before. Yet this is by no means the case. A number of national surveys tell us that we are not alone on the Search at all. People from a variety of philosophical and religious persuasions are making the journey with us. All are searching for deeper spiritual meaning in their lives, and most are unsatisfied with the conventional forms of religion that society offers. It is not unusual for people to reject religion yet feel a yearning for something spiritual.

What exactly is the difference between a spiritual way and a religious way?

Boiled down to essentials, religion applies to the outer aspects of worship: ritual, doctrine, and congregational practice. Spirituality, on the other hand, pertains to a person's deepest and innermost relationship with the sacred, with a Higher Power, with something that cannot be easily defined when the Search begins. Many of the seekers I have spoken with find rote, ritualized religion unsatisfying, and are looking for something deeper and more satisfying. Generally speaking, these searchers fall into three categories.

First, there are those who have never been formally religious, but who are nonetheless attracted by spiritual concepts and ideas.

Second, there are people who were brought up in a particular religion, but who have fallen away from this religion and are searching an alternate tradition, either Western or Eastern.

Finally, there are seekers who are looking for a deeper and perhaps more hidden meaning in their present faith.

Further insight into the spiritual Search comes from an important national survey conducted by Professor Wade Clark Roof and his associates at the University of California at Santa Barbara. Roof's research group looked at a representative national sample of 2,620 households, focusing on baby boomers in an attempt to discover what assumptions and goals motivate these seekers. Roof's findings show that a majority of people engaged in the spiritual Search are independent-minded men and women anxious to go beyond the superficial aspects of religiosity and to find religion's inner core.

"They think more about questions of meaning and purpose in life," Roof tells us, describing a group of searchers he titles Active Seekers, "and about why there is suffering in the world. They tend not to accept necessarily the answers as provided them by a particular faith or tradition. They dwell on fate and the dilemmas of life simply because their understandings of why life is as it is are rooted more in their own biographies and experiences than in any grand religious narrative that purports to provide answers for all times and in all places."

One Roman Catholic respondent in Roof's survey went to the heart of the matter in her response: "To me religion is practicing . . . going to church . . . receiving Communion. Spiritual to me is just being in touch with your higher power, I guess."

Those who are engaged in a spiritual Search have certain common characteristics. Active Seekers are better educated: 72 percent have attended college. They tend to come from all the major Western religious denominations, and are likely to be well into their adult years: 62 percent are over thirty-five years of age, a figure that confirms the fact that the Call comes principally during the middle adult years. Finally, Roof's survey found that Active Seekers are far more likely than other respondents to go their own way, to follow their own inner drummer.

Roof and his colleagues were particularly interested in identifying significant life events that trigger a search for spirituality. Not surprisingly, they learned that the most powerful historical influence on the baby boomer cohort was that cluster of tumultuous events known as "the sixties," a time of upheaval characterized by civil rights, Vietnam, and, most important, a popular fascination with mysticism and Eastern religions. Among respondents, Active Seekers most affected by the 1960s were also most likely to show an interest in exploring different spiritual teachings (80 percent). Respondents who were minimally influenced were far more apt to stick by their childhood faith.

In Roof's survey, participants were asked if they agreed or disagreed with the proposition "People have God within them, so churches aren't really necessary." Among the Active Seekers, 60 percent agreed with this proposition. Active Seekers were also more than twice as likely to report that they practice some form of meditation. People in the stage of Search, in other words, tend to be people looking for a mystical and personal approach to spirituality.

How then do we begin our spiritual Search? Do we simply follow our instinct? Do we go by our intuition and gut feeling? Do we retrace our steps and attempt to find something we dropped on the road of life long ago and that we now recall as in a dream?

"I have forgotten something," said a man to the Sufi poet Rumi.

"There is one thing that must never be forgotten," Rumi replied. "It is as if a king had sent you to a foreign country with a task to perform. You go and perform many other tasks. But if you fail to perform the task for which you were sent, it will be as if you had done nothing at all."

Our situation in the midst of life is analogous: we also are sent by a king on a mission to a far country. In the midst of our lives we suddenly remember we have forgotten something momentous. But what? We crave to recover this disturbing memory. But what is it about? God? happiness? A cure for our psychological problems?

While in our teens many of us believe that by being "good" and following the dictates of moral behavior—by making sincere spiritual efforts—we will someday automatically become happy and holy, and drive the neurotic demons from our psyches in the way that Christ drove the money changers out of the temple.

But as we grow older, we come to look at things a little differently. By now we've overcome or outgrown certain psychological problems. And more to the point, we've learned to accommodate ourselves to the problems that are permanently part of us. Most important, we no longer judge ourselves as harshly as we once did for having psychological hang-ups in the first place. When they come along now we shrug and get on with the day's work. No more *Sturm und Drang;* or at least a lot less of it than when we were eighteen.

If nothing else, being older gives us permission to admit the inevitability of our fallibility. It allows us to savor the very human joy of accepting our own limitations.

This merciful act of self-forgiveness, besides helping us be more at ease with ourselves, spotlights a noteworthy truism: the spiritual Search is *not* a search for therapeutic cure or personality improvement. You may become a better person for making spiritual efforts, yes, and you may become more psychologically fit. But these are side effects of the journey, not primary goals. The immediate goal of the Search is simply to find a spiritual teaching you are comfortable with, and to follow it with all your heart.

How do we recognize such a teaching?

During the course of our lives we've all been touched by sublime influences that leave indelible marks on our sensitivities: encounters with great art, poetry, music; certain experiences in nature; times in love; even moments of danger when we feel intensely and heartbreakingly alive.

At such moments we realize that our customary life is by no means our real life, and that there is a quickened, magical state of being hovering just above the rim of our everyday awareness. "There have been striking events that have stood forth in our memory as impressive markers of our inner life," writes psychotherapist Ira Progoff. "In our view of them they possessed qualities that set them apart as distinct moments in our experience. . . . Each of them was so intense or dramatic that we thought of it as being unique and self-contained at the time. Now we see the connection of these events to one another, observing how a theme is carried in a particular experience, then dropped, and after some passage of time, resumes its development in another event."

Such "encounters with significance," as G. K. Chesterton dubbed them, leave a deposit inside us, a gathering of charged and enduring memories. As we grow older these memories accumulate. Finally, they form a kind of center of gravity inside us that acts as a "receiving station" for higher influences; so that when the Call finally does come it is this center that is able to hear it and respond. As the medieval alchemists proclaimed: "You must already have some gold before you can make more gold."

At such moments of recognition the Call turns into the Search. We realize that something of the Eternal is summoning us, but we cannot quite get there on our own. We need a trained helping hand to pull us toward it. "I feel there's some kind of divine mystery inside me," a friend once phrased it. "I just don't know how to find the key that unlocks the door."

How Do I Start?

A classic shaggy dog story tells of a man who feels a sudden yearning to understand the secret of life and who leaves his wife and children to find it. The man spends years crossing several continents and deserts. Arriving at last at the foot of the Himalayas, he learns of a wise guru living high on one of the peaks. He wanders through the mountains day and night searching for this man. One day, ragged, starved, practically on all fours, he comes to a temple in the clouds. Here, on a humble reed mat, sits the old man, his great white beard bespeaking centuries of wisdom.

"Master!" cries the searcher, throwing himself at the guru's feet. "I have come long and far to find you. Tell me, I beg you—what is the secret of life?"

The old man remains silent for some time, then smiles, leans forward, and in a trembling voice intones: "My son—life . . . is . . . a . . . bird . . . on . . . the . . . wing."

The man waits for more, but nothing is forthcoming. "Father," he finally says, "I've left my home, traveled halfway across the world, sacrificed everything to come before you and learn the truth. And this is all you have to tell me? That life is a bird on the wing?"

The old sage leans back on his mat, and looks puzzled. "You mean," he finally asks, "life *isn't* a bird on the wing?"

The fact that we recognize the clichéd props in this story so quickly— the tormented search, the bearded swami in the clouds—shows how common it is to assume that spiritual quests begin in a formal setting out "there" somewhere: on a mountaintop or in the temple. Indeed, during the 1960s and 1970s Americans explored caves and mountaintops all across the world searching for such teachers. They wandered the deserts of Iran in search of Sufis, and the snowy peaks of South America, seeking a bona fide shaman, preferably one cast in the image of Carlos Castaneda's Don Juan. Celebrities like the Beatles fused the romantic fantasies of a million young people to their own destiny by emigrating to India and living in a Hindu ashram under the watchful eye of Maharishi Mahesh Yogi. Though this arrangement ultimately went sour—rumor had it that John would not stop smoking marijuana and Ringo hated Indian food—other superstars like Mia Farrow and the Rolling Stones soon followed suit, and by the 1970s searching for a guru in exotic lands was a standard part of hippie youth culture.

Yet this practice of spiritual adventuring, glamorous as it appears, can be subtly diverting. For the fact is that you and I do not need to visit Zen monasteries or Shangri-la to rediscover our souls. The Search starts *anywhere* you happen to be, right now even, this very moment: at the dining table, raking the leaves, with the next step you take. All that is required is the decision to begin.

And yet, the custom of wandering the backcountry in search of enlightenment tells us something compelling and, I think, essential about the spiritual Search. Traditionally most Western seekers who make pilgrimages to foreign lands *are young,* and the reason for this is critical in helping us understand our own position as we age and mature. It centers on the fact that during the early years of adulthood the spiritual quest is powered by the need for roving activity. The impulse now is to overcome rather than accept, to seek rather than to find, to accomplish instead of simply to be—all that partakes of the knightly quest and its passionate wanderlust. It is no coincidence that in tales of knighthood and courtly heroism the majority of the hard work is done by youths and maidens under thirty.

As time passes things change. Most of us who are moving ahead on the life cycle no longer have the same infinite supplies of passion and ambition we set the world on fire with at twenty-one. But since passion and ambition are not necessarily valuable in themselves, and can even get us into trouble— it was, after all, Sir Lancelot's irrational passion for Lady Guinevere that caused the ruin of Camelot—this apparent shortfall works to our benefit; for passion and ambition are worthwhile *only* if accompanied by wisdom and experience.

This fact introduces us to an important lesson. After we have lived for three or four decades our fiery energies begin to level off, it's true; but in their place we now gain certain character qualities that are far more profitable. These include qualities that can only come from living on this planet a certain number of years and from coping with life's raucous ups and downs: qualities such as discrimination and shrewdness, acceptance and insight, patience and judgment, common sense and the ability not to take ourselves so seriously.

We accrue these virtues almost automatically as the years pass, simply by toughing it out in difficult times and paying attention to the details. We've all gained these qualities to some degree. They tend to come slowly over the decades, and sometimes we don't always realize how much they've changed us for the better. But they do come. "Only those who have lived a while," someone once remarked, "have all their five senses in keeping with their wits." The fact is that by the time we arrive at the middle years we've coped with enough painful relationships and made enough tense decisions, been fired enough times, dealt with enough fools and phonies, and gone down enough wrong roads to have a markedly improved eye for the right roads. This experience, in turn, helps us make the canny decisions and follow the right gut feelings when we search for a spiritual way.

This essential difference between the Search in youth and the Search in the middle adult years is well chronicled in wisdom tales and myths around the world. One story is especially enlightening, an Eastern European tale of the Search, couched here in strangely mystical and mythological terms.

Once upon a time, the story goes, there lived a farmer and his kindly wife. At one time wealthy and prominent in their village, the couple's land has been mysteriously losing its fertility through the years and each season their harvest is diminishing. No one in the village knows why their land is becoming so barren or how to restore it, and after several years the man and woman fall deeply into debt. Reduced finally to poverty, they go to their neighbors and children for help.

But though they've known their neighbors all their lives and have been unremittingly kind to their children, no one will come to their aid. The farmer and his wife return home empty-handed, more disconsolate than ever, rejected by the loved ones they have nurtured and by the earth that has sustained them.

Note at this point that there is a clear analogy here between the loss of fertility in the land and our own loss of vitality as we age. The devitalization of the soil mirrors the slowing of the biological processes that takes place within our own bodies as the years pass. This gradual drop-off can produce panicky feelings, just as it does for the farmer and his wife. Most difficult of all is the worry we feel over the further losses that may come in the future.

The normal thing to do at such anxious moments, of course, is to seek help from our family and friends. Unfortunately, they don't know the secrets of making soil fertile or of giving us back the brightness of youth. Nor do they necessarily understand the emotional vacuum and existential angst we encounter as we face an uncertain future. The emotional and psychological supports we've depended on up till today, in short, become inadequate.

One day the man and woman are sitting dejectedly in their house wondering what to do next when a beggar woman comes to the door. Her clothes are in shreds. She is gaunt and shriveled. The couple offer her their last supply of porridge; she seizes it greedily, opens her mouth as wide as a house, and swallows it down, bowl and all.

The couple are afraid the woman is a demon, but she calms their fears, thanks them for the meal, and takes a small box from her pocket. "To make your land flower again," she says, placing the box on the table, "follow the road west till you come to a three-headed tree. Sow a seed from this box beneath its branches. Then return and rise anew."

The beggar woman leaves the house and the couple look inside the box. Here, sure enough, they find a handful of seeds. But what are they to do now? Follow the road? Which road? And to where? A tree with three heads? Preposterous!

After much discussion they decide to do nothing at all and to ignore their visitor's advice. What does a beggar woman know, after all? They put the box away and resume their unhappy life.

But the old woman does not leave them in peace. Every night she appears to the wife in a dream offering the same words of advice: "Follow the road west and arise anew."

In our own life we know that when the Call to spiritual exploration comes there is a temptation to ignore it and do nothing. Then it comes again, this time in a different form, in a dream, in a book, as a piece of friendly advice. Once it begins, the Call is not easy to silence. Like Paul Bunyan's dog, it sinks its teeth into our leg and hangs on until we feed it, even if we, like Paul Bunyan, drag it along with us from one end of the continent to the other before giving in.

Finally, after the wife dreams her dream for the hundredth time, the couple understand what they must do, and they set out in search of the three-headed tree, carrying their box of seeds with them. Since there is no place to start from but the road in front of their house—or my house, or your house—they begin where they are at that moment, in the midst of life. The spiritual way, symbolically speaking, always starts at our own front door.

After walking many miles they come to a crossroads where a hundred paths diverge in all directions. Not knowing which road to choose, they sit down and ask the spirit of the old woman for guidance. Suddenly the wife has an inspiration. The answer is in the box. She opens it and removes one of the seeds. Instantly it bursts into flame, and in its place appears a hideous dragon.

Fire, smoke, foul smells—but the couple are not intimidated. Instead of running from the monster they stand their ground and face it bravely. After a moment or two they begin to talk to it in friendly voices and offer it food.

The moment the creature hears their kindly tones it lies down in front of them like a dog, and miraculously a gem-studded saddle appears on its back. The man and his wife mount the saddle and give the dragon free rein.

Instantly it gallops ahead, approaching the crossroads where it takes the right road, guided by its own mysterious instinct.

Now dragons, in both psychotherapy and mythology, are a symbol of the instinctive and libidinal energies that lurk in the unconscious and that threaten to devour us in times of passion or distress. Slaying the dragon in this regard is a symbol of a seeker's ability to successfully integrate these destructive forces into his or her life, and to maintain control over destiny. In the Western tradition, when a dragon threatens the land, our impulse is to kill it immediately. In myths down through the ages young dragon slayers like St. George, Sir Gawain, Hercules, and others have turned this fatal act of slaughter into a sacred rite.

In many Eastern traditions, however, and in certain schools of psychotherapy, the symbology of the dragon or monster is viewed in a different light. While these traditions have no illusions concerning the creature's dark, demonic side, the dragon force itself is not necessarily looked upon as something to annihilate, but something to harness—a source of power and strength. The spiritual Search, in other words, is not undertaken to overpower the external world but to balance and integrate the psychic forces that exist inside us. Like the courageous couple in the story, we need to make friends with our instinctive energies—our passions and our fears—rather than flee from them or put them to the sword.

From here on the story leads the farmer and his wife through many further perils, each one overcome by mature wisdom and patience rather than youthful aggression. In the end the man and woman reach the three-headed tree and plant their seed beneath it. This tree, mythologically speaking, is a version of the World Tree joining heaven and earth. Once the seed is in the soil, a blaze of light erupts, and the couple are rewarded with a cosmic vision: one head of the tree shows them their past, another their present, a third their future all at once. In mystical terms, they experience a Breakthrough into a state of higher consciousness.

The vision complete, the couple are then transported back to the village, where they find their cottage transformed into a splendid many-towered castle. Around it their land now grows not only abundant crops but trees of gold, silver, and precious gems. Their vision at the Tree of Life has changed them, making both their inner and outer life rich and magical once again.

THE SEARCH AND ROMANTIC LOVE

The Two Ways of the Heart

And so our couple lives happily ever after.

And this, naturally, is as it should be. For surely one of the most important searches any of us ever embark on is the search for a loving, lasting relationship with another human being.

And yet, despite the universality of this need, so many of the people I speak with in my groups have become cynical and bitter about love. They talk to me of heartbreak, of a partner's selfishness; of how a partnership inevitably takes wrong twists and turns no matter how much love and effort they bring to the relationship; and of how difficult it is to keep the flame alive once the headiness and novelty of an affair—or a marriage—wear off.

I hear these stories with profound interest and a good deal of empathy, for I've visited many of the same places myself. At the same time, I can't help wondering if there aren't deeper reasons to explain why we're so often hurt and disillusioned in our quest for love. I can't help thinking that a good deal of the problem stems from the fact that what we think we're looking for in life is not what we're really looking for at all.

Since early childhood we've been told that romantic love is the most thrilling, fulfilling, and transfiguring force in the universe, and that once we achieve it all the other headaches and heartaches of life will magically melt away. We all know the story. Love conquers all; all you need is love; love will save the day.

This vision of idealized love is by no means a new invention in Western culture. It goes back to the time of the Middle Ages and to the tradition of courtly love when roving bards and storytellers raised the romantic chase to a kind of secular sacrament. Romances like *Lancelot and Guinevere* and *Tristan and Isolde* were the popular entertainments of the day, all typical tales of star-crossed lovers swept so thoroughly away by love that they were willing to destroy themselves and their kingdoms to consummate it. Over a period of time these tales gave the attraction between the sexes an aura of both irresistible desire and forbidden fruit, and soon lords and ladies of the chivalric court were making the love-at-any-cost ethic into an ideal throughout Europe. From this time on, romantic love became *the* central theme in all of Western culture.

Today this view of idealized love rules the day more than ever, as evidenced in our films, novels, advertisements, popular songs, all of which take it as a given that the prime justification for human existence is achieved through peak love and sex with an ideal lover. Women especially are taught to feel dependent in this way; to believe that their salvation lies in the sex-love bond, and in the admiration they receive from men. Relationships are what define you, we are told. Without relationships you have no identity, no life, no name—and, by implication, no value as a social being.

Bombarded with such messages all our lives, we finally come to suspect that if we are not "in love" we are not in life. And so we spend a good part of our first decades searching for the promised land of Eros and Amor.

Then comes the passing of the years and with it the ebb tides of disillusionment and reconsideration. We now discover that our second marriage or our latest affair has brought us no closer to emotional fulfillment than when we were moonstruck teenagers. What's gone wrong? we wonder. Why have I given so much of myself so many times, and gotten so little back? If love is really all I need, why have I loved so much and have so little to show for it?

These themes of attraction and disillusionment are not, of course, limited to our own culture. They can be found in stories and myths throughout the ages, and in countries throughout the world. In many of these tales we find the same motifs of thwarted love and unfulfilled desires so common to our own lives. Yet in a select number of these works we find another element as well, one that I believe holds the key to many of the problems and frustrations that currently bedevil male-female relationships. This element pertains to the spiritual side of love and sex along with the physical. Indeed, what sets certain older schools of thought apart from contemporary sexual philosophy is that they are not simply love stories per se but metaphors of the interplay between the human and the divine.

The power of human love, for example, in works such as the Hindu *Gitagovinda,* is considered to be analogous to the force of spiritual love. Just as in Hindu lore the maiden Radha longs to embrace the deity Krishna, so the human soul longs to embrace the love of God. Indeed, sexual love in its highest form *is* an evocation of God.

To the eye of an outsider, perhaps such a conceit may appear to be pure eroticism, similar to the stone figures of penises and vaginas—lingams and yonis—one sees in villages across India, or to the statues of gods and goddesses embracing in every imaginable position on the towers of so many Indian temples. Yet as any devout Hindu will tell you, there is nothing prurient or even especially sexual about the way these stories and images are interpreted. If anything, an air of virginity and strict division of the sexes surrounds the worship of the god Krishna, and many of his worshipers are celibate. For them, carnal love and divine love are symbolic equivalents.

When listened to from this perspective the *Gitagovinda* takes on a fantastic world of hidden interpretation and double identity. An amorous look from Krishna, Hindu scholars tell us, stands for a moment of higher awareness. A raised eyebrow symbolizes a stage in meditation. There is the famous tale of Krishna going to one of the town women, a Gopi, and dancing with her in a circle lit by moonlight. When the frolic is over the excited Gopi runs to tell her friend. But the friend has also danced with Krishna that night. And so has her friend's friend. All of the Gopis, it turns out, have danced with the god simultaneously, each thinking that she alone was the object of his desire— just as the Divine Presence nurtures all the individual souls on earth at once.

Such religious motifs are masked in the form of love poetry. Though raised to a consummate art in India, they are not exclusive to this part of the world and can be found in civilizations both East and West. Hafiz, a favorite Persian poet, praises his lover's beauty and the joys of imbibing wine in the tavern with his cronies. But "beloved" in the Sufi lexicon is a code word for God; "wine" an emblem of spiritual intoxication; and the "tavern" a Sufi's prayer hall.

Similar spiritual puns are coded into the Song of Solomon from the Bible, in medieval Troubadour poetry, and later in Renaissance dramas like *Romeo and Juliet* and in the writings of the Metaphysical poets, especially the love poetry of George Herbert and John Donne. All these works can, naturally, be read as pure entertainment and romantic adventure. At the same time, they are informed by layer upon layer of esoteric code that if read in the proper way can guide readers through their own journey of seeking, struggle, and redemption.

What's more, many spiritual teachings spend a good deal of time probing the problem of love and its relation to our perception of life. Human existence, say traditional teachings, is ultimately a kind of cosmic dream. But since most of us cannot live without our dreams, better at least that we live them well and wisely.

Recall for a moment the *Kama Sutra,* the notorious "Hindu book of love" that seventh graders in the 1950s smuggled to their rooms in plain brown wrappers. Though it is filled with the most explicit and sometimes kinky depictions, Vātsyāyana, the legendary writer of this encyclopedia of sensuality, is quite serious when he tells us the "hundred thousand bedroom delights" are nothing more than physical manifestations of the Divine.

Similar accommodations are made in Hindu scriptures for other worldly enterprises besides sex: business, war, art, politics. These activities are all part of the cosmic design, Hindus believe, and deserve a place within religion's magic circle. Sacred writings exist in India, for example, telling merchants how to cheat their customers and manipulate their scales. Excerpts from the ancient *Arthashastra* lay out a course in realpolitik ruthless beyond Machiavelli's dreams. Manuals of war, agriculture, animal husbandry, all can be found in the Hindu scriptures, all telling it like it is. Even prostitutes have their special literature.

The message behind these texts, besides the practical advice, is simply this: If fate has made you a merchant or a lover or a prostitute, be the best merchant or lover or prostitute you can be. But as you practice your calling, do so with the name of God on your lips. Do so with detachment and with the recognition that the world is an illusion—and you will someday gain enlightenment.

The Message

What relevance does all this love and sexual symbolism have to the issue of the Search? Simply this: Through the centuries sacred traditions have recognized that the sexual drive and the spiritual urge originate from the same center of psychic energy inside us, and that at times these forces overlap. In societies where religion is part of everyday life, this blending of two related impulses is integrated into the order of things by combining them into a single myth like that of Krishna and Radha. Everyone in the society is brought up to understand the double meaning. Everyone knows that several levels of symbolism are operating at once.

In our own culture, however, sex and spirituality are hopelessly split apart and viewed as two opposing and in some cases hostile forces. There are no guidelines to help us determine where one stops and the other begins.

For those who've been treading the love mill year after year, but who never seem to find what they're searching for in another person, this is a vitally important point. How many shattered expectations must we endure? We wonder. How many sad, bitter nights? Will we *ever* find what we're looking for?

Perhaps. But perhaps not—at least not in the places we've been searching. For it may be possible that we're searching in the *wrong* places. It may be that what we are unconsciously hungering for at this stage of our lives is not completion through another human being, but completion through the power of inner unity. It may be that the force driving us from partner to partner is, underneath it all, the disguised power of spiritual yearning.

This is not to suggest that we become celibate, of course. Obviously the expression of love and sexuality is central to all our lives. It *is* to suggest that at least part of the energy that motivates our hunt for an ideal mate may actually be a longing for something larger, something beyond personal attraction. And that by making room in ourselves for both these fundamental human needs, the romantic and the spiritual, we advance ourselves several steps closer to wholeness. Both, after all, are intimately associated with the growth and feeding of the heart. Nuns, for example, speak of "marrying" Christ when they take vows, and in Tibetan Buddhism the supreme deity is portrayed as a male and female god merged into a coital embrace. Among Christian scholars two kinds of love are recognized, *eros*, the energy of human love, and *caritas*, divine love. Both exist in all of us, Christians believe, and both must be balanced within us if we are to become whole. Even Freud himself recognized a similarity between the religious impulse and the sexual drive, believing that the former is a side effect of the latter. Carl Jung took this idea one step further, maintaining that sexuality is part of something even larger and more universal, a vast life force that is both empowered and embodied in the craving for spiritual transcendence.

Can we learn to integrate these two mighty forces of the heart into our own daily rhythms, giving them both the attention they need to flourish? Do some people unknowingly hunger for spiritual unity just as intensely as they do for social fulfillment? Is it possible that at some level what we love in another person is not simply their good qualities, but also a Divine Essence behind the personality? The Krishna inside each of us? "For God hath mingled in the dusty earth," writes Rumi, "a draught of beauty from His choicest cup. 'Tis *that,* fond lover—not these lips of clay—thou art kissing with a hundred ecstasies."

"After my split with Ryan in 1988," a friend told me in a memorable conversation, "I sat through a lot of boring evenings. I went to shows by myself and with my boyfriends and with my girlfriends. I traveled, worked long days at the office. But when I got home each night the only thing waiting for me in my apartment was the silence. I felt vulnerable, like part of me was sticking out. Even the good times didn't fill that spot. You know? That hunger for something you can't put a name on?"

Knowing that my friend had become a Quaker several years ago and that she was deeply involved in her religious activities, I suggested that what she'd been searching for all this time was not romantic commitment at all but commitment to a higher ideal.

"In a way it's true," she replied. "I got involved with the Quakers because nothing else seemed to address the hole I felt inside me. I'd been telling myself each time I got involved with a man that *this* relationship, *this* love affair would be different from the rest. That *this* would be the person who'd make everything okay. But it never was. Finally I started to wonder if I was barking up the wrong tree. Two marriages didn't do it for me. Dating didn't do it. Even my friends and career didn't do it. Something wasn't the way it should be. And there it was all the time too, you know: the emptiness . . ."

"Does being part of the Quaker community fill that spot for you now?" I asked.

"It's not as exciting as having a hot affair," she replied. "But it's there next morning when you wake up. It doesn't ask you for a divorce the week after you lose your job at the agency. It sticks with you and gets bigger in your life. You don't get tired of it. It grows you in a way nothing else can."

"Do you think romance and a spiritual life are compatible?" I asked.

She shook her head in an ambivalent way. "I still go out. I still have all the fantasies about living happily ever after. But having a faith in something offsets my loneliness and nervousness, and gives me another focus in life besides the man thing and the work thing. I invest some of the emotions I might have given to a lover into another part of myself. I think it's safer and saner that way."

Other people I talked to had related things to say on the topic, some of them surprising.

"Learn to savor your aloneness," an ex-banker turned bookseller told me. "Learn to find your way in the mind and heart first. You have to be completely centered in yourself before you can give love to another person."

"Does that mean you have to withdraw all your affections from other human beings until you're a perfectly balanced person?" I asked.

"It means we fool ourselves," he replied. "We think it's other people that are going to make us happy. But we make *ourselves* happy and we do it by tapping into our inner spirit, our spiritual energies. Instead of dissipating them outside all the time it's better to keep some of these energies for ourselves. We have to plant them in our own garden and not give them away."

And how does one do that?

"Learn to be alone," he said, "even when you're with other people."

His remark made me think of a Zen proverb: "When alone, act as if with honored guests; when with honored guests, act as if alone."

A retired antique appraiser and devout Zen meditator told me, "I've been married almost all my adult life now. In the beginning of the marriage the physical thing was all-important. But this gets monotonous with one person after a while, and then you have to decide: cheat on your wife and let your genitals drag you around. Or use the energy for doing something more constructive. Channel it in the right ways and feel good about yourself rather than bad. That's when I started getting into volunteer work at Children's Village and driving across the river to work at a hospice for the dying. A couple of years later I joined the meditation center."

"The thing to do," said a woman who's been practicing Transcendental Meditation for eighteen years, "is to find the lover inside you."

"What about your husband?" I laughed. "Isn't that kind of like mental adultery?"

"You're mixing things up," she replied. "I love my husband a lot. We have a great thing most of the time. But you know, he can't get me to enlightenment. And he can't do my meditating for me. You die alone; and you say your mantra alone."

"What does that mean in practical terms?" I asked.

"I keep my husband and my spiritual practice separate—my inner lover and my outer lover. One helps me stay grounded in this life, the other helps me get to enlightenment. I give them both sort of equal time, because they're both important to me for different reasons. I try not to get the two lovers, the inner one and the outer one, mixed up."

Allen Parkinson, a professional model ship builder, a computer programmer, and Tarot card reader in his spare time, told me of a dream he had on his fortieth birthday. It was sent to him, he declared, by one of the cards in his Tarot pack, the one known as the Lovers.

Allen's dream was burlesque in its imagery but deadly serious beneath the surface. In the first part of the dream he is driving along an empty highway somewhere in the middle of the desert. He's been on the road now for many days and is starting to think he's lost. Suddenly he sees an unbelievably beautiful woman standing by the side of the road hitchhiking. One side of her body is clothed in sequined ceremonial robes marked with strange magical symbols—suns, moons, stars. The other half is stark naked.

He stops. "Where do you want to go?" he asks her.

"That's your choice," she replies, seductively climbing into his car.

"You can take me to the body ballpark or to heaven's gate." The next moment Allen's car snaps in two like something from a cartoon and forms two cars. One part of Allen drives off with the naked woman, the other part stays with the sequined priestess.

Here the dream ends.

"The female figure is sensuality and spirituality in one," Allen explained, laying the Tarot card of the Lovers on the table for me to see. It shows a young man standing at a crossroads with a woman on either side of him. One woman is dressed in a voluptuous way and smiles seductively. The other looks like Snow White.

"In some packs the sexy woman is naked," Allen explains, "and the other one's a nun."

"What does this have to do with your dream?" I asked.

"The woman in the dream represents the two parts of my own psyche," Allen explained. "The sexual side and the spiritual side. The two needs are so close in my head that they're incorporated into a single dream figure."

Allen turned over another card on the table. This one is called the World, and it shows a scene from the biblical Resurrection with bodies rising from their tombs. "I'm forty-two years old now," he continues, "and it's time to make a decision. The Lovers is always a card of decision. It's telling me I have to decide whether I'm going to use my life force to keep having fun in the body ballpark. Sex. Partying. Or for more grown-up purposes: to help people, do good works, struggle against my selfishness, reflect more on my life and my moral goals. This other card here that I just turned over—the World. This one is telling me my life can go either way; that I'm not a kid anymore; that someday there will be a reckoning; and that even though I've been flirting with spirituality for years it's time now to put up or shut up."

In all, a surprising number of people that I spoke with about the question of romantic love are aware that the instincts of passion and spirituality run along parallel tracks and that the search for one can blend into the other in strange and unaccountable ways. One woman's response rings in my ears louder than the rest. She's a college professor who has authored several books on spirituality.

"It's in our nature to love," she told me. "We can't keep ourselves from loving something. Some of us love money the most. Some of us love another person the most. Some of us love God the most. I'm trying to allow myself to keep loving the ordinary pleasurable things of life—I don't really have any choice in the matter anyway. But at the same time, I keep shifting bits and pieces of this love to my trust in the Absolute. There's room inside me for all kinds of different love—the heart has a lot of pockets—but as I grow older it just somehow feels more comforting and natural to use that love part of myself to worship the Highest."

Searcher Beware

We all know stories of gurus and evangelists who attract flocks of followers by preaching a gospel of light and love. And we all know of the intelligent, dedicated people who follow them; the educated people, the people of repute and discernment who leave their marriages, give up their jobs, sacrifice their families and fortunes to follow a master they believe will lead them to enlightenment. We have also seen how years later many of these same people come slinking back humiliated and in despair. How could I have made such a terrible mistake? they cry. Why didn't I see the danger signs?

But what are the signs? When can the Search lead us to a wrong or even destructive way? And what is a wrong spiritual way as compared to a right one?

A way is a wrong way when it harms us, deceives us, misleads us, or, worst of all, when it diverts us, forcing us to give up a portion of our precious time on earth to pursue a Search that leads nowhere. As a sage once remarked, the best method for recognizing the right spiritual way is to learn to recognize all the wrong ones.

Refusing the Call—and Search

Receiving a spiritual summons and opting to ignore it is not a wrong way exactly. In fact, it's not a way at all. Yet for this very reason it is also a dangerous way, perhaps the most dangerous of them all. Joseph Campbell identifies it in mythological terms as "Refusing the Call"; the process could as well be termed "Refusing the Search." This response—or nonresponse—is based on our reluctance to surrender the comfort of ingrained habits and behavior, even if these habits have brought us nothing but agitation and discontent throughout our lives.

Campbell cites the Greek myth of Apollo and Daphne as a classic Call and refusal story, and his choice is an apt one. The scene in this story opens with the divine Apollo falling furiously in love with a wood nymph, Daphne, who, in turn, repels his advances. In true sylvan tradition, Apollo pursues the object of his affections across boggy glen and fairy glade, begging her to hear his proclamations of love and to listen to his plans for making her immortal. But she will have none of it.

What exactly does Daphne fear? The deity's overzealous affections, no doubt. But even more, that he will snatch her away from her familiar home in the forest, from the trees and plants and stones she has known all her life. Since she is a daughter of the earth who has never beheld the dazzling realm of the gods, it is inconceivable to her limited perspective that any brighter, better place exists beyond what she can feel underfoot and see through the caressing leaves of the wild rose and fern. The more Apollo pleads his case and promises bliss in Olympia, the faster Daphne runs. But Apollo is persistent and quick in pursuit.

Only at the last moment is the maiden "saved" by her father, a river god, who transforms her into a laurel tree the moment Apollo is about to consummate his quest.

And so, given the opportunity to rise to godlike heights, to become more than she is, Daphne resists. And by so doing finds herself "reborn" as a lower form of life, a creature of the plant world, moving down the cosmic scale rather than up, all by her own choosing. Even today Daphne remains rooted to the earth, encased in her tower of bark and vegetation, unchanged and unchanging through the seasons, as she wished—but also denied forever her chance to be touched by the Divine. She has chosen to refuse the Call.

The Bible tells comparable stories of people who choose not to follow, even though they have heard the Call. Consider, for example, the disciples Judas and Peter in the New Testament. Judas is the embodiment of all those who are offered the Kingdom and refuse it. He does so because he is weak, greedy, deceitful—and human.

But he is not the only one to betray Christ that day. When the Roman soldiers walk among the Jews questioning them about the crucified criminal, the good disciple Peter denies all association with this man. He does this not once but three times while the cock crows, just as Jesus predicted.

Now, although interpretations vary, most scriptural stories have an inner psychological meaning as well as a narrative one. Here the message suggests that we all have a Judas inside us, a heedless, worldly naysayer who looks for the slightest opportunity to abort our journey and betray our highest yearnings. At the same time, we also have a Peter: a well-intentioned, good, and reflective soul who, when push comes to shove, is too frightened to make the final leap of faith. In an oblique way he is akin to another peculiar biblical personality, Nicodemus, a middle-aged Pharisee who comes to Jesus for guidance and who is told by the stranger from Galilee that guidance can only be given to one who is "born again."

Though he will eventually become a convert, Nicodemus's response to these words is astoundingly obtuse. We may suspect that Nicodemus has invested a great deal of effort in maintaining control and in appearing to be worldly-wise. This is sometimes the price of secular maturity—we do not want to seem vulnerable or unsophisticated to others; we do not want to become as little children again. And we *certainly* do not want to be reborn or go backward, to start over again after all these years.

How is it possible, Nicodemus thus asks, not understanding the deeper meaning of Jesus's words, to be born again at my age? And more amazingly, he wants to know how a man can "enter the second time into his mother's womb."

Misinterpreting the spiritual summons in such muddled ways not only exemplifies the blindness of literal-minded thought of Pharisees everywhere but echoes the excuses we ourselves make to postpone our Search. "I'm too old," I hear myself saying. "It's too late for me." Or another favorite: "I'm too young. I'll get to all that later on. When I retire. When I have more time to think about it."

But how much time do we really have?

Thanks to modern medicine most of us today, statistically speaking, can assume that we will live into our seventies or eighties. We take this longevity for granted, not fully aware that the present generation is *the first in all history* in which the majority of people can expect to live out the full course of their natural existence—the threescore years and ten promised us in the Bible.

This gift of longevity is enormously liberating, yet there's a price to pay for it. The very protection we are granted against premature death also deprives us of the powerful, bittersweet sense of urgency our ancestors once felt, the knowledge that our end may come at any moment, and that we had better live life to its fullest and make our peace with God while we can. Death for our ancestors was a constant presence, undisguised by euphemisms or hospital walls. This awareness gave their lives an immediacy and intensity we can no longer experience, and helped them turn to sacred matters with a passion we no longer understand. "As I was looking at Signorelli's painting *Descent into Hell*," says a character in one of writer Israel Zangwill's novels, "I was thinking how vividly our ancestors enjoyed life, how important each individual soul was, to have the ranged battalions of Heaven and Hell fighting for it. What an intense sense of the *significance* of life!"

Today, in the twilight of the twentieth century, like Scarlett O'Hara we imagine we have plenty of time to think about all that tomorrow; which often means never to think about it at all. The truth is, however, that despite medical science our tomorrows are by no means guaranteed, and that, as the Koran reminds us, "no man knows in which land he will die." In this sense, the extra years science gives us can be a false consolation and even a tender trap. Tomorrow, we gently assure ourselves . . . and tomorrow . . . and tomorrow, and this siren song becomes another form of denial, cutting us off from the Search for the sacred before it ever begins. "Dread the passing of Jesus," says the Christian proverb, "for he does not return."

When the World Is Too Much with Us

Rilke once wrote that he dreaded dying "with unlived lines" on his body. Like most of us, the great poet wanted to depart from this world having experienced his cycle of the years to the fullest, with no regrets.

It is a wish we all share, for we know, like Rilke, that we will not pass this way again. During the decades of our thirties and forties and fifties we especially need to make our mark. It is during these years that we are most likely to initiate major life changes, most likely to unmarry or remarry, jump-start a new career, explore parts of ourselves we thought were extinguished or that we never knew existed. Shortly after my fiftieth birthday I took up the piano after a thirty-five-year hiatus, and instantly fell in love with Bach all over again. Something about returning to music after all those years aroused feelings of an old companionship and made life seem newer and richer. Existence is not over till the last breath, and we all have an obligation, a mandate even, to plumb its depths.

All this is indisputably true. And yet—as the masters in all great spiritual disciplines might add—it is true, but only relatively true. Because the world is maya—an illusion that will pass away, leaving only our soul behind.

What might the spiritual masters say, for example, if you told them you had heard the Call and were responding by getting in all the living you possibly could before you die? That you were building your own sailboat and shipping out to Tahiti? Or going back to school and getting a Ph.D. in Japanese literature? Or becoming a race car driver at forty-seven and living life faster and harder than ever before?

How might the masters respond if you told them what the experts say: that now is the time—in your middle years—to *really* get into high gear. Now is the time to *really* start to live! If you've been an accountant up till now, the experts tell us, plan on owning the company before you retire. If you've been a wage slave at the agency for twenty years, go for the dream; buy that country inn in Vermont. Workforce drones can still go back to school and get their Ph.D.'s. Stay-at-homes can still make a tour of the world. And if you don't quite succeed, well, at least give it your best shot. Because it's all in the trying. Self-improvement, commitment, taking a chance. Aging is only a state of mind . . . You're only as young as you feel . . . Dare to dream! Helen Gurley Brown, *Cosmopolitan* magazine's chief editor and number one proponent of taking the bull by the horns, tells us in her book *The Late Show* that work and involvement is "our chloroform . . . our life . . . our freedom from pain . . . supplier of esteem." In a similar vein, critic and essayist Malcolm Cowley in his book *The View from 80* espouses the same philosophy when he writes, "Perhaps in the future our active lives may be lengthened almost to the end of our days on earth; that is the most we can hope for."

There is enormous seduction in these voices, certainly, and a generous helping of truth as well. The concept is a familiar one in the scientific study of aging where it is known as Activity Theory, or more informally, the "busy ethic." Statistically speaking, life-course psychologists have discovered that the more active and involved people remain in their middle and later lives, the more likely they are to achieve mental health, physical well-being, and personal satisfaction. Enterprise, challenge, daring, activity—all these qualities, psychologists tell us, are integral parts of existence and a tonic to our self-esteem. They make us vital and interested. They keep us alive. Without them, and without our dreams, we wither and turn old before our time.

What, then, might the spiritual masters say to all this?

They would say exactly what traditional spirituality has always said to people who seek fulfillment in the activities of this world. They would say: Yes! Bravo! It's a splendid thing to feel alive! To work and play. We must live our lives to the last breath. We must find meaning in our days. We must strive. "Your young men shall see visions," say the Psalms, "and your old men shall dream dreams."

But, they would ask, will you really find the ultimate gratification you're searching for by sailing to Tahiti or going back to graduate school at fifty? By inventing a "new self" for the second half of life, dedicated, as the beer commercial tells us, "to grabbing all the gusto you can"?

Don't such activities camouflage our existential dilemma rather than eliminate it? Aren't people really just escaping something? Denying something? Rather than facing the real issue, which is that time is running out, and that we still have not started the Search for the hidden parts of ourselves that can make us feel genuinely vital and free. "Man is fearful of things which cannot hurt him and he knows it," writes Rabbi Nachman, "and he longs for things which can be of no good to him, and he knows it. But in truth it is something in man himself of which he is afraid, and it is something in man himself for which he longs."

Wouldn't it be better, the sages ask, instead of palliating your fears of growing older with ever-escalating activity, to accept this fear, even go into it? "If you want to escape the heat," a Buddhist proverb tells us, "jump into the fire."

That's what the spiritual path is all about, the masters might say. Not about escaping from the transitoriness of life, or from terrors of aging and death; but about accepting these realities, embracing them, then using them as a fulcrum to launch ourselves into a Search for deeper meaning beneath the illusory surfaces of life. "Throughout the whole of life one must continue to live," says the Roman playwright Seneca, "and what will amaze you even more, throughout life one must learn to die."

What, then, does the spiritual Search ask us to do? To give up the active life?

Again, no. The Search encourages activity and involvement. It espouses joy and commitment. At the same time, it encourages you to rethink your life agenda in certain ways, and to reconsider your priorities. It asks you to slow down rather than to speed up. To look inwardly for your satisfactions as well as out toward the bottomless well of the world. To focus in on a few important essentials rather than to branch out on an inexhaustible search for ever-new sensations and experiences. To try not so much to "reinvent" yourself as to get to know the hidden parts that are already there.

As we grow older, many of us feel a sense of loss and diminishment. We're not sure what it stems from exactly, and we tell ourselves we'll get over it soon. We're still, after all, in the prime of life. Yet there are intimations that something is peaking, and passing. It's analogous to the story of the Persian ambassador who visits the court of the great Mogul king in seventeenth-century India. Full of praise for the Emperor, the ambassador compares the Mogul empire to a full moon, and the king is accordingly flattered. It is only after the ambassador leaves the court laden with gifts that the Emperor realizes the implied insult in his visitor's remark. For when the moon is full there is nothing for it to do but decline.

And yet ironically, the sense of contraction we begin to feel as the years pass does not always occur because we are aging. Nor might it go away even if we could freeze time in its tracks. The real problem is not necessarily related to concerns about getting older or physical decline. Its roots run deeper, I believe, tracing back finally to the fact that we have wandered so far from our original center; that our closeness to the wondrous faith of childhood has dwindled; and that we are now experiencing a kind of rebound effect after several decades of forgetfulness, yearning for contact with a magical "something" that we cannot put our finger on, but which we know we are missing. We are all like the Prodigal Son, longing to return home but not knowing where to find the road that leads us there.

But don't despair, the masters say. Because there *is* a road back home. And there *are* still enough years to search for it and follow it. I myself have seen people in their seventies and eighties at Elderhostel workshops for spiritual growth who understand this fact, and who are pursuing their spiritual muse with unconquerable gusto. These elders move through their lives like pixies or magical beings, as if part of them is made of fire or air. Some of them may be sick or partially handicapped. Yet an inner light shines through and gives them both a youthful air and a timeless one. They are people who have drawn closer to their inner center, and who, in so doing, have come closer to one of the great secrets of the life course: the secret that tells us *something inside never ages and never grows older.*

I remember a conversation I had once with my dear friend Larry Morris when he was ninety-seven years old. "How does it feel to be ninety-seven?" I asked him one day, and his answer cut to the heart of things.

"I live in the body of a very old man," he replied, "but in my soul I feel there's something in me that hasn't changed at all, hasn't gotten any older, hasn't been affected by the pain or pleasures of all the years."

Larry stared curiously at his withered hands. "I look at myself in the mirror and I don't recognize the person I see there. It's as if all the aging has happened to someone else, not me. As if my real being is sitting here unchanged in the middle of myself, young and exuberant as the day I was born." Then he quoted me a line from the philosopher George Santayana: " 'Nothing is inherently and invincibly young except spirit.' "

The great mystic Meister Eckhart once wrote: "Old age concerns only the soul's use of the bodily sense . . . my soul is as young as when it was created. Yes, and much younger! I tell you, it would not surprise me if it were younger tomorrow than it is today!"

As we proceed on the spiritual journey, a kind of miracle occurs. *We begin to erase time.* Not in regression to the infantile as Freud described, but to a place inside ourselves that no longer measures life by calendars and clocks, and that returns us to the timeless happiness and joy we knew when we were children. Isn't this what we really want in our deepest hearts? To return to some resting place inside ourselves, outside of all frantic activity, outside of time, that we sense is waiting for us, calling to us at every moment of our lives? Isn't this the *real* fountain of youth human beings have been searching for? "Is this not a better path?" asked a Sufi master of his disciple. "Is this not a way that goes backward, away from the body, toward the light from whence you came?"

The choice between searching for more and more stimulation in an endlessly stimulating world or searching for our souls is a choice each of us must make. What's important is that we make this choice from a place of knowledge within ourselves rather than from a conditioned response to today's deny-your-aging-at-all-costs mystique. This mystique tells us that there are only two options to choose from as we age: get with the action program and progress; or stay in a rut, grow old, and decline.

But this choice is wrongly framed. The French novelist Georges Bernanos wrote: "The worst and most corrupting of lies are problems wrongly stated." What this common-day wisdom doesn't tell us is that a third choice exists as well. Don't worry about progress, this choice says, or about decline either. They are both temporary states of mind. Just set a middle course for your own timeless center, and let the inner faculties of navigation do the rest. "But seek ye first the kingdom of God," the Bible tells us quite directly, "and His righteousness; and all these things shall be added unto you." Seek after the powers of your own soul, the third choice tells us, and the good things of life will follow. Pursue the Search with all your heart, it says, and let the powers of light and love guide you home from there.

Bypassing the Spiritual Candy Store

During the Middle Ages it was customary in Muslim countries for students of Sufism to travel vast distances in search of spiritual teaching. Seekers sometimes walked thousands of miles for a year or more, journeying, say, from Damascus to Samarkand, where they settled for a time and studied with a teacher. After they had learned what was necessary, the teacher then sent them on to another teacher, perhaps this time in Cairo or Seville. Some seekers spent their entire lives traveling from one point of instruction to another.

With so much contact between spiritual centers across the globe, a vast body of stories arose over the centuries concerning the words and the deeds of the great masters. These stories qualify as one of Sufism's greatest legacies and are still told to this day. Several of the most powerful concern the great master Bahaudin Naqshbandi, founder of a Sufi order that still flourishes in many parts of the East. Because of his great fame, searchers came from every point in the Muslim world seeking Bahaudin's instruction. As with many Sufi masters, his response was often an odd combination of the oblique and the literal. The following story is told.

One day a man came to Bahaudin Naqshbandi announcing that he had studied with many illustrious teachers throughout the East and that he now sought permission to drink from Bahaudin's vast well of truth.

Instead of saying yes or no, the master announced that dinner was served. He seated his guest at the place of honor and proceeded to ply him with one sumptuous course after another. First came the sherbet. Then the rice pilaf, followed by piles of sweet steaming bread and a savory stew with vegetables. All this was finished off with trays of fruit and pastries.

When the man had cleaned his plate and was painfully stuffed, Bahaudin called for another full-course meal to be served. Since in the East it is a great discourtesy to refuse one's host, and especially an illustrious sheikh, the visitor had no choice but to suffer through a second round complete with meat, bread, fruits, and dainties.

Finally the glutted visitor lay writhing on the floor holding his midsection in unbearable pain.

You have come, Bahaudin finally said to him as he lay there, to see me full of half-digested teachings. Just as the meat and fruit are now half digested in your belly. You thought of your discomfort as a hunger for spiritual understanding. But really it is nothing of the kind. It is simply a hunger for more knowledge for its own sake; a hunger for food you can never really digest. Because of this your real condition is now indigestion rather than understanding.

This encounter between master and student occurred almost a thousand years ago. Yet the same tendency to "path-hop" from teacher to teacher—and from teaching to teaching—is a familiar part of our modern landscape. Today all of us have access to a vast storehouse of multicultural religious choices. Indeed, it is possible to attend Bible class this morning, practice Zen meditation tonight, attend yoga classes tomorrow, and sit in on a course given by a Kabbalist master next Thursday: a truly modern phenomenon and quite remarkable. Even three decades ago religious historian Martin Marty was describing a similarly bewildering array of options that was being offered by the spiritual supermarket. "In search of spiritual expression," Marty writes, "people speak in tongues, enter Trappist monasteries, build on Jungian archetypes, go to Southern California and join a cult, become involved 'where the action is' in East Harlem, perceive 'God at work in the world,' see Jesus Christ as the man for others, hope for liberation by the new morality, study phenomenology, share the Peace Corps experience, borrow from cosmic syntheses, and go to church."

The question underlying all these choices is, do we really benefit from collecting random pieces of sacred wisdom in such a way? Do we come closer to self-realization by stuffing ourselves with as many sources of esoteric knowledge as we can find? Or do we get nothing more for our efforts than a belly full of Bahaudin's undigested food?

A similar Bahaudin story, also about food, shows another aspect of the same spiritual trap.

One day Bahaudin was preaching Sufi doctrine to a group of listeners. A man in the crowd interrupted, saying that if the master would just tell him one thing that was new and original he would become his follower.

Bahaudin immediately invited the man to dinner. When the man arrived the master handed him a plate. "I hope you approve of my lamb stew," he said. "I made it especially for you."

The guest lit into the meal with gusto, but after one bite spit it out in disgust. "You're trying to poison me!" he howled. "This isn't lamb stew!"

"It certainly is!" Bahaudin protested. "But since you don't like the usual recipe, I've prepared something entirely new for you. It contains lamb all right, but I've added vinegar, mustard, chili, cloves, and pepper to make it different enough to suit your taste for the unique."

The dinner guest's demand has a contemporary ring to it, doesn't it? It seems to echo the relentless searching for spiritual novelty and psychological gratification that we see all around us. In the early part of this century Carl Jung once visited a Southwestern Indian tribe, where he spoke at length with a Taos Pueblo chief. The tribal leader's words still have an almost prophetic sound to them. "See," said the chief, "how cruel the whites look. Their eyes have a staring expression: they are always seeking something. What are they seeking? The whites always want something; they are always uneasy and restless. We do not know what they want. We do not understand them. We think that they are mad."

In our ever changing consumer culture words like "new" and "different" and "original" have assumed an almost sacred meaning. This fascination with novelty carries over into the spiritual Search as well. Forget the traditional forms of spirituality, the voice of variety tells us. They're outmoded.

Select the "updates" and the inventions—the more offbeat and unorthodox, the better. And don't settle for one. Shop around. Experiment. Try two or three at the same time. That way you'll maximize your spiritual input and get to enlightenment that much faster.

But be careful. Traditional teachings have always cautioned seekers to avoid eclecticism and to walk with care along the pathways of novelty. If we're not careful, they warn, the Search can become an obsession, an end in itself. Until one day it stops becoming a quest and turns into one more form of entertainment.

This point was brought home in my own life when a close friend of mine decided to be baptized as a Christian, then backed out at the last moment. I asked him why he'd changed his mind. "Because," he answered, "the minister told me if I became a Christian I couldn't go to channeling sessions anymore."

Isn't the church enough, I asked?

"I guess," he answered, "but it would kill a lot of my fun."

A recent "Doonesbury" cartoon sums the matter up with typical irony. The first scene shows an affluent-looking couple talking to a hip, bearded minister about joining his church. The minister goes down the list of his congregation's benefits: 12-Step Christianity, overcoming denial, recommitment. "It's all in the brochure here," he says.

The minister adds that members of his flock consider themselves recovering sinners.

"Doesn't that imply guilt?" the woman wants to know. "We're looking for a place we can feel good about ourselves," she says. "I'm not sure the guilt thing works for us."

"On the other hand," her husband adds, studying the brochure, "they *do* offer racquetball."

"So did the Unitarians, honey," the woman replies. "Let's shop around some more."

"So many gods," a path-hopping friend of mine once said to me with a twinkle, "and so little time." Yet how many spiritual teachings do we really need? Isn't a single genuine spiritual way also, by definition, a whole way, a complete way? Doesn't it contain everything needed for the care and watering of the soul?

Years ago I wandered into a New Age bookshop in the Upper West Side of Manhattan and ended up having a lively conversation with the manager. A man approximately my age, he had converted to Islam a decade earlier and entered a Sufi order. Seeing the motley collection of spiritual books I was toting, he looked at me with a bemused smile. "I see you've been caught by the candy store," he remarked.

"What do you mean?" I asked.

"All the goodies on one big shelf," he said, looking at my selection. "The Kabbalah, Esoteric Christianity, Gurdjieff, est, Theosophy. It's hard not to want them all at once, isn't it?"

I had to agree.

"But you know," he added, "for me and the other members of our group our search is over. We've found what we're looking for. We don't need to read all these books anymore or make the rounds at the meetings. Our way gives us everything we need."

I didn't particularly like what this man was saying. I felt I'd heard it before: the sense of unquestioned conviction, the coolheaded surety. Yet there was also a disturbing ring of truth to what he said: "Our way gives us everything we need." These words aroused mixed emotions in me, and not a little envy as I stood there embarrassed, holding half a dozen books under my arm. For a moment I felt a little like an unmarried guest in a room full of happily married people. Why can't I find a commitment that satisfies me fully? I wondered. Like this man.

Almost immediately the answer flashed through my mind: because something in me doesn't really *want* to commit, doesn't really *want* to take the responsibility for my own spiritual destiny. I was, if the truth be known, having too good a time browsing the spiritual candy store. Just like my friend at his channeling sessions, I was having too much fun to want to stop.

And so my Search went on.

When to Run Like Hell

In 1985, Jack Kornfield, eminent American Buddhist and psychotherapist, published the results of a survey in the *Yoga Journal* that shed disturbing light on the guru-student relationship in the American Eastern religious community. According to this article, of the fifty-four Buddhist, Hindu, and Jain teachers interviewed, thirty-four *admitted* to sexual involvement with their followers, mostly of the female variety. Of the students interviewed, half told Kornfield they felt that such lapses of propriety and trust had "undermined their practice, their relationship with their teacher, and their feelings of self-worth."

These findings come as no surprise to most of us, having lived through several decades of scandals involving one prominent religious leader after another. We all know about the Jimmy Swaggarts and Jim Bakkers and Jim Joneses. We also know the more exotic varieties like Shree Bhagwan Rajneesh, who built a New Age religious empire on his estate in Oregon, complete with quarter-mile-long caravans of Rolls-Royces and special orgy rooms, and who was finally deported from this country for moral turpitude. Or Swami Rama, head of the prestigious Himalayan Institute, whose reputed celibacy vanished in a storm of sexual accusations from dozens of anguished followers. Perhaps the most notorious case is that of Osel Tendzin, onetime head of the Buddhist Naropa Institute in Colorado. Despite having received a diagnosis of full-blown AIDS, Tendzin indulged in sex with several of his male followers. At least one of them is known to have contacted the disease and died.

Certainly it's important that searchers have at least some understanding of the forces that drive this dark side of the spiritual journey. One day in my own life I happened to be scanning my college's twenty-fifth-anniversary report and I came across an article by a classmate who had spent his last twenty years on a spiritual odyssey. This man (whose name is withheld at his request) wrote at length about his present peaceful life on a small Hindu ashram in Arizona and about his Search. He then ended his article with some advice: "If I've learned anything at all about spiritual groups it's this," he claimed, "and I'd like to pass it on to those of you who are looking for a teaching: If you find a teacher who sleeps with his followers, run like hell!"

Though I hadn't known the author of these words when I was in school, I took a chance and wrote to him, asking for his observations on how the spiritual Search can go awry, especially for people in their middle adult years. He responded immediately, and a correspondence passed between us. His insights, I discovered, were articulate and direct, conveying a sense of personal experience that gave his advice an air of deep authenticity. According to his reckoning, there are four principal ways in which people can be exploited by spiritual teachings. With his permission, I quote verbatim:

"Here, as you asked, is a summation of the ways in which mature adults can, in my experience, be exploited by opportunistic teachings:

"*1. The teacher sleeps with the students.*

"There are a number of ways to rationalize this exploitative trick. There are ways to make it appear noble, plus clever methods for blaming the victim. They'll tell you, to take a case in point, that sex is an act of disinterested compassion on the part of the teacher. And that turning down the honor is a cruel slap in the face to his compassionate intentions. They'll tell you how the teacher is communicating 'spiritual force' or 'supernatural grace' to his sexual partners. They'll announce that you can only learn from a teacher when all psychological barriers are dropped and total intimacy is achieved. People with some life experience will be scolded: certainly *they* are mature enough by now to understand these grown-up things, and to participate without prissy hang-ups. I even heard of one pseudo-spiritual teacher years ago who quoted a phrase from Rasputin, the greatest spiritual seducer of all time. Rasputin's line was: 'You think that I am polluting you. But I am not. I am purifying you.'

"The list of sexual rationales is long and persuasive and entirely specious. These tricks prey on people's vulnerability and trust, and cause great pain.

"*2. The group makes unreasonable monetary demands on members.*

"Be wary of groups that charge a high 'initiation fee,' or of group dues that escalate sharply after you join, or of teachers who demand a percentage of members' earnings. Be highly suspicious when supposedly voluntary donations turn into high-pressure tactics and then into religious blackmail: if you don't give us your money you won't advance spiritually in our philosophy. A favorite line is: 'You don't really value a thing unless you're willing to pay for it.' Another favorite takes the line from the Bible about a rich man having no better chance of entering heaven than a camel has of passing through the eye of a needle. Sham teachers use this line as proof that people should give their money away—to the teacher in question, naturally.

"People who are middle-aged tend to be more affluent than the young, and are likely to be targeted with special intensity. They think they can't be conned now, and this makes them even more vulnerable.

"*3. The group puts undue emphasis on power.*

"Another sign to watch for is when members of a spiritual group are extremely competitive, both for the teacher's attention and for positions of authority within the organization. Genuine spiritual traditions tend to be hierarchic, it's true, like a Zen or Christian monastery, but not competitive. All decisions come from the teacher or abbot, who is presumably wise enough to know which people to put in charge. The moment you see infighting and jostling for influence, and a teacher who doesn't do his best to stop it, consider this a danger sign. Power corrupts.

"*4. The group puts the health or welfare of its followers in jeopardy.*

"I once attended the meeting of a religious organization where several visitors, all of them sophisticated people well into their forties, were given a 'spiritual task' by a group leader who was half their age. The visitors were instructed to walk down the middle of Fifth Avenue, the busiest street in New York City, waving both their hands over their heads like crazy people. The idea was to free them from their normal habit patterns and arouse the feelings of self-awareness that people sometimes get in dangerous circumstances. 'Don't worry,' the teacher assured them. 'You'll be fine. God watches out for people doing crazy things in His name.' In reality, the participants were endangered several times that day, and one of them ended up being questioned by the police.

"Anytime you find a group that compromises the safety of its members in the name of 'testing' them or of putting them through a 'psychological experience' that is also hazardous, know that this is well-meant ignorance at best, and sadistic powermongering at worst. The same holds true for groups that pressure members into severe diets, group meetings where members are degraded and ridiculed, and even the collective use of hallucinogenic drugs. Such demands, extreme as they seem, are more common than people imagine in groups today. At the first sign of such shenanigans, leave while you can."

Despite these and other miscarriages of trust, betrayals of the spirit have their useful side as well. They teach us the come-ons and seductions to be wary of, and hone our ability to recognize the real thing. By contrast they show us how valuable legitimate spiritual guidance really is.

David Michaelson, a forty-nine-year-old copywriter living in New York City, threw himself into a New Age spiritual movement several decades ago. As it turned out, this group practiced much of the knavery that my classmate warned about. (David asked that the name and affiliation of the movement be omitted.)

"When I first came across this philosophy," David told me, "it had a ring of truth about it that I found very exciting. So I jumped in. It was in upstate New York, a kind of communal thing, except that members had their own houses. I started throwing myself into it hammer and tong."

But there were problems. The teacher was an old, extremely charismatic man, in many ways enormously wise but also selfish and manipulative. He kept group members under his thumb by encouraging them to compete for important-sounding but essentially meaningless titles and positions within a complex power structure of his own creation. He assigned or withheld these positions in a whimsical way which members of the group's inner circle assured those lower on the pecking order was all part of the teacher's mysterious and ultimately benevolent teaching system. The teacher himself did nothing to disabuse his followers of the belief that he was supernaturally guided and aware.

The result of this weird game of spiritual power politics was that the ambitious group members, the more predatory and authoritative types, males and females alike, quickly scrambled to the top of the power pyramid and started lording it over the more reticent, passive members.

"Understand," says David, "most of these so-called group leaders were just kids in their early and middle twenties without any real contemplative training, and without the slightest sense of what an earthshaking responsibility it is to direct another person's spiritual destiny. Before long several of these young men began to fancy themselves sages and gurus, and predictably, the teacher encouraged their delusions.

"It was also the early 1970s," David continued, "and there was a lot of emphasis on back-to-the-land and building your own house. This enthusiasm was fueled in the group by the apocalyptic pep talks the teacher gave us every week about upcoming geological world changes and catastrophes—the kind of California-falling-into-the-sea paranoia that was in vogue at this time. He'd tell us how we'd better learn to become self-sufficient and knowledgeable in survival skills if we wanted to stay alive after the deluge.

"The natural result of this fearmongering was that most members of the group dropped out of their white-collar jobs and learned a manual trade. Soon it was the norm to be a carpenter, a plumber, a roofer. This was okay in itself, I guess. But if you also happened to work at a desk job or as an advertising exec, the group considered you to be a spiritual cop-out, and they shunned you.

"After a while a strange thing started to happen: a reverse hierarchy of values developed in the group where the dirtier you were, the more ramshackle your house, the more menial your job, the poorer you and your kids looked, and the more you scorned everything intellectual and artistic, the higher your rank rose on the group's spiritual ladder. Down and out was now equated with religious. The trades were holy. Bookish or commercial work was profane and sissy. It was your basic redneck, blue-collar disdain for intellectuals, really, but given a weird religious twist. What happened, you might say, is that the ideals of poverty and humility and hard work that you find in monastic settings got distorted into the worship of down-and-outness and menial labor for their own sake. As if some guy who works like a jackass humping sheetrock all day gains spiritual understanding simply by dint of the fact that he's doing physical work. It was crazy. They forgot the substance for the form."

Another disturbing element, according to David's testimony, was the indiscriminate sexuality practiced by the group.

"It was the 1960s–1970s pre-AIDS mentality," he says. " 'If it feels good, do it' was a bumper sticker you'd see around a lot then. Do it with anyone, anytime. Despite the fact that our group was supposed to be a 'religious' community. You can guess the outcome of this promiscuity: all kinds of bizarre living situations, multiple divorces, spouse swapping, kids abandoned, broken homes. The teacher himself, despite his pious protesting, was living with a girl fifty years younger than himself.

"Finally, after several years, I left the group and moved back to New York City. I was in my middle thirties by then. I had a bad taste in my mouth from contact with this group, but I was still anxious to become associated with a legitimate spiritual teaching. This time I approached my search with far more knowledge and sophistication than before. New York was swarming with spiritual movements in the late 1970s, and I must have gone to all of them. Wherever I went I encountered the same power games and the same forms of sexploitation. By now, though, I'd learned to read the signs pretty well. A lot of the eagerness and sense of commitment I'd felt in the early days was gone. At the same time, though, I felt more experienced than when I was a kid, less gullible and leadable. I knew what I was looking for. I had become, I guess you could say, a seasoned spiritual seeker. It would be hard to fool me anymore."

Eventually David Michaelson ended up returning to his Jewish roots, becoming an active member of the synagogue he had grown up in.

Answerless Answers

Spiritual journeys are best undertaken with the aid of a teacher, a teaching, and a community. This principle has been echoed by spiritual authorities throughout history.

Does this mean that one cannot follow the spiritual path alone with a simple faith in a personal God? Of course not. Many people feel no need for formal guidance or for the help of a community. Their own inner belief is enough.

On the other hand, others do feel a need for a formal religious struc-ture, not simply to make sense of a difficult world but to receive the companionship and counsel of others who share their longings. The challenge is to find the *right* structure and the right guidance in a world where religion can so easily be transformed into inquisition, and the urge to save souls into holy war.

How do we proceed? Do we throw out the baby with the bathwater and turn our backs entirely on organized spirituality?

Hopefully not. For despite its flaws, millions agree, religious devotion is still the best medicine human beings have come up with to heal the anguish of the soul. If it has also spawned wars and inquisitions we would do well to remember the words of American clergyman Henry Ward Beecher. "War and intolerance are not the fault of religion," he says. "They are the fault of those who misuse and distort its truths."

If you were religious as a child, then left the church, consider giving it another look. This doesn't necessarily mean you will go back to church. You may. But even if you don't, you'll gain a deeper understanding of your own spiritual roots and how they have shaped your present interest in the sacred.

"For any of us who return to faith," write psychologists Janice Brewi and Anne Brennan, "whatever that faith might be, the process is not a static one, not a single act in which by joining a church or synagogue we have completed our search, but rather, such an action means we're beginning again. 'Returning' to me does not mean 'going back' to something, but rather re-turning as in 'turning again,' for the process is continuous and lifelong, a constant renewal and discovery."

If you were not brought up as a practicing Christian or Jew, or if you find that the religion of your youth does not suit your needs, consider focusing your Search on the fertile field of the world's other great spiritual paths: Islam, Buddhism, Taoism, Hinduism.

Some people find themselves drawn to a Search for physio-spiritual body work like hatha yoga or tai chi. Or to the martial arts. (Though it's not commonly known, certain martial arts offer a contemplative tradition as well as a combat-oriented one.) Others find a home in what Jacob Needleman dubbed the "New Religions," such as the Gurdjieff work or the Course in Miracles. Much interest has also been generated in shamanism and in indigenous tribal practices. Those who are psychotherapeutically inclined will discover a variety of spiritually oriented regimens in the field of transpersonal psychology. And, of course, some make the journey without formal involvement of any kind, armed only with an abiding belief in a Higher Intelligence that informs everything they do.

This is only a sampling. There are many other possibilities in our multicultural civilization where the blending of different races and nationalities makes previously inaccessible teachings far more approachable today than even several decades ago. Each of us must make our own search and our own choices. Do remember, though, that seeking has one purpose only: finding. And that once you've found, this stage of the spiritual journey is completed. "There are many gates into the Garden," a Sufi aphorism says. "But to enter the Garden you must pass through only one."

How do you know when a spiritual way is the right way for you? The best touchstones are intuition and the voice of the heart. Sometimes the answer blazes forth right before our eyes.

I remember a TV program I saw years ago on Mother Teresa and her work with the poor in Calcutta. I don't know what it was about her exactly. Her appearance and manner are plain, slightly stiff, entirely without pretense. She wasn't even discussing spiritual matters. Yet something in this woman's presence exuded an ineffable air of peace that anyone, even the most cynical, would find moving. I later encountered the same sense of spiritual energy while watching the documentary film *Sunseed,* about the Zen teacher Suzuki Roshi. In one part of the film Suzuki Roshi is seated in a chair, drinking a cup of tea. That's it—just drinking tea. Yet my mouth fell open as I watched him. I was astonished at how inexpressibly graceful his movements were as he brought the cup to his lips and placed it on the table again; in the way he folded his hands on his lap and walked across the room.

What was it about this man that impressed me so profoundly?

I'm not sure. It's difficult to say. Yet somehow I and thousands of other people who came into his presence over the years recognized the spiritual energy beaming out of his every glance and gesture. Just to see him *be* was to receive guidance. "I did not go to the Teacher of Meseritz to learn Torah from him," a Talmudic scholar once remarked, "but to watch him tie his bootlaces." We instinctively know spiritual presence when we see it, in the same way that we know a sunset is beautiful, or a child pure.

People of such advanced spiritual states—the saints of our world—do not pass this way frequently, of course. Despite the saying "When you are ready your teacher will find you," our part in the equation still asks that we make the effort to search. During the 1960s Maharishi Mahesh Yogi visited the United States on tour. He was wildly popular at the time due to his association with the Beatles and the Rolling Stones, and his glamorous entourage attracted massive audiences wherever it went. I attended one of his lectures at Yale. He was holding forth alone that night, stage-center in the midst of a vast auditorium, a tiny man in white robes, white beard, smiling, beatific, so straight from central casting that he resembled the clichéd Indian wise man we've seen a thousand times in magazine cartoons. He might even have doubled for the swami in the "life is a bird on the wing" joke.

For an hour and a half that night a thousand listeners were held spellbound by the Maharishi's prescription for "instant nirvana."

All you have to do, he told us, is sit quietly a few minutes every day reciting your mantra, the sacred Sanskrit word or phrase chosen for you by one of the organization's "initiators." That's it. That's all. Otherwise do what you always do. Go to work. Eat, sleep, live as you please. In a few weeks you'll start to feel more spiritually attuned. More alive. More successful. Guaranteed.

After finishing his speech, the Maharishi announced that he would take questions from the audience. Something prompted me to stand up.

If your system is as effortless as you say, I asked, why is it that the world's greatest spiritual geniuses, Buddha, Jesus, Moses, Muhammad, and countless others, had to suffer so much and work so long and hard during their own search for enlightenment?

The Maharishi smiled impishly. "Maybe they just didn't know the right way," he shot back.

The crowd roared in approval and I sat down, a bit humiliated. But deep inside, at a level I cannot define, something positive had happened, and I was exploding with certainty. Yes, I said to myself, now I understand why I was impelled to ask this question. This man, despite the adulation of millions, does not know the full truth. He is not what I'm searching for. Can anyone who really understands the spiritual process tell others that the way is easy? That all you have to do is pull this switch, push that button, and presto: enlightenment! Like a quick oil change during your lunch hour.

Whatever the value of the Maharishi's teaching—and I could see that it had enormous value for many people—it did not seem to me to embrace the highest level of truth. The teachings of the great masters, I understood, always include an element of search, struggle, and overcoming. The stick needs the flint, say the Crow Indians, or there will be no flame. Without this search and struggle a journey is incomplete. Without them we can only go part of the way.

This sentiment is echoed in a telling passage by philosopher Jacob Needleman, who had also heard the Maharishi speak. "When the Maharishi so cheerfully brushed aside the whole idea of effort and inner struggle as a 'misunderstanding,'" Professor Needleman writes in a book on contemporary religious movements, "not only he but all his followers, including youngsters who had been tested in life by nothing sharper than a low grade on a term paper, were casting their understanding above that of Socrates, Augustine, St. John of the Cross, Rabbi Akiba, Maimonides, al-Ghazzali, and countless others, including, perhaps, even Jesus Christ himself!"

"There are no free rides," hippies liked to tell you during the 1960s. And there aren't.

Shot in the Act

Several years passed. One night I attended a lecture given by a recent arrival to the United States, the young Tibetan Buddhist teacher Trungpa Rinpoche.

The stocky, bespectacled master delivered a brief talk, then invited questions from the audience. Once again I found myself moved to speak. What, I asked, is the meaning of boredom, that state of restlessness and emptiness we feel at so many moments of our waking hours?

Without a word Trungpa reached under his chair, pulled out a water pistol, and squirted me in the face.

Laughing along with Trungpa, I sat down, fully satisfied this time that my question had been answered. With this surreal, wordless gesture, Trungpa had taught me more about the spiritual process than I had read in any book or heard at any lecture. I understood it all in a flash. Boredom and restlessness, his gesture seemed to say, arise from within me, the person who feels the splash of water, the person who is here right now. I alone create these feelings. They do not come from conditions outside me but from my own ego. Tame this ego and the answer to all such questions will be clear.

I was reminded of a passage I had read in a J. D. Salinger novel—about how if Abraham Lincoln had been really honest at Gettysburg he would have mounted the podium overlooking the bloody battlefield, gazed down at the crowd for a moment in silence, shaken his fist at them, and then sat down again. Very Zen. A kind of koan, really; and this is what Trungpa had given me also, a koan: a spiritual conundrum that can only be answered from the depths of one's understanding in wordless words. Trungpa's impossible riddle pointed me back to myself, to the original question inside me, and to the fact that I was the source of the very mental activity that had dreamed up such questions in the first place. The koan spurting from his water gun shocked me, in the way that whacks on the head or slaps in the face can sometimes do, into understanding that I exist this very minute; that I am; and that someday I will no longer be. And that this cycle is all part of the same vast silence.

———

Several more years passed, and I now found myself on a group retreat for a day devoted to discovering higher consciousness in the ordinary activities of life; exactly the path I knew I must take after my conversation with Sister Ann-Marie. The group spent their time in total silence that day, like members of a Trappist monastery. We cleared brush, dug trenches, chopped wood. The July weather was steamy, and I worked in silence, trying to remain constantly in the moment, a practice the Buddhists call "mindfulness."

Soon the intensity of these efforts bore fruit, and from time to time I began experiencing unusual states of consciousness. In the midst of chopping a log I suddenly "saw" the log with perfect, luminous clarity. In the middle of the day's quiet, I became aware of the vast sky above me and of the smallness of myself on the earth, almost as if I was becoming a tiny human traveler walking through the mountains of a Chinese landscape painting.

I experienced other unusual awarenesses in these early hours as well. But as the day wore on they diminished, and by midafternoon the elevated states had given way to tedium, then to utter fatigue.

I now began to feel more like a hired hand than a spiritual seeker as I sweated and toiled and cut my hands on the brush. A little voice kept telling me I was a fool to work this way for no reason and no recompense. Was I a slave? Was mindless labor really the way to spiritual joy and delight?

Then I would criticize myself for thinking these thoughts. Then I would criticize myself for criticizing myself. When it all seemed intolerable I'd glance into the eyes of the person working next to me and experience a strange kinship. Then I'd go back to work.

Toward the end of the day, as the sun neared the horizon, the sensations of heightened consciousness began to return, and I now realized what the ancient Benedictine monks had understood so well: *Laborare est orare*—to work *is to pray.*

My entire body became filled with energy and light.

In this mood of spiritual expansion I looked for my teacher and found him in a field planting seeds. Gaining permission to break the silence, I asked the question that had been forming in me throughout the day: *how can I have these states of consciousness all the time?*

Without a word the teacher slapped me across the face. Then he walked away.

I stood alone in the fading daylight, my cheek stinging and tears welling up in my eyes. I was stunned and humbled. But deep inside I was also content. There was not a trace of doubt in my mind about the meaning of this slap. It was a message about pain, about striving, about what it costs to get where I wanted to go. And about my arrogance in thinking I could get there in a single day with a magic formula, simply by asking a question. Yes, I understood, it is possible to achieve such states in the midst of life. With a kind of exultation I realized that moments of heightened awareness—the fullness and intensity of life—are possible not just in ancient monasteries but here and now, today, this very minute.

But to achieve them, I understood, required search and effort and a struggle of a far more intense kind than digging trenches or remaining silent for a day. And yet, savoring just a taste, just a crumb from the table of heightened awareness, I felt like the man in the Dostoevsky story who, having experienced one moment of mystical bliss, is told he must walk a quadrillion miles before he can have another, and who shouts out joyously that, yes, he will begin the journey immediately!

And so over time these three strange lessons—a guru's half-truth, a squirt from a Tibetan lama's water pistol, a slap in the face—filtered through my consciousness and powered my need to know more. On the surface each encounter seemed a roadblock at first: a glib answer to a burning question, then no answer at all. But they were not roadblocks. They were signposts on the Search, mirrors held up to my own reflection, asking me to solve that ancient koan of my own existence. And announcing that the answer lies in myself; that the Search is for something that is there already, waiting, watching, calling to me all these many years. "Console thyself," a celestial voice cried out to the amazed French philosopher Blaise Pascal as he stood in a mystical ecstasy within a pool of holy light. "Console thyself," the voice said to him again. "For thou would not seek Me if thou had not already found Me."

part two

The Struggle

The Buddhas do not tell the way; it is for
you to swelter at the task.

DHARMAPADA

Do men think they will be left alone
on saying, "I believe,"
and that they will not be tested?

KORAN

chapter 5

Learning to Let Go: The Struggle of Heart and Mind

INTRODUCTION TO THE STRUGGLE

If you happen to visit Istanbul one day and take the ferryboat across the Bosphorus from the European side to the Asian, somewhere in the middle you will notice a decrepit lighthouse set on an island so tiny a child could walk across it in forty paces. The first time I noticed this odd landmark I was sitting next to a loquacious English-speaking Turkish student who told me the following story. Every native of Istanbul, he assured me, knows that it's true.

Once long ago in the days when Turkish kings ruled half the world, the Ottoman sultan had a daughter who was terrified of snakes. Searching the kingdom, the ruler's courtiers reported that no snake-free town existed anywhere in the entire kingdom. In response, the princess begged the sultan to build her a miniature palace on this tiny island in the Bosphorus so that she might be forever safe.

The sultan complied, and from this time on the princess lived alone on this sheltered dot of land, where three times a day a royal boat arrived bringing food, drink, and amenities. Here the frightened lady stayed for many a year, protected from ever crossing paths with a serpent.

Until, that is, the day she opened her morning food basket, reached in for a piece of fruit, and was bitten by a poisonous snake, dying on the spot. The snake, it seems, had slithered into the basket back on land when none of the royal attendants were watching, and had made the trip to the island undetected.

And so, in attempting to escape from her worst fears, the princess ended up creating the very conditions that made them happen.

A typically Eastern story, perhaps, and a disquieting example of Eastern fatalism as well. In the West, by contrast, determinism of this order has always been considered extreme, and has been counterbalanced by concepts of personal choice and free will. Yet even in our less fatalistically inclined culture, all the great spiritual traditions agree on one point: no matter how far we run, even if it be to an island in the middle of the Bosphorus, there is one vicissitude of fortune we can never escape in this life—struggle.

Through the years, religion and philosophy have addressed themselves to this matter with great diligence, and have delivered a unanimous verdict: namely, that human beings often strive for impossible things, spend their lives in vain pursuits, then discover too late that they have sought illusionary goals and wasted their precious years in a wrong kind of struggle.

How, then, do we find the right kind of struggle?

The answer lies in realizing that every ordeal, every conflict in our ordinary lives, is not to be treated as a meaningless affliction, but as a potential ally that can be transformed into a life-affirming and even life-transforming vehicle. Yes, all living things must struggle, suffer, and die. But human beings are different. Of all the creatures on earth, we alone can use these struggles not only to take care of our survival, but to find meaning, fulfillment, and felicity. This epic opportunity is what separates humans from animals, and what marks us as potentially divine beings. It is also why the pursuit of meaning, not the pursuit of happiness or comfort, is the key to moving from the Search into the Struggle. "I come not to send peace," Jesus told the world, "but a sword"—the sword of effort and striving.

Up till now in this book we have moved through two of the five Stages of the Soul. The Call leads to the Search, then the Search to guidance. Now at the third stage of Struggle the real work begins, and certain of our idealistic fantasies about the spiritual process must be put into proper perspective. In his twentieth-century spiritual masterpiece, *The Screwtape Letters,* C. S. Lewis tells the story of a young man who has recently fulfilled his Search by joining the Christian Church. As often happens with converts, the young man's expectations turn out to be idealized and overblown. The thud comes when he realizes that his fellow churchgoers are just ordinary people like himself. Some are fat with double chins, he discovers. Some sing off key, or wear odd hats, or have boots that squeak when they squirm in their pews.

This disenchantment, claims Screwtape, the wickedly brilliant devil who narrates the tale, is all part of the plan devised by the "Enemy" (Screwtape's name for God). For the Enemy, Screwtape says, "allows such disappointment to occur on the threshold of every human endeavor. It occurs when the boy who has been enchanted in the nursery by *Stories of the Odyssey* buckles down to really learning Greek. It occurs when lovers have got married and begin the real task of learning to live together. In every department of life it marks the transition from dreaming aspiration to laborious doing."

But, adds the wicked devil, "Once they get through this initial dryness successfully, they become much less dependent on emotion and therefore much harder to tempt."

What we discover as we stand at the threshold of the third stage of the soul—the Struggle—is that once our Search is completed, the most intensive and dramatic part of the journey begins—what the Christian monastic tradition refers to as "the true work of the spirit." The following two chapters are concerned with this work—one, with the obstacles, puzzlements, and challenges that await people in this most critical stage, two, with how a number of different seekers have learned to navigate these difficult shoals, transforming the ordinary struggles of their lives into the very stuff of Breakthrough, understanding, and enlightenment.

Remembering Lucy

I had many talented classmates in my high school graduating class. Several have since made a name for themselves in the literary and corporate world. One even had a fling at elected office. But of all the people in my high school circle, Lucy Dulles was by far the most gifted.

You won't read her name today in the newspapers or Who's Who. In fact, I haven't heard anyone mention her for thirty-five years. But if any member of the class is still out there drawing hilariously revealing caricatures, still playing Villa-Lobos piano pieces from memory, and still writing captivating poems, it's Lucy.

I was jealous of her, especially after our high school poetry contest. A prize had been offered by the English teacher, Miss Fanning, dinner for two at Scappy's Steak and Sea Food House, something I coveted so much I could, well, taste it. But despite the time I spent working on my poem, Lucy's won in a walkaway.

And well it should have. While the rest of us were penning lines about smoldering sunsets and waves of passion breaking on the shores, she was turning out lyrics reminiscent of a young Emily Dickinson. One stanza from her winning poem struck me especially, and I memorized it.

> *The struggle of winning and losing*
> *Is the struggle of poniard and blow;*
> *But the struggle of heart and the struggle of mind*
> *Is the struggle to learn to let go.*

At the time most of us didn't even know that a poniard was a dagger, let alone did we think much about the difference between worldly contest and inner reflection. That phrase, "the struggle of heart and the struggle of mind," has stayed in my memory all these years. It's still the most appropriate description I know of for that part of the spiritual Struggle that involves our common psychology—our emotions and intellects, our fears and longings; the side of us that questions our identity and asks where our lives are taking us: Who am I? Who might I have been? What was I in the past, and what will I become in the future? What is it that weighs me down?

While the Struggle of mind and heart is inherently a sacred venture, it unfolds in daily life as a complex weave of secular, psychological, and spiritual influences, all three of which are interlaced into a single tapestry that forms the stuff of our inner growth. Every element of our lives, the seemingly mundane as well as the sublime, is a necessary thread in this weave; without each thread the pattern is incomplete. The path to the Supreme begins and ends in the daily rhythms of ordinary life.

There is, of course, always the temptation to separate the psychological from the spiritual, and to tell ourselves that whatever discontents happen to plague us stem simply from unrealized worldly goals or unfulfilled wishes. In such cases we assure ourselves that we can work through these conflicts, either on our own or with professional help, and thereby gain a measure of self-insight. After this process is complete, we tell ourselves, we will no longer have to go through these struggles again, and life will run smoothly ever after. Freud himself remarked that what is achieved by some people in psychoanalysis can be gained by others simply through the course of living.

The Stages of the Soul point in another direction. They tell us that each conflict we encounter in our daily activities is not only an ordinary transaction with life but a sacred transaction as well, and therefore an opportunity for spiritual growth. We grow not by escaping these daily conflicts or making them go away, but by using them as raw materials in the process of self-transformation.

Our struggle, in short, is much like the Jesuit ideal as defined by Ignatius Loyola: to "find God in all things." As ordinary people in a difficult world, we are asked to take the commonplace activities that occur to us hour by hour, and to discover the spiritual lessons inherent in them. The Struggle of mind and heart, when all is said and done, is a struggle to turn the ordinary into the extraordinary—and finally into the miraculous.

Learning to Read Our Own Foreheads

A Native American legend tells that every person on earth has the secrets of their life and death written across their forehead. They cannot read this writing, however, because they cannot see their own foreheads.

This intriguing notion turns up in various forms throughout the religions of the world, implying that within each of us is a kind of personalized instruction book revealing where we have come from and who we really are. A Christian monk once told me that the human heart contains knowledge of everything in the universe. "Like a book," he said. "But there is a veil that covers this knowledge. Many veils."

Later on, in the teachings of Gurdjieff, I came across a notion that makes this puzzling idea more accessible in psychological terms. "Every man has a certain feature in his character which is central," Gurdjieff explained to his students. "It is like an axle around which all his false personality revolves. Every man's personal work must consist of struggling against this chief fault."

This fault—or sometimes cluster of faults—is also recognized in psychotherapy where it is defined as the dominant illusion or network of defense mechanisms that keeps us from seeing ourselves clearly.

Each of us, in this regard, has our own version of the chief fault. For one person it's laziness. For another procrastination—he or she is always late, both psychologically and socially. Anger appears not just as rage and lashing out, but in passive-aggressive expressions—impatience, sullenness, and even more trivial incarnations ("I had a bad day"). In Jungian psychology, the segment of the unconscious where these variations on the same dark theme lurk is referred to as "the Shadow."

"When an individual makes an attempt to see his shadow," writes psychiatrist Marie Louise von Franz, "he becomes aware of those qualities and impulses he denies in himself but can plainly see in other people—such things as egotism, mental laziness and sloppiness; unreal fantasies, schemes and plots; carelessness and cowardice; inordinate love of money and possessions—in short, all the little sins about which he might previously have told himself: 'That doesn't matter; nobody will notice it, and in any case other people do it too.' "

"That doesn't matter: nobody will notice it . . ." Whenever we find ourselves saying these words, we can be sure we are covering ourselves with veils, with the deep, self-sustaining illusions that keep us from seeing the truth about our own behavior. This is one reason why confession of sins—sincere acknowledgment of fault—is such a necessary part of every spiritual path.

Each of us still has scar tissue from the wounds of childhood. In adulthood these scars become like psychic knots blocking our receptivity to spiritual influences. Yet just as the sun is always shining behind the clouds, waiting to break through, higher influences are there waiting for our psychological clouds to part. This is why the Christian mystics insisted that the spiritual process does not require wondrous powers or abilities, but simply a lessening of the vices that block the entry of the Holy Spirit. They speak of this process as the *via purgativa* or way of purification.

How then do we discover where our chief faults lie?

As with the writing on our own foreheads, we are unable to see our central weaknesses by ourselves. They are masked from us by layers of clouds and shadows. Others see them quite clearly. But to our limited vision these flaws remain invisible. We need skilled mentors to help make them visible. Without this help these traits remain unconscious and sabotage our spiritual possibilities, perhaps for the rest of our lives.

To make matters more difficult, a majority of our difficulties are triggered by these same psycho-spiritual problems time after time. The apparent cause of these difficulties may change as circumstances change. But beneath the surface lurks a core collection of behavioral reactions that, like a puppet master hidden behind the scenery, pulls our strings.

Part of the Struggle of heart and mind is thus centered on illusion and perception, two processes familiar not only to spiritual teachers and therapists but to professionals who make a living out of fooling others.

I once invited a sleight-of-hand artist named Carlos to entertain at my son's eighth birthday party. After an hour of baffling entertainment that charmed the adults in the room as much as the children, the show ended and Carlos and I struck up a conversation.

"What's more important," I asked him after we had chatted awhile, "fooling an audience's eye or fooling their mind?"

"The mind," he replied without hesitation. "Hands down."

"But it all seems to be happening right there in front of you," I said.

"If you want to understand how a real magician works," Carlos replied, sounding more like a professor of psychology than a stage magician, "you have to understand the way a magician thinks *you think.*"

I asked him to explain.

"You see, magicians know that you, Mr. and Mrs. Audience, have certain fixed habits of perception. Assumptions about reality. You expect things to look and behave a certain way because they've always looked and behaved that way in the past."

Carlos pointed to a nearby door.

"A magician assumes you'll think that what looks like a door *is* a door. Not a painted black rectangle. What looks like a floor *is* a floor. Not a swinging partition. That if you shuffle a deck of cards, the cards are actually mixed. 'Mental misdirection' we call it."

Carlos held up an empty palm. "Right now you assume that since you don't see anything in my hand my hand is empty."

He then closed his hand, sprinkled some "woofle dust" on it with a naughty raising of the eyebrows, and opened it. A shiny half-dollar appeared.

"It was here all the time," he said, showing me how he'd hidden it lengthwise in between the back of his middle and index fingers. "But you didn't see it. So you assumed it wasn't there. Hands that look empty *are* empty, you think to yourself. Very logical. But very wrong."

Carlos had said enough to convince me that I *could be* tricked. And enough to make me think that misdirection is an appropriate metaphor for the misapprehension of our own behavior patterns as well.

How often, for example, do we have the feeling of being caught in the illusion of our habitual assumptions? That feeling of being misdirected, fooled, forced to repeat the same errors over and over again because something in us assumes we already see things clearly.

One day not long ago I found myself frantically rifling through my papers at the office searching for a $10,000 check given to the Brookdale Center by an important donor. I was certain I knew where I'd filed the check. But though I turned my office upside down, it simply wasn't there.

Panic struck! How could I lose $10,000? Has *anybody* ever lost $10,000? What will I say to the donor?

Then an inner voice spoke up in my defense: "We can always tell the donor to stop payment on the check."

An opposing voice answered, "Sure, but the donor will *never* give us any money again. Not after we've put her to all this trouble; after she sees how careless and disorganized we are."

I started to feel dizzy. I ferreted through all my papers, my drawers, my files. Ten thousand dollars! People came by the office and glanced at me, aware that I was in a state of restrained but visible panic. This couldn't really be happening! I shut the door to avoid being seen.

Then in the midst of all this frenzy it suddenly dawned on me: I've been in this place before, haven't I?

Yes, I've been here before. Different stage setting, perhaps, but always the same three-act play: sleepwalking through an important transaction, waking up in hysteria, then the embarrassment when it's all over and resolved.

What was keeping me from learning my lesson? I asked myself. Why did I repeat this same comedy of errors over and over like an automaton?

Because, I realized, some invisible force of misdirection keeps assuring me that I don't have the problem in the first place. A voice within kept saying, "Hey, you may have done it this time. But it's an exception, not a rule. You won't do it again next time."

And yet here I was, *doing it this way again* for the umpteenth time, and suffering accordingly.

Twenty minutes later the check was found by my secretary after consulting with the bookkeeper. I had put it in the wrong file folder. Like the coin in Carlos's hand, it had been there all the time.

The panic departed as quickly as it had come, and soon it seemed like a bad dream. I straightened my tie, pretended that nothing had happened, and everyone went back to work.

But something had happened. I knew it, everyone in the office knew it, and I was accordingly embarrassed. The whole experience had that feeling of uncomfortable familiarity, like a recurrent nightmare. I found myself wondering what would have happened if someone had come along in the midst of my hysteria, taken me into the corner, and shown me in an unequivocal way the psychological forces that were causing me to fall into this recurring pattern of frenzy once again. Then at last I'd understand what was really going on inside me. Then at least I'd have a clearer picture of the forces I'd have to struggle against in my pursuit of spiritual awareness.

Then I thought again: Would I actually believe this person? Would I accept what this person said without arguing, rationalizing, denying?

Probably not. The personal demons we struggle with in life that keep us from our spiritual goals are so familiar a part of our everyday makeup, I realized, that we cannot see the woods for the trees. Gurdjieff once informed a man that his chief fault was the impulse to constantly argue. "But I *never* argue," the man argued back.

The obvious is *too* obvious. If we wear the same mask too long it becomes our face. Does a fish know it lives in water?

A Middle Eastern story tells of how the famous enlightened fool, Mullah Nasr Edin, is visited one day by his neighbor, who asks to borrow his donkey.

"I'm sorry," Mullah Nasr Edin replies. "My donkey died last week."

The neighbor is about to commiserate when the Mullah's donkey, who has been grazing contentedly in the Mullah's backyard the entire time, lets out a booming *hee-haw!*

"Liar!" shouts the neighbor. "Your donkey is very much alive, and in your backyard. I hear it braying."

The Mullah sniffs and raises himself to his full height. "And just whose word are you going to take on the subject?" he asks indignantly. "Mine or a donkey's?"

Even when confronted with the evidence right in front of our eyes, something in us refuses to acknowledge reality. This is why the sages tell us that enlightenment—seeing directly into our own nature—is always just a step away, hidden, as the Jesuits say, "in plain sight." Nothing but our own minds veil us from it.

The following story makes this very point in a similarly piquant way. Every day for years Mullah Nasr Edin crosses a certain regional border with several donkeys, all of them laden with overstuffed saddlebags. The customs inspector is certain that the Mullah is smuggling some kind of goods. But what these goods are he can never discover, even though he thoroughly searches the Mullah's saddlebags every time.

One day the inspector retires. On the eve of his departure he pulls the Mullah aside.

"Listen, Mullah," he says in a confidential voice. "I'm retired now and don't have any authority. But I know you were smuggling *something* all these years. I'm dying of curiosity. Please, tell me what it was."

"Donkeys," the Mullah replies.

The forces that keep us blind and against which we are obliged to

struggle are the donkeys of our lesser nature, our chief faults, present everywhere, visible nowhere. Just as the inspector in this story cannot see the
obvious because he has certain habits of thought and assumption that keep
him blind, so we must start looking at things within ourselves in a different
way if we are to see them clearly.

But how?

One way is simply by watching ourselves in action during the day,
striving to see our positive and negative qualities with an equally impartial
eye. Such advice may sound easy, but it isn't easy at all. It demands that we
give up the comforting illusion of "That doesn't matter; nobody will notice
it." This is why spiritual teachings urge us to behave at all times as if both our
inner and outer acts are seen by God. Never allow yourself to be convinced
that "nobody will notice it" or that an act is too small to matter.

A second means of help comes from other people, whether it be a
spiritual teacher, therapist, or simply family, friends, associates, even adversaries—especially from adversaries. "Our enemy's opinions of us come a good
deal closer to the truth," quipped the French wit La Rochefoucauld, "than
our own opinions about ourselves." To accept this help from others means to
be willing to see our adversaries as a tool for our own self-understanding.
Even, for example, as we turn red with anger or fret with embarrassment
from other's criticisms, some small part of us must be willing to recognize
that what has been said to us holds an element of truth. Later on, when we've
calmed down and thought about it a while, we can weigh and consider what
we've heard, see where the shoe fits, and begin the process of self-change. In
small ways like these, working with the very nitty-gritty of our ordinary
emotions and circumstances, spiritual forward motion can be achieved.

The conclusion we draw from following this advice is that it is indeed
quite possible at certain moments for that inner "inspector" in each of us to
detect Mullah Nasr Edin's smuggled donkeys and thus pave the way for self-
knowing. After all, the sought-after contraband is right in front of us, hidden
in plain sight. So what stops us from seeing it?

"One may sometimes surprise the Chief Feature of another in a chance
description or an off-hand remark," writes psychologist C. Daly King. "One
may turn on oneself in this sudden and unexpected way, and make an equally
striking discovery. But the sure way is to watch one's general and detailed
behavior over a considerable period impersonally, and to let the picture gradually form in our mind. Soon an outline will emerge. Suspicions will thrust
themselves forward. Disregard them for a long time until you are relatively
sure. Then go to someone competent to confirm or to deny your own judg-

ment. You can never be sure of this aspect of yourself by yourself. You will always need an outside confirmation."

Pruning: Learning to Let Go

The summer of my fiftieth birthday was the first time my family ever had a well-tended garden. The reason for the improvement was that my wife took over all the gardening responsibilities that year.

Handing over this little square of land was like passing the torch for me, a bittersweet midlife ritual that I acquiesced to outwardly because I was too busy to take the time anymore, inwardly because I was coming to terms with my own limitations. I noted the passing with both regret and relief, as one often does in rites of passage.

For years my wife had joked that men like to plant the seed but not stay around to harvest the crop. I had to admit there was some truth in her accusation, at least as far as my gardening style was concerned. Yet at heart I had not abandoned my little world of string beans and tomatoes. I loved it and cherished it. The very reason for our move out of New York City—or at least one of them—had been to get back to bare feet on warm garden soil.

No, the reason I gave up my garden the summer of my fiftieth birthday was not abandonment. It had more to do with the fact that whenever I worked my little plot of ground I found each baby plant so eminently deserving of life that I never had the heart to pull it out.

This act of compassion, or sentimentality some might call it, backfired when July rolled around, and I inevitably discovered that the result of my tender mercies was a jungle of plants all struggling with each other for limited light, water, and soil. My garden never worked, in short, because I had failed to *prune it*, to thin out a portion of the plants so that the rest might prosper and grow.

This inability to prune has flowed over into many other aspects of my life as well. Through the years I had never really understood that a small patch of ground cannot support unlimited growth—just as I had not accepted the fact that a single human being cannot do everything, be everything, and at the same time expect to cultivate an inner life.

Folklorist Barbara Kirshenblatt-Gimblett points out that for many people accumulating and collecting is actually a symbolic way of holding on to life as we age. Some people collect clocks, for instance, as a subconscious attempt to control time. Others build dollhouses or miniature furniture as a way of keeping the world orderly and manageable.

Social workers in particular are familiar with this syndrome, and often see it in its most extreme form. It's a rare caseload, for example, that doesn't include at least one client who belongs to the group euphemistically referred to as "collectors." You've seen such people. They are the sad solitaries who live in sixth-floor walk-ups piled to the ceilings with old newspapers or copies of *Look* and *The Saturday Evening Post;* rooms filled with orange crates, Popsicle sticks, candy wrappers picked up in the park. The saddest cases keep everything they find, including their own wastes.

Such people are extreme examples, certainly. Yet many of us accumulate comparable collections on an inward plane, psychological waste matter and emotional detritus. Our stockpiles consist of outmoded attitudes, useless behaviors, unreasonable expectations, impossible self-demands. You know the list: the inventory of "shoulds" and "oughts" and "musts" that have been drilled into us since we were young.

I think, for example, of the cartons of books in my garage, half of them never read, the other half unreadable. These books represent my own unfulfilled intellectual ambitions: everything from Hittite archaeology to French troubadour poetry. Someday, I've always told myself, I'll have time to master all this knowledge. But it's never happened. And the very presence of the books on the garage shelves is guilt-producing. "Read me!" they shout every time I walk out to get my car.

For years I was intimidated and depressed by these unread books, symbols of roads not taken. Then one day, out of the blue, I realized that I didn't *want* to read them really. And, more important, that I didn't *have to.* I had no obligation to their authors or to myself. None at all. I could be as free of these books as I chose to be, and spend this time on the inward-turning things that interested me more. All I needed was to prune them from my life.

Such inner voices deserve the same selective thinning as plants in a garden. Especially the "must" voices that keep us so submerged in the trivia of daily living that we forget our deeper aims. These are the nagging little creatures that tell us we absolutely "must" keep our home cleaner; we "must" start using a NordicTrack machine or spend more time practicing aerobics; we "must" learn to surf the Internet; or lose weight; or improve our cooking skills; or learn Spanish: all the "musts" we've come to believe will make our lives better and brighter, and which ultimately eclipse the spiritual ends that something in us is crying out for.

For years I allowed these voices to dominate my life. Though it was impossible to comply with all their demands, I certainly tried. The trouble was that the more I listened to these voices, the louder they became and the more their demands escalated. Here's a little secret: these voices never stop and they never go away. If you give in to one demand, two grow in its place, like a multiheaded hydra. Such voices are nothing more than inner recordings, really, audiotape loops that repeat and repeat like prerecorded messages on our own inner telephones. Peace will never come as long as we listen to them.

What do we do, then, to escape the clutches of these broken inner records? We prune them and weed them and thin them as thoroughly as we can.

A person who helped me most at this task is my friend Steve Carter, a man now in his early fifties who had himself been a serious gardener for many decades. Whenever I visited Steve he made a point of showing me his garden, a beautifully tended quarter-acre plot that put my own little patch of weeds to shame.

The last time I visited Steve's house and asked to see his garden, however, he gave me a strange look.

"Garden tour's canceled this year," he said. "Since I got downsized at work, I've scaled down a lot of things."

I must have looked surprised.

"They cut our entire division at the office," Steve continued. "Outsourced a lot of the work and gave me the choice of staying on as a 'director' rather than VP. That's a euphemism for limited options, lousy future prospects, no job security, and a major cut in pay. We're in the process of selling the house."

I stammered out my sympathies as we walked into his living room.

"Don't worry," he said, leading me to a sunny corner of the room. "I'm thankful I still *have* a job. As a matter of fact, I'm thankful for a lot of things."

We stopped in front of a piano. On top were four miniature bonsai trees, their reflections lustrous in the polished mahogany. The biggest tree, a pine, was no taller than my hand. All four had been perfectly trimmed and shaped to fit into their miniature planters, each tree a self-contained world that could be nurtured, managed, understood.

"From a quarter-acre to four trees on top of a piano," Steve said.

He went on to tell me how for the past ten years he had submerged himself in his work and ambitions. "I was going to be president of the damned corporation by the time I was fifty," he said. In the process he'd lost sight of the spiritual goals that had once motivated him so strongly.

"I was, you know, always trying to get bigger and better," he said, "to have more, do more, own more. Then all of a sudden here I was, literally cut down to size. I got shocked back to a sense of rightful measure. It made me remember who I was, and what the less materialistic parts of me wanted."

Steve picked up a small pruning shears and clipped several branches off one of the trees.

"It turned out to be the best thing that ever happened, this downsizing. Instead of a huge garden I have these little trees now. But, you know, one tree equals a whole garden in some funny way. The smaller things get, the bigger they get too."

The bonsai tree is beautiful because it is small: its beauty is the beauty of limit and proportion, of paradise resting in the palm of the hand. The efforts a caretaker makes on the tree's behalf are not aimed at forging something monumental, but at maintaining an equilibrium that hints at the Illimitable and Supreme through congruity, relationship, opposition, a harmony of all the parts rather than size for its own sake—through what is implied rather than what is stated. In this way the gardener makes the tree's very limitations into a signpost pointing to unity and perfection. "Consider the lilies of the field, how they grow," says Matthew 28:29. "They toil not, neither do they spin: And yet I say unto you, that even Solomon in all his glory was not arrayed like one of these."

Steve Carter had found contentment through a different kind of gardening. Gone was the showy quarter acre of land, and in its place was a one-foot-square patch of earth—but sacred earth, a tiny center of life that represented the growing end of his revived spiritual ambitions. This sense of achieving mastery through a narrow but highly concentrated band of focus is essential in our passage through the Stages of the Soul. We must all stop spreading ourselves so thin, I realized. We must try to achieve inner equilibrium rather than outer profusion. We must become compact, spare, like the bonsai tree.

The Spanish philosopher Ortega y Gasset put it this way: "It is the virtue of the child to think in terms of wishes. But the virtue of the grown man is to will. . . . Now we can achieve things only by concentrating our energy; by limiting ourselves. And in this limiting of ourselves lies the truth and the authenticity of our life. Indeed . . . He who has once honestly accepted his destiny, his own limitations, is imperturbable."

The same truth is expressed in different words in the *I Ching:* "Unlimited possibilities are not suited to man. If they existed, his life would only dissolve in the boundless." Artists are familiar with this principle. They intuitively understand that knowing where to stop is half their craft; just as ballet dancers know that without the force of gravity to keep them tied to the earth their attempts at achieving freedom from these restrictions would be without meaning or beauty. Our limits are also our tools.

After Steve talked more about his bonsai, he beckoned me nearer to one of the trees. "Look closely," he said, pointing to the tiny plant.

There at the foot of a gnarled ten-inch-high tree trunk was the miniature porcelain figure of a Chinese sage sitting in contemplation. As small as the figure was, I could see a tiny smile modeled on its face.

Steve looked at me. Perhaps it was my imagination, but there was something about his smile and the smile on the face of the sage that was the same.

Confronting the Death of Our Dreams

At some stage in our busy existence we must define the things that are fundamental to our lives and prune the rest. "Let us cultivate our garden," Voltaire wrote. If we are to be filled with a Higher Spirit, whatever name we give this Spirit, the first thing we must do is become empty enough to receive it.

One day a scholar visited a spiritual teacher and announced that he had come to attain knowledge.

The teacher said nothing but poured the scholar tea. The scholar waited for some words of wisdom; the teacher continued to pour.

Finally the tea filled the cup, then overflowed the brim and spilled all over the floor.

"What are you doing?" the scholar shrieked.

"You are like this cup of tea," the teacher replied. "Filled up, overflowing with your own opinions and plans and desires. Until you empty your cup completely there is no way I can fill it with the knowledge you request."

The middle years of life, we know from many sociological studies, are a time in which people typically begin to realize that their youthful plans and ambitions will never be fulfilled. In *The Seasons of a Man's Life*, Daniel Levinson talks a great deal about the dreams we fashion when we are young. "In its primordial form," Levinson writes, "the Dream is a vague sense of self-in-adult-world. It has the quality of a vision, an imagined possibility that generates excitement and vitality. . . . It may take a dramatic form as in the myth of the hero: the great artist, business tycoon, athletic or intellectual superstar."

In a subsequent work, Levinson turned his attention to midlife women respondents, where he discovered many parallels with his male subjects.

One major female subgroup, the Homemakers, as Levinson dubbed them in his study, had opted to bypass a career and "keep house." Now at age forty to forty-five this group found themselves facing a major life crisis. In their early married years the homemakers had made a conscious decision to devote themselves to the role of mother, wife, and keeper of the household. In return they expected a due measure of familial love, financial security, and the self-satisfaction that comes from domestic devotion.

Over and over again, Levinson discovered, women from the Homemaker category felt cheated and deprived. Many spoke of sacrificing their youth for an unreal dream. Others complained that they had done their duty but were never granted the promised rewards. The typical Homemaker respondent, according to Levinson, "felt totally trapped. Her marriage was almost intolerable, yet divorce seemed worse—she had no place to go and no adequate way to take care of herself financially and socially."

Levinson's findings are not surprising, considering the limitations that homemaking forces on today's career-oriented women. Strangely enough, however, women in the workplace who were surveyed fared no better in terms of fulfillment. Many complained of bumping up against a "glass ceiling," the invisible and unspoken corporate promotion barrier. But even those who broke through this barrier soon realized that expectation and reality were not converging. The death of the Dream comes in many different forms.

One case is Debra Rose, a participant in Levinson's Career Women group. At forty Debra captured her company's Holy Grail with a promotion to the position of regional director. "The job was a tremendous success," Debra reported. "It was a marvelous, beautiful, satisfying fulfillment of a youthful dream."

But there was trouble in paradise. Debra's promotion meant that her entire family had to move from New York City to Boston. Her family resented this upheaval, rebellion broke out, and eventually they moved back to New York. Torn between family and job, Debra now tried to commute between the two cities, but the effort proved predictably taxing. Before long it was clear that in her attempt to balance a career with a family, Debra was not receiving the fulfillment she craved from either quarter. "It was . . . a time of great crisis," she acknowledged. "I had everything I ever really wanted in life, and then I had to face up to the harsh realization that I still was not emotionally satisfied, and I had a need for something that I couldn't get out of either family or my career."

Debra was a victim of her own realized dreams. "I don't quite know where I'm going from here," she says. "I'm forty-four and trapped in a kind of success. I'm not prepared to stay where I am for another two years if I can help it. I may have to but I don't want to."

Similar sentiments are expressed by Megan Bennet, who at forty-five was awarded a highly coveted directorship at an academic science laboratory. While this advancement was a testament to Megan's brilliance and tenacity, she nonetheless had hesitations about leaving teaching. As a hedge against losing her scholarly roots, Megan gave herself a five-year timetable as director. At the end of this period, she promised herself, she would resume her academic work with students and colleagues.

Soon, however, Megan began to see that with public power comes a loss of personal freedom. In the process she realized that returning to her beloved teaching post "would be very difficult, perhaps impossible." "I don't yet understand in what direction to move or what to do with myself," Megan told an interviewer. "I have become a more and more public person with very little private life. It's such a comedy—everybody sees me as such a successful person. I have a great feeling of accomplishment, but I realize that I am somewhat trapped by my success."

Megan Bennet's story made me recall my own ambivalence when I became director of the Brookdale Center on Aging. This sensation of feeling "trapped" is a familiar one to anyone who has ever held a high-profile leadership position. Moving into such a role, one quickly discovers that colleagues, co-workers, even old friends start to perceive you in an entirely different way now that you've moved into a position of authority, and their perceptions are not always friendly, as Megan no doubt discovered.

Megan and Debra, in short, learned the same lesson that I learned: that the achievement of lifetime goals and lofty ambitions does not necessarily lead to the promised emotional Valhalla; that, in fact, it often leads to crisis, loss, and feelings of imprisonment.

Though neither of these women was involved in a spiritual struggle, as far as I know, the syndrome of being trapped by one's dreams in the middle of life is familiar to many in people on the spiritual path. In the stage of Struggle, one of the major tasks seekers face is to free themselves from their fantasies and dreams. In the attempt, they soon learn that these dreams, especially the youthful ones, do not die so easily—that they stand in the way of one's spiritual forward motion, drawing one back to the ordinary pursuits of money, name, and fame, and blocking the path ahead like giant stone idols.

Two psychologists, Charles Drebing and Winston Gooden, recently carried out studies to determine the importance of having a dream at midlife. Administering a battery of psychological tests, they collected data on sixty-eight men between the ages thirty-six and fifty-five. Results showed that three-quarters of these respondents had cultivated a dream as young adults. A majority of their dreams centered on successful careers, though some were related to interpersonal and even spiritual goals.

Drebing and Gooden's most relevant findings show that men whose dreams are still alive at midlife tend to be less depressed and anxious than those who have lost a vision for the future. Highly successful respondents, and even those who had not experienced success but still anticipated it, maintained a strong sense of purpose and optimism.

Several years later the investigators carried out a similar study on women at midlife, interviewing ninety women between the ages of thirty-eight and fifty-two. Respondents were asked whether they had formed a dream as young adults, and how close they had come to realizing this dream.

The findings were similar to those of the men. Ninety percent of women had a dream in youth; 78 percent still believed in these dreams. There was also evidence to show that the pursuit and realization of this dream is linked to positive mental health. Those women whose dreams had deserted them tended to be depressed and to see life in far more despondent and hopeless terms than the others.

The results of all these studies are ambivalent, and leave us in something of a quandary. On one hand, dreams are clearly a necessary ingredient for our mental and emotional well-being. "A life based upon a Dream has a special vital quality," Levinson writes. "Any other is at best a compromise and at worst a defeat." Without a dream we lose our hope and drive, and sometimes even our health—not a good state in which to pursue a contemplative practice. "Does any man doubt," asks Francis Bacon, "that if there were taken out of men's minds vain opinions, flattering hopes, false valuations and the like, but it would leave the minds of a number of men poor shrunken things?"

At the same time, our dreams can also disappoint and torment us, especially as we grow older and watch them crumble. Even dreams that come true do not necessarily lead to a happy ending. They simply bring a different set of complications. "Pursuing a Dream is risky," Levinson warns, "since the outcome may be grievously disappointing."

Does the fulfillment of a dream bring contentment? Or does it lead simply to another dream, and then another, and another? Is dreaming really what one writer termed "the mind's immodesty"? And might the endless pursuit of dreams be a disguised form of psychological consumerism, imprisoning and deluding us rather than helping us free ourselves from the profane world?

This troubling paradox of needing a dream to inspire us, yet finding that its fulfillment leaves us perplexed and empty, is vitally significant from the perspective of the Stages of the Soul. For in spiritual terms, we need *both* elements, the hope *and* the disillusionment, to see things clearly. This ambivalent reality was acted out for me several years ago on the stage of life in one of my own classrooms.

The occasion was a one-day seminar I gave in Philadelphia on the subject "The Search for Meaning at Midlife." Of the eighteen people who showed up that morning, by far the most conspicuous was a tall middle-aged woman with paper-white skin and bright red lips. Even in the simple act of sitting down, this woman had the knack of drawing the attention of everyone in the room. Her nametag identified her as Martha.

A major theme of the seminar that day was the concept of the dream at midlife and how it impacts, positively and negatively, on our spiritual Search and Struggle. As a rule, of course, seminars on midlife spirituality do not excite a great deal of conflict. Polite disagreement, perhaps, and some "sharing of opinions" that occasionally borders on the prickly. But outright war? In my experience, such things never happen.

That is, until today.

The pyrotechnics began when a bereft-looking woman in the front row began to talk about the role her dreams had played in keeping her sane through a painful divorce. In the middle of this heartfelt speech, Martha interrupted.

"That's a lot of crap!" she shouted.

The entire class froze. "Dreams are just a carrot on a stick," Martha went on. "I don't care what kind of hassles you're going through."

It's interesting to see the way a group of people react in times of conflict. On this occasion three-quarters of the class seemed cowed by the harsh interruption, and most of them stared at the floor in mute embarrassment. The remaining quarter, however, took Martha's salvo on a deeply personal level and prepared for combat.

"But our dreams are what make life worth living!" an Hispanic man in the back row protested. "How can you turn your back on hope?"

"I'd like to know what kind of life *you* must have had without dreams?" another woman said. "It must be awfully barren."

Martha gave a grim chuckle. "It's just the opposite," she replied, warming to the challenge. "How can anyone be happy living a lie? Your bubble has to pop someday. Then what?"

"If you don't have dreams, what's the purpose of living?" a nurse said with a pained expression on her face. "Dreams inspire us."

"It's your mind and intelligence that should inspire you," replied Martha. "Not a lot of opium smoking."

What Martha was saying had some sense to it, it was true, but her argumentative stance was disrupting the class. I tried to cut the discussion short, but she wouldn't let it rest. Finally a man in the back hurled an angry challenge.

"Let's get it straight what you're really talking about," he said. "You keep on throwing the word 'dream' around. Will you tell the rest of us what you actually mean by it?"

"I mean pie in the sky," Martha shot back. "Thinking the world owes you a living. Impossible fantasies about finding a man who'll take care of you for the rest of your life. Having a lovey-dovey perfect little family. Making a million dollars. The kind of fantasies that make people line up for hours in front of deli counters to buy Lotto tickets. And do you know who all those people are that are standing there waiting to waste their hard-earned money? They're you and me! We're the poor slobs standing on life's Lotto line waiting for that one in a hundred million chances to hit. And I'm here to tell you folks: All we're going to get out of it is a broken heart!"

Martha's phrase "life's Lotto line" struck a chord throughout the room. Are any of us really any different? I wondered. Aren't we all secretly expecting the big payoff in one form or another? That someday moment when fate intervenes and makes our lives perfect forever. I myself had been waiting for it in the form of a big grant in the sky, a call from the MacArthur Foundation or the Rockefeller Foundation, say, a call that would smooth the way in my ongoing research. Talk about dreams. It's all a bit like waiting for a visit from Michael Anthony, the character on that old TV program *The Millionaire* who knocks on your door out of the blue and hands you a check for a million dollars (tax-free, if I remember correctly). Haven't we all been waiting for Michael Anthony to knock at our door?

Yet while Martha's words conveyed some truth, she used them more as weapons than as tools for communication. A moment later she was on her feet trying to hog the floor again, but this time no one in the class was biting. She spent the rest of the day silent and brooding.

After the seminar was over I headed out to the parking lot. As I approached my car I heard someone call my name. I turned and saw Martha following me.

I had a momentary impulse to leap into my car and drive away before she could collar me. But my teacherly instincts prevailed. As she came closer, I saw tears in her eyes.

"Dr. Moody," she cried out, "I wanted to catch you before you left. To say how sorry I am for ruining things. I got . . . carried away. As usual."

Her apology took me by surprise.

"Can I talk to you for just a minute?" she asked.

"You want to have a cup of coffee?" I offered.

We talked for an hour that day, and it was difficult to realize that the quiet, rather dignified person sitting at the table in front of me was the same woman who had shouted down a classroom full of people a few hours ago.

The life story that Martha poured out to me was sadly familiar: two bitter divorces, a teenage son in recovery from a drug habit, a bright career as a graphic artist sabotaged by bouts with alcoholism. In the past year, Martha had entered therapy and done a great deal of work with her therapist on the very issue of not being led around, in her words, "by wish-fulfillment fantasies." Intoxicated with self-discovery, as people can be in the early stages of therapy, she had taken it upon herself to set the world straight.

"I wanted to tell all those people about the trap they were falling into thinking that everything's going to have a happy ending," she said. "Those kinds of fantasies ruin your life. I've lived through them myself, I know what those phony hopes do to you. I see my friends wasting their lives this same way, trying to keep it together with a lot of empty promises."

"But sometimes that's all we have," I replied. "There may have been some truth to what you were saying. But what those people in the group were saying is right too. Dreams can be noble and necessary. Or maybe they're just what we happen to need right now to work our way through hard times. They have their place, Martha, believe me!"

"I know, I know," Martha replied, tears coming to her eyes again. "I didn't mean to get so obnoxious. I just wanted to help."

While the evidence in psychological studies shows how important dreams are for our mental health, the Marthas of the world certainly have their point as well—in the long run dreams are nothing more than, well, dreams. These studies, what's more, tell us a good deal about how we adapt to the contingencies of life, but little about how we can change ourselves within it.

Adaptation is important, of course. We all need a bit of sage counsel to keep us on the right track. But from the perspective of the soul, adaptation is advice given to prisoners locked up in Plato's cave. It does not offer the wisdom we need to grow spiritually; it simply tells us how to get more enjoyment out of the sound-and-light show presented to us on the walls of our cave. From the standpoint of the spiritual Struggle it makes no difference whether our dreams of accomplishment and success are filled or unfulfilled. At a certain point success and failure become equally irrelevant. What *is* necessary to realize—and this is the key—is that we cannot "drop" our dreams at will. Even if it were possible to do this—and, try as we might, it is not—shedding hopes and attachments prematurely can be a blunting experience in our spiritual growth, and even an emotionally dangerous one. It's not, in the long run, that we must give our dreams up; it's that at a certain point on the spiritual journey *our dreams give us up*.

This, at bottom, is what the struggle of the mind and heart is all about. It's not that we are expected to sacrifice everything all at once like a fakir in the desert. All that is necessary as we traverse the Stages of the Soul is to persevere at our spiritual practice and continue grappling with the spiritual, emotional, and moral challenges we face. As a natural consequence of these efforts, illusions will drop away one by one of their own accord when the time is right and when our lives have no further use for life's lotto line.

The end of the dream, then, does not take place when our dreams fail us or turn sour. It occurs as a natural result of our spiritual Struggle when our dreams become irrelevant, and are replaced by a deeper, more dependable reality. This change comes about in its own time, as part of a process. It grows on its own. We need only plant the seed, and keep it nourished with the water of hope, contemplation, and struggle. Until someday it blooms spontaneously like a plant in a well-pruned garden. "Seek ye first the kingdom of God," says the Bible, "and all these things shall be added unto you."

Once upon a time, a Sufi story tells, three men seeking guidance lived on a caravan route in the middle of the desert. These men had no knowledge of gardening, so they eked out a living trading whatever trinkets they happened to find in the sand. Deep in their hearts, each of them had a secret dream: to become a gardener and grow their own trees, flowers, and plants.

One day it was announced that a Master Gardener would be passing through on the next caravan.

The first seeker greeted the news with indifference. All the guidance he needed could be found in books, he told himself, or through his own efforts.

The other two men were more excited by the prospect of the Master Gardener's visit and they eagerly awaited his arrival.

When the caravan reached the town, the Master Gardener visited the house of the first man and soon discovered that this man was content to follow his own counsel.

So the Master Gardener went to the house of the second seeker, who begged to be initiated into the secrets of growing a garden. The Master Gardener was a kindly man, and he agreed, but only on one condition: that the second seeker follow his directions exactly.

The Master Gardener then asked to be left alone for several days on the site of the second man's future garden. When he finished his mysterious work he gave the seeker strange and unexpected instructions. Instead of delivering a dissertation on the principles of gardening, he showed the seeker a lever near the wall of the garden, and told him to turn this lever faithfully and without fail every day for a few minutes. Then he left without further explanation.

Now, as it turned out, this second seeker was a man of modest faith, and he was disappointed by these odd directions. He had expected to be told cosmic secrets of growth and fertility. Instead he was asked to perform an act that seemed irrelevant, even nonsensical. Though he did what he was told in the beginning, after a while he stopped turning the lever, and eventually forgot about it entirely. Nothing ever grew on his dry plot of land. When people asked him about his gardening lessons he replied that he had been duped by a charlatan.

Meanwhile, the Master Gardener continued on to the house of the third seeker. This man too was disappointed by the Master's instructions. But he turned the lever faithfully, as instructed. What the third seeker did not know was that this lever was connected to a skillfully hidden irrigation system that the Master had buried under his plot of land.

One day while the third seeker was inspecting his garden site he noticed that a few tiny shoots had broken through the soil, brought to life by the hidden irrigation system. The man's joy was mixed with dismay, however, for he did not know what to do next. Thinking on the matter for a while, he decided to simply keep following the instructions and turn the lever as told.

Then one morning he made a discovery that changed his life. Looking down at the growing shoots, he saw tiny words written on the leaves of each new plant. Rubbing his eyes in astonishment, he looked again and read. To his joy and astonishment, these words presented detailed instructions on what to do next and how to tend and care for every aspect of his garden.

The third seeker continued to work and study, and gradually he learned all the secrets of the lever, the plants, and of agriculture in general. Eventually his home was surrounded by a paradise of refreshing greenery and abundant fertility. "It all happened so naturally," said the third seeker when the people came to see. "I tried to have no expectations; I simply persevered."

Struggling Against Habituation

As a scholar and administrator, I have worked in the field of aging for nearly half my life. Yet I am still sorely puzzled by what it is in human beings that causes them, psychologically, to age. When does this process really begin?

A colleague of mine, psychologist Dr. Robert Kastenbaum, has also been intrigued by this matter—so intrigued that he has developed a rather startling theory to explain it. Psychological aging, he believes, begins in infancy.

What Dr. Kastenbaum means by this strange assertion is that as we grow older we develop a gradual decrease of response to persistent stimulation, a process he calls *habituation.*

In psychological terms, habituation means becoming gradually oblivious to a repetitive stimulus, a ticking clock, say, or the sound of shuffling feet in the apartment upstairs. At first these sounds hound us through the day and keep us up at night. Then a filter goes to work in our brains, and over time begins to block the sounds out. A week passes, then two. One day we wake up and realize we've become so accustomed to these noises that for all intents and purposes they no longer exist.

This "mental reducing valve," as Aldous Huxley refers to it, is essential as far as our everyday living and coping goes; without it we would become maddeningly distracted by the thousands of irrelevant impressions that strike our senses every moment.

Yet the habituation Kastenbaum speaks of is one step more subtle than pure physical reactivity; it is a reduction of our consciousness as well as our senses, a process in which the ordinary stimuli of life, the simple pleasures and small joys, lose their flavor over time by dint of sheer repetition.

This process starts in infancy the moment we begin to notice the world.

At first everything around us is brilliantly vivid and animate—the sparrow's chirp, the taste of ice cream, the sight of summer clouds. Then the years roll by. As we hear the chirping of a thousand sparrows, as we lick our ten thousandth ice-cream cone, as we watch our millionth cloud pass overhead, the immediacy of our response to these stimuli dims. Eventually we become deadened to their beauty. Habituation sets in, and with it a feeling of becoming fixed, hardened—older.

Aging, in this sense, is less chronological or physical than it is psychological. Its origins can be traced more directly to a self-induced loss of mental flexibility than to any natural decline in cognitive processing.

The reason we feel more alive when we travel, for instance, or when we find ourselves in unusual circumstances is that new impressions tend to loosen habituation's grip. Colors, sounds, tastes, smells, ideas seem more vivid when we are on the road and in new surroundings. Even time itself seems to slow down (which makes us wonder if our sense of time is not also conditioned by the speed at which we process impressions). This explains to some extent why we spend so much of our lives searching for novel experiences—a new film, a new restaurant, a new lover. Unconsciously, we are self-medicating against habituation.

In certain ways, of course, habituation is essential to life, making it unnecessary for us to respond to every fragment of sensory information that comes our way. Yet it also makes us old before our time. Habit, in short, is a two-edged sword, providing freedom from sensory overload, but also causing people to become set in their ways, even those who are otherwise brilliant and capable. I am reminded of the German philosopher Immanuel Kant. Intellectually one of philosophy's greatest champions of autonomy and freedom, in his private life Kant became so habit-bound as he aged that the citizens of his native Königsberg were accustomed to setting their clocks by his regular afternoon walks.

What does habituation have to do with spirituality?

In its most profound sense, habituation is more than just a chronic indulgence in routines and ruts. On a deeper level it can be looked at as the polar opposite of the mindfulness and attentiveness which are the pillars of spiritual life.

The Bible enjoins us: "Be still, and know that I am God." The goal in contemplative prayer is likewise to anchor our awareness to the present moment, and to keep our minds free from the stream of worldly thoughts that usurps our attention. If we do this long enough, and if we are able to still our minds in the proper way, something strangely wonderful happens. Some people experience a sensation that they are moving from a familiar dimension to an unfamiliar one. Others feel a sense of expansion, of moving outward beyond the ordinary limits of everyday perception. Still others discover a boundless space inside themselves that seems to contain everything. Words pale.

Try an experiment. Take a few deep breaths, then sit back, relax as fully as you can, and think of nothing at all. For half a minute, say, let your mind become a total blank, like a blackboard without any writing on it. Close your eyes, breathe normally, and focus attention on your breath. Breathe in and breathe out, keeping your consciousness fixed on the breath. Each time you find your attention wandering, bring it back to your breathing.

If you've never tried this rudimentary form of meditation, you'll be surprised first of all at how difficult it is to stop your thoughts; second, at how calm and rooted in the present moment you'll feel even after just twenty or thirty seconds of effort. This feeling of relaxed presentness is the beginning of mindfulness. It is the starting place of contemplative practice. All religions, all spiritual ways, adopt some variation on this method as part of their spiritual practice.

Habituation, on the other hand, is what we could call "unmindfulness" or "inattentiveness." If mindfulness means living in the here and now and being viscerally aware of what we do at each moment, habituation means living *out of the moment,* being *unaware* of ourselves, of *not* noticing what we do. It means allowing our minds to idle away the time thinking their customary thoughts and dreaming their customary dreams—I want, I don't want, I like, I hate, I remember, I forget. Habituation, viewed in this light, is a form of spiritual sleep.

How exactly do we struggle against habituation?

Before we answer this question we have to answer several that precede it: what is the difference between habit and habituation? And if habits are a necessary part of living, might it not be dangerous to eliminate them?

Habits, it's true, are necessary. Some, like putting your car keys away in the same place each time or flossing your teeth, are highly useful. Perhaps even most habits are good. "Could the young but realize how soon they will become mere walking bundles of habits," writes William James, "they would give more heed to their conduct while in the plastic state. Every smallest stroke of virtue or of vice leaves its ever so little scar."

The danger does not lurk in any one particular habit, though there are certainly many we would be better off without. Individual habits can be helpful or harmful, as the case may be. Habituation, on the other hand, in its most negative sense, is more a cumulative mental mechanism than a regulated accommodation to living. It runs during all our waking hours and causes the shutting down of our awareness to such an impoverished level of perception that we interact with the world only on the most superficial level via fixed ideas, canned assumptions, and a closed mind.

In their seminal study *On the Psychology of Meditation,* psychologists Robert Ornstein and Claudio Naranjo claim that our assumed view of reality is actually a subjective and biased mental construction in which we select a tiny group of ideas and stimuli and systematically tune out the rest. The ordinary man and woman believe that what they see around them when they walk down the street is an accurate reflection of what really is. This idea, insist Ornstein and Naranjo, is impossible to maintain even at the most elementary level if we consider the innumerable forms of energy surrounding us every moment—electricity, magnetism, radiation, light waves, radio signals, X rays, not to mention our own inner chemical and electrical discharges, our thoughts, feelings, senses, muscular impulses—on and on.

Since we are bombarded by this vast vibratory shower every moment of our lives, a good deal of mental energy must be expended toward making sense of it all. This we do by first discarding and simplifying a majority of the information that comes into our brains; and second, by sorting and categorizing this data into neat packets of awareness and response; bytes of consciousness, as it were.

The result of this mental organizing effort is that our universe becomes scaled down to the level of our own capability to understand and process it. We literally "tune" our consciousness to the channels that are most easy to access, and block out the rest. "As we become experienced in dealing with the world," write Ornstein and Naranjo, "we attempt to make more and more consistent 'sense' out of the mass of information arriving at our receptors. We develop sterotyped systems or categories for sorting the input that reaches us. This set of categories we develop is limited, much more limited than the richness of the input. . . . We expect cars to make a certain noise, traffic lights to be a certain color, food to smell a certain way, and certain people to say certain things."

As a result of this stereotyped processing, what we *actually* perceive, say Ornstein and Naranjo, are not real cars or real traffic lights or real foods at all. They are figments of our limited internal processing systems that see what habit tells us to see, and that are filtered through the lens of our own subjectivity, imagination and suggestibility. So that ultimately our entire sense of reality comes to be built not on things as they really are, but on interpretative models based on a heavily edited and intensely processed version of past experiences and future.

Habituation, then, is the by-product of all the routines, ruts, and pigeonholing that our minds have indulged in for decades. By midlife this mechanism becomes predominant in us, censoring, categorizing, distorting, judging, assuming, routinizing, mechanizing everything we see, feel, and think. Habituation sets in, for example, when we no longer hear what people are saying to us (because our preconceived notions tell us we know the truth already). It happens when we become blunted to the subtle beauties surrounding us, when we stop seeing things as if for the first time, as a child is capable of doing. Habituation is when we hear ourselves mouthing the same shopworn opinions, when we catch ourselves telling a story we've told a hundred times before in exactly the same way. Habituation is talking automatically of things we know nothing about. It is assuming without understanding, judging without weighing, reacting from bias rather than evident fact. It is, in short, a reduction of our awareness rather than an expansion of our consciousness.

How do we escape this trap?

In the past traditional societies have sometimes taken extreme measures to sever themselves from the bondage of habit. Among the Sioux tribes of the northwestern Americas, a few select members of the tribe volunteer to become a *Heyhoka*, which means quite literally one who has an obligation to do things differently from everyone else in order to break all patterns of habitual behavior. "Sometimes the *Heyhoka*'s actions are very humorous," writes Joseph Epes Brown, biographer of the great Native American shaman Black Elk (who himself was a *Heyhoka*), "because this is a part of the technique for shattering a person's perception of, and participation in, the everyday routines of life. To break through the habitual enables one to take some distance from oneself—to see things a little bit more objectively, and thereby on a higher level."

Taking their counter-habituation mandate seriously, *Heyhokas* literally do everything backward and upside down. They will pitch a tepee, Brown tells us, with the tent poles on the outside rather than the inside, and with the smoke flaps facing the wrong way. They will mount a horse on the wrong side and sit on it facing backward. They will lie in their tepees with their feet in the air. Instead of entering the main doorway of the tepee they will lift up the lodge cover at the back and crawl under.

Among the Sioux, it should be added, *Heyhokas* are often shamans as well as trickster figures, and are looked on with great reverence by those within their society, for whom the act of breaking the bonds of habit is given the rank of sacred institution.

In our own society, of course, such dramatic means are not open to us, and so we are faced with the question again: how do we break free of the many strings of routine that bind our consciousness so tightly and keep us from participating in life with full keenness and self-awareness?

This question troubled me in my own struggle for years, and it was the topic of conversation when I got together with my old friend Paul, one balmy Sunday afternoon in Pennsylvania.

Paul is a man who has worked as long and hard at breaking the rigidity of habituation as any person I know. Through the years his searching has drawn him down many strange alleys and byways of psychology, religion, and philosophy. At one point he considered becoming a Trappist monk.

Though Jewish, Paul eventually studied with a Christian monk who had left his order and formulated his own eclectic spiritual method based on ideas borrowed from modern psychology, Sufism, Gurdjieff, and Christian mysticism. Paul recounted to me his first meeting with this man, who went by the name of Father Frederick.

"I'll never forget the shock of that meeting," Paul said, shaking his head. "It completely turned my expectations upside down. I told Father Frederick I wanted to know God, to have an experience of Ultimate Truth. Father Frederick is a big man, you know. He's got a bushy black beard, craggy skin, piercing eyes, still wears his monk's robes. He looked at me in this half-mocking, half-compassionate way, and told me that this was very good, that it's right to want to know God. But before you can know God, he said, you have to remember to touch your nose."

" 'I'm sorry?' I stammered.

" 'What you say about God is a very big thing,' Father Frederick insisted. 'Perhaps it's possible for you, perhaps not. But let's start with something smaller. Let's see what *is* possible.' "

Father Frederick told Paul that every day at exactly ten o'clock in the morning and three o'clock in the afternoon he should touch his nose. Do this every day for a week, Father Frederick said. No earlier, no later. That was all.

"To make a long story short," Paul continued, "I found out that I was so caught up in my daily routines that I didn't have the presence of mind to do this seemingly little task—touch my nose. I'd remember maybe an hour late one day, an hour early the next. Some days I didn't remember at all. Or

I'd do it in the morning, then forget in the afternoon. Not a single day went by that I ever got it right. So here I was talking about making the efforts to know God, and I wasn't aware enough to remember my own nose.

"It was at this point," Paul went on animatedly, "that I started to realize how deeply caught up I am in my habit systems. I realized what change really means, how hard it is to make it happen. It's difficult enough to make spiritual efforts, I thought. But it's even harder to *remember to make* the efforts!

"I recall that Father Frederick once talked about how the church tells us we should love our enemies. Sounds great. Until you go out and try it. A few whacks at it and you discover that not only can't you love your enemies. You can't even love your friends. Or the people closest to you. Or even yourself, for that matter. How can we talk about something as big as loving our enemies or universal compassion when we can't even learn to love and accept ourselves?"

Paul smiled.

"Do you know the Yiddish words 'shlemiel' and 'shlimazel'?" he asked.

I said I'd heard of a shlemiel. But what's a shlimazel?

"A shlemiel is the guy who always spills the hot soup on you," Paul explained. "Count on it, he'll be there having an accident on your lap wherever you go. A shlimazel, on the other end: he's the guy who's always getting the hot soup spilled *on him.* They say if a shlimazel tries to sell an umbrella, the sun comes out. If he tries to sell a shroud, everybody stops dying. Everything always happens to the shlimazel. See the difference?"

I nodded.

"And the terrifying thing about it," Paul went on, his face darkening, "is that the shlemiel and the shlimazel, you and I, all of us, we're all chained to these deep-seated roles. They're part of us, like our own skin. We can't get away from them. That's how deep our habits of being go."

How then do we overcome this tissue of habits that keeps us so tethered and blind? One answer is simply: attention.

Roshi Philip Kapleau tells the story of how one day a man came to the Zen master Ikkyu and asked him to write a set of wise maxims for ordinary people to read and understand.

Ikkyu wrote a single word on a piece of paper, and handed it to the man. The word was "attention."

"Is this all?" asked the man, unable to hide his disappointment. "Can't you add something more illuminating?"

Ikkyu took the paper back and wrote the word "attention" twice.

"Really," the man said, "I fail to understand the meaning of what you have given me."

At this Ikkyu wrote the word three times: "Attention. Attention. Attention."

Immensely irritated, the man shouted, "What does this word 'attention' mean anyway!"

Ikkyu answered gently, "Attention means attention."

A good source for insight on the subject of attention is the *Philokalia,* a remarkable collection of writings of Christian saints. Here one of the great spiritual masters, Nicephorus the Solitary, equates attention with "sobriety" and guarding of the heart:

"Attention is the beginning of contemplation," he writes, "or rather its necessary condition: for, through attention, God comes close and reveals Himself to the mind. Attention is serenity of the mind, or rather it is standing firmly planted and not wandering, through the gift of God's mercy. Attention means cutting off thoughts. It is the abode of remembrance of God."

How do we start practicing attention on an everyday level?

We begin by paying heed to the events happening around us—by entering into daily life with full focus on ordinary activities. Opening a jar. Typing a letter. Turning on the light. Picking up the phone. Eating breakfast.

Years ago my wife and I had the privilege of spending several hours meeting privately with Dr. Martin Lings, Keeper of Arabic Manuscripts at the British Museum and a distinguished scholar of Islamic mysticism. As I was leaving his office, Dr. Lings showed me to the door. "You know," he said, "for the enlightened even the act of walking through a door can be a sacred act."

According to the *Spiritual Exercises* of St. Ignatius Loyola, a recommended practice at the end of each day is to narrate to oneself everything that has happened, and to replay these events in one's mind one after the other. A related exercise is to narrate to oneself one's movements and activities at the very moment these activities are taking place. The inner dialogue might go something like this: "I'm sitting here at the word processor now. My hands are in front of me moving on the keys. Now my head is turning to the right, looking out the window. Now it's back looking at the screen again. Now I'm getting up from my seat. Now I'm walking to the kitchen. Now I'm standing at the sink. Now I'm pouring myself a glass of water. Now I'm drinking the water. . . ."

One woman I know, a minister in a Protestant church, has spent many years studying the writings of the Eastern Orthodox masters. One of the features she is most drawn to in these writings is the specific direction they provide on attention and awareness. On the basis of her readings in the *Philokalia* plus other translations from Greek and Russian texts, this woman carries their advice into her everyday practice and shares it with her congregation.

For example, one of the readings from the *Philokalia* advises that when we wake up in the morning we should sit on the side of the bed and become aware of the simple in-and-out rhythms of our breath. After centering ourselves in this way, we then say our prayers, whatever these may happen to be, remaining conscious of this in-out rhythm as we recite. In this way our mind is automatically centered and kept from wandering while we pray.

Another woman, Barbara, is the mother of twin two-year-old girls and a son of seven. At one time a serious follower of Christian prayer and contemplation, in her early years of motherhood Barbara found it impossible to split her attention between child rearing and spiritual effort. She finally took time off to attend a half-day Christian meditation seminar that stressed contemplative prayer, especially constant repetition of the name of Jesus in all acts throughout the day. Fortified with what she learned, she now goes through her busy day of child care and at the same time remembers her spiritual roots.

"God is everywhere," Barbara told me. "Even in diapers and bottles. That's what we have to see. Why not? Why should we think that God is only in church on Sundays and not present with us every day of the week? I try to keep to this by not letting my mind drift, by returning to the name of Jesus whenever I can. I try to fix my mind on what's before me right now. And in this I try to see God as much as I can when I wash the children's clothes or bathe them. It's like a meditation in movement—just stay focused on the remembrance of God. Keep your mind calm and serene. I give thanks that we have food on our table, and that we're so well taken care of. It's all in the remembering, in keeping your attention focused on what's happening in your life right now. God is there in the simple acts of cleaning up and hugging my child. I try to understand this and keep focused."

This is the same message that the eighteenth-century monk Brother Lawrence taught in *The Practice of the Presence of God,* telling us that he "had no other care but faithfully to reject at once every other thought, that he might perform all his actions for the love of God." And on an even more esoteric level: "I make it my only business to persevere in His holy Presence, wherein I keep myself by a simple attention and an absorbing passionate regard to God, which I may call an actual *Presence of God;* or, to speak better, a silent and secret conversation of the soul with God." In recent years Father Thomas Keating has made a variant of the Presence of God technique, conjoined with the Jesus prayer, familiar to thousands of devotees through the method he calls "Contemplative Prayer."

Those who are drawn to the spiritual life in such intense forms often find it extremely demanding, and at times need to break free from the world entirely: if not by taking monastic vows, then by spending time in retreat. There is, indeed, nothing like a trip to the world of silence to shock the powers of habit and routine, and to help us refocus our attention on spiritual goals. In recent years both Christian and Zen monasteries have opened their doors to temporary retreats for laypeople seeking a taste of the contemplative life.

Still other seekers try to bring the contemplative life into the world outside monastery walls by breaking the bonds of habit in everyday life itself. For example, certain modern Sufi orders are so concerned with matters of habituation and attention that they never remain in the same location longer than a week or two. In the early 1970s I became acquainted with one such group, known as the Fuqara. Mostly British and American, these wandering mendicants dress in North African style, and live and travel in vans, like hippies, never settling or putting down roots. Once I asked the leader of the Fuqara, a burning-eyed Englishman, why his followers never stay in the same place. "Moving constantly keeps you awake," he answered with a wink.

We might not want to do what the Fuqara do, of course. But we can achieve a similar condition, even at home, as Barbara, the mother of twins, was able to do. We *can* prevent ourselves from falling into ruts of behavior and from dwelling on the past. Such efforts are within our power. We have but to see the need for making them. We *can* change our own "inner environment." We can resist getting hung up in the same old habits of thought day after day. We *can* live as though each day is our last. Perhaps it is.

In Asian cultures, especially those inspired by spiritual ideals, exercises are likewise employed to cultivate mindful attention. One of the best-known of these is the Japanese tea ceremony. Far from being a picturesque Eastern version of a coffee break, as an American GI once termed it, the tea ceremony is deeply imbued with the spirit of Zen, and is a living exercise in mindfulness for all attending. Each movement that the tea master makes during the ceremony—and, ideally, that the guests echo back—is a purposeful one. Nothing is out of place, nothing random or accidental. At the same time, despite such precise rules of behavior, there is, as in all sacred art, boundless latitude for creativity and spontaneity.

The story is told of a famous tea master who once invited a high-ranking dignitary to his teahouse. In those times it was customary for a tea master to give his guests a small, appropriate gift. Yet on this day, as the ceremony proceeded, no gift was forthcoming.

The master brewed the tea and served it. The dignitary and his entourage drank the tea, admired the ancient teacups, and paid the proper compliments. But where were the gifts? Could the greatest tea master in Japan be committing such a breach of etiquette?

Then, just as the guests had finished their tea and were preparing to leave, the tea master stood up, walked to the window, and pulled open the shade. Outside, framed perfectly by the window, a glorious full moon was just that present moment rising up out of the sea, its reflection glittering majestically on the ocean below. The master had not forgotten to give his illustrious visitors a gift. He was simply waiting for precisely the right moment to give it.

To be a master of attention means to experience everything as if for the first time; to see the world, as the poet and mystic William Blake describes it, with the doors of perception cleansed. In such a state of awareness we consider no action to be trivial. We do our best to act with knowledge and intention in all matters whether large or small. In the small, we know, we will find the great; in the present moment, all moments; in the ordinary, in the everyday, we will find the holy.

This honing of the perceptive faculties and treating every moment as if it was the *only* moment, is not simply a picturesque metaphor, but has a solid grounding in the behavior and functioning of those who master it. Several decades ago two Japanese neuropsychiatrists, A. Kasumatsu and T. Hirai, performed EEGs on a control group of nonreligious men and women, and then on a group of Zen monks. Both groups were wired to an EEG machine in a soundproof room, and both were exposed to a clicking sound that was repeated once every fifteen seconds.

When the ordinary control group listened to the clicks their sensory selection mechanism began tuning out the sound after the third or fourth click. Within several minutes no brain-wave response of any kind was registered in response to the clicks. The people in the control group had simply stopped hearing the sound. Habituation had set in.

Then the Zen monks were tested. Their EEGs showed that when exposed to the same set of stimuli, they maintained a steady level of attention from the beginning of the test to the end. Unlike the control group, their attention never flagged. For these long-practiced meditators, each click was, in a manner of speaking, the first click, the last click, and the *only* click. For them each moment of this test was the *only* moment of their lives.

Such intensity of concentration is unusual, of course, and is characteristically demonstrated by men and women who have spent years cultivating powers of attention. At the same time, there are also forms of attention training open to all of us. Several years ago my children were passing through a phase in which every game they played ended in a howling argument. Talks, scoldings, separating them—nothing curtailed the fights.

Then my wife got an inspiration. One day while one of these brawls was in full swing, she walked into the children's room with a tape recorder and put it down on the floor between them.

"Keep on arguing," she said. "Don't let me disturb you. I'm just going to tape you. When you're finished you might want to play the tape back."

That was it. None of the usual lectures. Just a tape recorder spinning its wheels in the middle of the floor.

Later that afternoon, long after their quarrel was over, I heard my son and daughter playing the tape back. Both were howling with laughter and a bit of incredulity at their own carryings-on. "Do I really sound like that?" they kept asking one another. I could tell from eavesdropping on their conversation that both were experiencing the diffident embarrassment people feel when faced with irrefutable evidence of their own foolishness. The tape recorder showed them the cold truth of how habitually sputtering and spiteful their voices sounded in the middle of an argument, how full of bluster, how silly.

From this time on whenever an argument began, one of my children ran for the tape recorder, turned it on, and recorded what followed. It became a kind of sport for them, but a meaningful sport. Because the more they taped their arguments, the fewer arguments they had.

What my children had stumbled on, quite unconsciously, is an oblique version of what Eastern Orthodox Christianity speaks of as "sin eating." This phrase refers to the act of observing our own negative behaviors with a detached, impartial eye. During such moments, part of our consciousness splits off, as it were, becoming a separate observer. This observing faculty simply watches: no more, no less. It does not try to alter what is observed. It does not try to stop the negative behavior or change it in any way. The process does not involve thinking or introspection, nor does it analyze or judge. It simply *sees*. "Two birds sit on the same branch" goes the Hindu parable. "One eats of the berries and the leaves, the other looks on in silence eternally."

The use of self-observation as a tool of change—specifically, through videotape playback—is familiar today in fields ranging from marriage counseling to sales training. For years I myself have used this tool to teach public speaking in seminars and workshops, and have repeatedly seen how visual feedback can produce spectacular advances in habit correction. The camera tells the truth in direct, nonverbal form: unnecessary hand movements, slumping posture, too many "you knows" in a speech, all are registered and recorded impartially. Seeing their manifestations mirrored back on-camera is a jolting shock to most students, and usually a therapeutic one. Participants not only self-correct with amazing speed; many seem to derive a greater quotient of plain self-knowledge in the process. As a result, habits are magically transformed, sometimes without a word being said.

Why the act of self-observation should have such an altering effect on behavior is a mystery. Yet, as religions have known for centuries, somewhere in the process of watching ourselves impartially and nonjudgmentally, a strange transformative magic takes place, the same magic that my own children grew so fond of. Once habits are caught in the act, it seems, some strange inner combustion goes to work, and over time these habits burn themselves up and vanish on their own. Even our deeper "habits of being" eventually reveal themselves and dissolve when scanned by the cold eye of what Hinduism terms "the witness" and Christians call "watchfulness."

This process has roots in the deeper structure of the physical universe itself, where, according to Heisenberg's Uncertainty Principle, the act of observing a thing changes the nature of what is observed. Observation, in some cosmic way, modifies reality. We do not directly oppose negativity or habituation within ourselves; we simply focus the beam of attention onto it and let the principle of light dispelling darkness do the rest. Attentive self-awareness, in this sense, is a universal solvent, the most powerful we have at our disposal.

As the Zen master Ikkyu said: Attention, attention, attention.

DEALING WITH REGRET

Reclaiming Our Right to Remorse

It was six o'clock in the evening, and David Hobler was driving to the Claremont Hotel to meet his uncle for dinner.

Feeling nervous, he stopped off at a package store to fortify himself with a beer and several premixed tequilas, then he drove straight to the hotel. "It was how I handled any social situation during those twelve drunken years, even one as simple as having dinner with my uncle," David told me in a phone conversation from his law office outside San Francisco. "Take a little false courage from the bottle, you know."

David Hobler's story is one of both triumph and regret. A highly successful defense attorney in headline homicide cases, David began drinking as a way to relax from professional pressures; then the drinking turned into a social crutch, and finally devolved into a physical disease.

"How I had attained all the dreams I could imagine," he told me, "and I was drinking peppermint schnapps at Husby's Tavern in Sister Bay at ten o'clock in the morning. I had come to think of drinking as a natural part of life, like paying a mortgage or having a family."

For several years David was in and out of recovery programs, but inevitably the pressures of a tense marriage and a demanding profession drew him back to alcohol. The situation darkened dramatically when his fifteen-year-old son, Kawika, was knocked off his bicycle by a car and left paralyzed from the hips down. Remaining by his son's bedside day and night in the recovery ward, David now began to rely on alcohol as an emotional analgesic as well as a social stimulant. The downward spiral accelerated.

Soon he was drinking alone in parking lots and at sporting events, or nodding off on a portable futon on the floor of his law office. Before long he found himself living alone, with a divorce winding its way through the legal process. "I kept telling myself that tomorrow was going to be better," David informed me. "Tomorrow was a new day. But, drink or no drink, tomorrow was always worse. More terrifying, because the relentless progression of alcoholism is so insidious, My reality was a living hell."

David finished his beer in the parking lot and walked to the hotel. His uncle was waiting for him in the lobby, fidgeting nervously with some papers.

"I sensed something was up when my uncle told me we had to run upstairs to his room for a minute. I didn't know what was going on. But something was about to happen. I could sense it. Like being asked to go to a strange new place."

They rode up in the elevator and walked down the hotel corridor in ominous silence. Outside the door of his uncle's room a stranger was waiting. She introduced herself as an "interventionist," then took David by the hand and led him through the door.

Inside, the room was filled with fourteen members of David's family who had come from all across the country, and who were waiting, as David described it, "in ambush." Most of them had been in San Francisco for at least a day or more comparing notes, conferring, and carefully scripting the things they wanted to say. In the group were David's mother and father, his estranged wife, two daughters, assorted sisters, cousins, and aunts, plus his nineteen-year-old son, Kawika, in a wheelchair.

For the next three hours each family member took turns saying their piece to David about his drinking, his reckless behavior, and the future consequences of his habit if he didn't get help. Some accused him. Some pleaded with him in tears. Some told long, painful stories of how his drunken behavior had sabotaged their lives.

Finally it was Kawika's turn. Moving easily now, a wheelchair athlete, he recalled how David had helped him through the nightmarish aftermath of the accident when the doctors announced he would never move the lower part of his body again. It was his father's inspiration, Kawika told everyone in the room, that had given him the courage to fight back, to go on with his life, to enter college and eventually become a U.S. Open Tennis Wheelchair Tournament champion.

Now he wanted to return the help. "You've been my recovery for three and a half years," Kawika told his father with tears in his eyes. "Now I'm going to be yours."

"When I heard my son talking this way," David said, "everything in me seemed to swell inside emotionally, then break like a dam and flow into every part of me. The arrow had struck its mark."

Later that evening several family members drove David to an alcoholic intervention center, where he remained for several months. He never took a drink again.

"Something happened in the intervention that's difficult to put into words," David told me. "The harsh things that were said to me and the praising things—both had their effect. For the first time I felt like I could let down my pretenses and be vulnerable. I had external permission to be the person my soul or essence had always told me I was supposed to be. I could finally admit to myself and others that I was bankrupt spiritually, an emotional wasteland. That I needed help."

But there was something else too. "Kawika's heart was the catalyst," David said. "His forgiveness relieved me of the crushing burden of condemnation. I no longer felt evil. He offered me a partnership and support as an ally. He knew the reality of disability, knew I was sick but not bad. His gifts were forgiveness, gratitude, and charity, and they turned me around that very moment.

"You know," David added, "if I had to sum up what happened to me in the hotel room that day I'd say I became repentant—I guess 'repentant' is the right word—for the destructive things I'd done to my family and others. It made me own up to the guilt I'd kept inside me all these years because of my addiction. The intervention permitted me to admit to myself, to others, and to my Creator that whereas I might not be responsible for having the disease, I was *totally* responsible for my own recovery, and for making amends."

As I listened to David tell his story, I was struck by his choice of certain words such as "repentance," "guilt," "amends."

These words had a strongly "Victorian" ring. Hearing them reminded me of how such notions as contrition and remorse, once so central to our Judeo-Christian sensibilities, have fallen out of fashion. I thought of how insistent so many members of the psychotherapeutic community are on relieving patients of their guilt feelings, even if these feelings happen to stem from genuinely unconscionable behavior; of how certain professionals work with an almost religious fervor at convincing patients of their blamelessness, without at the same time reminding them of their accountability.

Hearing these words also made me realize to what extent we are encouraged to avoid self-blame of any kind in other sectors of life and especially in our relationships; of how the right to feel shame and to perform expiation has been taken from us; and of how the relativistic ethic of "no blame, no shame" now rules as the undisputed standard of self-judgment. I thought of the motto at one time attributed to the Bank of England: "Never apologize, never explain."

Are we losing an essential part of our humanity, I wondered, when we eliminate concern with remorse? With apologizing and explaining? Do we harm our spiritual possibilities when we extol notions of soul development, but in the process overlook the Bible's warning to remember "from whence thou art fallen; and repent, and do the first works." To err is human, surely.

But it is also human to feel sorry for our erring. And it is human to experience the joy and relief that comes from paying off our moral debts.

We do not gain self-esteem, Christian texts remind us with special urgency, by telling ourselves how wonderful we are, or by soft-pedaling our misdeeds. We gain it by sincerely facing our flaws, correcting them as best we can, resolving with all our hearts to do better in the future, and putting our finest virtues of the soul into daily practice—unselfishness, generosity, kindness, patience, and love.

We gain real self-esteem, in other words, not by "getting comfortable with ourselves," or "becoming our own best friend," or any of these other trendy prescriptions. We gain it by *cultivating good character,* an obvious fact, perhaps, but one that has been largely tossed out with the bathwater in what Christopher Lasch referred to as our "Culture of Narcissism."

Some years ago I saw a cartoon in *The New Yorker* that seemed to sum it all up. The drawing shows an urbane devil greeting a group of new arrivals in hell. Looking them over with a TV announcer's smile, the infernal welcomer informs his cowering wards, "Down here, we just want you to know, there is no right or wrong; only what works for *you.*"

David Hobler's talk of repentance made me think of a memorable conversation I had some time ago with psychiatrist Robert Butler, one of the fathers of modern gerontology and the originator of life review—the practice of formally examining one's past and noting its patterns, trends, and lessons.

I talked with Dr. Butler in his office at Mount Sinai Hospital one rainy Saturday afternoon. Ruggedly handsome, in his late sixties, wearing a white doctor's gown, he looked every bit like a modern-day Dr. Marcus Welby. In our talk, I found it significant that he traced the origins for his ideas of life review not to psychiatry but to a spiritual encounter four decades earlier.

"When I was in Washington in the 1950s," Dr. Butler explained, "I had occasion to talk with the great Jewish philosopher Martin Buber about his idea of looking back over one's life and evaluating it; a concept I'd later call 'life review.' Buber emphasized that when looking back over your life you don't just pat yourself on the back and tell yourself, okay, I've gone over things, now everything's fine. No, there's a moral dimension to life review. You have to look evaluatively at yourself, your behavior, your guilt. You stand in judgment of the life you've led, and you admit where you've gone wrong as well as where you've gone right. It takes both sides, the dark and light, to make a life."

As with David Hobler's mention of the word "repentance," I was surprised to hear Dr. Butler invoking that most forbidden of all psychotherapeutic terms, "guilt." Erma Bombeck once described guilt as "the gift that just keeps giving." She was joking, of course, but there was method to her madness. Guilt *can* be a gift, if understood in the proper way. Spiritual traditions all agree that both guilt and regret play an indispensable role in our development as human beings. They help us to return to the path of conscience when we stray off course, and to pay our moral debts when we accrue them. Without these powerful self-correctives we become less than human.

"We can't really get away from guilt as we confront memories of the past with siblings and loved ones," Dr. Butler added. "Atonement, expiation, redemption, reconciliation, and the search for meaning are all powerful potential positive outcomes of looking back over our lives. It's necessary to explore our guilt, confess our wrongs, and not deny them. Also to experience atonement and reconciliation. Especially as we move into the middle and later years of our lives."

As if to underscore Dr. Butler's comments, soon after this conversation a colleague of mine shared with me a psychiatrist case history that was extraordinarily relevant. This history was related in strictest confidence, so I'll refer to the doctor in question with a pseudonym. Call him Dr. Mason.

"Not long ago," Dr. Mason revealed, "I treated a group of middle-aged Vietnam War veterans. All of them had tried to forget the horrors they'd seen in the jungles, and to get beyond their pain. Most of them couldn't do it. They were too deeply imprinted with post-traumatic stress disorder, with all the accompanying rage, anxiety, flashback experiences, and depression. The men who'd shot children or been forced to burn villages, that kind of thing, had the hardest time dealing with their past. Even though they had acted under unbearable mental duress during the pressures of a terrible war, they couldn't shake the memories of what they'd done.

"At first I treated these men in basically the same way," Dr. Mason explained. "By attempting to relieve their feelings of guilt. I tried to help them understand that what they'd done wasn't their fault, that they'd been under orders, that it was just what soldiers did over there at the time, that war is hell.

"This clinical strategy was perfectly correct by the book, I suppose. But after a while it became evident that my patients simply weren't responding. Some were even becoming more agitated—the treatment was stirring up repressed memories. So I decided to take a radically different tack."

As a boy, Dr. Mason had been brought up in the Catholic Church, and had gone to confession faithfully every week. Looking back, he recalled how cleansed and renewed he had felt after admitting his mistakes and performing the required expiation. He decided to try a version of this confessional-penitential approach on his Vietnam vets.

"My therapy began to focus on the hard realities," Dr. Mason explained. "Yes, you've committed a terrible act. To deny the seriousness of what you've done or to try to rationalize it away would be to make a mockery of your own inner feelings. It would also trivialize the pain suffered by the victims.

"Your feelings of remorse and anxiety, I explained to them, hurt terribly, I know. But these feelings offer a healing wisdom. If you listen to them in the right way they'll help you get better. They're telling you that even though you can't change things for the Vietnamese victims, you can make things different for yourself—by making amends."

Dr. Mason then sat down with each of the veterans and together they worked out a program of community service. One vet agreed to give his time to an agency that helped Indochinese refugees. Another performed volunteer work for an adoption agency that specialized in placing Asian babies. A third spent several evenings a week working with underprivileged teenagers. Other patients performed similar acts of atonement.

After a year, according to the doctor, the vets reported that the pain of their wartime experiences still haunted them. Most, however, felt that the quality of the suffering was now somehow different—that it had been transformed from a persistent psychic pressure into a strange, deeply sad sense of communion with their victims and a heightened feeling of connection with humanity at large. Several of the vets became religious as a result of these experiences.

"My colleagues would probably hound me out of the profession if they got wind that I'd used such unconventional methods," Dr. Mason said to me in a voice with a touch of sedition in it. "But if it works, well—then it works. What else can you say?"

What We Do for the One Person We Do for the Many

Some of us—maybe all of us at some moment in our lives—commit deeds that go beyond simple errors of judgment. We're talking about harmful things here, selfish things, sometimes immensely destructive things. Over time these acts tend to fester inside us. Until eventually they take on a heavy, sometimes unbearable weight, and we long to rid ourselves of the burden.

But how?

Traditional teachings and especially the Christian churches have always offered a clear-cut and unambiguous, if challenging solution.

First, we face the wrong things we have done in a direct and courageous way.

Second, we feel genuine compunction.

Third, we make amends in whatever ways we can.

Fourth, we look on this series of actions not as an isolated attempt at self-correction, but as an integral part of our devotional work. We make what might otherwise be a random struggle into a spiritual one.

The point is that repentance is not self-chastisement or self-abuse. It is not regret over things done and past that cannot be changed. In its truest form repentance is a kind of conversion or "turning," a starting again. First comes a self-cleansing, then a self-forgiveness, and finally a self-renewal. "Remember not the former things, nor consider the things of old," says Isaiah 43:18–19. "I am doing a new thing; now it springs forth, do you not perceive it?"

Here we take a lead from the famous 12 Step method originated by Alcoholics Anonymous.

Like David Hobler, recovering alcoholics are often deeply bothered by the wrongs they have committed in the past under the influence of drink. AA's remedy for such feelings is systematic and very direct: Turn to a Higher Power. Become sober. Admit your guilt. Review your errors. Make amends to the people you've hurt. Stay on the straight and narrow. Help others avoid similar mistakes.

Here in capsule form is an A-to-Z course in expiation, complete with spiritual guidance, practical action, and final resolve. What makes this 12 Step method so popular today is that its healing magic is universal: it works for all those who sincerely wish to repair their past and improve their future.

Step 8 in AA's 12 Step plan, for example, suggests that we "make a list of all persons we have harmed, and become willing to make amends to them all." This is tough love, all right, and a hard thing to do. But even if we succeed just a little, the effort generates deep healing.

Simply going through the motions of making amends is not enough, however. Amends must be made, AA insists, with heartfelt sincerity as an act of contrition before a Higher Power. Here Step 2 tells us that we must come "to believe that a Power greater than ourselves can restore us to sanity." Step 3 then advises: "Make a decision to turn our will and our lives over to the care of God *as we understand Him.*"

As people in all walks of life have discovered, AA's 12 Step methodology is powerful medicine for a multitude of emotional ailments, and many of the organizations that apply its principles have become wildly popular. In the shuffle, a number of self-help groups have lost sight of the original spiritual underpinnings from which the movement draws its force, substituting humanistic and even political morality in its place.

Within the organization of AA itself, however, the principles of admitting one's mistakes, turning to a Higher Power, taking moral inventory of past misdeeds, and making amends are still recognized as the wellsprings of self-healing, not only for alcoholism but for many other diseases of the soul—guilt and regret among them. Indeed AA's method, when properly applied, is universal, principally because it returns people to an archetypal truth that religion has always known: that the only lasting remedy to serious misdeeds is spiritual repentance, sincere reform, and service to others.

A folk story that has been told for many years and in many forms restates this philosophy in social terms. One day a high government official decides to abandon his career in government and become a monk. He visits a great spiritual master.

"If you wish to be my follower," the master informs him, "you must find every person you have ever seriously harmed and make amends."

The official bows and does exactly as directed.

Returning home, he reviews his life and attempts to recall every person he has ever wronged. He spends the next three years finding these people and making restitution. At the end of this time he has found all of them but one.

"But where is that one?" the master demands when the official returns to him.

"I do not know," the official replies with tears in his eyes. "I simply cannot find him."

"It is well," replies the master. "The amends you made for the others will serve for this missing person. What we do for one person we do for the many as well."

The master then accepts the official into his monastery. *"That which ye do unto the least of them ye do unto me."*

Recognizing False Regret

At some point in our adult lives, therefore, we must all look back at the unwise things we've done to ourselves and others, and feel a corresponding sense of chagrin. This is a right and necessary way to heal ourselves, and should—must—be part of everyone's spiritual journey. At times, however, it's also necessary to cope with a subtle variation on this theme: differentiating between real mistakes in the past and imaginary ones, and learning to give up the latter, just as we redress the former. For the fact is that we often feel regret when none is necessary; in fact, at times the things we regret most are the things that have helped us most.

What is this life about anyway? What should we feel good about in our past, what should we feel bad about? Are the mistakes we made in the past really mistakes—the ordinary "should haves" and "shouldn't haves" we torment ourselves with as we move into the second half of life? And what really constitutes a "mistake" anyway?

These questions have been asked throughout the ages, not only by philosophers but by writers and artists as well. Recall for a moment the character of George Bailey in the beloved 1940s motion picture *It's a Wonderful Life*. Besides serving as an affirmation of American values and a postwar catharsis, this seamless piece of filmmaking offers a finely woven meditation on misplaced regret.

George Bailey—played, we remember fondly, by Jimmy Stewart—is a paradigmatic midlife hero, an affable American Everyman who grows from childhood to youth to middle age before our eyes in the small town of Bedford Falls, Anywhere, U.S.A. Along the way we watch him become increasingly frustrated, then overwhelmed, by the struggles that life puts in his way. Everything George wants from his life—travel, money, a career as an architect—seems to elude him. Everything he touches seems to turn to sand.

Finally, frustrated and embittered, his life one massive regret, George Bailey drives his car one snowy Christmas Eve to a bridge outside of town and prepares to leap into the icy waters.

But all is not as it seems. Someone else leaps in first: his guardian angel, an elderly cherub named Clarence. When George saves him, then protests that the world would be a better place if he had never been born, he is sent back to a world where he was *literally* never born.

A weird version of an after-death experience now unfolds, granting George Bailey a view into the secret mechanisms that drive his existence; not as he imagines this existence to be, but as it really is from a providential point of view.

As George gazes down from his perch outside of time, many of his seemingly inconsequential deeds now reveal themselves as pivotal moments in his life and in the lives of many others. Such moments, we and George discover, spread out in ripple patterns of cause and effect across the ocean of time, generating far-reaching consequences that can only be seen, as it were, from above.

As a young boy, George remembers, he rescued his brother from drowning. His brother grew up to be a war hero and saved the lives of every soldier on a troopship. In a world where George does not exist, the only trace that now remains of his brother is an inscription on a tombstone. Since George was never born, his brother did not live. Neither did the hundreds of people on the transport ship.

On the dark streets of the town, George sees his wife walking home from her job as librarian. Without George she has become a withered spinster. The town pharmacist, Mr. Gower, makes his appearance as a drunken outcast; George was not alive to save him from accidentally poisoning a child. In another part of town George finds his mother, an angry hag running a fleabag boardinghouse. Violet, an ex-girlfriend, has become a prostitute; George was not there to help her. Indeed, the town itself is a neon-lit hellhole of striptease joints, honky-tonks, and pawnshops, all bankrolled by the evil miser, Mr. Potter. George, we realize, was not alive to stop him.

As our hero wanders the streets of this melancholy Sodom, the hidden meaning of his life is revealed to him through his very absence from it; and we, the audience, share in the revelations. Up till the time Clarence appears, George's life unfolds in seemingly random increments. We the audience, like George, cannot fully understand the meaning and connection of these separate events—taking over the family business, marrying, having children, helping friends, working for the community. All are seemingly "ordinary" occurrences, the same "ordinary" events that happen in our own lives—events that we perceive in isolation, separated from one another by stretches of time, clouded by memory. And so George, like us, does not perceive the gradual creation of the tapestry of life as it is woven by the Fates from the threads of his very deeds.

It is only when George is allowed to glimpse the pattern of his life as a complete panorama from beginning to end that these isolated actions add up, take on cohesion and meaning in one vast, breathtaking arabesque, becoming the chronicle not of regret but of a wonderful life.

"Strange, isn't it?" Clarence says to George, as George stares in horror at the wasteland created by his nonexistence. "Each man's life touches so many other lives. When he isn't around he leaves an awful hole." What George Bailey understands in this tremendous moment is akin to psychologist Erik Erikson's famous definition of "ego integrity" as ". . . the experience of one's one and only life cycle as something that had to be, that permitted of no substitutions."

In the end all is made well again. Brought back to the present, George is spiritually reborn and rescued from financial ruin by the grateful donations of friends and townspeople. He learns to treasure the preciousness of his life and sees that up till now he has had everything wrong. Once he assumed that without college and travel and all the accomplishments his imagination told him were so important, his life would have no real purpose. Now he discovers that things are just the opposite. It is because he did *not* travel and go to college, because he *did* stay home, because he *did* make sacrifices and work hard for others, that his existence takes on such a rich and abundant meaning. The very events George looked on regretfully as deprivations were, he now understands, essential elements of his Struggle, and stepping-stones toward fulfillment. Up till now George Bailey had, in short, seen everything upside down.

Why upside down? Because George has done nothing wrong. His regrets are regrets over the ordinary twists and turns on the road of life—events that cannot be changed, and that would not necessarily make life better if they *could* be changed. Unlike the legitimate misdeeds of Dr. Mason's vets, say, or of David Hobler's alcoholic past, George's actions call for no expiation or remorse. The "if onlys" and "what ifs" in George Bailey's life are actually blessings—blessings misunderstood.

In psychotherapeutic terms such "what if" scenarios are referred to as counterfactual thinking—that is, thinking about how much better life would be *if I had only . . .*

Only what?

Well, if only I'd gone to a different college. Or married a different person. Or not married at all. Or not gotten a divorce. Or pursued another career. If only I'd been a teacher instead of a lawyer; a lawyer instead of a teacher. If only I'd gone into business for myself rather than worked for the corporation; or worked for the corporation rather than gone into business for myself. If only I'd had children—or not had children; or had more children; or not had so many. If only I'd lived in France rather than Los Angeles; lived in the country rather than the city; had an inn in the mountains rather than a house in the suburbs.

We all write our own counterfactual scripts, and each person's list is unique. It is a totally human response to the thwartings and frustrations of life, the George Bailey in all of us. But it can also be insidiously and needlessly self-punishing.

"From the time I turned forty to around my fiftieth birthday," a woman told me, "I spent a big part of that ten-year period regretting everything you can think of, including the fact that I hadn't become religious at an earlier age. I regretted my marriage, how I raised my children—that they weren't brought up with a good Christian foundation. I regretted the kinds of friends I'd had. I regretted that I hadn't spent my money in the right way.

"One day I sort of 'snapped out of it' and realized that this business of regretting things that can't be helped is a waste of energy, and something that I'd—well—one day regret. What I mean is that this kind of breast beating is a stealer of time. Even if what you think you did was so bad, which it probably wasn't, you just have to leave it and go on. We have to learn to give ourselves a break."

"Retrospect is dangerous," a college professor told me. "Very risky. It's like looking through the wrong end of the telescope—things are distorted, you don't always see them accurately in hindsight. Our instinct is to see our past as flawed. Everybody wishes they had done more, or done certain things better. That's the lens effect. But it's hard to be objective about our past. Just because we want something today, and because we're a certain person today, we tinge our past with recriminations. What for? What are we doing to ourselves? We were a certain person then, and we're a certain person now. Why beat up on a self that has long since gone away? Seems to me the wiser course is to plunge ourselves into our lives wherever we find ourselves, and try to become better people."

Some years ago I found myself growing increasingly restless and dissatisfied with my work. If only I'd gone into such and such a field, I started telling myself with increasing frequency, I'd be doing what I *really* want to be doing today. Soon I found myself fantasizing about finding a new job, one that allowed me to be more creative, to travel more, to teach more, to be more myself.

Musing in this manner, I decided to write a page or two outlining my dream job. I worked at this description for more than an hour, then sat down to read my wish list with a combination of sadness for what I was missing and longing for an ideal I could never attain. About halfway down the page, I realized something peculiar was going on. By the time I'd finished it was obvious what the problem was.

What this dream job summary was describing, down to the smallest detail, *was the job I already had!* "My God!" I said to myself. "If I saw a job description like this in the want ads I'd be on the phone in a minute!" Here was the perfect example of false regret caught red-handed, and unmasked.

"None of us die," goes a Jewish proverb, "with even half our desires fulfilled." As we get older there is a growing tendency to torment ourselves with self-accusations and mea culpas. Usually these accusations come in the form of nostalgia, whispering frustrations, siren calls. One is tempted to think of Odysseus on his journey home from the Trojan wars, passing the island of the Sirens, who lure sailors to shipwreck and death with their irresistible song.

Like Odysseus, we too can willingly listen to the voices of the Sirens for at least a moment, understand their powerful but destructive attraction, and then sail on. Such clever navigation is an essential part of the struggle of mind and heart.

A story is told of two Zen monks on a pilgrimage to a distant monastery. Walking through the wilderness for many days, the monks arrive at a river. Here they see a beautiful young maiden standing by the water's edge.

"Excuse me," the woman says to the monks. "I don't know how to swim. Would one of you be kind enough to help me across?"

"Of course I will," says the first monk, and without hesitation picks the maiden up, carries her to the other side, and puts her down.

The two monks walk the rest of the day in silence, finally reaching a way stop at sunset. Here over their evening meal the second monk says to the first, "You know, the rules of our order forbid us to have any contact with women. It was wrong of you to talk to that young girl, let alone to pick her up and carry her."

"Oh, her," says the first monk. "I put her down back by the river. You've been carrying her all day long."

The degree to which we torment ourselves with needless anxieties over the past became apparent to me several years ago in what turned out to be a poignant lesson in false regret. The roots of the incident go back many decades, to my freshman year in high school. One morning early in the ninth grade term I was walking through the school corridors when a burly, crew-cut twelfth grader named Ed DeBono picked a fight. Before I knew it I was being shoved back and forth from one twelfth grader to the next pinball style and banged against the lockers. This ritual continued for four or five minutes until the class bell rang. At this point everyone dispersed, leaving me standing there alone, disoriented, and deeply, deeply humiliated.

From that day on I harbored a bundle of grudges and regrets toward Ed DeBono. Why hadn't I fought back? I asked myself a hundred times. Why hadn't I been tougher and braver? What could I do to pay him back?

I began to fantasize. I'd study judo. I'd join the boxing team. At night before I fell asleep I pictured myself shoving Ed DeBono into the locker just as he'd done to me. I imagined him flying through the air from one of my judo flips.

Fantasy followed fantasy. But I never did get up enough nerve to challenge him directly, and he graduated that same year.

It was all very typical, I suspect. Many people have similar tales from their school days. The problem was that this unresolved bit of grand opera did not stop at graduation. Even after I went on to college and graduate school, even after I was married and had children, the memory of this humiliating incident haunted me. I replayed it over in my mind a thousand times through the years, promising myself that one day I'd find Ed DeBono and settle the score. This fantasy, with innumerable variations on the theme, I blush to say, continued until I was into my forties.

Then one day I happened to visit my hometown on Long Island, and stopped by the barbershop in my old neighborhood.

The barber, an old man now, was delighted to catch me up on local happenings, and to reminisce about the past. I steered the conversation around to high school days, then asked if he happened to know what ever happened to Ed DeBono.

"You didn't hear?" the barber asked with genuine surprise.

I shook my head.

"Eddy was one of our first boys to get killed in Vietnam," he said. "Stepped on a land mine, got blown to bits. Never found most of his body."

I was dumbfounded. The moment I heard this grisly story something in me began to rearrange itself. A moment earlier Ed DeBono had been the target of my fascinated loathing. A moment later I was feeling deeply embarrassed and ashamed over my petty lust for revenge. For decades, it turned out, I had wasted my precious time harboring hostile fantasies for a man who was dead—who had *not existed* for twenty-five years!

How foolish I felt! How sheepish and silly! And how emblematic the situation seemed to be of the false-regret trap we so often fall into. Like George Bailey, I had seen everything upside down and so made my own hell. I had frittered away good hours, good days of my life, for an illusion, for a fantasy, for a nothing.

That was one side of it. On the other, here I was, alive, with arms and legs kicking, time behind me and time in front of me—time that Ed DeBono would never know. He, it turned out, had been the victim, not me.

Something in my heart mingled with his memory at this moment, and compassion arose. What had been a source of grudge and resentment for half of my life was suddenly transformed into a fountainhead of gratitude and grace.

We spend our lives feeling sorry for imaginary things. Things that never happened, that could never happen, and that might not have been good for us if they had—this, instead of being grateful for what life has put on our plate; this, instead of deriving the profound contentment that comes from being thankful for what the Sufis refer to as our "portion"; this, instead of receiving with open hands the raw materials of our lives, the good and bad alike, and welcoming both as part of our Struggle.

I thought back to another day when this same conflict between gratitude and regret had been an equally large issue. It was 1967, just outside of Wapakoneta, Ohio, where I was racing along in my new Corvair at seventy miles per hour traveling across the country. As I took a curve I suddenly heard a loud clanking noise in the bottom of the car. The Corvair began to shimmy and vibrate, and I lost control. The car made a terrifying scraping noise as it slowed to a stop a foot or two short of a steep embankment by the side of the road.

Safe, but with a ruined vehicle on my hands and no tow truck in sight, I climbed out and gave my car the once-over. Sure enough, the rear axle had spontaneously snapped apart, just as Ralph Nader warned it would on all Corvairs that year (I had even read his book *Unsafe at Any Speed*).

I stood by the ruin of my automobile experiencing the usual emotions one feels in such situations: anger, self-pity, helplessness, regret that I'd bought the wrong car.

Then a little voice from the nether regions of my consciousness piped up: "But you're *alive!*" And still in one piece, what's more, with my Corvair obligingly perched on the edge of a cliff that would have made a sandwich of me if the car had skidded two more feet to the right.

Me: alive. And utterly thankless for the fact.

At this moment of recognition everything changed, just as it changed the moment I heard the news of Ed DeBono. The anger over the car wreck was suddenly transformed into feelings of safety and escape; what seemed like a calamity became a deliverance.

I realized at this moment that the antidote for my blasé disregard of the miracle that had just taken place, and for my petty regrets in general, was in the final count a simple one: gratitude for what I had, in this case my very life; this, instead of regret for what might have been, but which in fact could never be.

These are the lessons I learned from my Corvair that day, and that Ed DeBono taught me all the way from the grave. Like the worried Zen monk by the river, I was carrying a useless piece of the past around on my back. At any moment I was free to put this burden down. But I was the one who had to take the initiative; the decision was in my hands. I could make my life a nightmare of false regrets or a psalm of thanksgiving, depending on how I wished to look at things.

The choice was mine.

In the end, the struggle of mind and heart comes down to a small margin of choice. If the truth be told, we don't really govern many of the forces that shape our existence. None of us really have all that much personal power, despite the myths of "being in control" so dear to the hearts of so many in our society. If we are honest, and if we look back at the past with an impartial eye, it's clear that most of the fundamental circumstances that order our lives are out of our hands. We don't pick our parents. We don't choose our bodies, our talents, our temperament, or most of the other seminal elements that determine our fates.

What we *do* choose, especially as we increase in wisdom and years, is the way we approach the circumstances of our lives. Either we jettison the things that are no longer useful for our journey toward the light or we live in a world of "might have beens." Either we enter the fray and fight the good fight of mind and heart or we don't, and things will remain as they've always been and nothing will change. "Tell me what you want," said Chekhov, "and I will tell you what you are."

The wise have said that we repair the past and prepare for the future by living in the present. A committed contemplative regimen is what matters now: cultivate attention and mindfulness; give up what has to be given up, prune what has to be pruned, strive without embarrassment or apology to be virtuous; be discerning, choose wisely, struggle; and eventually you will surely find the means you need to live each day in the way you were meant to live it, and to become the person you were meant to be.

Herein lies the ultimate struggle of mind and heart. It is a choice that we can make, and it is the only choice that matters.

And that choice is ours.

chapter 6

The Struggle
and Spiritual Practice

"Even if it were a question of my head being cut off and the brain
removed, or my belly being ripped open and my heart cut out, or
any kind of transference or transformation, I would take on the job
at once," said Monkey. "But if it comes to sitting still and
meditating, I am bound to come off badly. It's quite against my
nature to sit still."

"MONKEY," Chinese folktale,
translated by Arthur Waley

Pray to Him in any way you like. He is there to hear you, for He
can hear even the footfall of an ant.

SRI RAMAKRISHNA

THE STRUGGLE AND SPIRITUAL PRACTICE

The Pinnacle of the Soul's Cathedral

In the town of Wakamatsu, a Japanese story tells, there lives a young Samurai
soldier named Zenkai who spends his time gambling and carousing. One day
Zenkai falls in love with the wife of a local magistrate, and the wicked woman
begs him to murder her husband and take his money.

Zenkai agrees.

On his way to commit the crime he passes an old Zen priest who looks at him in a sadly disapproving way. Disregarding the feelings this encounter awakens in his heart, Zenkai continues on. Reaching the house of the magistrate, he slits the man's throat, empties his money box, and together he and the magistrate's wife flee to another province.

No sooner do the couple settle down than Zenkai becomes disgusted with himself for what he has done, and sick of the woman; she is vain and greedy. What's more, Zenkai cannot get the memory of the Zen priest out of his mind.

One night he slips away, leaving the woman all his possessions, and sets out to find the priest. After many adventures he locates this mysterious presence high in a mountain monastery. Zenkai comes before him, admits his crimes, and begs to become his disciple.

For fifteen years Zenkai remains with the Zen master, meditating, studying the sutras, and attaining moments of enlightenment. During this time, however, he is never fully able to rid himself of the shame he feels for killing an innocent man. Finally one day the old priest calls him to his quarters. Before Zenkai can attain full enlightenment, the master says, he must find a way to make amends for the crime he committed as a youth.

Zenkai obediently leaves the monastery and wanders through the neighboring countryside, searching for an opportunity to atone for his misdeeds.

One day while climbing a mountain pass an idea comes to him. The trail is extremely narrow in this place, and through the years many people have fallen to their deaths. Zenkai decides to settle down in this wild part of the country and dig a tunnel through the mountainside so that travelers will no longer be endangered.

For twenty-five years the aging Samurai works night and day burrowing a passageway through the mountain, removing shovelful after shovelful until three-quarters of the tunnel is complete. Every night he then sits for many hours in silent meditation. In the process his enlightenment deepens and matures.

One day a young soldier arrives at Zenkai's hut and identifies himself as the son of the magistrate Zenkai killed many years before. The youth has come, he announces, to take his revenge.

"My life means little," Zenkai replies. "But I have been working at this tunnel for many years now, and am close to the end. Let me finish it. Then you may cut off my head."

Sensing Zenkai's sincerity, the young man agrees and pitches his tent near the hut. For the next few months he watches the aging warrior dig and shovel tirelessly. Finally the young man joins in.

Three years pass in this way. The two men work side by side, sharing their food, their possessions, their labor and meditations. At the end of this time the tunnel is complete.

"Now," Zenkai says, presenting himself to the son of the man he murdered so many years ago. "You may kill me. My work is done."

"How can I kill my teacher?" the young man replies with tears in his eyes. "How can I kill the man who has enlightened me?"

When I first heard this story from a Buddhist monk at a Zen center in New York City, it made a profound impression on me. As the years have passed, its impact has grown rather than dimmed—which is, after all, what a well-told wisdom story is designed to do.

What is it that so touched me in Zenkai's tale?

Many things, but particularly its portrayal of that most fundamental of human dramas, fall, expiation, and redemption. The story of Zenkai is the story of every human soul.

But there's also something else about this tale that captures my imagination: the high-intensity profile it provides of the spiritual Struggle itself.

In the beginning Zenkai's turmoil is psychological and emotional. Haunted by his past and conscience-stricken for what he has done, he becomes a monk.

But escape and seclusion are not enough. Even the investiture of holy robes cannot dissolve his regrets. To become free of his past, Zenkai must take his spiritual practice into the field, to the level of sweat and toil, making reparations in a physical way as well as a moral and spiritual one.

Finally, overarching these two levels of effort, comes the third and most central part of his Struggle, *spiritual* practice: meditation, contemplative study, prayer—our "work and regency," as Christian monks call it. This last element of the Struggle is made up of:

1. Faith and belief
2. Service to others
3. Prayer, meditation, and spiritual method

Let's begin at the beginning: with faith.

1. THE STRUGGLE OF FAITH AND DOUBT

The Will to Believe

As our boat chugs up the river of time, many of us reach a place in life where we sincerely wish to believe in something greater than ourselves. Basically we *yearn* to believe; it is human instinct. If we don't fill this need by honoring a Higher Power, then we invest it in another passion, in politics or art, in our profession, in basketball or love—*in something*, as long as it fills the need for faith inside us. We are all born to believe.

Certainly few words have been bandied around by religious and non-religious people alike as much as "faith." Have faith in the process, one person says. Keep the faith, baby, says another. "One by one, like leaves from a tree, all my faiths have forsaken me," Sara Teasdale writes, voicing an especially middle-aged sentiment. "Faith is believing what you know ain't so," says Mark Twain.

All in all, the most common use of the word "faith" is probably in a religious context. Yet even devout believers sometimes wonder: Why must I blindly believe. Why must I trust?

"I'd rather start with doubt," a friend of mine told me, "and work my way up from there."

If we've come this far, and if we find ourselves engaged in a spiritual Struggle of some kind, we must believe in *something*. Why else would we make these efforts? At times it's difficult to pinpoint exactly what we believe. But then, there's *something*, some presence deep in our blood that keeps calling, keeps whispering instructions we can't entirely make out, hinting that the only road to self-contentment is through the very things we can't see or define; something, as a master remarked, that "won't leave us to our dreams and let us sleep in peace."

The Magic Ring

A number of summers ago my family and the Stoner family—Marjorie Stoner, Phil Stoner, and their two children—arranged to meet at a guest lodge in the upper Lake George region of New York State. We would rendez-vous at the lodge during the last week of August, it was agreed, enjoy a few days of boating and fishing, then drive up to Montreal for some sightseeing before going our separate ways.

Late August rolled around, and our family made the four-hour drive upstate. When we arrived at the lodge the Stoners were nowhere in sight. I went to check in at the desk, where I was given a message to call Phil immediately.

The Stoner family, it turned out, would not be joining us, now or ever. A few days earlier, I learned, Marjorie and Phil had had a catastrophic argument with ultimatums issued on both sides, followed by a decision to separate.

Phil, a devout Christian, could not tolerate the idea of being married to a woman who no longer shared his religious beliefs. Marjorie could no longer put up with a husband who was "strangling" her with his religious ideals. Just around the time we were all supposed to be meeting at the lodge, I learned, Marjorie was moving out of the house with the two children. As far as both of them were concerned, the marriage was over.

But it wasn't to be this simple.

I first met Phil Stoner on one of my many business trips to Albany in the 1970s. Phil and I kept crossing paths at meetings and conferences—he worked for the state government—and finally we became friendly.

One day Phil invited me to his home for dinner, and here I met his wife, Marjorie, a woman in her early thirties who was just finishing up a long-delayed senior year in college with high honors in pre-law.

I asked where she planned to go to law school. "I won't apply for a while," she answered in a quiet way. "Phil and I have talked about it. We feel the children need me too much right now."

I visited the Stoners over the next seven or eight years on many occasions. I appreciated Phil's good humor, Marjorie's gentle intelligence, and I felt comfortable in their peaceful, orderly home. As a couple, they tended to be undemonstrative, but I sensed a bedrock of respect, if not affection, beneath their coolness. Both were also regular churchgoers and members of a local Christian prayer group. Between them Phil was clearly the more dedicated. This prayer group, I discovered, had innumerable rules, and Marjorie and Phil went to great lengths to obey them all.

From the start there was something mysterious about Marjorie. Her serene and disciplined presence, I felt, concealed currents of frustration below the surface that I could sense but not see; a purity leavened with a streak of earthiness and secret, perhaps impulsive dreams. She was sincerely religious, like Phil, but her sensibilities seemed colored with a closet skepticism that came out in her tone of voice and in her body language. When Phil talked about religion, her eyes glazed over. When she talked about her church group, a certain flat tone of voice gave her away.

Marjorie Stoner was, in short, a complex person, one of those people you liked instantly, yet whom you felt was carrying a burden she wanted you to know about but in the end would never reveal.

After their separation I didn't see Phil or Marjorie for almost a year. Finally Phil brought me up to date one day at lunch.

Marjorie, I learned, was living in a rented house just outside Albany, and Phil was making regular weekend visits to take the children. After a few false starts, Marjorie had landed a high-paying job as a legal secretary, and was seriously thinking of going to law school. Despite Phil's entreaties, she refused to give their marriage a second try.

I also learned that Marjorie had renounced their prayer group and had turned her back on Christianity. Throughout the time of their separation, there was never talk of divorce on either side. From Marjorie's standpoint it would be too painful for the children. For Phil it was a sin.

At the end of a two-year period I was amazed and frankly a little shocked to get a call from Phil. He and Marjorie were back together. Would I come up and visit?

It was with mixed emotions that I made the trip. Could a marriage really work after being rent asunder so completely? And over such fundamental issues? With Phil still devoted to his church group, what chance would they have of a happy reconciliation?

My first visit to the Stoner house was brief and rather awkward. Phil and Marjorie were both overpolite, not only with me but with each other. All night long the conversation felt forced and was clumsily steered away from any mention of the past. My worst suspicions were confirmed. In the year that followed I then made several more trips to their home, and lo and behold, at each visit the atmosphere seemed to lighten. By the third or fourth trip Phil and Marjorie seemed far happier and freer with each other than I had ever seen them before. What could have caused such a turnaround?

Marjorie brought up the subject at the dinner table one night, and quite unembarrassedly discussed the events that had led to their breakup. To an onlooker her loss of faith might seem like a sudden impulse, she explained. But internally her doubts had grown out of deep and ancient issues: the crisis of authority, the coming of age, and the quest to discover what spiritual belief really meant in her own life.

"It started around the time I turned forty," she told me. "A couple of weeks before my birthday my mother called and said she had a wonderful birthday surprise. Could I come over right away?

"When I got there my mother greeted me in a strangely formal way and ushered me inside, where she sat me down and held out her hand. She pointed to the emerald ring on her finger.

" 'It's yours now,' she said proudly. 'I wanted you to have it for your fortieth.'

"It was *the* ring. The one I'd loved and yearned for all my life. It had once belonged to my grandmother, and I remember playing with it on my mother's hand when I was a little girl. I used to ask my mother all the time if she'd give it to me someday, and she was always evasive. Now here she was slipping it on my finger. You'd think I would have been deliriously happy. But it actually had the opposite effect. Because of something I could never have foreseen."

While Marjorie talked, Phil was in the kitchen washing the dishes, well within earshot. I was amazed that they were both willing to talk so openly about such a delicate subject. Something had clearly changed between them.

Marjorie held out her hand with the ring on it and kept it extended as she talked.

"You see, when my mother held her hand out to show me the ring I didn't see the ring at all. The only thing I saw was *her hand*. It was all gnarled up with arthritis, worse than I had ever seen it before, like old tree roots. Suddenly I thought: Oh my God, my hands are going to look like this someday! I saw myself reflected in those hands, you know, like I was looking into a mirror. There I was thirty years from now, gnarled, broken down, old."

As she stared at her mother's hands an even more forbidden thought passed through Marjorie's mind. "What good will my religious beliefs do me then?" she asked herself. "How will they stop me from getting old and twisted up like this?"

Marjorie's mother was a formidable presence; I had met her several times at dinner. A successful buyer at a department store in an era when women had few career options, she had been driven into business partly from ambition, partly to survive. Her husband had deserted her shortly after she was diagnosed with multiple sclerosis, a diagnosis that, ironically, turned out to be incorrect. From this time on, Marjorie's mother became the dominant figure in Marjorie's life.

"My mother is a great woman," Marjorie continued. "But she's also very strong and domineering. The main thing I wanted when I was a child was be a Miss Perfect so I could please her."

Then Marjorie married Phil, and he took over the reins. "He was a fantastic guy, of course," Marjorie said, smiling at Phil in the kitchen. "But he had a lot of set opinions about how things should be. It got so I felt he was trying to pour me into his mold of Miss Perfect Little Christian Wife. I went along with it as usual, the way I did with my mother. But the anger was building up.

"Then came the prayer group with its endless lists of dos and don'ts. At first I was convinced I'd found the certainty I was looking for. I admired our leader's confidence, and I knew that Phil was deeply committed. The confidence of both these men made everything seem certain to me. That's what I thought it meant to have the Holy Spirit: never having to doubt anything."

And so Marjorie went along with the schedule. But in her mind, as she described it, she was confusing religious faith with the acceptance of human authority and with never having to question anything. "I thought I had faith," she said. "But all I really had was dependency."

Then Marjorie's mother slid the ancestral ring on her hand that fateful day and something snapped. The ring had a strange potency, it seemed, like the magic ring in a fairy tale. It marked a turning point, empowering her in a way she still does not understand to this day.

"It was a couple of weeks after my mother gave it to me," she explained. "I was in my room praying one night. I raised my hands in supplication and noticed the ring on my finger. For a minute it seemed to kind of flash, to send out rays. Then the same sensation came over me I'd felt staring at my mother's hands. I said to myself: 'What am I doing this for? I don't believe any of this stuff the group tells me! I'm almost forty years old. I don't want to be a puppet anymore!'

"So I stopped praying, got up off my knees, and walked downstairs."

A week later Marjorie and Phil separated.

"I had made a lifetime deal with myself," Marjorie went on. "Trust the authorities in charge and believe implicitly in what they tell you. Then everything will be okay. It didn't matter whether it was my mother, my husband, my church—just trust, follow, obey. Blind faith across the board. Now I was a big girl and I realized the deal wasn't working. Maybe it never had."

Making the Covert Bargain

Marjorie's description touched on a familiar motif, variations of which we have met throughout this book. As psychoanalyst Roger Gould has pointed out, many of us go through life relying on a covert and often unconscious bargain that we made with life early on. If I obey the rules, the bargain goes, if I'm a good person and do everything that life requires of me, then life will treat me fairly and squarely.

This is what some of us come to call faith.

Then one day the grown-up realities hit, and with them comes a withering of the dream. Suddenly we understand that our bargain with life has been based more on wish fulfillment and the need for security than on any heavenly guarantees. We realize that the agreement we made with life was really just an attempt to manipulate reality, an attempt at striking a "you scratch my back, I'll scratch your back" deal with Providence. Unfortunately, the contract was signed by only one party—ourselves.

It's at this moment that we begin to see that what we've called faith is not faith at all; that our bargain is really a self-serving contract the ego makes with itself to protect itself. Harvard psychologist Gordon Allport suggests that in order to be truly mature, religious sentiment must first be "fashioned in the workshop of doubt." Without questioning and testing, Allport insists, people remain stuck in a mechanical form of belief that often imprisons them for life. "The route to an intrinsic religious orientation is by way of a 'dark night of the soul,' " writes Eugene Thomas, professor of human development at the University of Connecticut, "in which original convictions are subjected to doubt and skepticism. The resulting faith is no longer made up of one's inherited religious beliefs and parental values, but consists of one's personally embraced beliefs and convictions, a basic component of one's 'ego identity.' "

The combination of sudden doubt conjoined with the shock of recognizing that her faith was not faith at all, was the ghost that frightened Marjorie out of the closet and caused her to Search for a more authentic spiritual and personal identity.

For the next two years as a single woman, Marjorie told me, a battle raged inside her.

In the beginning she followed a predictably self-effacing course, taking low-paying clerical jobs, and even working as a salesperson in a bakery. But the longer she was on her own, the more she began to recognize her abilities.

This realization came both from a growing self-knowledge and from feedback she received from others. "People responded to me now as if I were a thoroughbred grown-up," Marjorie said. "As if I were an intelligent and resourceful person capable of doing interesting and original things. Maybe even wonderful things."

Eventually she found a job in a major Albany law office and began to entertain thoughts of law school.

In her interior life, meanwhile, Marjorie at first tried to run from anything that smacked of religion. She worked at convincing herself that she was really just a scoffer, an escapee from the ball and chain of dogma. She no longer went to church. She stopped her prayers. She even subscribed to a journal for atheists.

But it didn't work. Despite herself, she was a genuinely religious person. "I *did* believe," she told me. "That was the problem. I just didn't know in what, or why, or how."

After giving up on her attempts at nihilism, she decided to investigate other spiritual paths. On nights when Phil took the children she would launch herself into a Search, visiting every kind of religious group she could find and participating in a wide range of workshops and gatherings. Along the way she had several silly and unpleasant encounters, a few that were meaningful, and one that changed her life.

"It was at an all-day retreat in a loft in Troy," Marjorie said. "A nondenominational kind of thing, no particular religious affiliation. The session was run by an Episcopal priest and a Spanish woman who claimed to be a shaman. The idea was to meditate for an entire day from nine in the morning till nine at night with only a few breaks to stretch our legs and eat a meal. It was a lot like other meditation programs I'd been to. Except that it lasted so long.

"During the retreat nothing much happened. I got through it, that was about all. But later on at home that night I began to get really psyched up and couldn't sleep. I started to have funny thoughts. If I don't have any faith, I asked myself, why did I just sit there in that hot, smelly loft for twelve straight hours trying to talk to God? Am I crazy? Is this the way a person acts who doesn't have faith? Heavens no, this is quite the opposite. This is the way a fanatic acts!

"Then what *is* faith? I wanted to know. If I have faith, why do I also have so many doubts? What do I really believe in? What, what, what!

"I opened the front door and walked outside. It was a clear night. You could see a whole lot of stars overhead. Slowly a very quiet sensation began to creep over me. I started to feel a peace like I'd never known—real peace, I mean, not just a momentary lull. Everything in my body let go and sort of melted. It was almost like I was falling asleep, except that I felt extremely alert. At that moment I knew—no longer wanted to know, but *knew*—that God is real, and that He is always with me, watching over me, taking care of things. I just knew it. I don't know how I knew, or why I knew, but I knew.

"All this was fantastic. But here's the main thing. After a few minutes I went back inside and started to come down. Before long I was normal again. The absolute certainty I'd felt was gone. And that's when I realized what faith is."

Phil had stopped washing the dishes in the kitchen and was watching Marjorie across the room with loving eyes. I waited. It was as if she were waiting for something too. I urged her to go on.

"Faith isn't really a mental belief," she said. *"It's a state of consciousness.* It's a condition that comes to you like grace after you've struggled for a while. It's not something you automatically get. That's why I needed to go through everything I did up to that moment. I had to pay the price of admission."

Doubt and Faith

"The price of admission"—"a state of consciousness"—here was a changed Marjorie Stoner indeed.

Her words confirmed the point that real faith is not a birthright or a given, but a kind of reward. We don't need to have enormous amounts of it to begin traveling the Stages of the Soul. A small, persistent intuition is enough. "Nothing will ever be attempted," Dr. Samuel Johnson once remarked, "if all possible objections must first be overcome."

Marjorie's crisis of faith, it was clear in retrospect, was not based on any deep loss of personal conviction, or on the fact that her husband and her prayer group had feet of clay. It was galvanized by the realization that everything she had believed up to this point in her life was a mere mental construct, a collection of reassuring thoughts and ideas that supported her dependency neuroses, but that did not reach to the deepest levels of her heart and soul. Unlike true faith, which, as the great Hindu saint Ramakrishna once remarked, "is like a child calling for its mother in the night," faith for

Marjorie had been both a theoretical concept and a psychological fulcrum which she had used to shoehorn herself into the passive position her upbringing had taught her was so necessary.

What Marjorie had called faith up to that time was actually an obstacle on her path rather than an aid. Later on, when the "state of consciousness" burst on her that night under the stars, she understood that faith is more than simple hope or comfortable feelings of sanctuary. It is palpable knowledge, literally an organ of inner perception; with it she received a taste, an aroma, of her own spiritual possibilities.

Marjorie's experience is not a unique one, of course. Variations on her theme are cited in psychotherapeutic literature as examples of what is termed "transitional faith." James Fowler has perhaps done the most to identify and map these levels of what he calls "faith development" as it evolves over time toward its full maturity in a spiritually oriented person. Fowler charts the growth of individual belief through ascending levels, starting with childish literalism and extending to universal faith.

A recent study done to determine ways in which ninety-two terminal cancer patients and their spouses cope with the stresses of illness gives empirical corroboration to Fowler's ideas. This study determined that subjects who embody a more mature stage of faith, as measured against Fowler's categories, demonstrate a higher overall "quality of life" count in most essential areas. Other studies, including cross-cultural investigations by my colleague Eugene Thomas, reach the same conclusion, that persons with a deeper and more mature level of belief fare better in times of crisis than those with a rote, dogma-driven faith.

Philosopher Miguel de Unamuno once remarked that those who believe in God but who do so without anguish, uncertainty, or doubt, actually believe only in "the idea of God, not in God Himself." In truth it is our doubts, not our beliefs, that inspire us to go beyond rote acceptance and comfortable conformity. It is our doubts that prevent us from accepting half-truths and safe havens of security, as in the case of Marjorie Stoner. Doubts make us question and search; they force us out of bed and into battle; they refuse to let us sleep. Without them to stir the human mixture, real faith can never rise to the top.

This is perhaps the most important lesson Marjorie learned throughout her long dark—and light—night of the soul: that Struggle does not mean eliminating doubts. It means facing them, allowing them their place, occasionally embracing them, and realizing that when viewed correctly they point to the place where true faith lies. Ironically, it was only when Marjorie Stoner was able to turn her back on what she believed that her real spiritual work began.

I asked Marjorie if she had ever again experienced the same state of faith and certainty that visited her that night under the stars.

"No, I haven't," she replied. "But I don't feel deprived. I know it will happen someday again."

Marjorie looked over at Phil. "And I really don't think it matters what vineyard a person labors in to do this work—Christian, Jew, yoga, shaman, I don't know. You just have to do the work, that's all. After you've labored for a while, the vineyard Master comes over to you, places a hand on your shoulder, and says, 'Well done, good and faithful servant.' And then the vineyard Master gives you faith."

Now in her last year at law school, working hard to find herself both inside and out, Marjorie Stoner is still seeking. She hasn't ruled out Christianity or any other spiritual possibility. On the other hand, she doesn't know if she will ever again settle on a single belief.

And this is okay as far as Phil is concerned. Just as Marjorie's Struggle taught her to redefine faith, so Phil's gave him the tolerance to allow others to follow their own course.

"I feel like I'm wandering," Marjorie told me the last time we met, "I don't know where I'll end up. I have the prospect of a career to anchor me, and in some way it has anchored my believing life too."

"What about your doubts now?" I asked.

Marjorie gave a happy laugh. "Doubts. Faith. They work together, you know, one with the other. I have a suspicion that they're really two sides of the same coin."

2. STRUGGLE AND
THE PATH OF SERVICE

Just Grooving

I hurriedly took a seat among the 1,400 people in New York City's Ramada Hotel ballroom. Many of the most prominent scholars in the field of spirituality and life span psychology were here. The occasion was the first Conscious Aging Conference of the Omega Institute.

As I sat there listening to the greetings from the host, Omega's founder, Pir Vilayat Khan, I became aware of a balding, gray-haired man sitting next to me, taking notes at a furious pace. Since the first speech had not officially begun, I was intrigued. What was he writing about?

Then I glanced at him again. There was something familiar in the round lines of his face and the peering look in his eyes. I couldn't place who he was, but I knew he was *someone*.

Then it came to me.

I remembered a brisk spring day back in 1967. I was a senior at Yale living in New York's East Village doing fieldwork on the culture of psychedelic drugs. It was here that I first saw this man. He was standing in front of a store called the Head Shop (the first store to carry this name) chatting with a group of admiring young people. The windows of the Head Shop were adorned with water pipes, cigarette papers, posters of caterpillars smoking hashish and Allen Ginsberg levitating on a cloud of marijuana smoke. But this man seemed unconcerned with such trappings as he discoursed messianically to the young people on dropping out of the "robot culture" and on eternity in a grain of sand.

Now, several decades later at a conference on aging, I was sitting next to the same man, Baba Ram Dass, formerly Richard Alpert, the onetime Harvard professor who, along with the late Timothy Leary, achieved both celebrity and notoriety in the 1960s for his sponsorship of Oriental spirituality and psychedelic drugs.

As it turned out, Ram Dass and I would eventually become personally acquainted and would cross paths many times in the future. Today, however, I was just a listener and he was a guest speaker; the notes he had been penning so frantically were notes for his own lecture.

When it came time for him to take the stage, Ram Dass's speech did not center on the usual aging issues. He talked in more personal terms, specifically about his deceased father, George Alpert, former president of the New Haven Railroad, and a dyed-in-the-wool old-line Western capitalist.

This archconservative representative of a bygone era, explained Ram Dass to the audience, was both perplexed and dismayed by his son's implacably unconventional career: fired from a promising professorship at Harvard for giving LSD to students, then a champion of Flower Power and the counterculture, and finally a spokesman for mysticism and Eastern religion. Even Ram Dass's Hindu name was a thorn in the old man's side, and he quickly gave it his typically acerbic spin, referring to his son every chance he got as "Rum Dumb."

In short, Ram Dass told us, it would be difficult to imagine two more different human beings: one a pillar of conformity and the business world, the other a Hindu New Age renegade. As might be expected, the twain did not meet.

Then one day fate took an ironic twist: Ram Dass's father became chronically ill, and there was nobody in the family to take care of him except his son—Rum Dumb.

This situation put Ram Dass into a quandary.

This man *was* his father, he told himself. As someone who purported to talk the spiritual talk, perhaps it was time for Ram Dass to walk the spiritual walk. The hour of reckoning had come.

So Ram Dass made a decision: he would dedicate himself to the care of his estranged parent, not so much out of affection as from a sense of filial responsibility and spiritual service.

Years passed, Ram Dass told us, and he was as good as his word. The thing was, though, the more time Ram Dass spent washing and feeding and caring for the old man, the more he began to see him in a different light. As his father grew increasingly feeble, the inner light that his social manners and worldly concerns had hidden so well now began to shine out.

Ram Dass, on his part, became more open, more sonlike and affectionate. Eventually a bond formed between the two men that transcended both love and hate, a bond based on an almost cosmic tranquillity and unspoken bliss. At times father and son became one.

"I had an extraordinary image of aging when I was taking care of my father," Ram Dass told the audience that day. "Over the years my father had been very active in the political and social realms, very successful and busy in the world. But as he got older, during the last three years of his life—he died at ninety—he turned very quiet inside. He'd just smile a lot and not speak. I used to sit with him and hold his hand, and we'd look at the sunsets together. We'd never done anything like that in all our lives. Not only because we didn't get along. But because both of us were always so busy. Now we could take the time; we could meld."

One day a relative came to visit the Alpert home. Ram Dass's father had never liked this person. When the relative greeted him, George Alpert's only response was to smile. The relative stormed out of the room. "That bastard!" he said. "He still won't talk to me."

Later Ram Dass's aunt came visiting. She and the father had always been close. But when she greeted the old man he smiled in the same way and remained silent. The aunt was reduced to tears. "Poor George," she said, "what have they done to you? Where are you? You've gone away."

"But he hadn't gone away at all," Ram Dass told the audience with a mischievous smile. "He was right there all the time, grooving. It was all the same to him now, love and hate, enemy and friend—all the same. There he was, there I was, both in ecstasy together, just sitting and smiling, watching it all go by with dispassion. We were totally at peace. When I looked at him it was like looking at the Buddha."

The efforts that Ram Dass made to take care of his dying father, he told the audience that day in closing, were in reality also the efforts he made on his own spiritual behalf. That's the secret of service, he said—that which we do for others we really do for ourselves.

What We Do for Others
We Do for Ourselves

A recent study examined the lives of sixty-five men and women between the ages of thirty and ninety, all of whom were caring for a loved one suffering from advanced cancer. Respondents were given a battery of tests designed to probe for cognitive uncertainty and a sense of meaning in life (titled by the investigators "purpose in life").

Results showed that people who dedicate themselves to caring for a loved one not only gain a stronger sense of purpose in life but, interestingly, tend to have better physical health in the process. There is, the study suggests, a positive correlation between helping another and helping oneself.

Unlike Ram Dass, I have never taken care of an ailing parent. My mother and father are still alive and in good health. Yet in the past I've had the benefit of a similar education.

My lessons in caregiving as an aid in the spiritual Struggle began not long after my wife and I returned from a sabbatical in California in 1985. At the time we had already known our friend Larry Morris for more than twenty years. Widowed for a second time, Larry had recently relocated to our area outside New York City and was a frequent guest at our house for dinner.

In his heyday Larry Morris had been a formidable intellectual and spiritual presence. A longtime student of comparative mysticism, he was one of the last living souls on earth to have personally known Gurdjieff, Ouspensky, and A. E. Orage. During World War I he drove an ambulance at the front lines, and later served on the staff of *The New Republic*. In the years that followed he was an official in the Federal Writers' Project under Roosevelt, then Chief Cultural Attaché for the State Department in both France and Brazil. Now, at age ninety, his mind remained sharp and brilliant, his body strong and vigorous.

Yet we worried. Larry's eyesight was declining slowly but surely, and he was beginning to limp, the result of a joint condition for which the diagnosis was uncertain. My wife and I fell into the habit of checking on him in his apartment every few days and regularly bringing him dinner. He was always grateful for our company, and as usual held us spellbound with his conversation and spiritual insights. The bond between us deepened.

Soon we came up with a mutual agreement. Using his own money, he would build an addition onto our house, a separate apartment with its own kitchen, bath, and living space. He would live there and help defray our household expenses. At his death the apartment would belong to us.

My wife and I had always shared a vision of our children consorting on a daily basis with a wise, kindly grandfather figure, and now here was an opportunity. Construction on the apartment began soon afterward, and ten months later Larry moved in.

The arrangement turned out better than any of us could have imagined. For several years Larry lived happily in his handsomely decorated suite of rooms, preparing breakfast and lunch for himself, entertaining visitors, taking care of his voluminous correspondence, and even making short trips to New York City on his own. For dinner he regularly joined us at our table, cementing his relationship with our family even more.

The whole arrangement corresponded perfectly with my own romantic picture of how family life should be—kindly paterfamilias by the fireplace, children at his feet, harvest table with three generations of family members raising their glasses to life's abundance. At times I felt positively expansive, even self-congratulatory. How benevolent my wife and I had been to take this elderly friend into our home. How grateful he always was. How wonderfully the whole arrangement was working out.

But this cameo of home and hearth was not to last. As time passed, Larry's health deteriorated severely. After years of independence he began to lose his physical mobility and was finally confined to a wheelchair. Not long after that he became entirely bedridden, too weak to even roll over on his own.

Though stoically uncomplaining and invariably cheerful, the more Larry's body deteriorated the more needful he became. Barely able to read, sitting in a wheelchair or lying in bed, the brightest moments in his day were visits from others. This meant that every time I walked into his room to hand him the mail or bring him lunch, he seized on me with the special intensity of the needy, reminiscing about the past or engaging me in conversation.

I listened and nodded as Larry talked. But inwardly my mind was racing and my irritation level rising. Didn't he realize that I had to leave for the airport in half an hour? Didn't he know that I had to be at my office for a meeting of the Board of Overseers, or that I was a keynote speaker at a conference? Here I was in the midst of my busy, frantic life, trying to care for a man who lived in a shrunken world where the overriding concerns were where he'd put his eyeglasses and who would wash his hair. The more helpless he became, the more his demands increased. There simply seemed no end to it all, and no relief.

"How much of this can we take?" I muttered to my wife one day, pacing around our living room. "He wakes us up three times a night ringing his bell. He expects us to wash him, clip his nails. We wait on him endlessly. How did we get ourselves into this!"

Frustrated, I walked out into our yard and sat down on a tree stump. My wife waited an appropriate amount of time, then joined me.

"How do you put up with all this so cheerfully?" I asked her after a few minutes.

"I don't know," she answered. "I guess it's just a chance to help him." She looked at me for a minute. "And help us too."

I shot her a skeptical look and shook my head. She stayed a few minutes longer, then quietly got up and left.

I continued to brood. But the longer I sat there on the tree stump, the more I started to hear what she had just said to me. Slowly it sank in. Here I was being given an opportunity to turn this difficult real-life exercise into spiritual coin, she was saying, and I was missing my chance.

I thought of all the classes and seminars I'd given on the subject of the ethics of caregiving with the elderly. I remembered how often I'd told people that by helping others we help ourselves; that by being of service we somehow bring ourselves closer to wholeness. Now here was a chance to put my ideals into practice, here was an opportunity to break free from the bonds of egotism by focusing the spotlight away from my own needs and onto another's. Here it was—and I was letting the opportunity slip through my fingers like sand.

From this moment on, something changed in my relationship with Larry. It wasn't that I never got angry or impatient with him again. It was that I was now able to see this anger and impatience as *part* of the process rather than an impediment to it. I could let the anger do what it was going to do. I could struggle against it, accept it for what it was, and continue to serve. I was, in short, involved in an active and ongoing spiritual discipline, and not just grudging, purposeless servitude.

Larry, in turn, sensed the change, and we became closer than ever before.

As fate would have it, Larry died a few months after this incident took place. He passed away with dignity, as he had lived, surrounded by loved ones and with the name of God on his lips. A few weeks before the end he and I attended a high school graduation party for a friend. It was a beautiful afternoon that day in June, and all the guests were gathered on the lawn. I pushed Larry's wheelchair toward a cool spot in a grove of maples where we could watch the parade of life before us.

As we were sitting together quietly, I turned to him and pointed to a group of young people talking and bantering. "Did you ever think that all these people will one day be dead?" I asked.

This was not a comment one usually makes at a happy graduation party. But Larry picked up on it right away, grabbing my arm and looking at me with great conviction. "Never forget that thought," he said. "Try to hold on to it. If you can, that thought will free you."

Weeks later I found myself standing at the edge of a newly dug grave throwing a handful of earth onto Larry Morris's wooden coffin. As I bid my farewells, I remembered what he had said to me that day at the party, and I thought of the knowledge and insights he had given me through the years. Most of all I remembered those last precious days we'd had together and the lessons they'd brought me: that service helps the server as much as the person served; and that by using the serving process to see our own fears, angers, and resistances, serving can become a path to inner betterment as well as a means of doing good in the world. "Those whom God wishes to bless," goes the saying, "He puts in their hands the means of helping others."

The More I Serve, the Freer I Feel

By changing our attitude toward struggle in life, we change the struggle itself.

Consider, for example, the story of Estelle Goldman, a middle-aged Chicago real estate broker with whom I spent an evening several years ago on the recommendation of a mutual friend. Estelle, my friend assured me, had a poignant and uplifting story to tell about caring for her aging mother who had died a year earlier. "And believe me," the friend promised, "Estelle will tell it like it is."

Tall, fashion model thin, with alert eyes and frizzed hair, Estelle smoked incessantly as we talked, and was up and down innumerable times bringing me snacks from her well-stocked kitchen. Jewish by culture though not religion, in therapy for many years, Estelle had been extraordinarily successful selling suburban real estate. She pointed proudly to the plaques on her wall: three Real Estate Salesperson of the Year awards in five years.

In her personal life things hadn't gone so smoothly. Estelle had been married twice, she told me, once to an orthodontist, once to a teacher, "two nice but world-class nebbishy guys," she said. "After my second divorce four years ago I stopped going out with men completely."

"What happened?" I asked.

"I married my mother instead," she said.

She looked at me with a mock frown for a minute, then giggled.

Estelle's mother, I learned, had been in the clothing business much of her life, and at one point had owned her own retail store. The business brought a hefty chunk of money into their house, Estelle admitted, and enabled her family to live far better than they might have on her father's income alone (he was a leather broker). But it also turned Estelle's mother into an absentee parent.

"A father you expect to be at the office all the time," Estelle declared. "But a mother? Couldn't she have been home *once* in a while? My grandfather had to take care of me most of the time. Even when my mother was home, she was always busy. She'd be yakking away on the phone, potchkeeing with those stupid fabric samples. She'd be reading a trade journal, doing a crossword, listening to the radio, all at the same time. Everything in the world but paying attention to me. I felt like I was priority number zero."

What happened when you did ask for her attention? I was curious to know.

"Oh, then I get the guilt and manipulation trip," Estelle replied. "She'd end up making me think *I* was the one who'd done something wrong for asking her to pay a little attention to me. She'd say things like 'For God sakes, Estelle, when are you going to stop your nudging!' Or 'It's not enough your father and I work sixteen hours a day? You have to make me feel like I'm a neglectful mother too?' I'd also get a lot of lines like 'Learn to be more grateful, Estelle,' or 'You're just trying to get my attention, aren't you?'

"There was another goodie too," Estelle went on. "My mother was an expert at—this name came to me in the middle of the night once—she was an expert at what I call the 'whalebone technique.' You know what that is? The Eskimos used to hunt seals, remember? They'd take a sharp piece of bone, bend it like a spring, and tie a chunk of whale meat around it. The poor seal would eat the meat. Poom! The bone would pop open and cut its little insides to pieces. A cheap way to make a living.

"So that was my mother's trick too—time-delayed put-downs. She'd say something to you that sounded very nice at first, like 'Oh, that dress you're wearing is so much prettier than the ones you usually wear.' You're flattered. Then later on you realize she's zinging you. But the knife doesn't go *boing!* in your stomach right away. You have to think about it for a while.

"Or she'd say, 'Thank you so much for coming to see me, dear. I'm happy you can finally find the time.' You leave, and in a little while you realize what she was really saying was *'Bad girl! Bad girl!* For not coming to see me more often.' The whalebone goes off and sticks you one good."

After Estelle grew up, her relationship with her mother became predictably prickly and ambivalent. Though mother and daughter talked frequently on the phone, Estelle was incredibly busy with her real estate deals and saw her mother only on holidays and special occasions. By now Estelle's father was dead and her mother lived alone in a luxury apartment near Lake Michigan.

"She'd call me up practically every day and tell me how lonely she was, how much she missed me. She was always trying to get me to visit her, you know. But in a sneaky way. She couldn't just come out and invite me. Oh no. She'd always have to do it with the inferences, the innuendos, the guilt trips. She'd say things like 'I'm so alone, no one ever comes over to see me.' Typical, huh? Almost like the joke: 'You don't call, you don't write, you don't fax.' As she got older, she got more and more and more dependent and clinging, the opposite of how she was with me as a kid. But underneath it all, the same old 'what can you do for me?' attitude was always there."

Then one day came *the* call.

"It was a week before I was going to take my first real vacation in five years—to Aruba, in the Caribbean. My mother phoned. She'd just been to the doctor. He told her she had diabetes and serious circulatory complications. 'For God sakes, you can't leave now, Estelle!' my mother screamed into my ear. 'I was there for you when you were a little girl. I need *you* now!' What chutzpa! Years and years of therapy trying to get out from under her thumb, and in one minute she drags me back with her guilt and games. It was 'Take care of me or else.' "

"Or else what?" I asked.

"Or else I won't love you. I'll stop talking to you. I'll get sick. I'll take to my bed. I'll withdraw. I'll die. Take care of me, Estelle, or I'll die—and it will be *your* fault."

Swallowing her anger, Estelle canceled her travel plans, and soon found herself in the role of daily caregiver for a woman who, as she perceived it, had given her so little caregiving in the past.

The picture of Estelle's love-hate relationship with her mother emerged with increasing clarity as we continued to talk that evening. In many ways the relationship seemed to echo so many other mother-daughter relationships I'd heard about over the years. But where, I started to wonder, was the uplifting part of the story?

"Wasn't there a positive side to it all?" I finally asked.

"Not at first," Estelle answered with a grimace. "My mother wanted me there all the time. Every time she needed *anything* I was supposed to drop what I was doing and come running. If I didn't, I'd get the guilt. My mother really was physically sick, you know. There was no kidding around about that. It got so bad I tried to get her a nurse, but she didn't want to pay for it. She had plenty of money, you know, but she wouldn't spend any of it. 'I want to keep it so I can leave it all to you when I die,' she'd tell me."

As the months passed, the relationship between mother and daughter grew increasingly tense and claustrophobic. Her mother talked nonstop whenever Estelle visited, primarily about her infirmities, pausing only long enough to comment on Estelle's hair, her figure, her cooking, her choice of friends.

"You can't believe how crazy-making it all was," Estelle went on. "I felt like a kid again. I can still hear her. 'That chicken you cooked was so good, Estelle dear, but I just hope I don't get salmonella.' 'Careful with that tea, Estelle! You'll spill it on the couch! Tea stains don't come out, you know!' "

Feeling trapped and hopeless, Estelle finally decided she needed help, and turned to the therapist she'd been seeing on and off for years.

The therapist urged Estelle to protect herself against the "self-sacrifice syndrome." "Learn to put your own priorities first," the therapist said at every session. "If your mother's demands interfere with what's critical in your life, have the strength to say no. If your mother keeps insisting on making you feel guilty every time you do anything for her, consider the possibility of not visiting her for a while."

The therapist also suggested that Estelle fill her mother's obsessive hunger for companionship with a pet, something Estelle was deprived of as a child because of her mother's cleanliness fetish. ("Mother always had sheets of clear plastic fitted over the furniture, you know. God forbid I should get a spot on the Naugahyde!")

Estelle liked the idea. It would be a project she and her mother could share. One day she went to the pet store, purchased "an adorable black-and white kitten," and presented it to her mother.

"Right from the get-go I could tell this was going to be a disaster," Estelle said sadly. "My mother kind of shrank back from the thing, you know, as if it had a disease. She didn't want to touch it, even look at it. She seemed frightened, anxious—like, you know, something will happen, maybe the cat will die, it will pee on the sofa.

"I tried to tell her what fun it was, how nice it is to have a living thing around the house. But she didn't want to know from it. And I'll tell you why. Not because she didn't like animals. She liked them enough, I'd seen her with them. It was because she was frightened of the responsibility. She'd be responsible for taking care of it, feeding it, cleaning the cat box, giving it affection. She just couldn't do it—couldn't put herself out for anybody or anything, man or beast. Finally I had to take the animal back to the pet shop. The poor thing, I swear, it would have starved to death if I hadn't gotten it out of there."

Estelle paused for a minute and took several quick drags on her cigarette. "But you know, when I saw how my mother reacted to that little kitten, a lightbulb went off in my head."

"What happened?" I asked.

"Something big," Estelle went on, her eyes glowing in a way I hadn't seen up till now. "I realized that the way my mother was relating to this cat was exactly the same way she'd related *to me* when I was a kid. She just didn't want to be bothered. Couldn't make the effort. Didn't have enough time for anything or anyone but herself. If she couldn't get something out of this poor animal, she didn't want to put anything into it. I'll tell you, I learned more from that cat about my mother, and about myself, than I learned from eight years of therapy."

At this point I suggested that perhaps if Estelle hadn't been in therapy for so many years she might not have noticed the parallel.

"Maybe," she acknowledged. "The therapy helped me bring the thing to another level, that's true. But the cat got me across the finish line. In fact, the cat thing made something snap in me. It was as if I saw my mother for the first time, just the way she was. I'd been trying to get her to be the mother of my fantasy all those years. I wanted her to be responsible, share the work, love the pet, love *me*. It would all be great. But that was somebody else's mother. It wasn't mine.

"And you know what?" Estelle continued. "The moment I saw my mother clearly this way, without illusions, I began to accept her. Suddenly I didn't resent her anymore. And more important, I could *forgive her and even love her*. That was the really big thing: I could forgive and love."

After this inner realization many things changed for Estelle. For some time her therapist had been urging her to separate and cut her mother off entirely. Estelle should not sacrifice her own needs on the altar of her mother's codependent selfishness, the therapist insisted.

"But, you know," Estelle told me. "I realized that I didn't agree with this advice. It sounded good and shrinky, all right, but something about it was off target. I realized that the more I put myself out for my mother—and this is weird—the more free of her I became. The more I served her, the less of her servant I was. After that things became more autonomous for me in other parts of my life too. It got so I didn't care what she said to me—guilt trips, clinging, whalebone, whatever. It was all okay. She was okay. I was okay. The world was okay. Something in my head had opened up the day that little cat came into the house."

The more we talked that evening, the more it became apparent to me that the real healer in this story was not Estelle's psychotherapist, but the spirit within her that was able to turn a negative into a positive. Where Estelle's therapist saw only to the level of her guilt and manipulation, Estelle looked beyond, seeing the potential good in the situation and recognizing it as an opportunity for enrichment. Estelle's approach shows us that in certain cases the language of mainstream, secular psychotherapy is simply not adequate to describe or diagnose people like Estelle; people who are, I believe, suffering as much from a spiritual crisis as a neurotic one. When I heard her story I couldn't help thinking that the psychotherapist in charge might have served Estelle's needs better by prescribing three or four basic spiritual exercises: forgiveness, say, along with compassion and patience. Or perhaps a combination of psychiatric and religious discipline would have been best.

Such religio-psychiatric approaches are becoming increasingly accepted among psychotherapists today. Dr. Mark Epstein recommends that therapists treat their patients with a version of Buddhist psychotherapy in which the therapist stresses detachment from a neurosis as well as working through it. My psychiatrist friend Dr. Seyyed Abdullah emphasizes forgiveness in his practice, along with the application of specific attributes of God to problem-

atic life situations—the Merciful, the Appreciative, the Provider, the Pre-
venter, the Patient—in what he terms "Koranic psychotherapy."

When a parent becomes physically dependent in old age, I realized from
Estelle's story, it reopens certain childhood wounds that we thought were
closed forever. Estelle assumed that she was immune to her mother's manipu-
lations now that she was an independent grown-up. But distance and time
are no guarantees. Once Estelle was thrown back into the parental vortex
with all its familiar associations, she realized that her old buttons were still
there and as vulnerable as ever, and that her mother was pushing them with
the same ease and expertise she had when Estelle was a child.

Estelle crushed out her cigarette in the ashtray, leaned back on the
couch, and let out a sigh that said it all.

"Sometimes, you know, we have to bite the bullet if we want to work
through things. Just plunge in up to our necks, even if it hurts. As soon as I
saw how sad and empty this poor woman really was, I started to feel compassion for her, as if she was some kind of injured animal that I had to protect. I
realized that I *did want* to make sacrifices for her. At least to a certain extent.
I wanted to keep visiting, keep waiting on her, keep cooking for her in that
gloomy apartment, keep taking care of her. Not because she was so wonderful. But—I really don't know how to put it—because she was my mother,
and she needed me, and for the first time in my life I felt like I was acting
from some selfless part of myself. The more I gave, the freer I felt. The freer I
felt, the more I could give."

Estelle stood up and walked toward the kitchen to get more snacks. At
the kitchen door she stopped and smiled.

"And you know what else? You know what else? Something simple. It
just felt good to help. It just felt good . . ."

3. FINDING ONE'S WAY
WITH PRAYER AND MEDITATION

The Reopened Wound

There are moments in life bursting with a meaning and beauty that we
somehow fail to recognize while they are taking place, and that we can savor
only in retrospect, sometimes many years later.

One of these moments occurred in 1986 when my wife and I were visiting a fraternity brother of mine named Carter and his new wife, Jacqueline.

Several months earlier Carter had called and announced that he and Jacqueline were coming East from their home in Boulder, Colorado, for the first few weeks in July. Could we join them at Jacqueline's family house in East Hampton for the weekend of the Fourth?

I told him we'd be delighted.

As it turned out, Jacqueline's family lived in a sprawling Gold Coast château complete with pool, stone towers, and a hundred yards of what must surely be the most flawless lawn on the planet. My wife and I were a little intimidated by it all until we met Jacqueline and Jacqueline's mother, the widow of a powerful Washington diplomat. The two of them were so warm and attentive that within an hour we felt comfortably at home in this regal world, like members of the family.

Jacqueline herself was a study in graciousness—delicate yet energetic, with a touch of the tragic about her and a touch of the blithe. Her chiseled features and beautiful eyes reminded me—I'm not sure why—of Lady Guinevere from the Arthurian legends. She was one of those magic souls who put you at your ease in such an expert way that they make it seem that *it's you* who are making things so spontaneous and relaxed. Knowing of Carter's unhappy first marriage, I was delighted that he had met someone so right.

The first night in East Hampton, Jacqueline's mother gave a dinner party for a glittering cast of celebrities and remnants of East Hampton old money. Jacqueline was the perfect hostess, as I expected she would be, greeting everyone as if she had known them forever, and drifting from guest to guest like a well-bred wind sylph. After making the rounds of the room several times, she finally joined our conversational circle. A servant came by with a tray of drinks, and Jacqueline helped herself to a glass of red wine. Just as she was raising it to her lips, several loud explosions went off outside.

To my amazement, our hostess let out a muted cry and dropped her glass, spilling wine all over me and creating a blotch of red on my shirt that looked every bit like blood from a suddenly opened wound.

For a moment she became ashen—I mean *white*—and seemed to stagger. The next moment, by what I imagine was an act of sheer will, she regained her composure and spent the next five minutes apologizing to me and everyone in our group. Meanwhile, Carter, who had seen the whole thing from across the room, was at her side in an instant, wrapping his arm around her protectively as if she were a child.

A few minutes later Jacqueline seemed entirely herself, though I noticed that her hands were trembling at the dinner table and then afterward, on the veranda. The explosions, it turned out, were Fourth of July firecrackers set off by the children of one of the cooks. The rest of the evening went off flawlessly, and nothing more was said about the incident.

And yet, there was something strange about this episode that left a peculiar after-impression on me, like the imprint of a flashbulb exploded in your eyes. I was gratified the next day when Carter brought the subject up.

"Sorry about that wine thing last night," he said with a forced laugh. "Jacqueline's still pretty embarrassed. She wants me to buy you a new shirt."

"Don't be ridiculous," I replied. "Tell her I want to buy her a new bottle of wine."

Carter laughed a real laugh this time and seemed relieved. Then I added, "She's okay, isn't she?"

"Oh yeah, sure," he replied, avoiding my eyes. "She's great. Just gets a little high-strung."

I knew at that moment there was something he wasn't telling me.

Six years passed. Though I didn't see Carter and Jacqueline during this entire time, we exchanged Christmas cards each year, and occasionally talked on the phone. Then in the summer of 1992 I learned that I'd be in the Boulder area for a weekend to give a speech. I gave them a call. Always hospitable, Carter invited me to spend the weekend at their house. With both a touch of amusement in his voice and a touch of pride, he also announced that Jacqueline was off on a forty-day meditation retreat just then, but that she'd be back in time for my arrival.

Meditation retreat? I asked. For *forty days!*

Actually, Jacqueline had become a member of a Tibetan Buddhist community in Boulder, Carter informed me. She was making meditation retreats now on a regular basis.

I was intrigued. "Maybe I can talk to her about it," I suggested.

"Worth a try," Carter said breezily, then went on to give me the latest fraternity news.

My first night in Boulder I began quizzing Jacqueline about her involvement in Buddhism. It didn't take long to see that she had a profound knowledge of the subject. I asked if she would be willing to do a taped interview. Carter had obviously told her of my interest in spiritual autobiographies, and she replied with a combination of, I thought, enthusiasm and resignation. Tomorrow first thing in the morning would be fine, she said.

Next day at 7 A.M. sharp I was awoken by a knock. "Time to talk dharma talk," Jacqueline said cheerily outside my door.

I showered, dressed, and went down to the kitchen. As I walked past their bedroom, I heard Carter snoring loudly. Jacqueline and I would have the early morning all to ourselves.

Breakfast was waiting for me on the kitchen table. Outside everything was quiet; Saturday morning in the Boulder foothills. Jacqueline sat across the table from me in her silk bathrobe looking frail and queenly, her long hair streaming down over her shoulders. The image of Guinevere again came to mind. I placed my tape recorder in the middle of the table and turned it on. Before I could ask a question, she started talking.

"I was trying to figure out where to begin. It occurred to me that I should start with . . ."

For a moment her voice faltered. "Do you remember that time I spilled wine on you in East Hampton?"

"Of course," I said.

"It's all connected," she went on. "Carter wasn't sure I should get into all this with you. But I think it's part of the big picture, and I want you to know." She laughed nervously. "If I can't buy you a new shirt, at least I can give you an explanation about why I ruined it."

She then told me the following story.

When Jacqueline was in her early twenties, she lived with an artist named Christopher in an old Connecticut farmhouse. Christopher was talented, romantic, spontaneous, all the things she'd hoped an artist would be. He was also exceedingly high-strung, childish, and oversensitive.

One day they had a violent argument and Jacqueline threatened to end the relationship. Attempting to cool down and collect herself, she walked out into a field behind their house. Christopher called to her to come back and make up. Still seething, Jacqueline replied that she was *never* coming back. A few minutes later she heard a gunshot. Running into the house, she found Christopher sitting upright in his studio chair. He had blown a good deal of his head off with a shotgun.

From this time on, Jacqueline said, any gunshot-like sound made her hysterical and faint. I understood now why she had reacted so violently to the firecrackers that weekend in East Hampton.

Sitting there silently for several long moments, I wondered what I could say to such a tale?

I also wondered why Jacqueline was letting me in on such an intimate confidence, and how this heartbreaking story related to her spiritual search. Jacqueline sensed both my embarrassment and my questions.

"I almost never tell anybody about this," she went on in an intimate voice. "But it's a crucial part of the story."

I nodded and waited.

"After Christopher died I sort of went crazy. I was in a state of shock. Heavens, the anger it took to commit such an act! I never realized people could be so cruel to one another!

"Before Christopher died I hadn't spent much time thinking about death or religion. I'd been brought up an Episcopalian, which in my family was a very social thing. Then without warning I was split open by what happened. There I was in the middle of life, hanging on by my fingernails. What would help me? I didn't know. A wounded spirit is hard to heal.

"So I started looking around for things to give me support. I thought of psychotherapy at first, but it had no appeal. I don't know why exactly. Maybe I had such a gaping wound in me that I felt none of the usual therapies could help. I instinctively felt I needed some kind of super medicine that you can't find in the drugstores. The shock of this whole thing turned me inside out. Sometimes I thought I was going insane."

Fleeing the Northeast with all its memories, Jacqueline traveled to Colorado to visit her cousin, and here she met Carter. Within several months they were engaged, and a year later they married.

In Boulder, Jacqueline also came in contact with the Tibetan Buddhist community. At first she attended their meetings simply out of curiosity. Soon her fascination and commitment grew, especially as she realized that meditation seemed to be having a healing effect on her troubled spirit. Before long she was taking daily meditation instruction and was following a rigorous program of regular sittings. Finally she took formal Buddhist vows.

Jacqueline's spiritual biography interested me deeply, especially as it pertained to the practice of meditation. Prayer and meditation are the pillars of the spiritual Struggle, and I had talked to many seekers on the subject. But Jacqueline's case was different. Here was a woman suffering from a trauma so deep that it threatened her very sanity. Her response to this pain was to immerse herself in a religious community. She had come to Buddhism, as it were, looking for a cure. Was she using religion simply as a safety net? As an analgesic? And if so, was there anything wrong with this approach?

That Secret Place of Objectivity

While the term "meditation" is used in a variety of ways, it has a precise and unequivocal definition that should be stated here in full before we discuss the matter further. Meditation, in a nutshell, is a means of stilling the mind by focusing attention on a single point of concentration. This point of focus can be a single thought or a fixed mental image. Christian orders, for example, meditate on the image of the Madonna and Child or on the Stations of the Cross. A meditator can focus on a single word, a liturgical phrase, a mantra, even a mental puzzle such as the Zen koan. The actual object of attention varies according to the spiritual teaching, but the purpose behind the exercise is always the same: to quiet the mechanism of discursive thought so that states of consciousness normally cut off by the ordinary thinking mind can emerge.

How does meditation differ from prayer? Generally speaking, these two forms of practice make up the halves of the contemplative whole. The difference between them is that meditation requires single-pointed attention, while prayer is less concentrated and can take broader and less focused forms: petition, internal dialogue, confession, even a purely emotional and spontaneous outpouring of gratitude and love. If meditation is a single word spoken over and over again to the Divine, prayer is an entire conversation.

"In the beginning," Jacqueline said, "I got involved in Buddhism because I hoped it would cover over the suffering and guilt I felt from Christopher's death. I thought of religion as a painkiller. Take two spoonfuls of meditation and let it chase away the bad thoughts and memories.

"Later, when I sat in meditation for long periods of time, I saw I had it all wrong. The point was not to make the pain go away. It was to become *indifferent* to it. To let the pain exist along with all the other thoughts and feelings in my head. But to be separated from it, as if you were watching a stranger from a distance.

"Once I found this place of detachment inside myself the pain of remembering Christopher's death could wallop away at me all it wanted, negative memory after memory, like waves hitting the shore. But it didn't matter. With Buddhist meditation you never reject anything and you never accept anything. You just let it all wash in and out of your mind, like the waves, without judging and without analyzing. That's the posture: neither accepting nor rejecting. Keeping in the middle. Just being."

A statement from American Zen Buddhist master Bernard Glassman expresses this sentiment in different but complementary terms: "If a sound comes it comes, and if it goes, it goes. This is called 'mirror mind.' It's the same kind of sense as when something passes in front of a mirror and is reflected there. Whatever appears, appears. When it leaves, it's gone. No residue stays in the mirror. That's the process we're looking for in meditation. We're not trying to create silence or some euphoric state, or to keep anything out. Whatever occurs, occurs, and then falls away."

"After I discovered this secret place of objectivity inside myself," Jacqueline went on, "I could look at my pain and allow it to exist, and that was that. It was still there, all right, every time I looked. Christopher's face would even pop up in my mind during meditation sessions. Or I'd hear the sound of the gunshot. But now it didn't matter. It was just another mental impulse floating through my brain, no better and no worse than the others. I looked at them all with the same impartial eye."

I thought of a statement of Krishnamurti's: "Meditation is to be aware of every thought and of every feeling, never to say it is right or wrong, but just to watch it and move with it. In that watching you begin to understand the whole movement of thought and feeling. And out of this awareness comes silence."

When I asked if it was difficult for Jacqueline to remain seated and motionless for long periods of time, she nodded. "Like I said, the negative thoughts do come. How could they not? But this flood of thoughts is okay. Matter of fact, it's wonderful. These thoughts are all part of the feast that's offered you. The feast of phenomena, the feast of your own mind. You don't try to stomp out negative thoughts. You don't try to repress them. You just watch them. Like you watch the pain in your legs that comes from sitting. Or like you listen to the voices in your head that keep saying, 'Get me out of here!' You listen, you note them, then you keep on sitting."

"What kind of progress do you feel you've made with meditation?" I asked.

For many years, she replied, she had made none at all.

"No Breakthroughs of any kind?" I asked. "No sudden insights?"

She shook her head. "Nothing."

I asked her how she was able to bear these grueling stretches without getting any results.

"Well, you know, I gradually came to see that we can't push ourselves to understand anything more than we can understand. It's all going to happen someday to us, this ripening process. But it happens at its own pace.

While it's happening we don't necessarily see any evidence of it. We struggle away and struggle away, sitting there day in, day out. And nothing happens. But, you know, it *is* happening, really. Below the surface, in the capillaries beneath our regular consciousness. Something's growing in us all the time when we meditate. We just don't see it. It's like time-lapse photography. You glance at a rose for just a minute and it appears to be unmoving. But take a time-lapse movie of it for a week and you see the rose budding, opening, flowering. That's what our progress is like. We can't see it because it's happening in its own time frame. In fact, we're not allowed to see our progress. It's kept from us quite intentionally. If we knew how close we were to enlightenment—the enlightenment we've been trying to get to, maybe, for a hundred thousand lifetimes—we might get a swelled head. We'd say, '*I'm* doing this. *I'm* the one responsible, *I'm* the one making progress.' Our ego would take over and run wild, and muck things up.

"So we just have to keep slogging on," Jacqueline added, "even if there are no visible signs of getting anywhere. Eventually we'll succeed."

There was something else that Jacqueline wanted to impress on me about her struggle with meditation.

"There's one thing in Buddhism that's at the heart of all our meditations," she said. "When I began meditating I was hurting so much from Christopher's death. I had this very dualistic view of things. I thought to myself: I'm in here, and the world's out there. I've been deeply hurt, and the world has inflicted this pain on me. Therefore I want to escape from this cruel world into the quiet little meditation cell.

"But, you know, the more time I spent meditating, the more my point of reference changed. After sitting for a long time, I realized that meditation and life are the same. That the understanding I get from meditating is what I've got to bring to my life, and use *in* my life. Everything around us *is sacred*. Everything. It's holy, all of it—the thoughts, the material things, the feelings, all of it."

What Jacqueline said reminded me of a Zen proverb: "To one who knows nothing of Zen, mountains are mountains, waters are waters, trees are trees. When a person meditates and knows a little Zen, mountains are no longer mountains, waters no longer waters, and trees no longer trees. Then when a person has penetrated to the heart of Zen, mountains are once again mountains, waters are waters, trees are trees."

I was about to quote this saying when the kitchen door swung open and Carter staggered into the room. "Coffee, coffee!" he moaned, plunking himself down next to me at the kitchen table and holding his head.

My old friend's arrival broke the spell. Jacqueline the Buddhist instantly became Jacqueline the wife, and I realized that our interview was officially over. As she puttered lovingly around the kitchen making coffee, preparing breakfast, fussing over Carter while he thawed out, I looked on in silence until I could restrain myself no longer.

"From heaven to earth, eh, fellow traveler?" I said as she mixed the waffle batter.

She looked at me for a moment with a plain housewifely gaze, then turned on her Guinevere smile. "There's a Buddhist saying," she said. "First enlightenment, then the laundry."

The Return of the Repressed

Talking to Jacqueline that day made it more clear to me than ever that part of the reason we don't identify our own progress during the Struggle is because the deeper we go with our chosen form of contemplation, the more we feel we are getting worse, not better.

Why worse?

Freud himself, as we have seen in an earlier chapter, spoke of how at a certain age we experience a return of previously repressed mental materials. As with free association in psychoanalysis, the meditating or prayerful mind opens up its own Pandora's box, allowing certain psychic fragments to float to the surface, strange mental bits and pieces that sometimes arise from the lowest, most primitive depths of our mind. Seeing these fragments and experiencing them firsthand forces us to confront certain unsavory thoughts and feelings, and to own them. In the process we may make the mistake of thinking that these thoughts have been created by the effort of meditation itself, when all meditation has done is churn them up from the depths and force us to look them squarely in the eye. These unpleasant emotions are not gaining a greater hold on us. We are just seeing them more clearly than ever before, in the same way that we see the objects around us in a dark room more clearly as the light of day slowly comes up. Prayer and meditation, in this sense, are tools of psychological discovery as well as methods of transcendence.

Thomas Merton once remarked that if we meditate in the proper way we should feel ourselves becoming drier as time goes on. Like the spiritual process quest itself, meditation becomes increasingly difficult as we advance, not easier. "Aridity itself," Merton remarks, "can be taken as a sign of progress in prayer, provided it is accompanied by serious efforts and self-discipline." As Freud tells us too, the closer we get to the truth about ourselves, the easier it is to fall off the path.

"There were times when prayer itself brought up uncomfortable, distressing thoughts and feelings," writes Dan Wakefield in *Returning: A Spiritual Journey,* "emotions that shook me up inside, and I remembered our minister telling us once of a Yiddish proverb that said 'God is an earthquake, not an uncle.' "

Jacob Wrestling with His Angel

Not long after my interview with Jacqueline I got in touch with an old friend and colleague, Jacob, a man who understands prayer and meditation better than anyone I know. "Still wrestling with angels as usual," Jacob told me as we spoke on the phone. "And getting pinned to the mat every time."

Jacob is a professor of psychology at a midwestern university, a man now in his early fifties, balding, slovenly, acerbically brilliant, loved by everyone who can stick around long enough to see through his sarcasm and self-pitying poses. A native of Baltimore, he taught at Yeshiva University in New York City for several years until an offer came his way in the late 1970s and he and his French wife migrated to the Midwest. Here he has lived the life of a Yiddish Mr. Chips ever since, assiduously, if in a covert way, introducing generations of students to the spiritual implications and ideas that are so often overlooked by mainstream psychology.

And this is ironic. Because Jacob is not a religious man. At least, that's what he'll tell you. "Not *conventionally* religious," he'll say. "Not religious in your synagogue-praying, shul-sitting way. But, you know, interested in the mystical stuff, the Kabbalah, the hip rabbis from the Middle Ages."

Despite his disclaimers, Jacob also believes in God. In his own way, and at times, it would seem, bitterly and even unwillingly, he believes.

"A lot of Jews," he told me, "can't stop themselves from being faithful to God. Even when they feel like rebelling. You know, there's this story about a bunch of Jews who were sitting around one day griping about how hard life was. They decided that if there really was a Yahweh He was so cruel and unfair that He didn't deserve to be worshiped. They decided they'd quit worshiping Him this minute. So they started to draw up a pact to this effect when suddenly someone stuck their head into the room and hollered, 'Come on, you fellows, we need a minyan and you're going to be late for prayers.' At this everyone in the room dropped what they were doing and bolted to the synagogue. So much for Jewish revolution."

Though he hasn't set foot in a synagogue in thirty-five years, Jacob spends an hour each day in prayer.

What kind of prayer? I wanted to know.

"Occasionally I recite verses I memorized for my bar mitzvah," he says. "Just to keep up my Hebrew. But mostly I just talk to God. Converse with Him. I think that prayer is our heritage, the thing that makes us real. During medieval times Christian theologians described the Antichrist as a person whose knee-joints are put on backwards. That way he can't kneel in prayer like real men and women. The fact that we can pray is what raises us above the animals and makes us human."

"Yes, but it seems to me," I suggested, "that when you talk about prayer you're sometimes just talking about shaking your fist at God."

I reminded him for the hundredth time that for me he was forever the character of Tevya from *Fiddler on the Roof,* the confused, beleaguered, menschy Jewish Everyman arguing with God over his fate, scolding God, prodding Him, kidding with Him, praising Him.

"That's right," Jacob answered. "Because that's the Jewish relationship to God. Argumentative. Intimate. Boggled in the mind by the cruelty and suffering that God allows in this world and by the terrible things that have happened to our people. Amazed that God does these things century after century. But still drawn to Him. We ask Him why, why do you treat us like this? Why did you make your world so full of suffering and evil? And God answers us back—by sending more trouble and *tsuris.*"

Jacob was clearly the person to talk to on the matter of prayer. In our many conversations over the years on theological matters I had found his earthiness and warm subjectivity tremendously appealing, if for no other reason than that my own religious upbringing was in a more austere Protestant milieu. It was also clear that Jacob had been around the barn several times trying to understand the meaning of prayer, and trying to fathom what the "right" way to talk to God might really be. In the process he had cycled through many variant forms, sometimes coming dangerously close to what many might think of as heresy.

One day Jacob visited my family in New York and we talked at length on these matters. "God will provide," Jacob said, quoting an old Jewish saying. "But if only He would provide until He provides."

I talked with him about the relationship between prayer and meditation. The definition of meditation was relatively clear-cut, I said. You quiet your mind. You keep it fixed on a single point of attention. You try to go beyond the mere thinking process. But prayer is more complicated. There were so many different forms—petitionary, passional, scriptural, personal. It's hard to lump so many varieties under one umbrella.

Jacob thought about this for a minute. "Yeah, but it's great—we get to try them all. Sometimes you need something, right? So you ask. Sometimes you want to give back to God. So you thank. Sometimes you just want to praise and groove because you feel so lucky and thankful. Sometimes you want communion. Sometimes you want quiet. Sometimes you want to recite some scriptures you like. That's prayer too if you pay attention to the words, and try to feel them and think about them. And me, sometimes I want to punch God in the *kishkas*. I've tried every approach. Begging, shouting, crying, thanking, punishing God, telling Him I'm not going to talk to Him anymore since He doesn't listen to me anyway. You can combine them all into one big prayer if you like. Or pick and choose. I think God likes it whatever you decide. He just wants you to remember Him, that's all. Not forget Him. That's the big thing—not forget Him."

"What do you yourself want from prayer?" I asked.

"I don't know," Jacob replied. "But I know what I *don't* want."

"What?"

"Silence. The stonewall treatment. And that's all I've gotten for forty years."

"What do you expect?" I answered. "God to talk to you out of the Burning Bush?"

"Your famous Breakthrough experience," he said. "That's what I expect. You know what happens to people who have these experiences. Their prayers get answered in concrete terms. They see visions. They see light. They get wisdom and exaltations, wonderful things. God talks back to them in His own way. That's what I want."

"Sure," I answered. "But most of the people who've had breakthroughs have struggled for years. Breakthroughs don't come from nowhere. Not in most cases anyway."

"Struggled?" Jacob said. "Suffered? Listen to me, buddy. I've spent years struggling to talk to God. To get Him to return my calls. I beg Him to send me a sign. To let me know that He's out there listening. He doesn't have to stop the sun in the sky, I say to Him. Just drop a flower or two once in a while to let me know You're around."

"Why do you keep at it then," I asked, "if you think it's so hopeless?"

"I can't help it." Jacob replied. "I believe. Despite the evidence of my senses. Despite the fact that God keeps sending *tsuris*, I believe."

He paused and looked at me. "I know what you're going to say now," he said. "You're going to tell me that sometimes our pain *is* the answer to our prayers. Right? That suffering isn't always the problem; that sometimes it's the solution. Right? Isn't that what you're going to tell me?" I could feel his familiar, friendly, argumentative presence poking at me.

I smiled and said nothing.

"But you know what? That's not good enough, buddy. I want something better than a kick in the pants every time I talk to God."

"What is it you do want?" I asked again.

"Just like I said, some kind of tangible answer. Something I can sink my teeth into. If not your famous Breakthrough experience, at least some light in the dark. A sign that He's really there. That doesn't seem like so much to ask."

"Did it ever occur to you," I said, "that you're not *ready* for a Breakthrough? Did you ever think that if you were suddenly thrown into a state of altered consciousness you might go crazy? That you might not be ready to handle it? Did it occur to you that God knows what He's doing? That He'll know when your time is ripe? That He won't give you what you want a moment earlier—even if you stamp your feet and carry on like a little kid?"

I wasn't entirely convinced of what I was saying. But I knew that if you're going to argue with Jacob you have to give back as good as you get.

"I'm ready, I'm ready," was all he said, and lapsed into silence.

We sat together without speaking for several minutes.

"Look," he said. "I know all this stuff. I know the intellectual reasons why God doesn't fly down in a fiery chariot. I know all the rationales about how He answers our prayers with what we need, not what we want. How we have to learn patience—all of that. It's fine. I *teach* that stuff, you know. At least when I'm not pretending to be a psychology professor.

"But it's only my head that knows these things. In my heart I'm hungry for something more than promises. I want to receive something that's powerful. Beautiful. Loving. Doesn't go away. When it comes right down to it, I guess what I want from God is just a little peace."

I went to my bookcase and took down a volume of Kierkegaard's *Journals*. The passage I was searching for was folded down. I opened the book and showed it to him. He read it out loud: "The unreflective person thinks and imagines that when he prays, the important thing, the thing he must concentrate upon, is that God should hear what he is praying for. And yet in the true, eternal sense it is just the reverse: the true relation to prayer is not when God hears what is prayed for, but when the person continues to pray until he is the one who hears, who hears what God wills."

Jacob closed the book. "The beat goes on," he said. I thought I saw tears in his eyes.

"But you know, buddy," he continued, "there's just that one thing I can't figure out."

"What's that?" I asked.

"Why's God make it all so hard?" He wiped his eyes. "Why so much suffering in this world? Why so damned much suffering for all of us? All most of us want to do is just find a little peace and quiet for ourselves in this crazy world. Right? Come in out of the rain. So why's He gotta make it so hard?"

I had no ready answer. Not at that moment.

Nor did I have any answer to Marjorie Stoner's question when she spoke of her Struggle with despair and pain. Or for Estelle Goldman. Or for Jacqueline. I had no ready answers for any of these good people about why the way to God is so long and hard. None of us do.

But in the back of my mind I also knew how I would answer the question if I had to. I would answer it with a wisdom story, one of the most instructive I'd ever heard. In its own way this story answered Jacob's question, and at the same time addressed the entire issue of why we must Struggle so long and so hard to achieve the coveted state of Grace.

Once very long ago, the story goes, a hermit had a vision in his desert monastery.

He saw a vast ocean. On one of its shores a monk was standing. The monk leaped high into the air, and with bright wings soared effortlessly across the great body of water to a heavenly land on the other side.

As the hermit wondered over this strange revelation, he saw a second monk approach the shore. This monk also spread his wings. But his flight did not go so smoothly. Though the monk finally arrived at the other shore, he had all he could do to keep from falling into the lashing waves.

Finally, a third monk appeared. This smallest and frailest of the three monks, he soared into the air like the others, but his wings were weak, and he fell into the roaring waters over and over, practically drowning each time. Only with the most heroic efforts and titanic struggles did he eventually arrive, half dead and thoroughly drenched, on the other shore.

After much pondering the hermit went to his spiritual guide and asked the meaning of this vision.

His guide interpreted it in this way: "The first monk you saw was the believer who aspires to fly to heaven in our own time—now, when religion and good people are everywhere, and when reaching heaven is a simple matter.

"The next monk stands for those who wish to reach heaven in the years to come. Their journey will be far more difficult.

"Finally, the third monk is the believer who makes spiritual efforts in the very distant future, when religion and righteousness have almost vanished from the earth. During this dark time it will be difficult beyond imagining to find one's way to the other shore.

"So rejoice that you live in our blessed time," the spiritual director concluded. "But remember this—remember this above all: the third monk's efforts are worth far, far more than those of all the rest."

part three

Breakthrough
and Return

Eyes, you have seen it all . . .
come back now,
come back to the white
chrysanthemum.

ISSO

chapter 7

The Breakthrough

When you have entered the way, God Most High bestows on you kingdoms and worlds that you never imagined; and you become quite ashamed of what you desired at first. "Ah!" you cry. "With such things in existence, how could I ever seek after such a mean thing."

RUMI

UNDERSTANDING THE BREAKTHROUGH

To the Center

"Go deeper," the Zen Buddhist roshi said. "Question: What is the mind to the very bottom?"

> Deeper and deeper I went . . .
> My hold was torn loose and I went spinning . . . To the center of the earth!
> To the center of the cosmos! To the Center.
> I was There.

"Then all at once I was struck as though by lightning, and the next instant heaven and earth crumbled and disappeared. Instantaneously, like surging waves, a tremendous delight welled up in me, a veritable hurricane of delight, as I laughed loudly and wildly: 'Ha, ha, ha, ha, ha, ha! There's no reasoning here, no reasoning at all! Ha, ha, ha!' The empty sky split in two, then opened its enormous mouth and I began to laugh uproariously."

These two elemental encounters, one described by an anonymous American artist studying Zen Buddhism in Japan, the other by a middle-aged Japanese executive, are characteristic Breakthroughs. Significantly, both episodes take place after long and rigorous spiritual searching.

And this is well in line with the principles that inform the Stages of the Soul.

For though there are exceptions, and though the Stages of the Soul do not invariably follow one another like rungs on a ladder, the moment of Breakthrough tends to occur over time after intense efforts and struggles have helped to bring it to flower.

What is a Breakthrough experience exactly?

An ambiguous term, certainly, like "faith" and "meditation," a "Breakthrough" is difficult to define, not because people experience it so rarely or because it is so hard to describe, but because Breakthroughs vary so widely in their content from person to person.

For our purposes, a Breakthrough is any experience of heightened awareness and sudden insight that fundamentally changes the way people look at themselves and the world around them.

The Italian psychiatrist Roberto Assagioli characterizes the Breakthrough in the following vivid terms: "A harmonious inner awakening is characterized by a sense of joy and mental illumination that brings with it an insight into the meaning and purpose of life; it dispels many doubts, offers the solution of many problems, and gives an inner source of security. At the same time, there wells up a realization that life is one, and an outpouring of love flows through the awakening individual toward his fellow beings and the whole of creation. The former personality, with its sharp edges and disagreeable traits, seems to have receded into the background, and a new loving and lovable individual smiles at us and the whole world, eager to be kind, to serve, and to share his newly acquired spiritual riches, the abundance of which seems to him almost too much to contain."

A person who passes through such a superordinary occurrence is obviously deeply touched and comes out the other side psychologically and spiritually transformed. In many cases, however, the aftermath of this transformation lasts only a limited time and then fades. As Assagioli points out: "Such a state of exalted joy may last for varying periods, but it is bound to cease. The inflow of light and love is rhythmical, as is everything in the universe. After a while it diminishes or ceases, and the flood is followed by the ebb." In rarer cases, and particularly in deeply felt religious and mystical illuminations, this change does not wane but lasts for long periods of time, and in some instances for a lifetime.

Of course, change of one kind or another is always taking place within us, whether it be ordinary or superordinary. Every minute of the day brings fluctuations in our awareness and oscillating states of receptivity. Like viewers in a movie theater, we sit watching a film entitled "the world." This film stars our thoughts, perceptions, imaginings, fears, memories, desires, plus the sights and sounds we take in through our sense organs from the external world: in short, the vast stream of consciousness that circulates through our minds each day.

As we sit in this dark theater of life enchanted by the spots of light and dark before us, it happens on rare occasions that we suddenly "come to" and realize that the images are illusory. In these rare instances we understand that the only real things around us are the theater we are sitting in and the projectionist who is showing the film. At such moments we see the great cinema of life for what it really is: the dance of shadows in Plato's cave, the endless weaving of matter, time, and space that the Hindus call *maya* and the Western mystical tradition refers to as Cosmic Illusion. For an instant we come to our senses. For a moment we are awake.

These brief interludes, rare and sought after in all spiritual traditions, are Breakthrough moments.

The Sufis speak of the Fall of humanity as originating from a forgetting both of who we are and of the Covenant of loyalty we all made long ago with our Creator. We suffer, the Sufis say, not for our ancestors' wickedness, but from a monumental amnesia concerning our origins and our destiny.

According to the Sufi masters, the years go by in all our lives, and we remain in this state of spiritual blackout. Then one day, if we are fortunate, we hear the Call and begin the Search, remembering now that we have forgotten. We may not be sure what it is we've forgotten. But the scent of an enticing "something" lures us on. So we Struggle and we strive; until suddenly the floodgates of the mind burst open, and like the prince in "The Hymn of the Pearl," we remember our royal heritage—and our mission.

In this moment of Breakthrough we realize we have come home.

Anatomy of Breakthrough Experiences

The moment of passing from ordinary awareness to higher consciousness goes by many names, depending on the tradition naming it.

St. Paul refers to transcendent consciousness as "the peace that passeth understanding." In Zen it is *satori* or *kensho,* and in other forms of Buddhism, *dhyâna.* Hindus speak of *samadhi.* The mystically minded Canadian psychiatrist R. M. Bucke talks of "cosmic consciousness" in his famous book by the same name. Abraham Maslow coined the phrase "peak experience." Thomas Merton uses the term "transcendental unconsciousness." Roberto Assagioli talks of "superconsciousness." The Sufis carefully distinguish certain *hals*—higher states—and the final stage of ego extinction, *fana,* equivalent to the Buddhist nirvana and the Hindu *mokshu.* For the Quakers there is an experience of "the inner Light."

Not all these Breakthroughs are qualitatively the same—this is an essential point to understand: some experiences are higher than others. All, however, belong to the same wavelength, just as ultraviolet light, radio waves, and cosmic rays have their discrete vibrational frequencies, yet all are part of the same electromagnetic spectrum.

The following qualities, though by no means universal, are common to all Breakthrough states. The degree to which these qualities are experienced, and the frequency of their occurrence, depends on the depth of the episode itself:

- A perception of timelessness and "placelessness." A person feels as if the ordinary world, with its boundaries and limitations, is dissolved, or, at least deeply altered. In certain profound moments, people speak of "living in eternity" or of being entirely "outside of time."
- A conviction that the Breakthrough experience comes closer to a direct perception of reality than is possible in one's ordinary state of consciousness. Subjects feel that up till this moment they have been living in a fictitious or incomplete world—that now they see life as it really is.
- An intuition of freedom and lightness of being. A sense of liberation from one's everyday cares, worries, angers, and neuroses.
- Perceptions of light, serenity, and at times universal love.
- A loss of fear, terror, and dread of death. These feelings are often

accompanied by a sense of immortality and a belief in the imperishableness of one's own soul.

- An impression of renewal and of receiving a fresh start. During especially powerful Breakthrough experiences, seekers speak in terms of dying and being reborn.
- A belief that none of what one has seen or heard in this experience can be adequately expressed in ordinary language. After St. Paul's Breakthrough, he remarked that he listened to "unspeakable words." Dante's experience of paradise was "greater than our speech, which yields to such a sight."

Breakthroughs may seem to occur suddenly and seemingly out of the blue. In reality, these moments usually come after many years of daily struggle and time spent in the care of the soul. Unseen and unrealized, day after day, these golden drops of effort accumulate in our hearts and minds; until one day they overflow the rim of the vessel, and a single explosive moment results. What seems to be a spontaneous opening in a fraction of a second is, in truth, the product of thousands of small efforts made over a period of many years.

This subtle process of accretion, as we know from complexity theory in physics, is mirrored over and over again on all levels of nature, from the infinitesimally small to the infinitely large. A single chemical element dropped into a supersaturated solution can cause the entire liquid to suddenly coalesce into one shining crystal. A single sound made at precisely the right moment can bring down an avalanche. Why should things work differently for the human soul? The process is reminiscent of the time the great American painter James McNeill Whistler was asked how long it took him to paint a certain picture. Whistler replied that it took him less than half a day. Whistler was then asked if he really believed the price he was asking for this painting, many thousands of dollars, was justified by a few hours' work.

"I don't ask this price for a half day's work," Whistler retorted. "I ask it for the work of a lifetime."

The Vision Quest

Throughout history Breakthrough experiences have changed the course of the world. If St. Paul had not experienced his blinding vision on the road to Damascus, Christianity as we know it would not exist. The Roman Emperor Constantine, after seeing a flaming cross in the sky glowing with the words

"In this sign conquer," embraced Christ's gospel and went on to Christianize the Western world. Likewise St. Francis of Assisi's sudden Breakthrough visions in Spoleto inspired the founding of the Franciscan order, a religious movement that changed the face of Europe. Several centuries later Martin Luther's religious inspirations led to the formation of Protestantism and epic-changing upheavals. Across a continent, Buddha's Breakthrough to enlightenment beneath the Bodhi tree transformed Asia. The Prophet Muhammad founded the religion of Islam after receiving a visitation from an archangel.

Far from being an eccentric conceit cooked up in New Age meeting halls, the experience of Breakthrough is as old as the human race. The search for it was an integral part of life for primordial people across the globe, especially as practiced in the shamanic tradition, where in North America it was at the heart of tribal society centuries before the white man arrived. Among the woods and mesas of virgin America people took it for granted that the attainment of higher levels of perception—known to Native Americans as the *Vision Quest*—was not only at the heart of life but the very reason for it. Among Native American tribes men and women alike gave the Vision Quest a central place in their philosophy, and by so doing pursued a magical worldview that is largely lost to us today. The last lights of this ancient tradition flicker bravely in the reminiscences of Native American shamans like Black Elk and even in the controversial shamanic revelations of Don Juan, as described by Carlos Castaneda.

This journey of the Vision Quest proceeds through clear stages, each of them carefully delineated and each, when completed, joyously celebrated. Among primitive people, most rites of passage embody a separation from the group, then a transformation through struggle and suffering of the ordinary self to a higher, better self—a symbolic death and rebirth. Anthropologist Bronislaw Malinowski writes: "Such facts as the seclusion of novices at initiation, their individual personal struggles during the ordeal, the communion with spirits, divinities and powers in lonely spots, all these show us primitive religions frequently lived through in solitude."

So common, indeed, is the human hunger for breaking away from ordinary, ego-bound consciousness that we moderns, denied traditional tools such as tribal ceremonies and Vision Quests, turn to a variety of substitutes and simulations. "The great malady of the twentieth century," writes Thomas Moore, "implicated in all our troubles and affecting us individually and socially, is 'loss of soul.' When the soul is neglected, it doesn't go away; it appears symptomatically in obsessions, addictions, violence and loss of meaning."

Take, for example, dangerous sports like mountain climbing and skydiving. Such hazardous diversions can stop the customary flow of associative thought for a few remarkable minutes and transport risk-takers out of themselves into a state of terrifying bliss. Referred to both as "the poor man's mysticism" and the "Hemingway syndrome," this perilous strategy achieves its greatest intensity during moments of life-threatening danger. Witness the many reports of superordinary experiences that happen to people during times of war or disaster. Even the act of watching an exciting sporting event can thrill and absorb us so entirely that we escape from ourselves, if just for a moment, into another world. Intense sexual encounters can do this as well. So can driving at high speeds, prolonged dancing, drugs, even the thrill of fear we feel in a horror movie or when reading an engrossing story. All are quasi-conscious attempts to, as Jim Morrison of the Doors used to sing, "break on through to the other side."

Unfortunately, none of these experiences lasts very long or brings us remotely near the borders of the other side. These momentary feelings of exhilaration or oblivion should not be equated with genuine Breakthroughs that result from years of Search and Struggle. They are, as we shall see, mere shadows and imitations of the real thing.

The Neglected Vision

Clearly Breakthrough experiences are major agents of human change and have helped create the very foundations of world culture.

How strange it is then that so little attention is paid them by the scholarly and professional establishments today. Textbooks in psychology go into enormous detail on the subjects of learning, memory, personality, intelligence. But where, one asks, is mention made of altered states of consciousness and superordinary reality? Usually in the section on abnormal psychology, if it is there at all. This is ironic, considering that in the late nineteenth century the father of modern psychology himself, William James, was intensely interested in Breakthrough moments, and saw them as being the most accurate window we have into the human soul.

"One may say truly, I think, that personal religious experience has its root and center in mystical states of consciousness," James wrote in *The Varieties of Religious Experience*. "And I think I shall at least succeed in convincing you of the reality of the states in question, and of the paramount importance of their function."

James sums up his argument for cosmic consciousness in a single famous paragraph: "It is that our normal waking consciousness, rational consciousness as we call it, is but one special type of consciousness, while all about it, parted from it by the filmiest of screens, there lie potential forms of consciousness entirely different. We may go through life without suspecting their existence; but apply the requisite stimulus, and at a touch they are there in all their completeness. . . . No account of the universe in its totality can be final which leaves these other forms of consciousness quite disregarded. How to regard them is the question, for they are so discontinuous with ordinary consciousness. . . . At any rate, they forbid a premature closing of our accounts with reality."

Despite the voices in the wilderness of men such as James, and later on of Jung and Assagioli, the concept of Breakthrough gradually fell into disrepute, and by the middle of the twentieth century it was relegated to facetious footnotes in abstruse psychiatric journals. It was only in the late 1960s, after a half century of psychoanalysis made it clear that psychotherapy's methods were scarcely a cure-all, that a group of transpersonal psychologists led by Charles Tart, Ken Wilber, Abraham Maslow, and several others reopened the books on altered states and began to scrutinize them under controlled conditions.

Today notions of Breakthrough experiences are slowly gaining acceptance, and this is not surprising. For though official channels continue to assure us that extraordinary mental states are mere tricks of the mind, numbers of Americans report having experienced a wide variety of visionary encounters.

When, for instance, a 1985 Gallup survey asked respondents, "Have you ever been aware of, or influenced by, a presence of a power—whether you call it God or not—which is different from your everyday self?" 43 percent of people answered, "Yes." In a 1988 Gallup survey titled "The Unchurched American," a third of all Americans—33 percent—claimed to have had a life-changing Breakthrough of some kind. Their experiences ran the gamut from seeing visions, hearing voices, near-death encounters, all the way to mystical episodes involving union with the Divine. Respondents who reported these experiences came from all adult age brackets and from all walks of life.

Spiritual Breakthrough is thus not only a reachable goal for all of us, but a highly individual process that is not subject to the normal rules or timetables of ordinary psychology. Struggle and Breakthrough are private affairs, difficult to account for statistically and hard to classify within a given set of scientific categories. Aware of this danger, William James warned that "sharp divisions in this region [between mystical experiences] are difficult to make, and we find all sorts of gradations and mixtures."

On the other hand, while these divisions overlap in a variety of ways, we need to differentiate the real from the half-real, the quarter-real, and the outright false. For when we talk of Breakthroughs we are not speaking of a single level of heightened awareness but of a spectrum of experiences that differ substantially one from the other in degree of intensity, quality of insight, and duration of influence.

Thus in the end, we are entitled to ask: What can I expect from a Breakthrough experience?

And the answer is: For anyone who has weathered the difficulties and savored the joys of the Call, Search, and Struggle, the Breakthrough not only looms but beckons as the final confirmation and validation of what the entire spiritual journey has been all about.

Varieties of Breakthrough Experience

Peak Experiences

My first personal encounter with Breakthrough experience came in 1962 when I met Nina Graboi, mother of my girlfriend at the time, Nicole.

Forty-something, at the time, Nina was in the midst of a midlife transition that would transform her from suburban housewife to secretary for the late Timothy Leary during the psychedelic phase of Leary's bizarre career.

Nina Graboi was one of those people always searching for a way to break out, go further, probe the limits. Like many others who were attracted to the wilder shores at this time, she avidly consumed the writings of Alan Watts, Krishnamurti, Aldous Huxley, D. T. Suzuki, all the totems of 1960s mysticism and enlightenment— anyone who promised escape from the suffocating tract house environment of south shore Long Island that she, and I, knew so well. It was Nina who first introduced me to the work of psychologist Abraham Maslow, and to Maslow's notion of "peak experiences."

During the early 1960s, psychology was locked into a petulant quarrel between Freudian psychoanalysis and B. F. Skinner's behaviorism. Freud on the one hand promised patients a return to "ordinary unhappiness"; Skinner on the other offered a pain-free utopia of conditioned behavior. Against these two sterile options, Dr. Abraham Maslow appeared on the scene championing what he called a "third force," and laying the groundwork for what would later become known as transpersonal psychology. In 1962, the same year I met Nina Graboi, the Esalen Institute was founded in Big Sur, California, and Maslow published his groundbreaking book *Toward a Psychology of Being*. In contrast to current schools of psychotherapy, Maslow held out a warm alternative that would prove enormously appealing to those in the 1960s hungry for spiritual nourishment.

A psychologically healthy person, Maslow insists throughout his writings, is naturally motivated to achieve a state of *self-actualization*. By this he means an "ongoing actualization of potential, capacities, talents as fulfillment of a mission (or call, fate, or vocation) and . . . as an increasing trend toward unity, integration, or synergy within the person."

Unity? Mission? Call?

Concepts like these had rarely been heard in psychological circles up till now, and they generated a great deal of excitement in their time. Human beings, insists Maslow, need not look on themselves either as neurotic broken records or as Pavlovian stimulus-response machines. Those who attain self-actualization are balanced between such extremes. They are at peace with themselves, yet they also have their eye upon a star. Self-actualized persons have an unbiased perception of reality and a healthy acceptance of themselves and others. They love freely, give gladly, tolerate fully, but at the same time maintain a discrete sense of privacy and detachment. They particularly avoid blind conformity and identification with the herd. Most of all, a self-actualized person (and those on the way to self-actualization) enjoy what Maslow terms "peak experiences."

Exactly what does he mean by this now popular phrase?

Peak experiences, according to Maslow, are our healthiest moments. They are those times when we feel the most alive, the most tuned in and balanced—moments when we are clear, free, unencumbered, living at our optimum potential, the best we've ever been. Such moments may visit us in times of intense emotion, such as when a child is born, or in the throes of passionate sex. It can come while wandering in virgin nature or in the stillness of a contemplative trance. "A peak experience is, to a degree, absolute. Emotional reactions in a peak experience have a quality that can be characterized as awe, reverence, and humility. In a mystical/philosophical peak experience, the world is seen united into a total entity; in the love or aesthetic peak experience, the experience itself is given the quality of the complete world.

Fears, anxieties, and inhibitions are momentarily replaced by fulfillment, individuation, and great maturity."

Through the years I have talked to many people who have undergone such extraordinary flashes of awareness.

"On the beach once," a documentary film editor named Rowena told me in an interview, "I was watching the waves. I started thinking of the waves as my own beating heart. As I did, a great feeling came over me, as if the ocean was swallowing me up and I was underwater, hearing their thunder above me. I felt great calm, and at the same time great wonder and worship."

People undergoing peak experiences tend to lose track of time and place. The moment becomes "fuzzy," not beholden to the ordinary constraints of clock or measuring stick. "The first thing that happened when I started going into this state," Rowena explained, "was that I wasn't really on the actual beach anymore. I wasn't anyplace. Kind of in noplace. Limbo. Outside of everything."

Peak experiences can occur at the level of the mind as well as in the feelings. Writer Arthur Koestler describes an experience that took place while he was awaiting a death sentence in a Spanish jail during the Spanish Civil War. Whiling away the time to zero hour, Koestler began writing mathematical notations on the walls of his cell. Suddenly he found himself in a kind of intellectual ecstasy over the fact that one of Euclid's classic mathematical proofs expressed concepts of infinity using finite numbers. "The significance of this swept over me like a wave," writes Koestler, "I must have stood there for some minutes, entranced with a wordless awareness that 'this is perfect—perfect.' Until I noticed some slight mental discomfort nagging at the back of my mind—some trivial circumstance that marred the perfection of the moment. Then I remembered the nature of that irrelevant annoyance: I was, of course, in prison, and might be shot. But this was immediately answered by a feeling whose verbal translation would be: 'So what? Is that all? Have you nothing more serious to worry about?' "

In the midst of a peak experience people often feel "out of themselves." That is, outside their ego-bound, self-referencing circle of awareness. "For a few terrific moments my ego just wasn't there to bother me," a woman told me, "wasn't there to tell me I was happy or unhappy or pester me—remind me I'd left the lights on in the house this morning or something stupid like that." And another: "I felt as if I was no longer me," one woman said, "but more *me* than I ever was before." "I was no one, and I was everyone," a young woman explained.

Are peak experiences Breakthrough experiences?

Yes, but only after a fashion. And only to a limited degree. More specifically, they are preliminaries, a foretaste of states that are possible on the spiritual way, a kind of preview of things to come. People who have passed through the earlier stages of the soul's journey tend to have such moments with ever increasing frequency as time passes. We look on these incidents as serendipitous rewards of the Struggle.

There's a danger, though, that any spiritual traveler is well advised to heed. Peak experiences are almost exclusively pleasurable and sometimes ecstatic. They may be sexual, emotional, psychological. When they do take on a religious spin, they can easily set a seeker on the wrong course. People find themselves trying to duplicate these experiences over and over again, becoming literally addicted to the process. Meanwhile the notion of Struggle and of dealing with one's inner conflicts and pain is lost in the pursuit. Writes Jack Kornfield in *A Path with a Heart:* "Many people first come to spiritual practice hoping to skip over their sorrows and wounds, the difficult areas of their lives. They hope to rise above them and enter a spiritual realm full of divine grace, free from all conflict . . . [But] as soon as practitioners relax in their discipline they again encounter all the unfinished business of the body and heart that they had hoped to leave behind."

Compared with the way we feel a majority of the time, peak moments are an intoxicant. After experiencing such a moment we can't imagine anything better.

And yet from a higher point of view, such episodes are nothing more than a taste of what is possible in a total Breakthrough. The danger lies in believing that this peak moment is "it"; that we've gone as far as we can go, that we've arrived at the ultimate and seen Reality face-on. When, in fact, we have barely scratched the surface. "For someone living an uptight, head-restricted experience," writes Jacob Needleman, "a hot bath can feel extraordinary—but it's not a mystical experience. We live such constricted lives that the slightest triggering of a new vital energy gets labeled 'spiritual.' "

A friend of mine named Jerry told me the following story.

"My aunt Betty was a very devout woman," he related. "She once told me that she saw God. I asked her to tell me about it.

" 'Well,' my aunt said, 'one day I was in a movie theater, watching a particularly sensitive film. In the middle of the film I started to cry. Then I felt this very strong emotion. It filled me up entirely. I felt that I was lifting upwards, that I was very, very elevated. Everything in me felt loving and warm.'

"I asked my aunt how long this experience lasted. She said about five or ten minutes—she wasn't sure. I asked her what else happened. She said that was all. I asked her how she thought she'd seen God in all this. She said that the emotion was God. I suggested to her that God is something much greater than just a strong feeling. I told her that when saints talk to God they go into swoons, sometimes for days at a time. Usually people can't bear to be in the presence of God for more than a few seconds. When God spoke to Moses directly Moses went into a faint.

"But she wouldn't hear of this. 'That was God,' she insisted. 'I know it was.'"

Peak experiences have an ultimate quality about them that can sweep us away. They can thrill and elevate. But they can also mislead, making us think we have gone further on the spiritual path than we really have.

In truth, such moments are still very much of the ordinary world, very much a product of our senses and emotions and minds. True Breakthrough occasions go beyond sensory experience entirely, partaking of a realm that cannot easily be measured, described, or even imagined.

Peak experiences have their place, in short. But they are a beginning, not an end; the light of a candle, not of the sun.

Psychedelic Highs and Lows

In the spring of 1967 I was living in New York's East Village, that multicultural extension of Greenwich Village famed as racial melting pot, birthplace of Yiddish theater, and, in 1967, home of the psychedelic revolution.

The year was a magical-mystery tour. Flower children walked the streets by the thousands and I, as mentioned earlier, was spending my final college semester doing fieldwork for a senior thesis on psychedelics. It was a time when anything seemed possible, even a research project as outlandish as this one (fully approved by my advisors and professors at Yale, I should add).

As part of my research protocol, I stationed myself every day at the entrance to a local head shop known as the Psychedelicatessen. Here I accosted customers, each selected according to a rigorous random number table, and asked if they would grant me an interview. Despite the paranoia rampant on the East Village streets at this time, most agreed. In the months that followed I listened to literally hundreds of psychedelic adventures, some of them phantasmagoric and occasionally humorous, some dark and lurid, a few redolent of profound psychological and spiritual insight.

By May of this year I had interviewed a wide range of LSD and mescaline users, and was preparing to write the concluding chapters of my thesis. Having plumbed the heights and depths of the subject, I still felt there was one major stone left unturned: me.

How, I wondered, could researchers write in an informed and knowledgeable way about a state of consciousness they had not experienced?

By now I had seriously studied the clinical and medical literature on LSD and was satisfied that, despite a measure of risk, there was no way to do meaningful research on psychedelics without personally experiencing its effects. And so, along with seekers like Aldous Huxley and Huston Smith, and 1960s celebrities like Cary Grant and Steve Allen, I sampled a tab of LSD firsthand.

During the initial hour of my session I had no clear impression of change. By the second hour odd physical changes were taking place. By the third hour the walls of my Lower East Side pied-à-terre were pulsating like a beating heart, becoming so diaphanous and crystalline I fancied I could see their molecular structure. A thousand other sensory shocks followed. Yet oddly, my cognitive thought stayed lucid and my normal sense of self remained intact throughout all this. Where was the famed ego death I had heard so much about?

I mentioned this stubborn state of sobriety to the student who had administered the drug and who was participating in the session along with me. He smiled in a peculiar way and said simply, "Your mind is always in an egoless state. You just don't know it."

The moment I heard these words something inside me came "unhooked" and the entire universe seemed to collapse around me. The next instant I found my normal ego being swept away, and in a moment I was floating ecstatically in a timeless, endless world of light that, as William James had promised, was utterly beyond words.

A million other insights followed that day.

The essential point had now been made and understood: a Breakthrough is not the addition of something new to the mind, nor is it the subtraction of something old. It is simply a temporary parting of the veils that keep us from seeing what is always there—a glimpse into the depths of the soul that are normally barred from our view by angels with fiery swords.

I was appropriately humbled and deeply moved. I also felt a bit like a naughty cheater.

Soon after this experience I returned to Yale University, graduated, and never delved into psychedelics again. As Ram Dass himself later said, taking

LSD is like receiving a telephone call. You listen, you get the message, then you hang up.

Was my psychedelic experience a legitimate Breakthrough experience?

An experience, yes. Certainly. But a legitimate spiritual Breakthrough? I don't think so.

My encounter with hallucinogens proved to me without a doubt that the higher states described by saints and mystics are authentic and that all of us are capable of experiencing such moments. We all truly carry the Kingdom of Heaven within us.

But there's the dark side to this moon as well, and in my estimation it far outweighs the light.

Here I'm going to put aside discussion of the physical, psychiatric, and even genetic damage that psychedelics are reputed to cause, as well as the Chinese belief that such drugs degrade our primal *ching*—the fundamental store of vital life energy we receive at birth. More to the point, a psychedelic drug offers a Breakthrough of sorts, it is true. But it is flawed and incomplete. Psychedelics allow us to look through the window of the Spirit, as it were, and to play with the toys on the other side for a few brief hours. This experience does not give us anything permanent: no enduring inner change or transformation of being (except in a few cases a psychotic one), no wisdom or understanding, no lasting gift to take back to ordinary life. Only the memory of an encounter that soon fades; this plus, perhaps, a psychological craving to repeat the experience again, and again, and again.

The qualities that give a spiritual Breakthrough its legitimacy, I realize today, looking back on my own psychedelic experience, are the Call and Search and Struggle that lead up to it and in a sense produce it. A true Breakthrough requires preparation over time. It must be forged in the fires of effort and patience and sincerity; it must be drawn from the very stuff of our life. To allow oneself to be plummeted into a state of higher consciousness without adequate preparation and foreknowledge is dangerous business, not just psychologically but spiritually as well. One can become lost in the spiritual world as easily as in the material.

As with peak experiences, psychedelics awaken higher faculties in the mind for a few hours, causing the unwary to believe they are now permanently "enlightened." During the 1960s and early 1970s the streets of Berkeley, Harvard Square, and the East Village were filled with messianic young people who had taken too many acid trips and who had enjoyed free and unearned access to otherworldly visions once too often. These people believed they were on intimate speaking terms with God, and were now out "turning on" the world, preaching their own mishmash of drugs, religion, and delusional nonsense. As the Sufi saying goes: "The most misled is the one who misleads others."

In a postscript to his philosophical best-seller *The Outsider,* British writer Colin Wilson adds an interesting insight to this question, claiming that while drugs like mescaline plug people into a fascinating world of visions, they weaken their will and concentration, reducing them ultimately to "an animal level" of passivity and incoherence. Wilson quotes Aldous Huxley's famous sentiment: "A world in which everyone took mescaline would be a world in which there are no wars, but it would also be a world in which there is no civilization, for we just couldn't be bothered to build it."

This gap between drug states and genuinely mystical states was well expressed to me by Pat Ricci, a fifty-one-year-old advertising executive I met in Chicago. Pat is a person who has experienced both chemically altered states and several true Breakthroughs. "I had one experience on LSD a long time ago," she says. "I had just done a workshop with Stanislof Grof, and it helped me put the whole thing in perspective. At first I felt this wonderful sense of connection that people talk about from the drug. I saw that there was a reality much more real than this one. I felt I had woken up from a dream. I had feelings of love and compassion for everything and everyone. But then the experience wore off, and I lay around my apartment for days, mourning the loss of the experience and feeling this huge hole that I knew I couldn't fill. It was as if heaven had been handed to me and then snatched away. The only way I could get it back was to take the drug again. I knew that was a trap, and I didn't. I'll admit it, though—I was tempted."

Several years later Pat was traveling in Greece with a group of friends and seekers. She stopped for the night in an inn in a small village, and after dinner took a walk by herself down the ancient streets of the town. Suddenly the world became lit. "Everywhere I looked I saw faces of colored light," Pat told me. "It all happened so fast, out of nowhere. One minute I was strolling, the next the streets turned to glowing rainbow colors. The sky, and the sidewalk—all light. Everywhere I looked was shining. Behind that light I thought I could see the face of God. It wasn't a face, exactly, but that's the best way I can describe it.

"Later on I thought back to my drug experience and it seemed so pasty and unreal compared to what had happened to me that night. Unwholesome, you know, like a fake. If you asked me the difference between the two experiences I'd say it was like looking at a photograph of something as compared to the real thing."

"Reflect," advised Plato. "Is not the dreamer, sleeping or waking, one who likens dissimilar things, who puts the copy in the place of the real object?"

A Bolt from the Blue

At the conclusion to J. D. Salinger's short story "De Daumier-Smith's Blue Period," the nineteen-year-old hero, an ordinary and undistinguished young man, walks by a department store window where he happens to notice a hefty woman of about thirty changing the truss on a wooden dummy. The young man stares in fascination at this odd scene until the woman realizes he is looking at her and becomes self-conscious. To escape his gaze she steps back, then slips and does a pratfall, landing heavily on her bottom "like a skater."

Something about this spectacle of raw human frailty plays on the young man's sense of pathos. "It was just then that I had my Experience," he relates. "Suddenly (and I say this, I believe, with all due self-consciousness), the sun came up and sped toward the bridge of my nose at the rate of ninety-three million miles a second. Blinded and very frightened—I had to put my hand on the glass to keep my balance. The thing lasted for no more than a few seconds. When I got my sight back, the girl had gone from the window."

Here Salinger is describing a rare and shattering phenomenon, a spontaneous Breakthrough; that is, a sudden eruption into higher states of consciousness that is seemingly unconnected to one's efforts or to any larger religious context. For reasons no one entirely understands, and under circumstances that often make no sense, a person is simply struck by the Spirit. Such people may be lukewarm toward spirituality and may not have passed through the preliminary stages of Call, Search, Struggle. Their experience comes utterly out of the blue.

What is interesting about this phenomenon is that in many cases a person who undergoes such an episode—even one that triggers the most astonishing visions and emotions—often looks on it as a marvelous but essentially meaningless accident of nature. As time passes, the memory of this moment fades. Eventually it is forgotten.

From the standpoint of the soul, such moments are like free samples given away in a confectioner's shop, gilded invitations to a brief glimpse of the Beyond. Such gratuitous gifts come at the most unexpected times and to the most unlikely people, as the following narrative from a British schoolboy shows.

"The thing happened one summer afternoon, on the school cricket field, while I was sitting on the grass, waiting my turn at bat. I was thinking about nothing in particular, merely enjoying the pleasures of midsummer idleness. Suddenly, and without warning, something invisible seemed to be drawn across the sky, transforming the world around me into a kind of tent of concentrated and enhanced significance. What had been merely an outside became an inside. The objective was somehow transformed into a complete subjective fact, which was experienced as 'mine' but on a level where the word had no meaning, for 'I' was no longer the familiar ego. Nothing more can be said about the experience. It brought no accession of knowledge about anything except, very obscurely, the knower and his way of knowing. After a few minutes there was a 'return to normalcy.' The event made a deep impression on me at the time. But because it did not fit into any of the thought patterns—religious, philosophical, scientific—with which as a boy of fifteen I was familiar, it came to seem more and more anomalous, more and more irrelevant to 'real life,' and was finally forgotten."

Another fragmentary Breakthrough moment is described by Pamela Gordon, a writer who lives with her husband and daughter in Florida. Her mystical experience came when she was twenty-one, just out of college and living in New York. One summer evening she took a ride on the Staten Island ferry with friends. Standing on the deck overlooking New York Harbor, she suddenly found herself intensely aware of her deceased immigrant grandparents who had come through New York generations earlier. While immersed in the memory of her ancestors, a strange thing happened.

"Under the eerie sky," Gordon writes, "and the night wind I felt myself move beyond the immediate moment, beyond the time and place in which I stood. Not only were my grandparents surrounding me but each one of the many people who had traveled these waters over the centuries were there too. Time, it seemed, had both collapsed and expanded. What I'd always experienced as a continuous line, event following event from the beginning until now, was suddenly circular. I knew with a calm certainty that all of history had existed simultaneously; everything that had ever happened was happening, or would happen, flowed at the same moment in a continuous circle. The quality of the night, combined with the ride on the ferry, had allowed me to enter a reality outside my usual recognition, a fuller and larger reality.

"The realization was very strong—more an experience, really, than a realization. It was not in the least unnerving. Instead of confusing or upsetting me, it seemed to affirm something I had always known but had never felt so concretely and had never put into words to myself before. I didn't try to explain it to friends. I just breathed deeply and looked around and soaked it in until it faded."

What is this spontaneous Breakthrough, then? No one can say for sure. A gift of heaven? Or, as the skeptical suggest, a freak of body chemistry? Who knows?

Whatever its ultimate cause, to not take advantage of such a golden occasion is a spiritual blunder indeed, and one that will not easily be remedied. For unless one quickly seizes the moment and follows the path that an invitation of this kind offers, the glow soon fades—and with it the opportunity.

A Sufi teaching story suggests, in a humorous and bittersweet way, how a sudden flight to higher states can devastate those who are unprepared.

The story tells of a tattered beggar named Rafiq who spends his life wandering the streets of Baghdad. One day Rafiq is making his usual rounds when a young boy accosts him.

"My mistress wishes to see you immediately," the boy announces. "I am here to lead you to her. Do not ask questions. Just accept this blindfold."

Having nothing to lose, Rafiq agrees.

The beggar is led through the city streets for many hours until he and the boy come to a magnificent mansion. Here the boy removes the blindfold and ushers Rafiq inside. Waiting for him is the most celestially beautiful young woman he has ever beheld.

The woman proceeds to give Rafiq the most ravishing night of love a man can imagine. The beggar falls asleep in her arms, wild with adoration, giving thanks for his miraculous luck. The next morning, however, two armed guards enter the room, drag him out, and drop him off on the exact street where he was picked up the day before.

From this day on, the story tells, the poor beggar waits for the boy to come to him again, and escort him back for another tryst with the beautiful woman. But the boy never returns. And the ravished Rafiq spends the rest of his days pining away for his single night of ecstasy.

Death as Our Teacher

Breakthrough experiences are not invariably joyous occasions. They can also be times of terror; when death becomes our teacher.

Take the case of James Fowler, a Christian minister and director of the

Center for Faith Development at Emory University. Today Professor Fowler is one of the greatest contemporary writers on the psychology of human development and religion. In much of his work he contrasts literalistic, dogmatic piety with higher, more universal levels of understanding. When Fowler actually sat down to write his own book, however, he did not begin with universal understanding, but with himself, his own spiritual vulnerability, and, most of all, his own existential terror. For it turns out that Fowler's years of Search and Struggle led him to a poignant Breakthrough moment catalyzed by a sudden awareness of his own death.

"Four A.M. in the darkness of a cold winter morning," Fowler writes, "suddenly I am fully and frighteningly awake. I see it clearly: I am going to die. I am going to die. This body, this mind, this lived and living myth, this husband, father, teacher, son, friend, will cease to be. My wife, beside me in the bed, seems completely out of reach. My work, my professional associates, my ambitions, my dreams and absorbing projects feel like fiction. 'Real life' suddenly feels like a transient dream. In the strange aloneness of this moment, defined by the certainty of death, I awake to the true facts of life."

Fowler goes on to explain how this Breakthrough gave him a new insight into faith. On the one hand, he tells us, faith can be a coat that screens us from the "naked abyss" of life's mysteries. On the other, faith can permit us to stand before this abyss with all its terror and wonder, and look fearlessly—or fearfully, whatever the case may be—into its depths. Following a Breakthrough we begin to doubt many of the things we once took for granted. But when death is our teacher, we also have the potential to break through to new levels of faith and meaning. And for Fowler, this is exactly what happened. After his experience he went on to write a book that helped inspire thousands of readers to find deeper meaning in their lives.

An intense awareness of mortal danger can, in other words, activate such great infusions of energy and attention that we are catapulted into higher planes of awareness. It is this thrill of walking the dangerous edge, as we have seen, that drives people to voluntarily risk their lives in hazardous sports and death-defying endeavors. The closer we come to our own death, paradoxically, the more alive we feel.

We often hear Breakthrough stories from soldiers in war. One tells of a British armored car officer hit by a German antitank gun during World War II. Hurled through the air, his body set ablaze with phosphorus, the officer lived to tell the tale, reporting that "the next experience was definitely unusual. I was conscious of being two persons—one, lying on the ground in a field . . . my clothes, etc., on fire, and waving my limbs about wildly, at the same time uttering moans and gibbering with fear—I was quite conscious of both making these sounds, and at the same time hearing them as though coming from another person. The other 'me' was floating up in the air about twenty feet from the ground, from which position I could see not only my other self on the ground, but also the hedge and the road, and the car which was surrounded by smoke, and burning fiercely. I remember quite distinctly telling myself: 'It's no use gibbering like that—roll over and over to put the flames out.' This my ground body eventually did, rolling over into a ditch under the hedge where there was a slight amount of water. The flames went out, and at this stage I suddenly became one person again."

The British officer's story brings to mind another testimony from Richard Wilhelm, renowned translator of the *I Ching.* In China during the First World War, Wilhelm was watching an old scholar read his sacred texts while the catastrophic battle of Tsingtao takes place all around them. "Happiest of all," writes Wilhelm, "was an old Chinese scholar who was so wholly absorbed in his sacred books that not even a grenade falling at his side could disturb his calm. He reached out for it—it was a dud—then drew back his hand and, remarking that it was very hot, forthwith returned to his books."

In Tolstoy's great novelette *The Death of Ivan Ilyich,* the author takes us into the mind of a dying man.

Throughout this sad and solemn tale the protagonist, an undistinguished petty bureaucrat named Ivan Ilyich, comes to a gradual realization that he is suffering from a terminal ailment and that death is inevitable.

As he loops himself through every form of denial and rationalization, every emotional contortion, we witness the creeping horror that comes over Ilyich as one by one the things that matter most are stripped away, as with the dying miser in *Everyman,* until Ilyich finds himself faced with the soul-wrenching question: "What if my whole life has really been wrong?" In the last scenes of Tolstoy's tale Ilyich approaches death suffering the most terrible agonies of abandonment. Just as he has given up hope, the light breaks through. The moment is triggered when Ilyich's son enters his room, kisses his father's hand, and breaks down in tears.

"It was at this very same time," Tolstoy writes, "that Ivan Ilyich fell through, saw the light, and it was revealed to him that his life had not been as it ought, but that still it was possible to repair it. . . . All at once it became clear to him that what had tortured him and would not leave him was suddenly dropping away all at once on both sides and on ten sides and on all sides. . . . 'How right and how simple!' he thought. 'And the pain?' he asked himself. 'Where's it gone? Eh, where are you, pain?'

"He began to watch for it.

" 'Yes, here it is. Well, what of it, let the pain be.

" 'And death. Where is it?'

"He looked for his old accustomed terror of death, and did not find it. 'Where is it? What death?' There was no terror, because it was not there either.

"In the place of death there was only light.

" 'So this is it!' he suddenly explained aloud.

" 'What joy!' "

In this powerful tale of life, death, and resurrection, Tolstoy frequently uses the images of "falling through" and "seeing light," two metaphors frequently reported in Breakthrough experiences and in near-death experiences. Passing through the Stages of the Soul, in this sense, brings about a "falling through"; not the falling through of death, but of our illusions and false notions.

My friend Carol Segrave learned this truth at the time of the death of her mother when Carol herself was in her mid-fifties: "There has been a dramatic crisis in my life," she explained, "and it was the death of my mother in her ninetieth year. That was just a couple of months ago. She really was my greatest life-love and the most reliable love relationship I had in my life."

I was aware that Carol had moved from California back to New York to take care of her ailing mother. Fortunately, she was able to find a good job with a real estate development firm, and reestablish her life on the East Coast. But the reason for her move was not motivated by business concerns; it was done out of conviction that she belonged with her mother. As with Ilyich, death would become her teacher.

"I watched her decline. I watched her die. I sat with her. I held her hand, and it was the most profound experience of my life. I am not the same. It was life-transforming for me because I got to see that's where life ends. So then I really began on a very deliberate, careful path to arrange for myself the best way to live the rest of my life. My mother's death gave me that gift: a new life."

When we fully accept our mortality, the result can change our lives.

"I've slowed down tremendously," Carol says. "Once I had to have so much energy. I had to perform, to be so great, so fabulous. My whole life had been dedicated to proving that I was efficient, useful, intelligent, unselfish, that I could do more than anybody else could do, and that I could take care of everyone in the universe."

Taking care of everyone in the universe—that's a task many people feel obliged in one way or another to perform. We've already talked a good deal about the virtues of service, and of its immense value both to ourselves and to others. What then exactly is wrong with taking care of everyone? Or with similar charitable impulses? Why should Carol, or we, or any of us castigate ourselves for wanting to be helpful and unselfish?

Because, on closer scrutiny many of the character traits that we think of as charitable or unselfish reveal themselves as having subtle ulterior motives. Often, for example, we celebrate qualities in ourselves that we believe make us kindly and special, qualities such as Carol speaks of: "taking care of everyone" or "being unselfish." When we hold these qualities up to the merciless light of self-examination, they sometimes turn out to be a self-serving means for making ourselves look good in the eyes of others. What we think of as generosity may expose itself simply as a need to control. What we believe to be selfless involvement in a spiritual group or philanthropic organization may turn out to be hunger for attention or the need to be liked by others. There is a Buddhist saying that after you have purified yourself of your vices, then purify yourself of your virtues.

In the Bible, Jesus rebukes the Pharisees for their self-righteousness in exactly this spirit. The Pharisees are not necessarily "bad" people. They are simply self-satisfied and self-deluded. They act from egotism and self-admiration, then dignify their behavior with high-sounding terms: altruism, caring, self-sacrifice, humanitarianism. These Pharisees of the world would be well advised to heed the message of the great spiritual teachers, many of whom warn us to be careful lest we use our virtues as a weapon of manipulation rather than as a tool of the spirit; and who tell us that when we behave in this way our "virtues" are no longer virtuous at all but subtle forms of self-delusion. The Tibetan teacher Chogyam Rinpoche refers to this practice of using spiritual means for gaining personal ends as "spiritual materialism."

"I pretended that I had an inner life," Carol Segrave told me. "I meditated, I'd go off to retreats. I wore this whole outer costume of 'I'm a spiritual entity.' But coming back to this profound experience with my mother—watching her stop breathing all of a sudden and have her spirit leave. There were no fanfares, there was no drum. It was a quiet, peaceful slipping away into another form. I just said to myself at this point, 'Stop. Live the rest of your life in that spirit.' "

There is a common assumption that Breakthrough moments must be high-energy occasions, parades, as Carol says, of fanfare and drums.

But this is not always the case. There are quiet Breakthroughs as well, interludes that embrace us in the stillness of the night or when we sit by the bedside holding the hand of a dying parent. During much of life our relationships with others, even those we deeply love, are paved with a veneer of taking-for-granted. Then along comes the awareness of death, forcing us to separate the real from the unreal, thrusting back the veils, showing us that life is running out like the sands in a glass, and that there is precious little time for us to reach out and care for those we really love—our children, our spouses, our parents, our friends.

Such a moment can shake a person to the core. When it arrives, as it did for Carol Segrave, we are not necessarily swimming in light. Yet we are changed. Our new truth is direct and simple, without pinwheels and stars. It says simply what Carol says: "Stop. Live the rest of your life in this spirit of quiet and peace."

Breakthrough Experiences: A Sudden Shattering

The Zen master Hakuin once compared the moment of enlightenment to a great structure of ice suddenly melting and collapsing—just as our ego collapses under the weight of spiritual force, and we fall into our own Supreme Identity.

Hakuin tells how one day while he was studying the *Lotus Sutra* he became aware of an insect buzzing near his ear. The next moment he was catapulted into illumination. "Suddenly I saw through the perfect true mystery [of the *Lotus Sutra*] and broke through all doubts. I comprehended the error of my earlier greater or lesser enlightenments. Unexpectedly I called out and wept. One must realize that the practice of Zen is by no means easy."

The Indian poet Rabindranath Tagore underwent a similar mystical opening while looking at the sun come up one morning. "As I was watching it," Tagore tells, "suddenly, in a minute, a veil seemed to be lifted from my eyes. I found the world rapt in an inexpressible glory with its waves of joy and beauty bursting and breaking on all sides. The thick cloud of sorrow that lay on my heart in many folds was pierced through and through by the light of the world, which was everywhere radiant. There was nothing and no one whom I did not love at that moment."

Bernard Glassman, a contemporary American Zen master, tells of his Breakthrough under more prosaic circumstances, as it happened to him one morning while riding to work in his car pool.

"A powerful opening occurred right in my car, much more powerful than the first. One phrase triggered it, and all my questions were resolved. I couldn't stop laughing or crying, both at once, and the people in the car were very upset and concerned, they didn't have any idea what was happening, and I kept telling them there was nothing to worry about! . . . Luckily, I was an executive, and had my own office, but I just couldn't stop laughing and crying, and finally I had to go home. That opening brought with it a tremendous feeling about the suffering in the world; it was a much more compassionate opening than the first."

Glassman emphasizes the importance of the last stage of Return that follows Breakthrough. "Even after having a *kensho* [enlightenment] experience it can take many years to clarify it. Without work, it just fades away into a memory." Glassman compares a Breakthrough experience to an entrance exam at school: it is only the beginning, he says, of real study in a higher curriculum that has an endless number of courses.

Robert Atchley, a professor of sociology and a follower of Hindu Vedanta whom we met in an earlier chapter, makes a similar comparison while discussing his own Breakthrough experience. About a year after his initial spiritual experiences, Atchley went to India, where he spent five weeks with his teacher, Guru Maharaj. "I have no clue what he talked about," Atchley said. "I don't remember the specifics, just as I don't remember so many of the words and ideas I've read in textbooks over the years. The words didn't matter. After a while I stopped talking and he stopped talking. We just sat there and didn't say anything for at least a week. I wasn't thinking, I wasn't talking or analyzing. I was just being.

"After having shut up for a while, verbally and mentally, sitting near Maharaj, the questions started coming up subvocally in me, and then, at the same moment, answering themselves entirely on their own, one after the other, until all my questions were satisfied. I began to understand, really *understand*, what it was all about. The process had taken so long because we all have these conceptions that get in our way. Higher understanding is so subtle. It's not flashy or brilliant. For some people it may be. I don't know what anybody else's experience is like. I can certainly say, though, that for me spirituality is a very subtle and, at the same time, very powerful force. Yet I had to quiet my mind way down before I could see it, and sense it, and receive it."

Christianity interprets the idea of Breakthrough in terms of what the New Testament calls "transfiguration"; that is, the act of changing our shape of being. Not our physical shape, of course, as in the sudden appearance of a halo over our head, but our inner being. A firsthand account of transfiguration has come down to us from a disciple of one of the greatest saints in the

Eastern Orthodox Church, St. Seraphim of Sarov. Here the disciple (who is speaking) has just gone through a soul-shaking mystical opening, and Father Seraphim is helping him put it into perspective for him.

"What do you feel?" asks Father Seraphim.

"An immeasurable well-being," I replied.

"But what sort of well-being? What exactly?"

"I feel," I replied, "such calm, such peace in my soul, that I can find no words to express it."

"My friend, it is the peace our Lord spoke of when he said to his disciples, 'My peace I give to you, the peace which the world cannot give, the peace which passes understanding.' What else do you feel?"

"Infinite joy in my heart."

Father Seraphim continued: "Then the Spirit of God descends on a man and envelops him in the fullness of his presence, the soul overflows with unspeakable joy, for the Holy Spirit fills everything it touches with joy."

One of the characteristics of enlightenment often spoken of is how obvious the lessons are once they are revealed to us. And yet, many people struggle for a lifetime and never find it. What stubborn force keeps seekers from attaining what the illuminated ones tell us is so close at hand?

The obvious response is to point the accusing finger at selfishness and anger, and all the psychological bugbears and bullies that get in our way. Yet below these powerful impulses lies an even more elemental drive—desire itself.

In India generations of monkey catchers have used an ingenious, apparently foolproof trick to snare their prey. Monkey catchers take a hollow coconut shell and carve a hole in the center, cutting sharp teeth at the edges of the hole. Then they place a large sweetmeat inside the shell. They secure the shell to the ground, and wait for a monkey to pass.

By and by a victim appears. The monkey slips its hand into the coconut and seizes the bait. When it tries to remove its hand with the large chunk of bait, the hole is too small and the teeth along the edges cut too deeply. The monkey is trapped.

Understand, of course, that all the monkey has to do at this point to get away is release the sweetmeat. But no, it refuses to give up what it wants. Instead of running it sits there for hours on end screeching with rage and beating at the shell—*anything*, rather than let go. Until finally the hunters come along and take its skin.

We reach into the world to grab whatever the bait happens to be—money, fame, love, success—only to find ourselves trapped, then frustrated because we are trapped.

Like the monkey, we can free ourselves anytime by letting go of the desires that hold us captive. But our urges and our dreams will not allow it. Escape is possible only after the monkey inside us goes through spiritual reeducation, and learns that the secret of freedom has always been within our grasp—or, more accurately, within our release.

I remember once years ago spending a day visiting a meditation group. A young, highly intelligent lady was leading the affair, and she told us the story of how on a two-month retreat, she sat in her meditation cell every day saying to herself, "Okay, I'm ready to let go now. I'm ready to give it up. I'm ready to say goodbye to my ego. So okay now—let go. I said *l-e-t g-o*. But though I repeated this over and over every day, nothing happened. I stayed just as stuck as before."

Ripening is all, as we see in other Breakthrough stories.

Richard Jefferies, son of a British farmer and the author of a notable nineteenth-century spiritual autobiography, *The Story of My Heart*, tells how he migrated from disbelief to discontent to a resolve to break through to another world of comprehension. At the time of his writing, Jefferies held no orthodox doctrines about God or religion. The spiritual power of his ultimate Breakthrough is nonetheless unmistakable.

Jefferies' Struggle began in his youth. "My heart was dusty," he writes, "parched for want of the rain of deep feeling; my mind arid and dry. . . . A species of thick clothing slowly grows about the mind, the pores are choked, little habits become a part of existence, and by degrees the mind is enclosed in a husk. When this began to form I felt eager to escape from it."

Jefferies is describing the same process that Kastenbaum refers to as *habituation*—imprisonment in our fixed ways of seeing the world. Jefferies' solution was an ancient one—to lose himself in nature.

"There was a hill to which I used to resort at such periods. . . . The familiar everyday scene was soon out of sight; I came to other trees, meadows, and fields; I began to breathe a new air and to have a fresher aspiration."

So far Jefferies' story is familiar enough. We've all felt that special energy and sense of renewal in nature. But for Jefferies the Struggle led him one step beyond the outer surfaces of bark and flowers and stone: "I was utterly alone with the sun and the earth. Lying down on the grass, I spoke in my soul to the earth, the sun, the air, and the distant sea far beyond sight. . . . With all the intensity of feeling which exalted me, all the intense communion I held with the earth, the sun and sky, the stars hidden by the light, with the ocean."

Jefferies describes an important element in the movement toward Breakthrough: the surrender of the everyday personality. Here, in its own way, was the very letting go that the teacher in the meditation center had been seeking for years. Why it fell on Jefferies in such an effortless way we do not know.

"I hid my face in the grass," he continues. "I was wholly prostrated, I lost myself in the wrestle, I was rapt and carried away . . ."

The Breakthrough is not always accompanied by conventional prayer as understood in orthodox religion. For Jefferies the sacred text is the fine-textured vividness of the natural world itself: a prayer of leaves and birds and butterflies. And yet it is not simply the outer beauties of the forest that trigger these deeper episodes. It is what is behind them, or beyond them, the secret soul of the universe that gives hints of itself in the endless forms of the natural world. For Jefferies, and for many others, this divine code and all it reveals is enough to transport him to another world.

Another Breakthrough story that uses several metaphors of nature, like Jefferies', but which takes place in an urban setting, comes from the nineteenth-century collector of Breakthrough stories, Dr. R. M. Bucke.

In his famous book *Cosmic Consciousness,* Bucke tells how he had just spent the evening with two friends reading and discussing poetry. "We parted at midnight," Bucke tells us. "I had a long drive to my lodgings. My mind, deeply under the influence of the ideas, images, and emotions called up by the reading and talk, was calm and peaceful. I was in a state of quiet, even passive enjoyment, not actually thinking, but letting ideas, images and emotions flow by themselves, as it were, through my mind.

At this moment the Breakthrough occurred: "All at once, without warning of any kind, I found myself wrapped in a flame-colored cloud. For an instant I thought of fire, an immense conflagration somewhere close by in that great city; the next instant I knew that the fire was in myself. Directly afterwards there came upon me a sense of exultation, of immense joyousness, accompanied or immediately followed by an intellectual illuminating quite impossible to describe. Among other things, I did not merely come to believe, I saw that the universe is not composed of dead matter, but is, on the contrary, a living Presence; I became conscious in myself of eternal life.

"The vision lasted a few seconds and was gone. But the memory of it and the sense of the reality of it has remained during the quarter of a century which has since elapsed. I knew that what the vision showed me was true. I had attained to a point of view from which I saw that it must be true. That view, that conviction, I may say that consciousness, has never, even during the periods of deepest depression, been lost."

Breakthrough moments, by definition, have no limit, and at times can extend so far beyond human reckoning that any attempt to describe them is folly. Such a moment is described by an anonymous woman known only by her initials, C.M.C.

By way of background, C.M.C. was a believing Catholic and an apparently well-adjusted wife and mother. In her late forties she suffered a serious physical illness which shook up her old faith and in a strange way served as a Call. "There was always that undercurrent," said C.M.C. "A vein of sadness deep down, out of sight. Often as I have walked out under the stars, looking up into those silent depths with unspeakable longing for some answer to the wordless questions within me."

Recovering from her illness, she began a Search, not so much for a new religion as for a new kind of faith. "I had been living on the surface; now I was going down into the depths, and as I went deeper and deeper the barriers which had separated me from my fellow men were broken down, the sense of kinship with every living creature had deepened."

Now followed the Struggle: "The pain and tension deep in the core and center of my being were so great that I felt as might some creature which had outgrown its shell and yet could not escape. What it was I knew not, except that it was a great yearning—for freedom, for larger life—for deeper life."

C.M.C. waited patiently and vulnerably for something in her to grow and expand. In the meantime she struggled to give herself entirely to her beliefs. "I felt the Power in whose hands I am, that it may do with me as it will. It was several days after this resolve before the point of complete surrender was reached. Meantime, with every internal sense, I searched for that principle, whatever it was, which would hold me when I let go. At last, subdued with a curious growing strength in my weakness, I let go of myself."

There comes a moment in every Struggle when we glimpse, however fleetingly, what is ultimately at stake in our striving—nothing less than extinction and total loss of our worldly persona. This is one reason why the philosopher Kierkegaard puts such emphasis on the "leap of faith." Not because we must have rote confidence in a system of ideas. But because despite our doubts, our hesitations, our terrors even, we must be willing to trust in the greater possibilities of our soul, and throw ourselves headlong into the dark night of the Nameless.

The Roman Catholic monk Bede Griffiths in his autobiography likens this process to a small child standing at a trapdoor. In a basement below, the father is standing, urging the child on. The cellar is dark and frightening. The father tells the child to jump. The child knows the father will protect him, but there is much hesitation before the child finally lets go and leaps into the void, ultimately to be caught in loving arms. This is what the leap of faith that Kierkegaard speaks of is like—the extreme vulnerability of trusting and surrender.

For C.M.C. this inner release led to "the supreme event in my life. . . . I had never before realized how divinely beautiful the world was. . . . In that same wonderful moment of what might be called supernal bliss, came illumination. How long that period of intense rapture lasted I do not know—it seemed an eternity—it might have been but a few moments."

But the consequence of her Breakthrough was decisive.

C.M.C. describes the acute sensation of "being centered, or of being a center." This return to the center characterizes Breakthrough experiences the world over. It mirrors the many traditional civilizations that attempt to make their cathedrals and monuments and even their private homes symbolic centers of the universe. It is here in this sacred space that, symbolically, heaven and earth are joined in a single axis, and the seeker returns to the center of the self and the world.

C.M.C. emerged from her ecstasies permanently expanded and with a new sense of certainty. "Out of this experience was born an unfaltering trust," she says. "Deep in the soul below pain, below all the distraction of life, is a silence vast and grand—an infinite ocean of calm which nothing can disturb; nature's own exceeding peace which passes understanding. That which we seek with passionate longing here and there, upward and outward, we find at last within ourselves."

Breakthroughs are like boxes within boxes: within each category on the spectrum of experience greater and lesser examples can be found. My own Breakthrough moments do not, of course, compare with those of the spiritual masters; yet they are instructional in their own right as examples of what is possible for all of us.

One summer I took a trip to Los Angeles to visit friends. For weeks before the trip I was engaged in strenuous inner efforts to see certain undesirable traits in myself, to look over the wall of my own ego and catch sight of something beyond it. But my inner demons of defensiveness and self-delusion barred the way.

One night not long after I arrived in L.A., I was lying in bed wrestling with these same demons. I could feel the cool night air on my face. But I could also feel the heat of emotion rising in my chest as I struggled to see beyond my succession of masks. No matter how hard I tried, all I could discern was a collection of different selves, like Escher's magic boxes, all nested one into the other, extending in a spiral to infinity.

Then it happened. Quite unexpectedly and without warning, these masks were ripped away, by what agency or force I do not know, and in an instant the nest of boxes collapsed. In their place a great emptiness engulfed me as I started to tumble internally, to lose my orientation to time and space. Then I fell through the air of my mind as if with arms and legs outspread, first through one layer, then another and another, like plummeting through an endless succession of windows in a skylight, each pane of glass shattering and giving way to another—until finally there were no more windows, and there was nothing at all between me and the vast sky.

I was embraced by a Reality I had been looking for, a Reality that had always been there. In one moment I understood that nothing had been hidden from me from the start; that in fact there was nothing to hide: it was all in plain view for those with eyes to see. What I had been seeking all this time was present all around me. "Then shall we know even as we are known."

More than a year later I had another mysterious encounter that helped me understand how the Breakthrough is related to time and to something in us that is beyond time.

It was a cold Saturday afternoon in February. My wife and I were speeding along Route 9W on our way to a Broadway show in Manhattan. The winter sky was dark and a light snow was beginning to powder the roads. I glanced at my watch. We were late. The matinee was due to begin in half an hour, and we were still fifteen minutes from the George Washington Bridge. I accelerated to make up the time, then realized I was taking a chance speeding on an icy road. I stepped on the brakes, but with too heavy a foot. They locked.

The next thing I knew our car was spinning out of control. The events that followed unfolded before me like a dream underwater, a stop-action film in which I was cast as both the observer and the observed.

The first thing I noted was that even though our car was turning, time itself was slowing to a crawl, and everything around me was moving in slow motion. I seemed to have all the time in the world to notice the snowflakes patterning themselves on the windshield, the dull glow of daylight off the vinyl dashboard, the rough texture of the steering wheel under my hands. I observed these details with far greater acuity than I would under ordinary conditions.

More extraordinary, the center of perception that was observing this scene was located both inside my body and outside. Part of me was serenely gazing at the revolving world outside the car, another part was above me watching me watching. These two points of view operated in concert, one from within, one from above, as if I were simultaneously living in two worlds.

I had undergone such experiences before in my life. The most memorable took place once in the middle of a formal dinner party at a colleague's house. In the midst of animated table conversation I suddenly found that every face at the table was glowing with light, and that I was observing this remarkable sight from a perspective point up on the ceiling. Now here I was again with this same out-of-the-body sensation, this time at a moment of danger and perhaps imminent death. Throughout this experience my mind remained clear but concurrently seemed to slow down, or speed up—I'm not sure which—giving me hours, or rather days, even years, to think all the thoughts I liked. At the same time, as this seemingly endless parade of thoughts and images filed past, I was *simultaneously* aware of the external circumstances around me down to the smallest detail. The most prominent sensation I had at this moment, experienced without a tinge of fear or anxiety, was: "Well, guess I'm going to die now. That's just the way it is. That's just what's happening at this time." There was no emotional charge to this observation, nothing personal. Just the impartial recognition of an impending fact.

All of these impressions, understand, took place in a period of no more than four or five seconds by clock time. During this interval what seemed to be a lifetime's worth of memories, emotions, and sensations passed through my head at the most leisurely pace. When the car finally stopped spinning and came to a halt by the side of the road, jerking me back to ordinary time and reality, I was almost annoyed that this remarkable event was ending.

In the sudden motionlessness that followed, my wife and I sat there without saying a word. Somehow we knew exactly what the other was thinking. She had undergone an out-of-time encounter as well. I knew this instinctively, and she knew it about me.

I turned the car motor off. Our Broadway matinee was long forgotten as we sat unmoving, watching the snow swirl silently outside the window, listening to the occasional caw of a crow in the trees. I'm not sure how long we remained here, lost in a sort of trance between worlds, our normal consciousness not fully back in our bodies, yet not entirely out of them either.

Finally, as in a fairy tale, the magic spell lifted, and we both came back to life. I started up the car, and without saying much we drove on. To this day my wife and I rarely discuss this extraordinary moment on Route 9W. All that can be said about it was said in the silence between us.

What actually happened that afternoon on the snowy road to New York City? And how does my experience of being "out of time" and on the fringes of a different reality shed light on the Breakthrough?

An altered experience of time is often a hallmark of the Breakthrough voyage. Like others who have had such experiences, my wife and I had been transported to a place outside ourselves where our awareness was supernaturally keen, and where we could almost see past the veil of time and space. Both of us, it seemed, had lived a mini-life in a compressed moment of time; or, more accurately, in no time at all.

As we emerged from this enchantment, it was clear that time does not *have* to exist as we know it; that time can flow both forward and backward in a single instant; and that under certain conditions any one of us can be lifted out of the flux of ordinary reality and transported to a higher state where past, present, and future are joined. My magical encounter on Route 9W gave me a clear conviction that such glimpses of higher reality are possible, and that they are always a potential within us, waiting to be triggered by a strong enough stimulus—in this case a brush with death.

The experience also caused me to see the Breakthrough in a different light, even more mysterious than before. It made me think of the comment by physicist Sir Arthur Eddington, that the universe is "not only stranger than we suppose but stranger than we *can* suppose." Such moments of higher reality cannot be explained in logical terms (although thinkers from St. Augustine to Einstein have struggled heroically to do so). They are outside our circle of intellectual comprehension. Yet a direct taste of them, a single flash, and their power is obvious. Uncountable numbers of people have had such experiences, sometimes during prayer and contemplation, sometimes triggered by moments of danger, sometimes in near-death experiences. All of these encounters provide glimpses into the invisible world of the soul.

After these two episodes many things in my life changed.

I began to look on my existence as a renewed story and as a second chance to set certain matters right. I was also aware that my experiences were more a beginning than an end, as Breakthroughs often are.

Yet I also made a classic mistake. In fact, I made two mistakes.

The first was believing that I was responsible for making the Breakthrough happen. Such a conceit is tantamount to thinking that because I can walk I am also responsible for having created my own legs. In fact, the Breakthrough was not my creation. In retrospect, the entire experience was less like making an effort that produced a result, more like letting go and allowing a higher force to fill the vacuum. The Christian mystics conveyed this point long ago in saying, "Finding does not come from seeking; seeking comes from finding."

That was my first mistake.

The second was feeling proud that I had been granted such a peek into the Infinite. Breakthroughs are a kind of reward for service in the spiritual trenches, I told myself; not in so many words, but by inference, assumption. Effort produces results, after all, and results are a reward for good work. I was, therefore, *a special person.*

Yet somehow in the process of reaching such a conclusion, I had managed to forget that the great Zen master D. T. Suzuki used to sign his letters "No special person." And so my second mistake—spiritual pride—followed from the first.

Fortunately, this delusion did not last. It was not long before it would be quietly and quite thoroughly demolished in a way I would never forget.

Saints and Poets, Maybe

"Now we see through a glass darkly, but one day we shall see face to face," wrote St. Paul. I remember having a conversation at the Holy Cross Monastery on the subject of normal consciousness versus Breakthrough with Brother Robert, whom we met in an earlier chapter.

"We do see the face of God," Brother Robert told me one day in a confidential voice. "The few times it happened to me it was just for a second or two. But it was the kind of experience that knocked my socks off. I don't think people can live in these states very long. They're too intense. Theologically I would probably say they're given to us as stepping-stones to encourage us to keep going in our prayers. But they're not for a regular diet. If we were in a state of God consciousness all the time we would never want to come back to this world again."

Brother Robert's comments made me think of certain laboratory experiments in which rats are connected to electrodes and taught to self-stimulate the hypothalamus regions of their own brains. As soon as the stimulation begins, the animals immediately lose all interest in normal pleasures, including food, sex, and the company of other rats. Instead they become utterly absorbed in what must be a kind of rat nirvana. Once hooked up to the electrodes, the only thing they care about is continuing the stimulation. This they do with such persistence that they eventually drop dead from exhaustion.

Under comparable circumstances, humans too find themselves unwilling to come down and back to mundane reality. I remember a chilling picture story I saw as a child in *Life* magazine. The article showed a sequence of photographs of a deep-sea diver descending toward an unexplored part of the ocean. At the point where the diver should have stopped and turned around, the pictures show him drifting deeper toward the bottomless depths. Oxygen narcosis had set in, and with it the indescribable euphoria it produces, luring the diver on, Siren-like, until he disappeared forever in the dark depths. Mountain climbers, intoxicated in the same way by high altitudes, occasionally forget the goal ahead of them and wander off into the snows to die in ecstasy.

"I forget who the poet was who said that human beings can stand only so much reality," Brother Robert remarked. "But for the rest of us it's measured out in small doses. We can't take too much at a time. The Light of God is always around us. But, you know, you only see what you can see, and you filter out the rest. That's true of the Divine Face. It's staring at us everywhere, in people, nature, in our dog. It's there right in front of us. Sometimes I'm a little bit more open to it and I catch more of a glimpse of it."

Why is it we have so much trouble seeing what Brother Robert calls "the light of God" when it is there in front of us all the time? In the heartrending last scene of Thornton Wilder's great play, *Our Town,* the heroine, Emily, has died in childbirth, and now finds herself sitting in the cemetery next to her deceased mother-in-law, Mrs. Gibbs. From this eerie place Emily watches the people come and go at her own funeral:

EMILY: Live people don't understand, do they?
MRS. GIBBS: No, dear—not very much.
EMILY: They're sort of shut up in little boxes, aren't they? I feel as though I knew them last a thousand years ago.

Troubled by the abruptness of her separation from the world, Emily asks if she can visit her family again.

Mrs. Gibbs allows that it's possible, but she and the rest of the spirits in the graveyard caution against it. Some have tried, Emily is told, but they soon come back.

Emily listens thoughtfully, and despite the warnings decides to return. In a flash she is back in her family home in Grover's Corners, reliving a moment from her past.

The instant she tries to speak with her mother, however, she realizes that the spirits were wise: she is forever barred from the world of the living. Not because the living forbid it. Not because she knows the sad things awaiting them. But because the living are "in the dark . . . From morning till night, that's all they are—troubled." Only the dead, it ironically turns out, can understand the electrifying and stupendous value of life—of, as the Tibetans say, "the mighty opportunity it is to be born a human being."

Finally Emily can bear it no longer. She turns to the Stage Manager, a character meant to be a cross between master of ceremonies and God.

"I can't, I can't go on," she cries. "Oh! Oh! It goes so fast. We don't have time to look at one another."

Sobbing, Emily turns and bids farewell to life in a speech that could be made by any of us about to depart the fair, flowering world of the living.

"I didn't realize," Emily cries out. "So all this was going on, and we never noticed. Take me back—up the hill—to my grave. But first: Wait! One more look. Goodbye, goodbye, world. Goodbye, Grover's Corners . . . Mama and Papa. Goodbye to clocks ticking . . . and Mama's sunflowers. And food and coffee. And new-ironed dresses and hot baths . . . and sleeping and waking up. Oh, earth, you are too wonderful for anybody to realize you."

Emily turns to the Stage Manager: "Do any human beings ever realize life while they live it—every, every minute?"

"No," the Stage Manager answers with finality.

Then he reconsiders. "The saints and poets, maybe—they do some."

Meeting a Remarkable Man

The saints and poets. Maybe.

Yet the man I met who lived so much of his time as if awake and aware was neither saint nor poet.

One day I received a phone call from Wendy Klein, the former advertising executive whom we met in a previous chapter.

Wendy proceeded to tell me that she was making regular visits to a Sufi center in New York—known as a *tekke* or *khaneghah*—where a group of American Sufis or "dervishes" were pursuing the path of Islamic mysticism. She had found a man there, she told me, a stained-glass maker named Jeffrey whom she felt had genuinely experienced a major spiritual Breakthrough.

"He's one of the few American dervishes who's had an experience of what they call 'an opening of the heart,' " she told me.

Translated, this meant the glass maker had, in theory at least, experienced the kind of Breakthrough that Sufis consider a major stage in the unfolding of God consciousness. Wendy promised she would call him and see if he was willing to speak with me.

Jeffrey, it turned out, lived in a small ranch home on a tree-lined, residential street just outside of New Brunswick, New Jersey. His garage was a small but prettily decorated studio with several extraordinary specimens of stained glass hanging in the entrance, including a remarkable replica of a panel from a window in Chartres Cathedral. Entering the shop, I found the man in question sitting behind the counter assembling a lampshade. His shop was tidy, well lit, and filled from floor to ceiling with the most astonishing specimens of stained glass I'd ever seen. Jeffrey himself was tall, bonily built, and late-fortyish, with a long face and thick head of hair that was starting to go salt-and-pepper. He nodded in a homey way, and gave a shy smile. For a moment the image of Gary Cooper flashed through my mind.

Jeffrey, I learned, was born in Texas and brought up in Venezuela. His father had been a production worker in the international oil business, and an ardent Catholic. "If he'd had his way I'd have gone to Mass every day," Jeffrey told me. Eventually the experience of being constantly dragged off to church left him with a profound distaste for religion.

As a young man in the 1960s, Jeffrey was attracted to the hippie commune movement, and lived for a time on the Hog Farm in Tennessee and other utopian communities. Along the way, despite his early rejection of religion, he found himself drawn to Eastern mysticism and to various alternative forms of spirituality.

Finally one day he met a Sufi teacher at a friend's apartment. At the time, he explained, Islam conjured up the usual stereotypes of sword-wielding Arabs and terrorists at the airport. Meeting this elderly Sufi teacher changed all that.

"I sort of had . . . well, when I first met him my heart exploded in me. I felt like I'd always known this man; always wanted to be with him. Something like that—it's hard to describe these things."

At the request of his teacher, Jeffrey converted to Islam. "I didn't know anything about Islam, but I started reading the Koran, like he told me to do. One passage in particular got me: 'Wheresoever you look, there is the Face of God.' That pretty well said it all, I thought. After that I didn't have any trouble being a Muslim."

Jeffrey walked over to a hot plate and, without asking, started making me a cup of tea. I wanted to know more about his teacher.

"I liked the way he did things," Jeffrey said. "He didn't talk much or give lectures. Sometimes he'd just come into the room and sit there in silence with you for an hour and then leave."

"Wendy told me you've experienced what the Sufis call an opening of the heart," I finally volunteered. "Could you tell me about what it's like—the kinds of things you saw and felt when you were in that state?"

Jeffrey thought for a moment. "These big experiences can be important in some people's lives," he said. "They do happen sometimes."

I waited for him to go on. He didn't.

"What about your experiences?" I continued. "Can you describe them?"

"Well, there are so many kinds," he answered. "It's hard to tell you exactly. Everyone's experience is different."

I decided on another tack.

"I know that lots of people who've had Breakthroughs find them hard to talk about. But as I understand it, there are certain elements that all Breakthrough experiences have in common. A sense of timelessness, maybe. Enormous love and compassion. Being in eternity."

Jeffrey nodded. "If I talked about seeing visions or angels you'd get a certain picture in your mind. They'd just be some little pictures your imagination cooked up."

This was interesting and I waited for him to continue. But he fell silent again.

Our conversation went on in this start-stop manner for some time until my frustration got the better of me.

"Listen!" I said, startled by the intensity of my own voice. "I know it's hard for you to talk about all this. But you've been there! You've seen the fire and the light! I don't know how I know it, but I do. So give me some of it back. *Talk to me!*"

Instead of being nonplussed by my sudden outburst, Jeffrey almost seemed to be expecting it.

"Come on," he said, "let's take a walk."

As we walked, Jeffrey talked to me about the perils of discussing inner experiences—the dangers of misinterpretation on the part of the listener, and the dangers of complacency and self-importance for the person who has had such experiences.

"You know, seeing God isn't for everyone," Jeffrey said. "In Sufism we talk about a person's heart being open. People assume that this is the goal, that all of us have to get to this place. But it isn't true."

I waited for him to go on.

"The reason for being on a path is not always to have 'experiences,' " he said. "You struggle spiritually because that's what you're put on the earth to do. It's your job as a human being. Whether or not you get to the light is not what matters. If you do, great. If you don't, great. We can't really understand how it all works. It just happens to some people and not to others. That's another reason why it's better not to talk about it—it makes people feel badly that they haven't experienced what you've experienced. Better to just keep it to yourself."

Jeffrey's carefulness reminded me of a Sufi saying: "The more one talks about their vision of God, the faster you should run away."

"If your heart opens and you see light or angels, whatever," Jeffrey went on, "afterward when it's over you feel small and invisible. You realize you didn't do anything; you didn't really make the thing happen. It was given to you, and that's all you can say about it."

We walked on for some time without speaking, then headed back. As we neared his house, the words burst out of my mouth: "What should one do, then?"

I was amazed at the intensity of my own emotion.

"Small things," Jeffrey replied, again as if he was expecting the question. "Start with small things. Efforts that are in your power. Everyday efforts to be nice to somebody, to be patient. Try to see the matter from the other guy's point of view. Try to understand that maybe this person is having a bad day. Be generous. Give away something you like to someone who needs it. Be cheerful when you're not feeling so good. That's a hard one, but it gets you a lot of points. Try not to make things into tragedies if you can help it. Little things."

He shrugged.

I'd heard it all before, of course. On many occasions. But there was something in these plain, not terribly articulate words that went straight to my heart, as if I were hearing them for the first time. Yes, of course: small things. That's what's needed to make this world into the better place everybody wants it to be. How obvious; how deep. Small acts of tender mercy. We don't have to go on pilgrimages to Mecca or bathe in the Ganges. It all starts right here and now. Being kind to our friends, our parents, our children; being hospitable, slow to judge. Exerting ourselves for others, especially those in need. Being trustworthy, forthright, true to our word. Avoiding gossip, backbiting. Giving others the benefit of the doubt and wishing them well in our hearts. Having tolerance for people's shortcomings. Controlling anger. Being steadfast in hard times. Learning to forgive.

It was all so simple and obvious.

"Little by little, being kind changes us in big ways," Jeffrey added. "It's not a temporary change either. It's forever."

There was a power in his voice now, and a light in his eyes.

"The big experiences you talk about can come to any of us. Kings, street sweepers. Doesn't matter. It can happen to us anytime. We just have to keep going, keep trying. And wait."

At this moment I felt certain that his words came from his own experience, and from some place of deep understanding inside him.

"Let me say something else," he continued as we drew near the house. "Most of us are easily distracted. We're pulled along by the current of things. But, you know, if you want to become an accountant you don't study law one year, art the next, medicine the next. You'd never make it that way. You have to make a commitment. Choose something and stay with it. It's the same with spiritual things. If you keep jumping around you won't get anywhere, and you'll keep losing what you've gotten. You don't get any help this way, you don't satisfy that craving for truth if you get ten people's versions of it. Make the commitment; that's important. A person has to go at this with deep sincerity. Then if you do have an opening of the heart, hey, that's great. If you don't, hey, that's great too. The commitment is what's important. Let the rest take care of itself."

Jeffrey became silent again. But this time the silence between us didn't matter. The interview was over, and I had been given not only what I wanted intellectually but what I needed spiritually. As I stood there on that suburban New Jersey street, I remembered the concluding lines of the poem *The Conference of the Birds*. In this classic Sufi work the author tells of a group of birds who set out on a spiritual quest, in search of a magical bird of paradise, the Simurgh, symbol of the Supreme.

Following many trials and tribulations—and after many of the birds have given up or become distracted—thirty birds reach the destination: the "being which is beyond human reason and knowledge."

Here, like the escaped prisoners from Plato's cave, the birds are so blinded by the light that they do not see the Simurgh. Before they can receive this vision they must pass a final test, given by the Chamberlain who guards the palace door. Will they now abandon themselves utterly to the Divine, as a moth voluntarily flies into a flame?

After passing this test, the birds are granted the final Breakthrough, and are ushered into the presence of the King.

"When they were completely at peace and detached from all things, they became aware that the Simurgh was indeed there with them, and a new life began for them in the Simurgh. All that they had done previously was washed away. Thereupon, the birds at last lost themselves forever in the Simurgh—as the shadow was lost in the sun—and that is all.

"All that you have heard or seen or known is not even the beginning of what you must know. And since the ruined habituation of this world is not your place, you must renounce it. . . . So long as you are identified with the things of the world you will not set out on the Path. But when the world no longer binds you, you enter as in a dream; but, knowing the end, you see the benefit. Do you know what you possess? Enter into yourself and reflect on this."

We take each step along the Stages of the Soul with confidence that our motion will bring us forward to some felt but little understood destination. It is the same when we walk—each step is a kind of fall that rights itself, then leads to another fall, and another, and so we make progress by stumbling to our goal.

"To walk, we have to lean forward," British psychotherapist Robin Skynner tells us, "lose our balance, and begin to fall. We let go constantly of the previous stability, falling all the time, trusting that we will find a succession of new stabilities with each step."

And so it is with the Breakthrough: a letting go, a leaning forward, and a falling ahead in a moment of trust; trust that the Way itself will take us to our destination—and then return us home again.

chapter 8

The Return: The Last Stage and the First

Truly it was a sight worth looking at, to see how the souls choose their own lives—yea, a pitiful sight, and a laughable, and a wonderful sight.

PLATO, The Myth of Er

When the ten thousand things become one, then we return to the center, where we have always been.

CHUANG-TSE

UNDERSTANDING THE RETURN

After Going to the Mountaintop, What?

"I thought it would never, never end," Linda Purcell told me. "When I was in that place of glorification I saw that the Lord is everywhere all the time; that everything that happens is God's plan. We all have the light of God inside us."

Linda is an eighth-grade schoolteacher and a devout Christian. After years of worship and prayer, she attended a weekend church retreat with a group called Cursillo. Here she underwent a genuine Breakthrough, a moment of God realization, and for several weeks afterward was, in colloquial terms, on a spiritual high.

"I thought to myself," Linda said, "now I've changed forever. I see the world as the light and glory it really is. This must be like what the early Christians experienced, that sense of love and community."

But over the course of several weeks these feelings began to dwindle. "I felt like a queen who's had her kingdom snatched away," she said. "How do I deal with life now that I've been to the mountaintop?"

Like others who have experienced Breakthroughs, Linda wanted to believe that her state of illumination was permanent and that her life would be lived from now on in a state of spiritual rapture. Then her state began to fade, as high states tend to do. No matter how profound an experience one has, Linda learned, no matter how transforming the Breakthrough may be, the alarm buzzer still goes off the next morning at 6 A.M.; the lawn still needs mowing and the traffic is just as heavy getting to work. Nothing, in a sense, is different in the outside world from what it was before the Breakthrough. Nothing has changed, at least not as far as the hassles and needs of everyday life are concerned.

Linda soon found herself faced with the question that arrives after a moment of higher consciousness has come and gone: how do I readjust to ordinary reality and integrate what I've seen into my daily routine?

When my daughter was four years old I took her to see her first movie, the animated version of *Cinderella*. From the moment Disney's phantasmagoric images started to dance across the screen my daughter was enthralled. For an hour and a half she sat there wrapped in a cloud of bliss, taking in the color and fantasy and bibbidy-bobbidy-boo of it all. Then suddenly, unfairly, the movie was over and the fluorescent lights flashed on. All around us the heavy forms of human beings rose from their seats and plodded out of the theater in a decidedly unanimated fashion. For a few minutes the universe had been made magical for my daughter. Then without warning the magic was snatched away.

She burst into tears.

There are few better portrayals of this heaven-to-earth effect than that described in the autobiography of astronaut Edwin "Buzz" Aldrin, the second man to walk on the moon. Returning home from one of the greatest adventures in all human history, Aldrin tells us in his appropriately titled book, *Return to Earth*, he soon became listless and depressed. "I'd gone to the moon," he writes. "What to do next? What possible goal could I add now?"

To fill the hole, Aldrin began drinking heavily. Then came the collapse of his marriage and reliance on antidepressant drugs. It was not until age forty-one that he managed to sort out his priorities and pursue a search for deeper meaning. The whole ordeal, he tells us, "taught me to live again, at an age when it is very possible to begin anew."

To begin anew is what the fifth and final stage of the soul is about, the stage of Return. As Linda Purcell and many others have discovered, one goes up and then goes down again. But one does not go back. The Breakthrough and the Return together, they learn, are not a conclusion to the spiritual journey, but a consummation, and at the same time, a continuation into new and uncharted territory.

Finding this continuation is the task given in this last, and in many ways most challenging, phase in the Stages of the Soul.

Understanding the Return

People who have been through the Breakthrough begin to understand that their relationships and activities, even the burdens and hardships they once thought were so intolerable, are necessary pieces in life's mosaic. "We do not understand that life is paradise," says Father Zosima in *The Brothers Karamazov,* "for it suffices only to wish to understand it, and at once paradise will appear in front of us in its beauty."

Then, like an astronaut, we return to our everyday life. But this time we are charged with new tasks.

What are these tasks? First, to integrate what we've experienced into our daily lives. Second, to continue making efforts in hopes of further spiritual growth. Third, to give back to others something of what we've learned.

"The unitive life," writes psychotherapist Frances Vaughan, "is not lived apart from humanity. On the contrary, having at last come to full consciousness of reality, the circle of being is completed in returning to fertilize those levels of existence from which it sprang. The mystic is portrayed here as a pioneer of humanity, an activist among saints, a practical and intuitive person."

In Somerset Maugham's book *The Razor's Edge,* the hero, a nondescript young man named Larry, goes off on a long Search and Struggle after seeing his closest friend shot down in the war in Europe.

Larry finds his way to an ashram in the Himalayas, where he eventually undergoes enlightenment. Afterward he returns to the United States, where he vanishes into faceless anonymity. When last heard from, the author tells us at the end of the book, Larry is living in a big city somewhere driving a taxicab.

A taxicab? I thought to myself when I read this book as a young man. How absurd! Could anyone really live through a moment of cosmic consciousness in the Himalayas and then return home to drive a *taxicab?*

Today I understand why Maugham chose to end his book in this way. After the Breakthrough, the next step is not withdrawal or seclusion. It must be followed by concern and involvement with the world that has helped us achieve this state. There is work to be done now and lessons to be learned. In Erik Erikson's terminology, we owe the world our "generativity."

Some, of course, argue that spirituality, and mysticism in particular, are simply forms of psychological escapism. When Freud looked at mysticism he saw nothing more than infantile regression and self-centered withdrawal from adult responsibility. Since Freud's time psychoanalysis has followed suit, treating religion in general as a neurotic inability to cope with reality.

Today this criticism continues. Since the 1960s mysticism and the Human Potential Movement have been tarred with the same brush, targeted as childish me-generation fixations on "self" or as ersatz substitutes for true community involvement. Familiar images are trotted out of middle-class suburbanites rushing off to weekend retreats at chic resorts while the poor are trapped in ghettos.

But sweeping indictments of mysticism miss the mark. Such criticisms mistake superficial forms of religiosity and even pathological conditions for bona fide spiritual attainment. The mysticism of a St. Francis of Assisi is clearly more legitimate and authentic than the mysticism of lunatics or weekend groupies. There is even evidence that people who have undergone Breakthrough experiences are more deeply committed to social involvement than those who have not. Beginning in the 1970s, for example, sociologist Robert Wuthnow collected data showing that people who report mystical or spiritual peak experiences tend to be far *less* materialistic and status-conscious than those who have had no spiritual involvement. His research shows that people reporting mystical experiences are far more concerned with social action than their secular brothers and sisters.

These findings are supported by the example of the great saints and mystics of history. Many of these remarkable men and women, after ascending to unimaginable spiritual heights, returned to their lives, where they became intimately and sometimes controversially embroiled in everyday affairs.

St. Teresa, for example, died on one of her many tireless visits to the Spanish countryside to help found a monastic institution. St. Ignatius Loyola was a soldier, St. Louis a king, St. Joan of Arc a warrior and leader of a nation. St. Francis of Assisi, besides founding a lay order dedicated to involvement in the world and service to common humanity, participated in the Crusades and once traveled to the Middle East to preach Christianity to the Sultan of Egypt.

Devout participation in the world, what's more, does not belong only to the saints. Dag Hammarskjöld, to take a contemporary figure, was known to millions as the vigorous Secretary General of the United Nations and as a Nobel Peace Prize recipient. Three years after his death in a plane crash, quite another picture of Hammarskjöld emerged. In his book *Markings* readers discovered that this seemingly worldly man was in fact a committed mystic and an intense devotee of the spiritual life.

"Now you have been there," he writes with the sincerity of the world-weary sage, "and it wasn't much. Throughout life, how many steps must we take, how many hours must we spend in order to have heard, to have seen—what?"

To judge from his writings, Hammarskjöld's interior journey brought him to moments of Breakthrough and Return. "In the point of rest at the center of our being," he writes, "we encounter a world where all things are at rest in the same way. Then a tree becomes a mystery, a cloud a revelation, each man a cosmos of whose riches we can only catch glimpses. The life of simplicity is simple, but it opens us a book in which we never get beyond the first syllable."

"One *satori*," a Zen saying has it, "is all *satoris*. Yet it is still only one *satori*."

As Meister Eckhart explains: "If a person catches just one fleeting glance of the joy and bliss [of God], it will compensate him for everything he has ever had to suffer."

Yet despite the fact that the Return places one in a new relationship to life, there are pitfalls. These dangers may not be obvious at first, but they are very real. The first and perhaps most common of these is the "failed Return."

THE FAILED RETURN

Into the Labyrinth

When seekers achieve a Breakthrough, they not only gain new levels of perceptivity and power; they are also given new obligations. "To whom much is given, from them much will be asked." If someone fails to discharge these new responsibilities in the right way, there is a chance that what has been given will be taken away.

Many allegories are found in scripture and myth telling of such failed Returns. A classic example is the story of Theseus and the Minotaur.

This tale of many dimensions from the legacy of ancient Greece begins when a young Greek named Theseus is urged by the gods to travel to Athens to find his father, King Aegeus, and to learn of the mission that awaits him. When father and son are reconciled Theseus's Call and Search are complete.

Their rejoicing is quickly dampened, however, by the realization that the dreaded day of tribute is near. Minos, king of Crete, has levied a terrible burden on the Athenians. Every seven years the people of Athens must send seven youths and seven maidens to Crete, where they are herded into an inescapable labyrinth and fed to a beast known as the Minotaur.

The moment Theseus learns of this fatal ritual, he volunteers to become one of the human sacrifices. In the process he hopes to slay the Minotaur.

Aegeus begs his son to reconsider. But Theseus stands firm. Theseus, however, makes a sacred promise that on the return journey he will raise the ship's white flag if he has killed the Minotaur. If not, the ship's black flag will be left in place. Bidding a tearful farewell, Theseus and the sacrificial youths set sail for Crete. Here they are taken from their ship by the jeering crowd and paraded before a gloating King Minos and members of his court.

Now, among these spectators, it so happens, is the King's beautiful daughter, Ariadne. The moment she sees the handsome prince she falls in love with him. Arranging a secret meeting, she promises to show Theseus a way out of the labyrinth and a means of killing the Minotaur. In return he must promise to take her to Athens and marry her.

Once the compact is sealed, Ariadne wheedles the blueprint of the labyrinth out of its architect, Daedalus, then reveals it to her beloved hero. She also gives Theseus a small dagger and a ball of golden thread. While wandering through the labyrinth's passages, she instructs him, let the string unwind behind you to mark your trail. After slaying the Minotaur with the dagger, follow the golden thread back to the labyrinth's entrance.

The next day, thoroughly prepared for the encounter by his queenly guide, Theseus and the young Athenians enter the labyrinth. But while Theseus inhabits the same sealed prison as the youths, for him this prison is not a prison at all. Ariadne's wisdom has transformed it for him into a sacred space, a location not to die in, but to find new life. Armed with the provisions his beautiful guide has given him—knowledge, power, and love—Theseus perceives an order and purpose to the labyrinth that the ignorant youths cannot see. For Theseus the maze is not a deadly trap at all. It is a pathway to spiritual rebirth.

Finding the Minotaur and slaying him with Ariadne's dagger are thus practicable goals for our hero, and he accomplishes them with deadly precision. The monster thus dispatched, Theseus and his wards follow the golden thread back to the labyrinth's entrance, where Ariadne is waiting to guide them to their ship. Together they joyously set sail for Athens.

Now, up to this point Theseus has performed his mission in an unerringly proper and righteous way. He has answered the Call, fulfilled the Search for his spiritual destiny, then seen his Struggle through to Breakthrough with the defeat of the Minotaur. He is ready now for the Return, which, in comparison with what he has suffered and won so far, seems a small achievement.

But it is not to be so. Theseus now makes several critical mistakes on his Return, and pays for them in blood.

The first occurs after he and his crew put in for the night at the island of Naxos. Here our hero does something inexplicable and unbelievable: he waits until Ariadne falls asleep, then rouses his crew and they set sail in the dark of night, abandoning Ariadne to her fate.

Why Theseus performs this ungrateful and self-degrading act we never learn. Such behavior is tantamount to Dante throwing Beatrice to the hounds of hell, or Cinderella murdering her fairy godmother. Ariadne has been Theseus's lover and guide. Ignoring this fact, our hero deserts his benefactor and sails for home, and in so doing lays the groundwork for several more mistakes.

For as his ship approaches the harbor in Athens, Theseus, through sheer inattention, forgets the promise he made to his father and fails to replace the black flag with the white. Sitting in the Acropolis watching for signs of his returning son, Aegeus spies the dark pennant and assumes his son is dead. In despair, he leaps into the sea and drowns. From this time on, legend has it, these waters are called the Aegean Sea.

By the time Theseus completes his Return he has thus amassed an inventory of sins: ingratitude, untrustworthiness, inattention, breaking a sacred vow to his father, abandoning his dearest lover and friend. These acts will teach him two fatal lessons. One, that there are implacable laws of behavior demanded of those on the sacred quest. And two, that to break these laws causes even the greatest heroes to lose everything, even in the final hours when success seems so near. For though our hero eventually becomes king of Athens and sits on his throne for many years, the Furies pursue him to the end. Through the intervention of an angry god, he inadvertently murders his innocent son, and for this act is expelled from Athens. Finally he dies in banishment at the hand of a friend who betrays him—just as he betrayed his guiltless lover many years before.

A Shrinking Margin of Error

What's behind Theseus's strange behavior? And what warnings can we discover in this myth to heed in our own Return?

As we progress along the Stages of the Soul, and as our understanding grows, so does our responsibility. Phrased another way, the further we progress along the spiritual path, the smaller our margin of error becomes, and the fewer mistakes we are allowed. Along with the privilege of making the quest, we are given a set of boundaries and moral obligations. Step outside these boundaries and catastrophe follows. Tolerance for error diminishes in proportion to the degree that our understanding increases.

A good case in point is that of Dr. Jon Dorman, a neurologist and follower of Sufi teachings, who today spends half of each year practicing medicine in Virginia, the other half as a doctor in the Middle East.

Living in Sonoma County in Northern California during the 1960s, Dr. Dorman began attending meditation ceremonies at a nearby Zen monastery, and soon became a regular visitor. Before long he was waking up at 3 A.M. and driving to the monastery for morning meditation sessions.

"The thing that won me over about the roshi," he explains, "was one time when I was meditating. Our group would sit in a small room about twelve feet by twelve feet, half a dozen of us facing the wall, sitting on pillows. The roshi would sit in a corner of the room watching us.

"I was trying hard to meditate one morning. But my mind kept wandering and my body kept leaning. All of a sudden I felt a kick in my side. No one was near me. I looked over at the roshi. He hadn't moved. He was just sitting there, staring at me in a strange way. I straightened up and concentrated harder. A few days later I asked him if he had kicked me psychically. 'No one has ever called it a kick before,' he answered, laughing. 'They usually call it a smack.' "

Dr. Dorman stayed with the roshi for several years, becoming more and more immersed in his practice and occasionally experiencing moments of a deeper reality.

"When I meditated I began to have this sense of the utter diamondlike perfection of the world," he told me. "This intense realization that everything around me was perfect. Like a cut jewel throwing off rays of light. When I told this to the roshi he seemed to acknowledge that it was a kind of stage on the way, and he started me on rosary training. I thought seriously about becoming an ordained monk."

Then, like Theseus, Dr. Dorman made an egregious mistake. At the invitation of several friends, he went up into the mountains, where he spent a weekend taking magic mushrooms—psilocybin. When he returned to the monastery the next week, the roshi sensed what he had been up to and dismissed him on the spot.

"The roshi told me I had done something very wrong, against the tenets of Buddhism. He told me that I knew better but I did it anyway. This, he said, was a sign of disrespect and ingratitude toward the teacher. Taking drugs of any kind is an act of disobedience and shows a basic lack of attentiveness to one's practice. It meant that despite any progress I may have made, I wasn't serious. He told me to leave immediately."

Dr. Dorman tried several times to get back into the teacher's good graces, but the teacher was adamant and would not discuss the matter again.

This incident taught Dr. Dorman a hard-earned lesson: that there are certain lines one does not cross on a spiritual way and certain rules one does not break. Forgiveness has its place; but so does the law. "The lessons I learned from not being able to come back," Dr. Dorman said, "were as important as the ones I learned in meditation."

It was only many years later that Dr. Dorman found another guide, this time within the Sufi tradition. "At this juncture," he told me, "I knew that you can slip and fall at any point on the Way, even after you've been at it for a while and have taken some forward steps. I now try to be acutely aware of what I'm doing and how I'm behaving before God at every moment."

"I think what sabotaged me most in the monastery was my own feeling of progress," Dr. Dorman added. "I thought that because I had some experiences I was a spiritual big shot and that I could kind of do anything I wanted. Secretly I thought I knew better than the teacher—it would be all right for me to take drugs. He wouldn't know the difference. I'd had these big experiences now; I could handle it. A little psychedelic interlude would help things along, that's all. It would be an interesting experiment. So I went ahead and did what I wanted despite the fact that I knew it was disrespectful, and harmful to my practice. I went against my teacher and the dharma, and I paid the price."

The ancient Greeks had a word for it: *hubris,* a belief that one is greater and wiser than the gods. Just like Icarus, who, against his father's warnings, flew too close to the sun on wings his father had fashioned from feathers and wax, Dr. Dorman flew too high and suffered a fall.

These myths and the life experiences of countless other people warn against the risk of a failed Return. They tell of seekers who push too far, who think they are more spiritually advanced than they are, and who pay the price. Christians refer to this quality as "spiritual pride." In traditions of contemplative psychotherapy it is known as "inflation."

The Perils of Inflation

"I use the term inflation," writes the psychiatrist Edward Eddinger, "to describe the attitude and the state which accompanies the identification of the ego with the Self. It is a state in which something small—the ego—has arrogated to itself the qualities of something larger—the Self—and hence is blown up beyond the limits of its proper size."

A woman told me: "My sister has been part of a religious group now for ten years. I won't name names, but the more involved she gets, the more she looks down on absolutely *everybody* who isn't part of her group, even other Christians."

A retired magazine editor told me, "I stopped with my meditation group because I was getting uncomfortable. Some of the people had a few electric minutes while meditating, and suddenly they thought they were teachers. They were laying down the law to everyone."

"Watch out for the big moments," a friend told me. "Especially if you don't have others around you to bring you down and put things in perspective. You start thinking that because you've had these higher flashes now and then, you really know where it's at."

When inflation sets in, spirituality ceases to be a vehicle for positive change and becomes a weapon instead, a tool to bolster one's own self-importance. This phenomenon is well known in all spiritual traditions. "Christianity also practically equates sin with inflation of the ego," Eddinger tells us. "The beatitudes, approached psychologically, can be best understood as praise of the non-inflated ego."

One memorable lesson in the perils of inflation came to me personally via a classmate of mine, Richard, whom I had known since graduate school. For many years Richard and I had been extremely close. I was the best man at his wedding, and for several years we were neighbors on Morningside Heights in Manhattan.

When Richard and I first became acquainted he was keenly interested in Eastern Orthodox breathing techniques, and soon after that in tai chi, yoga, Rolfing—indeed, any esoteric physical technique that promised integration of body and mind.

After practicing a number of these methods, Richard claimed to have had successive Breakthrough experiences, and to have undergone, as he described to me, "a new integration of all my mental, physical, and emotional faculties."

The problem was that the more "integrated" Richard got, the more insufferable he became, not only to me but to everyone who knew him. Soon he was lecturing all his friends on what to eat, how to stand, how to sit. He developed the habit of interrupting conversations to inject non sequiturs about postural alignment or being more "bodily aware." Did I know where my center of gravity was right now? Did I realize how much my body was tilting forward when I walked?

Perhaps Richard believed he was being genuinely helpful, but his patronizing attitude finally became impossible to take, and one day I told him so.

"I was just offering suggestions, that's all," he said in a wounded tone of voice. "If they don't make sense to you, don't do them. I was only trying to show you a few techniques I'd found helpful."

As time went on I saw less and less of Richard. Finally we fell out of touch. Then one day about five years later I learned that he was seriously sick: a gall bladder problem requiring an operation. The day after the surgery I visited him at the Klingenstein Pavilion in Mount Sinai Hospital. I wasn't prepared for what I saw. Richard seemed to have shrunk since we last met, and I immediately felt something changed about him, as if the surgery had figuratively cut him down to size. There seemed to be less "Richard" here than before, and more of the vulnerable, sensitive human being I remembered. After we talked for a few minutes I asked him how his involvements in tai chi and body work were going.

He gave a wry smile. "See for yourself," he said, nodding down to the bandages over his midsection.

That was all I heard that day about body positions and finding your center. The Richard I once knew, I was delighted to see, had returned.

All Breakthrough states are gifts. The moment we think we've produced them ourselves or earned them through our saintly efforts we can be certain inflation is lurking. The ego never sleeps: a prideful little sense of self-satisfaction always waits in the shadows looking for a chance to wax holier than thou and to spoil our Return.

Living in Carefree

One reason why it's so tempting to fixate on the Breakthrough state, to think we've gone as far as we have to go, and by extension to neglect the stage of Return, is that so many of us are accustomed to thinking of fulfillment as a state of perfect quietitude and freedom from care. Hugh Downs, the noted co-host of ABC's weekly *20/20* show, once explained his own version of this misapprehension to me. A member of the board of the Brookdale Center, he and I talked at lunch one day, about his episode of "liberation" from the humdrum of everyday life.

"When I was just fifty," he told me, "I got tired of doing the *Today* show and of my other broadcasting duties. At that point in my life I had financial independence, so I decided it was time to liberate myself from it all. I'd retire early, I thought, and live the kind of quiet, stress-free life I wanted to live. I ended up leaving New York for a town in Arizona called Carefree."

"There's actually a town by that name?" I asked.

"Yes, there sure is," he replied. "And yes, Carefree, Arizona, is exactly what you imagine it to be."

Hugh Downs went on to tell me a bit about the laid-back lifestyle in Carefree, and about how after a year or two it dawned on him that escaping from the stress of daily living was not what he was looking for at all. In fact, he was spending most of his time just trying to keep busy.

"One day my wife, Jean, turned to me and said, 'Hugh, I wish you'd go back to work. Then you'd have more time.'"

Her comment stopped him in his tracks.

"I suddenly asked myself: What am I doing here anyway? I realized that the problem with goals in life is not that they can't be achieved, but that they can. And then what? You just have another goal in front of you after that. I realized that real fulfillment lies in the journey itself. Real fulfillment lies in giving back to other people whatever you've been given. It was time, I decided, to return to life again."

Soon thereafter, Hugh Downs moved back to New York City, where he once again threw himself into the world of television and public service, eventually becoming chairman of UNICEF as well as a busy network TV host. This time he approached involvement in the world from a new angle, attempting to remain detached in the midst of the high-powered realm of broadcasting where he now felt he could do good for society—and for himself.

"Selfless involvement in the midst of life is the key," Hugh Downs emphasized. "I once knew an old actor who had just finished his seven hundredth performance of a Broadway show. Someone asked him if it didn't get stale repeating the same performance again and again.

" 'No,' the actor replied. 'Because as far as the audience is concerned each performance is the first performance. When I go on that stage I think about them, the audience, not about myself—how I can please and entertain them. If I thought about myself each night I'd get stale after ten performances.'

"That's what my life was like after I returned to New York," Hugh Downs went on. "I tried to think about all the people tuned in to my show, and about taking what I'd learned and how to give some of it back to them. That way life never gets stale."

Like Hugh Downs, doesn't a part of us also want to live in the magical town of Carefree? Where no one makes demands on us, and where we can simply be? Especially after we've traveled the journey of life for a while and paid our debt to the gods of duty and responsibility?

But also like Hugh Downs, wouldn't we also discover that peace of mind does not come from escaping the demands of ordinary life? As Dr. Hans Selye, the noted medical researcher, explains in his book *Stress, Not Distress,* our bodies do not require an eradication of all stress to function properly. In fact, a total absence of stress leaves us listless and unmotivated. What our organism needs, Dr. Selye insists, is a balance between emotional activity and emotional lulls—a rhythmic alternation between states of pressure and states of relaxation, between escape from life and participation in it.

To function at our best, we need to participate in life fully, and yet maintain a silent place within ourselves that is impervious to the clash and clatter. "I move through the world paying homage to the ten thousand things," goes a Chinese poem. "I give to the outstretched hand. I speak to the people. Yet within my heart all is peaceful. Here there is only the One."

Refusal of the Return

In *The Hero with a Thousand Faces,* mythologist Joseph Campbell dedicates a section of his book to the notion of spiritual Return. He terms this section "Refusal of the Return." "The full round," writes Campbell, "the norm of the monomyth, requires that the hero shall now begin the labor of bringing the runes of wisdom, the Golden Fleece, or his sleeping princess, back into the kingdom of humanity, where the boon may redound to the renewing of the community, the nation, the planet, or the ten thousand worlds."

The Return, in Campbell's mythological language, demands that we take the treasure gained in the spiritual world and share it with others. The return and reintegration into society, Campbell asserts, "is indispensable to the continuous circulation of spiritual energy into the world." But there's a problem. "The responsibility has been frequently refused," he goes on to add.

This makes us ask: What forces in our own life could possibly make us refuse the Return?

Several things:

Self-doubts and temptations. Campbell cites how the Buddha, having achieved supreme enlightenment under the Bodhi tree, doubted whether he would ever be capable of communicating his message. When the Prophet Muhammad first received his Breakthrough revelations he thought they came from demons, or that he was going mad.

In the Odyssey of Homer, that singular meditation on the stage of Return, Odysseus makes his voyage back to Greece in several short weeks. Within sight of Grecian shores, his crew disobeys his instructions and opens a bag of winds, causing their ship to be blown farther from home than when they started. As with the twisting and turning pathways of the labyrinth, there are times when we are literally one step away from finding our own spiritual center. Then we take a wrong step, make a single incorrect turn, and our mistake carries us far from the goal. "Ninety-nine right turns, one wrong," goes the saying, "and you still lose your way."

From this point on it takes Odysseus ten years to accomplish his Return, and along the way he struggles with repeated doubts and temptations: Sirens who lure, poppies to put him to sleep, the hypnotic enchantments of the witch Circe, who tries to transform him into an animal, and when this fails, to ensnare him in a web of sex and passion. At times even Odysseus, that greatest of heroes, wonders if he will be able to complete his Return.

Skepticism. Sometimes people are inclined to doubt the legitimacy of what they have witnessed as time goes by and as memory of the Breakthrough wanes.

Linda Purcell voiced doubts about her own experience at the Cursillo Christian retreat. "You know," she said, "the further you get from this kind of heavenly moment, the more you begin to dissect it. Oh, it was real. But *how* real? I don't know. Is the world made of light like I saw that day? Did I really see God? If I didn't, what did I see? I don't know. I just wish it would happen again."

In the aftermath of superordinary experience, the interpretative mind steps in and tries to reduce the sublime event to familiar categories.

Some amount of analysis and questioning is healthy, of course. But too much distorts memory and trivializes legitimate experience. "The longer I'm away from that incredible glowing feeling I had in church," one woman told me, "the more it all seems like a fantasy. Was my mind playing tricks on me?"

Why dampen such a unique moment with endless evaluation? You're in the stage of Return now. Let the Breakthroughs happen as they will, accept them as a gift, and get on with things.

Falling in love with the Breakthrough. Behavioral scientists Brown and Engler surveyed a sample group of experienced meditators. At the beginning of their study the investigators expected confirmation of the common notion that seasoned meditators have more peace of mind and serenity in daily activities than people who do not meditate. But they found nothing of the kind. Experienced meditators, they learned, have the same internal conflicts as the rest of us.

Yet there's a fundamental difference.

Meditators are more *aware* of their internal conflicts, and are a good deal more willing to look at these conflicts and work on them than those without contemplative experience.

To put it another way, moments of higher consciousness do not resolve psychological problems or take away anxiety. Seekers are changed by these moments, yet they continue to fight the same internal battles over yes and no, right and wrong, joy and sorrow. What these experiences *do* accomplish is to raise a person's level of self-awareness and make one's personal problems more transparent—and thus more responsive to working through.

Yet in the process of working through there comes a point of fateful temptation. A seeker may begin to feel the need for ever greater jolts of spiritual experience. Like Narcissus in the Greek myth, after catching a glimpse of their higher Self in the waters of the unconscious, seekers fall in love with what they see. Instead of taking this impression back to process it in ordinary life, they crave another look, another Breakthrough, then another after that. They wait breathlessly by the water's edge for one more glance at the naked soul. When this occurs a person literally becomes Breakthrough-possessed.

What's wrong with falling in love with the Breakthrough? Isn't the Breakthrough the goal of all spiritual journeying?

The answer, in a word, is no, Breakthrough is not the goal of spiritual journeying. It is simply one of the stages.

Consider the story of American Zen master Charlotte Beck.

Now known by her Japanese name as "Joko" Beck, Charlotte Beck knew absolutely nothing of Buddhism until she was forty. Up till this time she had been a schoolteacher, a secretary, and the mother of four children. One night she attended a lecture at a local church delivered by Maezumi Roshi, a Buddhist monk, and was immediately attracted.

After spending the next ten years studying Buddhism, Beck took early retirement and immersed herself entirely in a Zen way of life. Eventually she was picked as the successor to Maezumi Roshi and became a renowned Zen teacher in her own right.

Beck explains how after sitting in meditation for several months at one period in her training she experienced a sudden insight into the clear and utter truth of the *Heart Sutra,* a key scripture in the Buddhist religion. For two weeks afterward she was in an expanded state.

Then, gradually, her certainty began to fade. For the weeks and months that followed, she tried desperately to push herself during meditation to recapture this luminous understanding, but never with success.

Then one day she realized these efforts were self-defeating. She was not only living in the shadow of her Breakthrough; she had glorified and embellished its memory to such an extent that it had become a false idol. Beck was pursuing the desire for enlightenment but not enlightenment itself. As she tells us: "You have to fully experience something before you see that it's empty. If you're evading fear, you're never going to see the fear's empty. . . . You may sit in deep *samadhi* and see the oneness, but it's almost a concept, because when you stand up, there you are, land mines and all. And someone comes along and criticizes you, and you fall into rage. And you're supposed to be enlightened now!"

Thinking the journey is complete. Joko Beck's admission of fallibility struck a chord in me when I first encountered her story. It reminded me of a remark Jeffrey the stained-glass maker made in our interview. "Anyone who tells you he's enlightened," Jeffrey insisted, "is not enlightened."

Maybe that's the benefit of the "land mines" Beck talks about, the angers and vanities we suddenly catch ourselves at, sometimes at the most embarrassing moments. These little booby traps stop us in our tracks. They take us down a peg, reminding us that many of our inner demons have yet to be exorcised. It's difficult, after all, to think of oneself as special or enlightened while raging at a well-meaning friend or shouting impatiently at our children. Such moments are reminders of our fallibility, and serve as wholesome correctives. Without these reminders of our flaws we would imagine ourselves to be flawless.

"How to live more meaningfully with those we love, how to earn a living, how to find love and be loved, how to be a member of a family and community and planet, how to make play, health, art, sex and business a reflection . . . of our spiritual lives." These are the challenges of bringing heaven down to earth, as American Buddhist Rick Fields puts it. Everyday experience must become our teacher. "I think the biggest koan study is the study of our life," says Maurine Stuart, an American Zen Buddhist teacher in Boston. "I give people koans like: How are you going to get through whatever it is you have to do tomorrow? Literally, how are you going to deal with this particular life situation?"

Writer Emilie Griffin reached the same conclusion from a Christian perspective. A prominent advertising executive on Madison Avenue, Griffin was in her thirties when she first heard the Call. After a long series of inner efforts, her Breakthrough came in the form of what she terms her conversion to Catholicism. At first this drama unfolded with great zeal and euphoria. "It seemed to me I had been entrusted with an enormous secret," Griffin writes, "one which really ought to be shared."

But the euphoria didn't last. "The day-to-day realities crowd in," Griffin tells us. "The celestial music dies away; the energy which has been set loose within us has to be integrated into life in some practical way. . . . There comes a day, for some sooner than others, when the sense of an extraordinary event begins to ebb, a day which is as humdrum and unexciting as the days before conversion began. At this moment, the convert may have a rude awakening."

Griffin reacted to her own rude awakening in two ways.

First, she had to come to terms with a vexing desire to share her spiritual secret with everyone she met, to broadcast her "achievement" everywhere, and thus allow her ego to take full credit. To protect against this impulse, she gradually learned to make her practice of faith "invisible"; that is, something to guard, to keep to herself and disclose only in the most subtle ways.

This was Griffith's first lesson. The second began when she thought seriously for a time of going into a nunnery. It was only after a great deal of time and reflection that she began to comprehend that the ascetic ideal does not require us to physically renounce the world. Griffin, like Thomas Merton, recognized that the "world" she needed to be freed from was actually inside herself all the time.

Merton himself tells the story of leaving his Trappist monastery one day in Kentucky and visiting downtown Louisville. In the midst of the city's hustle and bustle a sudden sense of oneness gripped his heart: "In Louisville, at the corner of Fourth and Walnut," Merton writes, "in the center of the shopping district, I was suddenly overwhelmed with the realization that I loved all those people, that they were mine and I theirs, that we could not be alien to one another even though we were total strangers. It was like waking from a dream of separateness, of spurious self-isolation in a special world, the world of renunciation and supposed holiness. The whole illusion of a separate holy existence is a dream."

At this moment Merton understood that his idealization of a "separate holy existence" in a monastery was for him a vain conceit. Paradoxically, it was in the welter of crowded streets and honking horns that he was able to see that the world is the very face of God.

"Perhaps the things I resented about the world when I left it," he writes, "were defects of my own that I had projected upon it. Now, on the contrary, everything stirred me with a deep and mute sense of compassion. . . . I went through the city, realizing for the first time in my life how good are all the people in the world and how much value they have in the sight of God."

As for Emilie Griffin, far from retreating to a nunnery, she found it possible to return to her familiar existence and to live a Christian life while maintaining a high-powered executive job on Madison Avenue.

Can one imagine any profession immersing one more in the mundane world than advertising? Yet Griffin's spiritual work had given her the detachment and inwardness she needed to carry it off—to Return to the world but not be of it.

There is, in this sense, not one Return but many. We are always in a state of Return, always going back to life for further lessons and further elucidation in matters of the soul. Three decades after the appearance of his youthful autobiography *The Seven Storey Mountain,* Thomas Merton expressed this idea with sublime concision. "We are not converted only once in our lives," Merton insists, "but many times, and this endless series of large and small conversions, inner revolutions, leads out to our transformation in Christ."

THE SUCCESSFUL RETURN

Many Gates to Paradise

"There are as many gates to paradise," goes a saying, "as there are human hearts." The same can be said of the Return: there are as many responses to spiritual awakenings as there are human hearts to express them.

In previous chapters we have witnessed a variety of such awakenings, and seen how personal and individual these moments can be. We also know, from interviews and excursions into sacred tradition that failed Returns are possible, and that the period of time that follows a spiritual encounter can be fraught with pitfalls and allures.

What, then, constitutes a "successful" Return?

Success in such an endeavor is gauged by the degree to which a person is inspired by the Breakthrough to continue striving, both personally and for others. In practice, a successful Return brings the evocation of harmony and deep love, both toward ourselves and toward the people around us: the family unit, close friends, spiritual associates. For others it can be a new and deeper commitment to a religious belief or to the lost faith of one's youth. A successful Return may involve doing good works in the community through teaching, volunteering, working in a helping profession. For yet others the Return is a continuation and deepening of one's chosen practice through meditation, prayer, cultivation of virtue, and association with a spiritual community.

People who have passed through Breakthrough experiences, what's more, tend to pursue virtuous behavior for its own sake rather than with an eye toward the outcome. Harvard psychology professor David McClelland spent many years studying human motivation and the way it relates both to charitable behavior and to personal well-being. In an interview, McClelland talked about how spiritual well-being impacts on both our physical and emotional health. "Some kind of tender loving care seems to be a crucial ingredient in healing," he claims. "So the idea was that this kind of care had a positive effect on the immune system."

McClelland performed a fascinating experiment to test his idea. Assembling a group of college students, he showed them a film on the life and work of Mother Teresa. As the students watched, their immune reactivity was monitored by measuring a protein secreted in the saliva.

While viewing the film, it turned out, a majority of the students registered measurable positive physiological changes, including a dramatic elevation in the number of proteins linked to their immune system. These responses, interestingly, took place whether a student approved of Mother Teresa or disapproved of her. This surprising result, moreover, was only the beginning of the story.

At the onset of the experiment McClelland assumed that people with a strong need for social affiliation would score highest in immune system elevation. But analysis of the data turned up quite a different finding: the students who showed the most significant immunological elevation were those who responded most positively to the notion of doing good for other people without being overly concerned with the results of their actions. Unwittingly, McClelland had discovered an actual physiological benefit that results both from doing good in the world, and from being in the world but not of it; that is, being in a state of detachment where, in McClelland's words, "the person is not invested in the outcome of the thing—the person is not fixated on the goal of the activity." Such people, McClelland concludes, live without the usual fear of failure, obsession with success, and negative emotions that so many of us are burdened with.

In the film viewed by the students in McClelland's experiments, significantly, Mother Teresa herself manifested the same sense of detachment that a group of the experimental subjects found so stimulating. For example, when she was asked how it is possible to expend such enormous efforts caring for terminally ill babies who will die anyway, Mother Teresa replied that the sheer act of love transcends its outcome. A spirit of disengagement in the midst of action, spiritual traditions have always understood, is the key to genuine happiness, and is one of the primary experiences reported by seekers on the stage of Return.

Throughout previous chapters we have met a variety of men and women who are living out their spiritual destinies in surprising and compelling ways. A number of these people seemed mercilessly and even hopelessly caught up in pressing life situations at the time I spoke with them. Their problems, I thought at the time, were so daunting that any form of progress seemed unlikely. Later on, when I met many of these people again, I was amazed to discover that they had escaped from the quicksand of their lives and had gone on to experience profound moments of inner discovery and enrichment.

Rita Cole is an example.

Rita, you will recall, is the woman who accosted me in the hallway one day after an Elderhostel class complaining of being caught up on a treadmill and of not knowing where to find satisfaction in life. After giving what advice I could, I lost touch with this unhappy woman—only to cross paths with her years later at a benefit dinner in New York City.

At first I had trouble recognizing Rita. Dressed simply and elegantly, she had lost her brittle nervousness; in its place she expressed a quiet, depthful ease.

We talked for several minutes outside the ballroom. Rita, I learned, had dropped out of her many frantic political and cultural involvements, and had transferred her search for meaning to a group that spent two or three days a week doing volunteer work in depressed inner-city grade schools.

I asked Rita what made her turn in this direction. She told me that several years earlier she had been dragged to a religious retreat by a friend, and that during this session she had undergone such a profound "sense of grace" that she lost consciousness for several minutes. Coming to, she felt that she had received a mandate from a Higher Power to use her life as a tool for helping others. "I was just so damn unhappy before because I was always thinking about my own needs," she told me in the intense few minutes we talked. "I knew the thing I had to do now was get out of myself and work with other people, mainly kids. This was the fast lane to happiness that I was missing. So simple, huh?"

A number of others interviewed for this book, I learned over time, had also lived out their own unique versions of the Return.

Anna Dreyfus, the mountain hiker who witnessed the glowing deer in the New Hampshire woods, was so inflamed by her vision that she began studying meditation in earnest. Today she is a teacher at a Transcendental Meditation center in Boston and is planning to spend a year abroad in India studying meditation.

David Michaelson is the New York copywriter who belonged to a troubled utopian community in the 1960s and who later began attending the synagogue he grew up in. In subsequent conversations it turned out that

David's Jewish roots so fascinated him that he developed a yearning to study the mystical side of Judaism. The rabbi at his temple was reluctant to discuss these matters, and told David that he was neither old enough nor mature enough to probe such weighty ideas. Not to be daunted, David made several exploratory trips to Israel in search of a mystical teacher and eventually found the man he was looking for in Tel Aviv. The last letter I received from him included these telling lines: "No one, not even good Jews, has any idea at all of what remarkable jewels of secret prayer and atonement exist beneath the outer surfaces of the Jewish faith. I've found what I've been looking for all my life here, the inner kernel not only of the Jewish faith but, I really believe, of all faiths."

Jacqueline, my friend from Colorado who recovered from the suicide death of her artist lover with the help of a Buddhist community, today works directly with Tibetan refugees here and in Asia. Besides donating a good deal of money to help Tibetans displaced from their homeland by the Chinese, she has traveled to Nepal in the past year and worked directly with homeless refugees in hospitals and camps.

In some cases, of course, the Return is not only a return to service and good works, but also a rethinking of previous ideas of faith. Joan Lamming, whose belief in God was shattered as a child when she learned there was no Santa Claus and who joined the Pentecostal Church as an adult, began to tread still another stepping-stone when she left the church to pursue a very private relationship with God.

In a later interview I asked her why she took this dramatic step.

"It wasn't anything wrong with the church per se," she informed me. "I'd been having a series of these amazing experiences where I felt the presence of something holy in me all the time. Much of the day I walked around feeling—I don't know exactly how to say it—totally at one with my inner spirit. So I tried to talk about this experience to several ministers, and to one in particular who'd helped me a lot before. I wanted to know what was really going on, and where this was taking me. But all I got from them was a lot of canned doctrine. One minister actually told me I was having hallucinations and that I should see a psychiatrist! When I heard this I thought, heck, no one here really understands where I'm coming from. If they did they'd reach out with some real advice and understanding."

Joan gradually drifted away from the church, limiting her visits to religious holidays and special occasions. In the meantime, she began to look inward in an unusually intense way. "I've spent a lot of time alone in prayer since I left the church, and it's had a good effect," she insists. "It's like, I've gone off on my own into new country, and I'm plugged into something that gives me everything I need there. They say Christ is within you. I'm trying to take this idea seriously. I've gotten little peeks at what it means. Now it's my goal to explore it, and understand it more fully on my own."

Joan Lamming's reaction to her moments of spiritual bliss and her consequent Return brings up a larger question of faith: how can seekers reconcile private, intensely individual insights with participation in organizations that are based on ritual, doctrine, and shared experience? Throughout history this issue has worried religious thinkers, creating an uneasy tension between the mystically minded individual and the group-minded community.

An especially interesting example of this tension is spotlighted in the odyssey of Robert Atchley, a colleague of mine whom we have met in earlier chapters. After his moments of expanded consciousness in a Hindu ashram in India, Atchley returned to Ohio, where he resumed his job as college professor. Here he taught classes and administered his academic department as before. He even went back to work on a revision of the sixth edition of his popular gerontology textbook.

Yet all the time Atchley was reentering ordinary life he was also searching for ways to combine what he'd learned in India with the more familiar context of American religious life. The problem was that after being back in the United States he realized how thoroughly Western his outlook really was, and that any notion of practicing Hinduism in this country was out of the question.

Finding himself caught between two cultures, Atchley sought a compromise. During the next year he began searching for a local spiritual group that would allow him to practice the meditation techniques that had inspired his Breakthrough episodes in India and that would at the same time afford him the support of a caring community.

After visiting a number of local churches and affiliated groups, Atchley discovered the Quakers, the venerable congregation of Friends. Here elements of personal, unstructured religion were combined with social activism in a way that perfectly reflected his needs. "With the Quakers you pray as you see fit," he told me, "you follow your Inner Light. They stress good works and involvement in the community too. This gives me the room I need to continue my inner practices and at the same time reach out to others. It's a rapprochement between self and community, you could say, between personal experience and social belonging; and, for me, between East and West."

Today Bob Atchley is living out his Return practicing Eastern meditation methods in a Western religious community that includes the notions of charitable activism and a nonhierarchical church structure. His major religious impulse, he tells me, is a feeling of shared love. "It's like loving your spouse or loving God. You think that you've loved as much as you can. But then next week you realize there's more to do, more you could actually do, more ways to help; and you find yourself doing more because of it. There are no limits to our possible growth and to our capacity to love."

The attempt to convert one's Return into a rapprochement, as Atchley describes it, between community and self is mirrored, though in a different way, in the continuing saga of the Stoner family.

Marjorie and Phil Stoner, you will recall, separated during Marjorie's crisis of faith, then reunited several years later. During their period of separation Phil remained devotedly involved in his prayer group. Later on when they reunited, Marjorie was more convinced than ever of the validity of the indwelling Spirit, yet less certain of how she wished to pursue it. Her Return involved a waiting game, as well as a revamped version of faith.

Phil, meanwhile, had for many years been the more intransigent and intolerant of the pair. Now all that has changed. Today there is a quality of quiet benevolence about him that simply wasn't there before. It's an elusive thing to define, but an obvious one to people who know him. I once read a short story that opens with a lengthy description of a modest and kindly person. After a few pages the author breaks off the narrative and apologizes, saying he can't go on with the story any longer; he's going to have to end it right here. Why? Because, he explains, it's impossible to write a story about simple goodness. It's just too subtle and imponderable a quality to describe in ordinary words.

This sentiment, I felt, described Phil Stoner. What was once a matter of faith now seemed for him to be part of his own deeper experience. One day I asked him point-blank if he had undergone a Breakthrough. He replied quietly that he had, but that he felt it was inappropriate to talk about it.

And so I never learned his story. What's important for our purposes here, however, is that in the past several years Phil and Marjorie have both gone their separate inner ways, yet at the same time have been able to develop a loving and solid rapprochement, each following the Return in their own way. Today Phil is more involved in community efforts than ever before, and has intensified his commitment by working weekends with underprivileged children and performing intensive ministry work on the side. Marjorie, meanwhile, continues to search, to cultivate her private relationship with God, and to wait.

Bernadette Roberts, author of *The Path to No-Self,* spent years of struggle and retreat at the Snow Mass Christian Monastery in Colorado. Writing about her experiences there, she pays special attention to the stage of Return: "I see Christ first and foremost as a mystic," she tells us, "who had the continuous vision of God, and whose mission was to share it, give it to others."

Drawing on her own moments of awakening, Roberts tells us that even with the best of intentions, the act of setting out heroically to save the world after gaining insights into the spiritual realm is fraught with dangers. Roberts believes that a Return to the unitive life is better and more gently done when it occurs in small, kindly ways, in what Thomas Moore refers to as "the transfiguration of the ordinary."

Giving up the false self, Roberts writes, "takes place on a totally mundane level of practical, everyday living. It does not come about by some great insight or enlightenment—which is transient at best. It is not lost through some psychologically traumatic event, or lost in a state of ecstasy. The self is not merely seen through, it is lived through—lived to its dire end."

"One reservation is needed," Thomas Merton adds, "which is: However transcendental and above all forms of conditionality this experience itself of 'breaking-through' may be, we are liable to formulate a distorted interpretation of the experience. The Zen Master therefore will tell us to transcend or 'to cast away' the experience itself. . . . Then and then only do we find ourselves again to be the ordinary Toms, Dicks and Harrys we had been all along."

Bernadette Roberts compares her Return to the life of a caterpillar that after a painful period of metamorphosis emerges from its chrysalis as a butterfly. Now a butterfly is a beautiful creature and a changed creature. But it is also, Roberts implies, still a being of this world, and still heir to all its imperfections. "Somewhere in the back of the contemplative mind," she warns, "is the creeping illusion that union with God means to be a little more divine than human, a little more extraordinary than we actually are. We keep waiting for this to happen, and cannot understand why the union realized in the depths of our being does not come forth to the outside, or why it does not possess us completely, take over our humanity—make us completely divine."

The Return, in short, does not mean that we become metamorphosed into gods, only that we are more reflective of God's grace, and hence more human. After seeing a ray of the Truth we come back, as T. S. Eliot wrote at the end of *Four Quartets,* to the place we started from, but we see it now as if for the first time.

"Having always been a person who expected perfection from myself," a professional sculptor named Diane Hanson told me, "it wasn't surprising that I'd transfer this drive to be Miss Good and Perfect Woman into a spiritual framework. My self-actualization exercises were like spiritual fireworks for me, and gave me a fresh start. I thought: Wow, now I'm different! Now I'll be able to act the way I've always wanted to act: never get mad, not get flustered when things fall apart; be a rock of help and support to others; never lose my cool. But the next day I found me waiting there for me, the same person I was before. Nothing was different about me. I was exactly the same. Where had all my spiritual enhancements gone? It took me a long time to realize that just because you get out of your ego for a few minutes and catch a look at another reality, this doesn't make you a perfect person. In a sense, it just makes you feel more like the same old person than ever before, with all your warts showing."

"What, then, is the difference," I asked her, "in the way you look at the world now and in the way you looked at it before your experiences?"

"Even though you don't seem different to other people," she replied, "inside your spiritual sense gets stronger. You feel more self-assured that you're on the right track. You're happier, more centered. But it takes a long time until this shows up enough to make you into a different person."

This tendency to think that since we have been touched by something higher we should, ipso facto, behave forever in a saintly way is a sentiment that Priscilla Brager, ex-opera singer and ex-Madison Avenue executive, was also struggling with when I first interviewed her.

In our initial interview Brager was not shy about acknowledging her contempt for the ordinary. She spoke of her impatience at having to get her children ready for school each morning, and expressed irritation at the idea of "sitting on a hard chair in the kitchen balancing the stupid checkbook." It was all so different from the glamorous years she had spent as an executive, and before that as a promising international opera singer. She seemed to choke on the contrast. Brager also felt that these humble endeavors were "pipsqueak stuff" compared with the powerful Breakthrough states she had encountered.

Interestingly, I saw Priscilla again two years after our first interview, and her attitude had changed profoundly. She was now a volunteer in a nursing home and was preparing to enter a music therapy training program to help elderly people. She had experienced enormous satisfaction in her visits to nursing homes, she told me, and had decided to make this her life's work. Brager, quite clearly, had overcome certain illusions concerning what it means to be a "spiritual" person. In the process she had come to terms with the unglamorous sides of her life and with the "ordinary" practice of helping others.

Successful Return does not mean turning ourselves into a spiritual colossus or a teacher of all humanity. Quite the contrary: success in the post-Breakthrough period requires a leavening of spiritual acquirements with the gratitude and humility that legitimate spiritual traditions invariably identify as the touchstone of genuine progress.

"For me the idea of a true spiritual life means more than praying or formal visits to the synagogue," David Michaelson told me. "It means seeing God in the traces and finding treasure in the ruins. Remembering the holiness of things even when I'm down and upset. Trying to keep up the inner dialogue with God wherever I am. Seeing the high in the lowly, and the extraordinary in the ordinary. Trying to keep that inner fire going and well stoked."

Rachel, a student in one of my classes, described yet another variation on the theme of successful Return.

On her fiftieth birthday, as if to flaunt her age by admitting it, Rachel surprised her friends by joining the American Association of Retired Persons. She also started attending synagogue on a regular basis, a fact that shocked the people who thought her to be an ardent nonbeliever. Raised in a liberal, secular home, Rachel had several powerful dreams in her late forties that disturbed her deeply. She then experienced a moment of unexpected spiritual shock while touring Jerusalem. Walking by herself in the back streets of the Holy City one afternoon, she suddenly felt herself in the mystical presence of Sarah, wife of Abraham.

"Why Sarah I have no idea," Rachel told me. "But I know it was her spirit that was close to me, and that seemed to be . . . well, she was holding my hand and pressing against me, like a child."

After this experience Rachel determined to recover her Jewish religious roots. She even arranged to have a bas mitzvah, a Jewish ritual normally performed for girls at the age of twelve.

"I was in good company returning to my origins," Rachel told me. "The comedian Henny Youngman had his bar mitzvah when he was in his seventies. There are lots of us Jews who grow up one day and realize, hey!, we're connected to more than just a cultural tradition. We also have this glorious religion that goes back to Abraham, a gift of our forefathers and foremothers that tells us life is something bigger than our little selves, and that there is more to living than driving a Mercedes."

For Rachel the bas mitzvah represented an essential rite of passage, and a spiritual Return.

"The idea to have a bas mitzvah started that day in Jerusalem. It made some cycle in my life complete, some kind of return to the holy part of me. But without my actually having to do anything big or accomplish anything big. After that day in Jerusalem the spirit of Sarah stayed with me and guided me. I feel renewed now, and excited about whatever lies ahead. Coming back to God is like coming alive again—like having all the luck in the world fall on your head at once."

Paying Back God

Ann Medlock is the founder of the Giraffe Project, a Washington State-based organization dedicated to encouraging and rewarding people for helping others. She is also the wife of John Graham, whose story of rescue and conversion in the North Atlantic was told in an earlier chapter. Medlock began her Struggle in Princeton, New Jersey, when her first husband walked out on her for another woman, even as she was giving birth to his baby in the hospital. Her comfortable life shattered, a year and a half later Medlock turned to a Hindu master for help.

The teacher, it turned out, taught in highly traditional ways, giving his students mantras and meditation techniques and asking them to dress in saris, eat Indian food, and adopt a Hindu lifestyle.

"I was totally resistant to the clothes and food part," Medlock explains. "I just wouldn't do it. I was much more intrigued by the mental and spiritual work. I started devoting myself to these exercises, and very quickly came up out of the psychic hole I was in. I not only came out of the hole; I went shooting into the stratosphere. The whole adrenaline burst people get from trouble and problems stopped for me. I became totally calm and concentrated inside no matter what was happening. I was just so present to life, so at the top of my game, that I felt invincible. I did my meditations in the morning, then the rest of the day I walked around feeling untouchable, as if nothing could bother me. I was centered and awake."

I listened to Ann Medlock's story with fascination, but I also had some questions. For most people, I thought, this degree of detachment doesn't last very long. Maybe once in a while we float above it all, but not very often. How long did this state last? I asked. Did it eventually come to an end?

"It lasted about three years," Ann Medlock said. "Then I started to come out of it. The doors just slowly closed, and I kept waiting for a new magic door to open. But it didn't. So I went to my teacher and complained. He just sort of laughed and said, 'Who told you it was permanent?'

"So now the magic was gone and I was back to earth. I knew it was critical that I find the right game to play; that I take all the work I'd done when I was in that expanded state and use it in the right way."

In 1980 *Quest* magazine launched an in-house project called the Giraffe Society—an organization designed to encourage people to "stick their necks out" and to take a chance by helping others in an unselfish way. Readers were encouraged to send in their stories, and the most courageous "Giraffes" were honored.

This idea attracted Medlock, and she took over at *Quest* as Giraffe Society director. Shortly afterward the magazine failed, and after a good deal of soul-searching, Medlock decided to use the Giraffe name and continue the society's work. The Giraffe Project, as it is known today, has been encouraging people to stick their necks out for others ever since.

"That was, you could say, my way of thanking God for what had been given me during that time period," Ann Medlock said. "For me, coming back after my spiritual high was based on knowing that I had certain God-given skills, especially as a persuasive communicator. How could I use these skills honorably? I wondered. Well, I thought, this spiritual state I'd had gave me *an imperative to do service* that was absolutely overwhelming. The inner voice said: You've got to serve. You just have to. It's not a thing to be questioned."

Had Medlock's spiritual high ever returned? I asked.

"I think I live with a version of it a lot of the time now," she replied. "But it's not at that same intense level as before. It just kind of informs my life in a gentle way You kind of fold it into your everyday awareness, and try to help as much as you can."

Ann Medlock's story is a story of successful Return. Refusing to become obsessed with her Breakthrough, she forged ahead, put what she had learned into practice, and made the delightful discovery that aspects of altered consciousness continue to illuminate our lives in subtle and unexpected ways, even after the fireworks die down. In this sense the Return is a natural extension of the Breakthrough, just as the Breakthrough is the fruit of the Struggle. The Stages of the Soul are not walled off from one another. They are living states of mind that in the end fuse into a single unified spiritual autobiography.

This coming together of the elements of the soul is expressed in many personal stories like Ann Medlock's, but also in a more universal way in art and literature. In one of the best-known of these tales, Charles Dickens's *A Christmas Carol,* we encounter both a classic version of the Return and a dazzling recapitulation of the Five Stages of the Soul.

Closing the Circle: The Greater Return

As *A Christmas Carol* opens we find the story's hero, Ebenezer Scrooge, to be a bullying, pitiless miser, seemingly beyond all redemption. And yet an invisible spiritual faculty has been mysteriously smoldering inside our protagonist all these years. On this particular Christmas Eve it reaches its flash point, and the Five Stages of the Soul unfold, recapitulated this time in a single night.

First comes the Call, Marley's voice and rattling chains, a sound straight from the hell that Scrooge is bound for if he does not mend his ways.

Next follows the arrival of the ghosts of Christmas Past and Present, and with them a Search for signs of goodness and meaning in Scrooge's earthly existence. Just as in the case of George Bailey, a ghostly life review now unfolds. But in this instance it is a condemnatory review in which our wicked hero observes his past and present behavior in horror, reeling with the shock of recognition as he witnesses his own decline from young idealist to aged curmudgeon. As each successive tableau is revealed, the ghostly messengers force Scrooge to face the gap between his youthful hopes and the shrunken reality of his present life. Compelling him to go beyond his own denial, they confront him with the loss of his dream. It is as if on this sacred night the invisible powers hold up a mirror that Scrooge has never gazed into before, the mirror of self-awareness. Up till now our hero has literally never seen himself as others see him, and as he really is. Spiritually speaking, he has been asleep. Now, as his life passes before him in one dreary episode after the other, the inescapable evidence of his own reflection awakens him.

Scrooge's moment of cosmic self-recognition has many parallels to the afterlife traditions of world religions. According to both ancient Egyptian and Buddhist doctrine, a mirror is held up to the souls of the dead when they first arrive in the post-death state. This mirror reflects every moment of their lives down to the tiniest detail. Observing their good and bad actions in the glass, the souls of the dead come to a final judgment about themselves, by themselves, based entirely on the evidence of their own deeds. As Emerson once remarked: "We are punished by our sins, not for them."

The cycle of Scrooge's Struggle with its testimony of past and present is finally completed by a visit from Christmas Future. Transported now to his own funeral, and then to his own grave, Scrooge comes face to face with the recognition that he must someday die; and more to the point, that this someday is soon, perhaps tomorrow. Death now becomes Scrooge's devilish tormentor—and also his teacher.

This collision with mortality is the coup de grace that triggers a repentance so forthright and sincere that in a single moment of Breakthrough Scrooge dies to his old self and undergoes *metanoia*—a spiritual change of heart. In the process he becomes what the Bible terms the "New Man." Quite simply, in the Christian sense, he is reborn. "I don't know anything," he cries out as he awakens on Christmas morning (both literally, sitting up in bed, and figuratively, into higher consciousness). "I'm quite a baby. Never mind. I don't care. I'd rather be a baby."

In an oblique but vivid way Scrooge's Breakthrough and Return echo enormous cosmic themes. One of the most essential is the Buddhist ideal of the Bodhisattva. The Bodhisattva is a human being who has achieved total nirvana—full and complete liberation from the illusory world. Yet instead of vanishing forever into timeless bliss, the Bodhisattva voluntarily accepts rebirth and Return into the illusory world in order to help others achieve this same state. He is like the prisoner breaking free of a jail cell who stays back to help other prisoners over the wall and who will not save himself until everyone else has escaped. In the Buddhist Mahayana tradition, the Bodhisattva's compassion is so great that he will not enter final nirvana until every sentient being in the universe is saved "down to the last blade of grass."

After Scrooge's conversion our hero spends his last days on earth helping others and doing good where he can. In the end it is said of him that no citizen of London was ever a better friend, a better master, a better man.

I remember when I first read these words at the end of Dickens's story. They gave me a deep sense of gratification, but they also roused my curiosity. What happened next in Scrooge's life? I couldn't help wondering. Exactly what *did* he do in his later years to receive such universal praise? How did he assimilate the moral precepts taught to him that fateful night into his business, his social dialogue, his friendships, his life?

I sometimes even imagine an epilogue to Scrooge's biography that spells out these details in fine print. Suppose for a moment that in the remaining years of his life Scrooge decides to use his tremendous fortune to set up . . . well, why not a charitable foundation? Call it the Jacob Marley Foundation, in memory of the man whose ghostly appearance inspired his Call.

The Marley Foundation's philanthropic mission, we imagine, is designed to help bright but impoverished youths like Tiny Tim and Oliver Twist get a proper education. Since we know that Tiny Tim himself survived to see many a merry Christmas, we assume that in the years to come he will take his place as a high-level employee at the Marley Foundation, working under the loving tutelage of his godfather, perhaps on programs to help the disabled. Most likely he will be groomed to take over as director someday.

But before we romanticize the Marley Foundation too much, let's bear in mind that to run a successful foundation it's necessary to turn away many legitimate requests for money. It's all part of a day's work in the philanthropy business.

And so we wonder: How will the now kindhearted Scrooge handle such appeals? Will his generosity cloud his common sense? Will he give to every outstretched palm, and by so doing bankrupt the foundation? Or will he turn a deaf ear to certain entreaties, and be racked with guilt as a result; not to speak of making personal enemies across London? Either way there will be problems to reckon with.

Then there's the Bob Cratchit question.

Scrooge's sudden charity and Cratchit's gratitude is heartwarming, no doubt. But what now? Certainly Scrooge will increase Cratchit's salary and give him a more liberal vacation plan. But would Scrooge be wise to raise a relatively unsophisticated clerk to the level of manager? Scrooge's converted heart tells him one thing and his business acumen quite another.

Still, our Ebenezer is a canny fellow. We instinctively know he will somehow navigate these ambiguous waters, keeping his foundation generous and at the same time remaining a tough-minded competitor.

Most important, while Scrooge has undergone his spiritual transformation, and while he is truly a new man, he nonetheless remains a man on earth. This means he must continue negotiating the swamps and lowlands of the world's daily affairs, dark places that do not magically disappear the moment the light comes into our hearts. Like all of us, Scrooge must keep making the tough decisions, must say no as well as yes, must even break hearts. All this is necessary, mandatory even, on the Return trip to this less than perfect world.

The seeds of goodness lie in all people, and anyone with a willing heart can be saved. This is the message Dickens wished to bring to the world. Had he written an epilogue to his story he would, I hazard a guess, have made the added point that the way we behave *after* we are saved is as important, spiritually, as what we have done before. Our new life begins where our old one ends.

Besides the obvious moral of Dickens's story, there's another dimension to this masterpiece that is rarely brought to light, an esoteric message that is not necessarily apparent at first reading. This hidden message shows how we are to live our lives during the stage of Return, and, more important, how the stage of Return ties all the other stages together and, in a sense, compounds them into a still larger and more universal form of greater Return—a Return to the primal source and center of our being.

In his Christmas odyssey Scrooge passes through the Five Stages of the Soul in a single night. He is, in a sense, a living exemplar of the Gospel parable of the three laborers in the vineyard who each work for different lengths of time but who all receive equal pay. God, the parable implies, is always waiting for us, always inviting us to return to Him. It makes no difference at what age we begin the voyage or how long we struggle. The rewards are equally tremendous for all those who answer the Call.

But why is this? How can it be that the amount of time spent in the Struggle is not taken into account by the divine powers?

This is because the Stages of the Soul do not correspond to time as we understand it. From a higher point of view, time is a relative process and an immeasurable one. Passing through the soul's stages in a single night for Scrooge is tantamount to passing through the experience both in a lifetime and in no time at all; or, better said, in a condition that is *outside of time.* Note, for example, that when Scrooge wakes up the next morning he has no reckoning of how long the phantoms have been visiting him, or how long he has tarried in his own future and past. Time no longer has any meaning; it has ceased to exist. "I don't know what day of the month it is!" he croons to himself merrily. "I don't know how long I've been among the Spirits. I don't know anything." His experience has occurred, as it were, not in time at all, but in eternity. And it is here in this timeless, spaceless world beyond matter and form that the final Return is made.

Scrooge intuitively understands this fact. He senses that his entire life has passed before him in what the Australian Aborigines call "dream time." That is, the enchanted chronology we experience in our dreams where past, present, and future meld into a single continuum; where an eternity is passed in a heartbeat, an instant is an eternity. The process is akin to a late medieval painting technique known as "continuous narration," whereby an artist depicts several time-separated incidents—the journey of the Three Kings, for example, their arrival in Bethlehem, and the Adoration in the manger—all occurring simultaneously in a single continuous panorama. "I will live in the Past, the Present, and the Future," Scrooge promises the spirit of Christmas Future. "The Spirits of all Three shall strive within me. I will not shut out the lessons that they teach."

A haunting passage at the end of Plato's *Republic* provides a similar portrait of what Carlos Castaneda calls "a separate reality." This passage embodies both Scrooge's journey and, more essentially, Plato's deepest intuitions about time, eternity, and spiritual rebirth. As a philosophy professor, I used to teach my students all the intricate dialectical arguments found in this book, which is perhaps the greatest masterpiece in all Western philosophy. Each time I taught the work, I never ceased to be amazed by the fact that here, at the very finale of this magnificent monument to pure reason, Plato breaks off his philosophical argument and ends not with definitive statements about life and death but with a puzzling story, the so-called Myth of Er.

Why does he do this? Why does Plato abandon ordinary language and logic just at the point where we are waiting for the final answers to life? What message was Plato trying to communicate? And why did he choose the medium of myth in which to do it?

The answer is that many metaphysical concepts, Plato knew, can be effectively communicated using ordinary philosophical reasoning. Certain transcendental ideas, however, are so far beyond the grasp of the rational mind that they can only be conveyed through the medium of symbolism. In an attempt to explain the inexplicable—why we are born, why we live, suffer, and die—Plato thus turned to myth, and to the story of a soldier named Er, who undergoes what today we would call a near-death experience.

The story begins when Er, a soldier in the Greek army, is cut down on the field of battle and left for dead. Several days pass and his comrades finally discover him in a pile of stinking corpses. Just as he is about to be cremated, Er regains consciousness, sits up on his funeral pyre, and proceeds to describe to the soldiers ranged around him the strange experiences he has undergone in the afterlife.

"He [Er] said that his Soul went out and journeyed together with a great company," writes Plato, "and they came to a certain ghostly place wherein were two open mouths of the earth."

Here Er sees two divine tribunals judging a group of human souls. Some of these souls are being sent to Hades in the bowels of the earth, others are drifting up to heaven. When Er is brought before these heavenly judges they inform him that he is not yet dead. He has been picked, they tell him, as an emissary. His job is to return to earth and explain to people exactly how the afterlife works.

Now follows Er's depiction of this strange heavenly kingdom, which, like the Christian vision, is depicted as a timeless world populated by hierarchies of angels, prophets, and endless numbers of human souls. What marks the difference between the two versions of the afterlife, the Christian and the Greek, is that in Er's heaven every soul is given the opportunity beforehand *to select the life he or she will lead on earth.*

Er explains how human souls gather in a great celestial meadow, and how a prophet of old lays out a number of lives on the ground before them. The sage advises these souls to carefully examine each life and choose the one that best suits their spiritual needs.

Some of these souls, Er says, quickly grab for a life that seems glamorous, the life of a king, say, or a rich person. On closer inspection they then discover that this seemingly pleasurable life is filled with misery and abasement. But the die is now cast, the selection is made; it is too late to change.

Other souls, meanwhile, inspect the array of lives with a more reflective eye, searching out, as they are urged to do, lives that will afford them an opportunity for spiritual enrichment, "calling that life the worst that will lead his soul to become more unrighteous, and calling that life the better which will lead it to become more righteous."

After choosing their fates, the human souls must then return to earth and live out their destiny. On the way to being born they first cross the river Styx. Here they are made to drink from the Waters of Forgetfulness. Henceforth they will remember nothing of heaven or their choices, and many will eventually come to despise the life roles they themselves have so carefully picked—the role, say, of camel driver or insurance agent, of bag lady or editor, of New Guinea chieftain or President of the United States. Forgetful that their lives are the products of their own choosing, they blame their unhappiness on other people, or on fate, bad luck, even God Himself. Like the prince in "The Hymn of the Pearl," these people forget that they have been charged with a mission, and that someday they must give a full accounting.

Plato's depiction of heaven, significantly, employs imagery of the afterlife that is found in cultures throughout the world, and that Plato could not possibly have known about—the Taoist, for instance, and the Tibetan. Versions of this story with their themes of heavenly worlds, divine judgment, and souls standing before their Maker are universal, and turn up with surprising frequency even in our own dreams.

Jacob, a close friend of mine whom we met in an earlier chapter (he's the psychology professor and commentator on prayer), once had a powerful and disconcerting dream along these lines that he and I discussed at length. Besides the fact that, in Jacob's words, "the dream was so goyish it was like something out of the Book of Revelations," he also found its similarity to classic near-death experiences compelling and baffling.

"I was standing in Grand Central Station," Jacob began. "Near me was a group of angry people hitting each other with sticks. A voice inside me told me this was the regular world with its troubles and strife. Then I noticed two large arched entranceways in one of the station walls. Both of them led to a very dark passageway of some kind. In one of the entrances an angel-like form was standing, beckoning for me to come."

When Jacob mentioned the large arched entranceways, I was reminded of the "ghostly place wherein were two open mouths of the earth" that Er describes.

"I went in," Jacob continued, "and the next moment I felt like I'd left everything that was familiar behind me. I was entering a psychological place I'd never experienced. But it was also strangely familiar, like I'd been there before. There was a different time and rhythm here. There wasn't the usual rigid separation between past and present.

"I found myself walking in a tunnel. A number of other people joined me, and a tour guide started leading us through a series of rooms. We stopped in one room that had a lot of crosses on the wall and other mystical symbols. The guide identified this room as 'texture and color.' In another room he said 'size, shape, and form.' In another he said 'time and space.' Each room, I suppose you'd say, represented some property of the physical world.

"At this point I started studying the people next to me. Right away a chill passed over me. They all had a dull, zombielike look to them, as if they were hypnotized or in a daze. I understood it all in a flash. These people were *dead*. They were souls of the dead. But they didn't *know* they were dead. They didn't know they were in the hereafter yet.

Naturally the next logical question was: So what was I doing here? Had I also died? I didn't think so.

"Next I was standing at the foot of a long bridge. On either side of the bridge everything was dark, but the darkness was lit by thousands and thousands of tiny lights. I could hear a pleasant murmur all around me. It was like the sound of people eating and talking in a restaurant. There was a refreshing coolness in the air. Something in me knew that each of these lights was a human soul. Then I looked up. At the end of the bridge I saw a gigantic wooden door. It was closed and bolted with a big iron bolt. I knew instinctively that God was on the other side waiting to judge me. I started to walk toward the door, but something gently pushed me back. A voice told me that it was not time yet. I had to go back to the world and carry a message. Two messages, actually. The first was that when you die, if you haven't developed your spiritual side you won't know that you're dead. That's not good. You'll be like the people in the tunnel. It's bad not to know you're dead. The voice didn't tell me why.

"Second, I was supposed to explain to people that the afterlife is a real place, and that we all go there. It's no fooling around. It's real. Don't doubt it."

Hearing Jacob talk about his strange dream, I was struck by how closely his description approximated the near-death experiences that have been so widely published over the past several decades. The ghostly guide, the tunnel, the angel, the hordes of souls, the judgment chamber, the sense of being beyond time and space—these images are not only found in eschatological traditions around the world but are frequently described by people who have been pronounced clinically dead and who, like Plato's Er, have returned to tell the tale.

One of the most illuminating of these near-death accounts comes from one of the major founders of modern psychotherapy, Carl Jung.

Hospitalized by a heart attack in 1944, Jung chronicles his brush with the hereafter in astonishing detail. His vision begins while he is on the operating table. Suddenly, he tells us, he feels himself being lifted up from the surgical room miles into outer space. Hovering above the earth, Jung looks down and sees actual topographical landmarks—the Himalayas, the Arabian Desert, the Mediterranean. Gazing about in space, he notices a cube of stone floating nearby. It is approximately the size of a house and has an opening on one side. Entering the stone, Jung finds himself in a candlelit temple and is greeted here by an ancient sage. He prepares to visit a second room, where, in his words, he will "at last understand what historical nexus I or my life fitted into. I would know what had been before me, why I had come into being, and where my life was flowing."

About to enter this sanctum sanctorum, Jung is accosted by a spirit from earth who informs him that his life's work is not finished and that he must return to his body immediately.

Jung obeys. But like many others who report being forced to return from a near-death experience, he is deeply dismayed at having to reenter the mundane landscape of the material world, which he now finds ugly and inhospitable. "The view of the city and mountains from my sickbed seemed to me like a painted curtain with black holes in it," he writes, "or a tattered sheet of newspaper full of photographs that mean nothing. Disappointed, I thought, now I must return to the 'box system' again. For it seemed to me as if behind the horizon of the cosmos a three-dimensional world had been artificially built up, in which each person sat by himself in a little box. And now I should have to convince myself all over again that this was important!"

Returned from his soul flight to the afterworld, Jung now spends the next several weeks convalescing in a hospital bed, where every evening he beholds a sequence of angelic and Solomonic visions, a carryover from his near-death encounter. "I would never have imagined that any such experience was possible," Jung tells us. "It was not a product of imagination. The visions and experiences were utterly real; there was nothing subjective about them; they all had a quality of absolute objectivity."

As the weeks go by, Jung soon finds himself caught between the repeating joy of his Breakthrough moments and the dread of the Return to his habitual life, where "everything was too material, too crude and clumsy, terribly limited both spatially and spiritually. It was all an imprisonment, for reasons impossible to divine." Yet as time passes, the ordinary world begins to draw him back despite himself. "It had a kind of hypnotic power," he admits, "a cogency, as if it were reality itself, for all that I had clearly perceived its emptiness."

Finally the visionary ecstasies cease, and Jung makes the conscious decision to return to ordinary existence and to live out his days in service to his profession.

Within several months he is back at work. Here he soon makes an exhilarating discovery: he is now able to draw upon materials from his Breakthrough experiences and incorporate what he has learned and understood into his psychiatric practice. A remarkably fruitful period of work now follows in which many of his most critical contributions to psychiatry are made. "The insight I had had," Jung tells us, "or the vision of the end of all things, gave me the courage to undertake new formulations . . . thus one problem after the other revealed itself to me and took shape."

"Something else, too, came to me from my illness," Jung adds. "I might formulate it as an affirmation of things as they are: an unconditional 'yes' to that which is, without subjective protests—acceptance of the conditions of existence as I see them and understand them, acceptance of my own nature, as I happen to be." Most compelling for the great psychiatrist was the beauty and enduringness of the Breakthrough moments themselves. "We shy away from the word 'eternal,'" Jung writes, "but I can describe the experience only as the ecstasy of a non-temporal state in which present, past and future are one."

The message we come away with from these and other spiritual encounters is that it is possible for us to achieve a state in which we see our entire existence in a single instant, and in which we grasp the reason why we are here, what we must do, and who we are.

This condition is analogous to Erik Erikson's concept of ego integrity, wherein at some point we look back at our past and see that the life we have led is "something that had to be, that permitted of no substitutions." During such moments of recognition all masks are pulled away. We see clearly and without illusion that our little self, our ego, covers over something far greater within ourselves, and that beneath the jagged exteriors of this "boxlike world" lie secrets unimaginable.

We all have a particular life to live with particular difficulties and joys to experience. We are given this life not through accident or bad luck or good luck, but through the ineluctable destiny that belongs to each of us and that in some vastly mysterious way we have chosen for ourselves. We cannot escape from our destiny but must embrace it, and say yes to it, down to the last detail.

I can't help but think again of the aged Larry Morris, ninety-seven years on this planet, who in a moment of frailty once cried out to me, "Why does God keep me alive so long!" Neither of us knew the answer, of course. But I do know that Larry Morris taught me many life lessons even in his final years. Perhaps this is why he was destined to survive so long despite himself. Perhaps all of us have such missions for ourselves and others, even if we are unaware of them.

Here also, I believe, lies the answer to the question of how long the Return lasts: it lasts as long as it takes us to complete the tasks we've been given in this life. The Return, in this sense, lasts until every moment of our lives becomes a testimony to what we remember and forget, and then remember again—our spiritual mission. It is a never-ending story whose center is everywhere in our lives and whose circumference is nowhere. The meaning behind this mystery can only be hinted at, or, better, expressed in parables and stories. Here is one of the greatest.

Making the Greater Return

One day, a story from an ancient Hindu scripture tells, God and a sage named Narada are walking across a vast desert. Narada turns to God and asks, "O Greatest Lord, what is the secret of this life and the appearances of this world?"

God smiles and makes no reply. They continue on.

"Child," God finally says. "The sun is hot today and I am thirsty. Ahead you will find a village. Go there and fetch me a cup of water."

Narada sets off. Arriving at the village, he approaches the first house he sees and knocks at the door. A beautiful young woman answers. The moment Narada looks into her eyes he forgets God's command and the reason for his mission.

The woman ushers Narada into the house, where he is warmly welcomed by her family. It is as if everyone in this gentle household has been expecting him. Narada is asked to eat with the family, and then to stay the night. He gladly accepts, enjoying the family's warm hospitality, and secretly marveling at the young woman's loveliness.

A week goes by, then two. Narada decides to stay on, and he soon begins to share in the household chores. After the appropriate amount of time passes he asks for the woman's hand in marriage. The family has been expecting nothing less, it turns out. Everyone is overjoyed.

Narada and his young wife settle down in her family's house, where she soon bears him three children, two sons and a daughter. Years pass. When his wife's mother and father pass away, Narada takes over as head of the household. He opens a small shop in the village and it prospers. Before long he is an honored citizen of the community and a prominent member of the town council. Giving himself up to the age-old joys and sorrows of village life, Narada lives contentedly for many years.

Then one evening during monsoon season a violent storm breaks overhead, and the river rises so high from the sudden rains that the village begins to flood.

Narada gathers his family and leads them through the dark night toward higher ground. But the winds blow so violently and the rain pelts down with such force that one of Narada's sons is washed away. Narada reaches for the boy, and in so doing lets go of his second son. A moment later a gale wind tears his daughter from his arms. Then his beloved wife is washed away into the roaring darkness.

Narada wails helplessly and claws at the sky. But his cries are drowned by a towering wave that rises from the depths of the terrible night and washes him headlong into the river. All goes black.

Many hours pass; perhaps days. Slowly, painfully, Narada comes to his senses, only to discover that he has been washed onto a sandbank far down the river. It is daytime now and the storm has passed. But there is no sign of his family anywhere, nor, for that matter, of any living creature.

For a long time Narada remains lying on the sand, almost mad with sorrow and abandonment. Bits of wreckage float past him in the river. The smell of death is on the wind. Everything has been taken from him now; all things life-giving and precious have disappeared into the swirling waters. There is little to do, it seems, but weep.

Then, suddenly, Narada hears a voice behind him that makes the blood stop in his veins. "Child," the voice asks, "where is my cup of water?"

Narada turns and sees God standing at his side. The river vanishes, and once again he and God are alone in the empty desert.

"Where is my water?" God asks again. "I have been waiting for you to bring it now for several minutes."

Narada throws himself at his Lord's feet and begs for forgiveness. "I forgot!" Narada cries again and again. "I forgot what you asked of me, Great Lord! Forgive me!"

God smiles and says, *"Now* do you understand the secret behind your life, and the appearances of this world?"

Now do we understand?

The story of Narada tells the greatest story—the story of a return to the reality that is always with us. Narada begs God to explain the mystery of existence. God complies, not with words, but with a demonstration, the same demonstration that we all are living through this very moment, and that we call our lives.

The flashing eyes of the young woman that make Narada forget his spiritual mission are a symbol of *maya,* the interplay of time, space, and illusion that causes even the greatest sages to fall asleep in the comfortable household of this world. Yet ironically, the whole time Narada—and we—are immersed in the cosmic dream, the whole time we are growing up, marrying, bearing children, suffering the fortunes and pleasures of life, in reality we too are alone with God at our side in the endless desert of infinity that stretches out in all directions.

The Return then— the real and Greater Return—is not simply a revivifying of ordinary life after tasting states of higher consciousness. It is a Return to the center of the universe within ourselves, a movement back to the sacred point toward which our journeying has always inclined.

This book has been a story about a journey in which the Call, Search, Struggle, Breakthrough, and Return are all stepping-stones, each following one another like acts in a play or movements in a symphony. The artistic metaphor is helpful here because it reminds us that we cannot skip a stage or disregard any part of the sequence. We cannot be impatient for the ending because we need each of the steps along the way to experience the journey as a whole.

Yet once we do see the Five Stages of the Soul as a complete cycle, even the idea of a "journey" seems inadequate and incomplete. True, we do not make the leap from zero to the Infinite in one jump; but neither do we creep our way along a one-way corridor toward the hypothetical finish line of enlightenment. In truth, we are not moving at all. From a transcendent standpoint, from the perspective of eternity, we are already where we need to go, like Narada. We just don't know it. This is why we must return to earth and live our lives. But it's also why we are never quite at home in this glittering world.

The Stages of the Soul are progressive steps. But they are also revelatory states of mind that spring one from the next like a flower from the bud, and the fruit from the flower. In pursuing the Stages we do not discover something new. Nothing original is invented. "Not knowing how far the Truth is," says Zen master Hakuin, "we seek it far away. What a pity! We are like him who in the midst of water, cries out in thirst so imploringly."

It's as if we have been dreaming all our lives. Now suddenly we wake up. The world, we discover, is the same as it's always been. It's just that we see it—and ourselves—for what it really is. Like Narada, we have always been rooted in eternity, always in a state of Great Return, always in the Eternal Now. We just don't know it. We don't know who we are.

Who then are we?

Once the scales fall from our eyes and we see things as they really are, we realize that we are all incipient knowers and seers, all saints and sages in potential. As St. Augustine tells us, God has created each human being for Himself, and "our heart cannot be quieted until it finds repose in Him."

We do not live in a meaningless, spiritless world no matter what the pundits and the naysayers may insist. In this book we've heard the stories of people who have discovered that our world is alive and sensitive to the temper of our souls. All of them have understood that we have only to call out for help with a sincere voice, and help will finally come. "You do not need to call to Him far off," Meister Eckhart assures us. "He waits much more impatiently than you for you to open to Him. He longs for you a thousand times more urgently than you for Him."

"Knock, and it shall be opened to you." And the step after that will then be revealed, and the step after that. Thus the sequence of stages—Call, Search, Struggle, Breakthrough, and Return, all of them leading finally to a Greater Return that reaches beyond the limits of this life. Perhaps this cycle will not unfold with the speed and ease you might wish for. And perhaps not in the form you might expect. But it will come. Your task, my task, is simply to knock, to call out over and over again, "I am here, O Friend! Hear my cry!" And then wait.

But be assured: an answer will come. Eventually an answer will come.

There are, of course, dangers and difficulties that assail us on the spiritual venture, as we have seen throughout this book. Self-delusion. Spiritual pride. Discouragement. Misunderstanding.

This is why clear-minded guidance is needed from those who have walked the Five Stages of the Soul before us, and who know the route through the maze. With Ariadne's help, a golden thread will show us the way out of our own labyrinth. Search for this thread. Follow it no matter how difficult the route. At the same time, be certain from the start that it really *is* Ariadne who is leading you.

Most important: whatever has happened in your life up till now, whatever you may have believed in or hoped for or dreamed of, remember that all this is in the past. A new life, a new chance, now awaits you. You have only to reach out and take it. But remember: you *yourself* must do the reaching. Though the Way calls, it will not come on its own accord. It is up to you to take the first step.

So take this step; take it while you can. Even if you stumble—and you *will* stumble—remember your purpose and continue on. If you forget, if you wander from the path, bear in mind that forgetfulness is everyone's fate—but more importantly, so is remembering.

Most of all, know that in everyone's heart there stirs a great homesickness, and that a small voice is always asking us, *calling* us to return. For far in the western steppes of Turkey the marble tomb of a saint still sits silently, gazing down upon a thousand miles of wilderness. Above the tomb's gate, words are emblazoned in stone, words that have spoken to the hearts of people for seven hundred years—words that continue to remind us of a truth we already know deep in our souls.

"Come back," these words say, "O you who still have breath to read these words, come back. There is still time!"

And there is.

Notes

Chapter 1

Page 7: "By the late 1970s, Professor Daniel Levinson had worked out his soon to be famous theory of adult life span transitions . . ." See Daniel Levinson, *The Seasons of a Man's Life.* New York: Knopf, 1978. See also Gail Sheehy, *Passages: Predictable Crises of Adult Life.* New York: Bantam, 1976. Gail Sheehy, *New Passages.* New York: Random House, 1995. For the question of whether psychological "passages" are actually linked to chronological age, see P. Braun, and R. Sweet, "Passages: Fact or Fiction?" *International Journal of Aging and Human Development* (1984), 18: 161–76.

Page 7: "Professor Erik Erikson argued that the formation of personality . . ." See Erik Erikson, *Childhood and Society.* New York: Norton, 1963, Chapters 1–3.

Page 7: "While Western literary and religious tradition had long spoken of the 'Ages of Man' . . ." See Thomas Cole, *The Journey of Life: A Cultural History of Aging in America.* Cambridge University Press, 1992, p. 195.

Page 11: On life stages, see J. A. Barrow, *The Ages of Man.* New York: Oxford University Press, 1986. See also Thomas Cole, *The Journey of Life: A Cultural History of Aging in America,* previously cited.

Page 11: "Carl Jung writes in his famous essay . . ." See Carl Jung, *Modern Man in Search of a Soul.* New York: Harcourt, Brace, 1955.

Page 12: On consciousness of aging, see Howard P. Chudakoff, *How Old Are You? Age Consciousness in American Culture.* Princeton: Princeton University Press, 1989.

Page 12: "But aging comes as a surprise to *everyone.*" See Robert N. Butler, *Why Survive? Being Old in America.* New York: Harper, 1985.

Page 16: See Jacob Needleman, *Lost Christianity.* New York: Harper, 1980.

Page 16: "The luminous teaching tales of the Desert Fathers." See Benedicta Ward, S.L.G., *The Desert Christians: Sayings of the Desert Fathers.* New York: Macmillan, 1980.

Page 17: See J. D. Salinger, *Franny and Zooey.* New York: Bantam, 1981.

Page 20: "Plato likewise hinted at a mystical wisdom." See Plato's *Seventh Letter,* in which he talks about his "unwritten philosophy" and its relationship to mystical experience.

Page 22: "The worst of it all . . ." See Jung, *Modern Man in Search of a Soul,* previously cited.

Page 22: Marc Kaminsky, *What's Inside You, It Shines Out of You.* New York: Horizon Press, 1974.

Page 24: "I was already working with Elderhostel." See Gene Mills, *The Story of Elderhostel.* Hanover, NH: University Press of New England, 1995.

Page 27: See the famous opening lines of Jalālu'ddin Rumi, *The Mathnawi* (Reynold Nicholson, trans.), vol. I. London: Luzac, 1982.

Page 28: "Among Hindus the life course is divided into four stages." The Hindu life course is described in the classic *Laws of Manu* of Hindu tradition. See *The Laws of Manu* (Georg Bühler, trans.). New York: Dover Books, n.d.

Page 28: For information on Yeats's visionary theories, see William Butler Yeats, *A Vision.* New York: Macmillan, 1961.

Page 28: "This is a moment of great mystical importance." Joseph Campbell, *Transformations of Myth Through Time.* New York: Harper, 1990, pp. 26–28.

Page 28: "A recent Gallup survey designed to measure commitment to religion in America . . ." George Gallup, Jr., and Jim Castelli, *The People's Religion: American Faith in the 90's.* New York: Macmillan, 1989.

Page 29: "Roberto Assagioli, made spirituality . . ." See Assagioli's essay "Self-realization and Psychological Disturbances," in Stanislav Grof and Christina Grof, eds., *Spiritual Emergency.* New York: Putnam, 1989.

Page 30: " 'Aging,' he writes, 'forces us to decide what is important in life.' " Thomas Moore, *The Care of the Soul.* New York: Harper Perennial, 1992, p. 216.

Page 35: See Brother Lawrence, *The Practice of the Presence of God.* White Plains, NY: Peter Pauper Press, 1963, p. 2.

Page 37: See Assagioli's essay "Self-realization and Psychological Disturbances," previously cited, p. 37.

Chapter 2

Page 43: "In an engraving titled *Everyman* by the great Flemish artist Peter

Bruegel . . ." H. Arthur Klein, *Graphic Worlds of Peter Bruegel the Elder*. New York: Dover Publications, 1963, pp. 86–87.

Page 44: See P. D. Ouspensky, *In Search of the Miraculous*. New York: Harcourt, Brace, 1977, pp. 251–54.

Page 45: "What's going on here? we are certainly entitled to ask." Although it has never been known for certain, most readers of this passage assume that the two subjects "experimented" on by Gurdjieff were placed into a state of hypnosis. Scientific investigators have been studying this strange phenomenon for two centuries, since Anton Mesmer and his famous "Mesmerism" first swept through Paris in the years just preceding the Revolution, bringing trance states into the public arena. Hypnosis can be interpreted, as some investigators suggest, as a relative breakdown in a person's normal orientation to generalized reality orientation. It can also be understood, as psychologist Ernest Hilgard tells us, in terms of a radical dissociation of the self, revealing unsuspected parts of the mind: an "essence," as distinct from an everyday personality. It is this buried part of the psyche—not the "soul" per se, but some deeper and more essential element of a person's being—that Gurdjieff is attempting to expose in this "experiment." For more information on the subject, see E. Hilgard, *Divided Consciousness*. New York: Wiley, 1977. R. Shor and M. Orne, *The Nature of Hypnosis: Selected Basic Readings*. New York: Holt, Rinehart & Winston, 1965.

Page 51: " 'When [a person] is fully grown, and reaches forty years,' says the Koran . . ." On the spiritual significance of a person's fortieth year, see Stanley Brandes, *Forty: The Age and the Symbol*. Knoxville: University of Tennessee Press, 1985.

Page 52: "Contemporary author Andrew Harvey describes one such dream." Andrew Harvey and Mark Matousek, *Dialogues with a Modern Mystic*. Wheaton, IL: Quest Books, 1994, p. 103.

Page 54: For more on punctuated equilibrium, see Stephen Jay Gould. *Ever Since Darwin: Reflections in Natural History*. New York: Norton, 1977.

Page 54: Daniel Levinson, *The Seasons of a Man's Life,* previously cited.

Page 54: Carlos Castaneda, *A Separate Reality*. New York: Simon & Schuster, 1991.

Page 57: *The I Ching or Book of Changes*. New York: Pantheon, 1966.

Page 59: See Gerald Collins, *The Second Journey: Spiritual Awareness and the Mid-Life Crisis*. Ramsey, NJ: Paulist Press, 1978.

Page 59: "Joseph Campbell speaks of it in mythological terms as 'the call to adventure' . . ." Joseph Campbell, *The Hero with a Thousand Faces*. Princeton: Princeton University Press, 1990.

Page 59: ". . . a Gnostic tale known as 'The Hymn of the Pearl.' " For the narrative details of this myth, see Hans Jonas, *The Gnostic Religion*. Boston: Beacon Press, 1963. Giovanni Filoramo, *A History of Gnosticism*. London: Basil Blackwell, 1991.

Page 60: D. T. Suzuki, *Essays in Zen Buddhism First Series*. London: Ryder, 1949. See also William Barrett, ed., *Zen Buddhism: Selected Writings of D. T. Suzuki*. Garden City, NY: Doubleday Anchor, 1956.

Page 67: ". . . as psychiatrist Maurice Nicoll explains it . . ." Maurice Nicoll, *Psychological Commentaries on the Teaching of Gurdjieff and Ouspensky,* vol. V. London: Vincent Stuart, 1960, pp. 1538–39.

Page 67: "Most of us can remember the strangely moving power of passages in certain poems read when we were young . . ." William James, *The Varieties of Religious Experience.* New York: Collier Macmillan, 1961, p. 302.

Page 67: "If the Magnetic Center receives sufficient nourishment . . ." P. D. Ouspensky, *In Search of the Miraculous,* previously cited, p. 200.

Page 70: " '. . . a letter from God left unopened' . . ." See L. Savary, P. Berne, and S. Williams, *Dreams and Spiritual Growth: A Christian Approach to Dreamwork.* New York: Paulist Press, 1984.

Page 73: Plato's allegory of the cave finds its parallel metaphor in the analogy of "Flatland," a mythical two-dimensional world whose inhabitants cannot comprehend that a third dimension could possibly exist. See Edwin A. Abbott, *Flatland.* New York, HarperCollins, 1983. For more on the Flatland concept, see Ken Wilber, *A Brief History of Everything.* Boston: Shambhala, 1996.

Page 75: See Joseph Katz, ed., *The Complete Poems of Stephen Crane.* Ithaca, NY: Cornell University Press, 1972.

Page 76: The term "lucid dream" was first used by Dutch psychiatrist Frederick Van Eeden to describe a condition in which dreamers are fully asleep, yet in some mysterious way are able both to *know* that they are dreaming and in some cases to express a certain degree of volition and control over their dream. Tibetan Buddhist tradition describes the yoga of the dream state as part of a system for achieving enlightenment. Certain schools of Tibetan Buddhism even assert that human beings are as morally responsible for the things that happen to them in their dreams as they are for their behavior during the waking state. See Jayne Gackenbach, "Frameworks for Understanding Lucid Dreaming: A Review," *Dreaming: Journal of the Association for the Study of Dreams* (1991), 1(2): 109–28. S. LaBerge, *Lucid Dreaming: The Power of Being Awake and Aware in Your Dreams.* Los Angeles: Jeremy Tarcher, 1985.

Page 77: See Carl Jung, *Memories, Dreams, Reflections.* New York: Vintage, 1963, p. 160.

Page 80: "We have not even to risk the adventure alone . . ." Joseph Campbell, *The Hero with a Thousand Faces,* previously cited.

Chapter 3

Page 81: "Gilbert Brim, leader of the MacArthur national network . . ." Gilbert Brim, *Ambition: How We Manage Success and Failure Throughout Our Lives.* New York: Basic Books, 1992.

Page 82: Robert McCrae and Paul Costa, "Personality, Coping, and Coping Effectiveness in an Adult Sample," *Journal of Personality* (June 1986), 54: 385–405. Robert McCrae and Paul Costa, "Psychological Maturity and Subjective Well-Being: Toward a New Synthesis," *Developmental Psychology* (March 1983), 19: 243–48.

Page 83: C. Bernard Ruffin, *Padre Pia: The True Story*. Huntington, IN: Our Sunday Visitor, Inc., 1982, p. 249.

Page 90: Leo Tolstoy, *A Confession*. New York: Scribner's, 1923.

Page 93: "In a recent article in *Archives* . . ." Carlo Maggini and Riccardo D. Luche, "Acedia: da vizio capital a disturbo dell'affettivita" ("Acedia: From Deadly Sin to Affective Disorder"), *Archivio di Psycologia, Neurologia e Psychiatria* (April–June 1989), 50(2): 266–72.

Page 93: "The biblical lamentations of Job . . ." Wolfgang Hofmann, "La Plainte de Job: Esssai d'une interpretation psychiatrique" ("Job's Complaint: Attempt at a Psychiatric Interpretation"), *Psychologie Médicale* (March 1989), 21(3): 361–63.

Page 94: "Studies of clinical psychopathology suggest . . ." George B. Kish and David R. Moody, "Psychopathology and Life Purpose," *International Forum for Logotherapy* (Spring 1989), 12(1): 40–45.

Page 94: "These changes in the DSM-IV diagnostic system . . ." Robert P. Turner, et al., "Religious or Spiritual Problem: A Culturally Sensitive Diagnostic Category in the DSM-IV," *Journal of Nervous and Mental Disease* (July 1995), 183(7), 435–44.

Page 96: "In alchemy . . ." For the source of this quote plus more information on Madathanas and spiritual alchemy, see Whitall Perry, *A Treasury of Traditional Wisdom*. New York: Simon & Schuster, 1971, p. 1105.

Page 103: "The Fisherman and the Genie." For a more extended interpretation of this story that is somewhat different from my own, see Allan B. Chinen, *In the Ever After: Fairy Tales and the Second Half of Life*. Wilmette, IL: Chiron, 1989.

Page 107: "The Kansas City Studies of Adult Life, a landmark study of adult life span development . . ." See Richard Williams and Claudine Wirths, *Live Through the Years*. New York: Atherton, 1965.

Page 107: On Gutmann's work, see David Gutmann, *Reclaimed Powers: Toward a New Psychology of Men and Women in Later Life*. New York: Basic Books, 1987. For partial validation of Gutmann's theme with qualifications, see J. James, C. Lewkowicz, J. Liphaber, and M. Lachman, "Rethinking the Gender Identity Crossover Hypothesis: A Test of a New Model," *Sex Roles*, 32(3–4): 185–207.

Page 108: See Betty Friedan, *The Fountain of Age*. New York: Simon & Schuster, 1993.

Page 109: "Women, it seems, as they answer the Call . . ." For more on women's spiritual development in midlife and beyond, see Kathleen Fischer, *Autumn Gospel: Women in the Second Half of Life*. Mahwah, NJ: Paulist Press, 1995. Maria Harris, *Jubilee Time: Celebrating Women, Spirit and the Advent of Age*. New York: Bantam, 1995. Cathleen Rountree, *On Women Turning Fifty*. San Francisco: Harper, 1993.

Page 109: " 'One of the reasons I got interested in Zen' . . ." On women's perspective in Buddhism, see Lenore Friedman, *Meetings with Remarkable Women: Buddhist Teachers in America*. Boston: Shambhala, 1987.

Page 110: "The Lute Player" appears in full in Allan B. Chinen, *Once Upon a Midlife: Classic Stories and Mythic Tales to Illuminate the Middle Years.* Los Angeles: Jeremy Tarcher, 1992.

Page 113: ". . . united, completed—and redeemed." For a further discussion of spirituality and male gender psychology, see Robert Moore and Douglas Gillette, *The Warrior Within: Accessing the Knight in the Male Psyche.* New York: Morrow, 1992. For discussion of gender differences, ego development, and transcendence, see Michael Washburn, *Transpersonal Psychology in Psychoanalytic Perspective.* Albany, NY: SUNY Press, 1994.

Page 114: On St. Teresa, see Carol Lee Flinders, *Enduring Grace: Living Portraits of Seven Women Mystics.* San Francisco: Harper, 1993. Also see Teresa of Avila, *The Way of Perfection.* New York: Doubleday, 1991.

Page 115: For more on Hildegard of Bingen, see Matthew Fox, *Hildegard of Bingen's Book of Divine Works.* Santa Fe: Bear and Company, 1979. Also Gabriele Uhlein, *Meditations with Hildegard of Bingen.* Santa Fe: Bear and Company, 1983. On the role of women in Rhineland mysticism, see Emilie Zum Brunn, *Women Mystics in Medieval Europe.* New York: Paragon, 1989.

Page 118: " 'It is in realizing and in living this sacredness,' writes the religious historian Mircea Eliade . . ." Mircea Eliade, *Myths, Rites, Symbols.* New York: Harper Colophon, 1975, p. 288.

Page 118: "Christine Downing, professor of comparative religion . . ." This quote from Christine Downing's chapter "Female Rites of Passage" in her book *Journey Through Menopause* (New York: Crossroad, 1987) appears in Thomas Cole and Mary Winkler, eds., *The Oxford Book of Aging.* New York: Oxford University Press, 1994, pp. 69–71.

Page 119: " 'Through participation in such rites,' Downing writes . . ." See entry above.

Page 120: ". . . several studies of women at midlife . . ." See Ravenna Helson and Paul Wink, "Personality Change in Women from the Early 40's to the Early 60's," *Psychology and Aging* (March 1992), 7(1): 46–55. Also Valory Mitchell and Ravenna Helson, "Women's Prime of Life: Is It in the 50's?" *Psychology of Women Quarterly* (December 1990), 14(1): 451–47.

Page 123: For more on the life of al-Ghazzali, see W. Montgomery Watt, *The Faith and Practice of Al-Ghazali.* London, Allen & Unwin, 1963.

Chapter 4

Page 128: See Joseph Katz, ed., *The Complete Poems of Stephen Crane.* Ithaca, NY: Cornell University Press, 1972.

Page 130: Janice Brewi and Anne Brennan, *Celebrate Midlife: Jungian Archetypes and Spiritual Perspectives.* New York: Crossroad, 1988, p. 249.

Page 133: "Further insight into the spiritual Search . . ." See Wade Clark Roof, *A Generation of Seekers: The Spiritual Journeys of the Baby Boom Generation.* San Francisco: Harper, 1993.

Page 141: For more on the relationship between sex, spirituality, and the knightly tradition, see Denis de Rougemont, *Love in the Western World.* New York: Doubleday, 1956. Also Bernard O'Donoghue, *The Courtly Love Tradition.* Manchester: Manchester University Press, 1982.

Pages 149: "Joseph Campbell identifies it in mythological terms . . ." Joseph Campbell, *The Hero with a Thousand Faces,* previously cited.

Page 158: "Carl Jung once visited a Southwestern Indian tribe . . ." Jung, *Memories, Dreams, Reflections,* previously cited, pp. 247–48.

Page 160: "Jack Kornfield . . . published the results of a survey . . ." "Sex Lives of the Gurus," *Yoga Journal,* July–August 1985, pp. 26–28.

Page 161: ". . . several decades of scandals involving one prominent religious leader after another . . ." Tony Schwartz, *What Really Matters: Searching for Wisdom in America.* New York: Bantam, 1995, p. 155. See also Katy Butler, "Encountering the Shadow in Buddhist America," *Common Boundary* (May–June 1990). Anthony Storr, *Feet of Clay: The Power and Charisma of Gurus.* New York: Free Press, 1996.

Page 163: ". . . how valuable legitimate spiritual guidance really is." On the subject of choosing a legitimate spiritual path, see D. Anthony, B. Ecker, and K. Wilber, *Spiritual Choices: The Problem of Recognizing Authentic Paths to Inner Transformation.* New York: Paragon, 1987. See also Connie Zweig, *Meeting the Shadow.* Los Angeles: Jeremy Tarcher, 1990.

Page 166: " 'For any of us who return to faith' . . ." Janice Brewi and Anne Brennan, *Celebrate Midlife,* previously cited, p. 249.

Page 167: See Shunryu Suzuki, *Zen Mind, Beginner's Mind.* New York: Weatherhill, 1993.

Page 168: "Professor Needleman writes in a book on contemporary religious movements . . ." See Jacob Needleman and G. Baker, eds., *Understanding the New Religions.* New York: Seabury, 1978. See also Harvey Cox, *Turning East: The Promise and Peril of the New Orientalism.* New York: Simon & Schuster, 1979. R. Ellwood, *Religious and Spiritual Groups in Modern America.* Englewood Cliffs, NJ: Prentice-Hall, 1973.

Chapter 5

Page 179: "Every man has a certain feature in his character which is central." P. D. Ouspensky, *In Search of the Miraculous,* previously cited, p. 226.

Page 180: "When an individual makes an attempt to see his shadow . . ." See Carl Jung et al. *Man and His Symbols.* New York: Doubleday, 1979, p. 168.

Page 184: "One may sometimes surprise the Chief Feature of another . . ." C. Daly King, *The Oragean Version.* Privately printed (Business Photo Reproduction, Inc.), 1951, p. 102.

Page 189: See Daniel Levinson, *The Seasons of a Man's Life,* previously cited; and Daniel Levinson and Judy D. Levinson, *The Seasons of a Woman's Life.* New York, Knopf, 1996. See also Anita Spencer, *Seasons: Women's Search for Self Through Life's Stages.* New York: Paulist Press, 1982.

Page 192: "Charles Drebing and Winston Gooden, recently carried out studies . . ." Charles E. Drebing, Winston E. Gooden, Susan M. Drebing, Hendrinka Van De Kemp, et al., "The Dream in Midlife Women: Its Impact on Mental Health," *International Journal of Aging and Human Development* (1995), 40(1): 73–87. Charles E. Drebing and Winston E. Gooden, "The Impact of the Dream on Mental Health Functioning in the Male Midlife Transition," *International Journal of Aging and Human Development* (1991), 32(4): 277–87.

Page 198: "Aging, according to Dr. Kastenbaum, begins in infancy." See Robert Kastenbaum, "Habituation: A Key to Life Span Development and Aging?" in *Encyclopedia of Adult Development.* Phoenix, AZ: Oryx Press, 1993, pp. 195–97. See also T. J. Tighe and R. H. Leaton, eds., *Habituation.* Hillsdale, NJ: Erlbaum, 1976.

Page 198: "This 'mental reducing valve' . . ." See Aldous Huxley, *The Perennial Philosophy.* New York: Harper, 1944, p. 155. See also A. Huxley, *The Doors of Perception.* New York: Harper, 1963.

Page 201: "Robert Ornstein and Claudio Naranjo in their seminal study . . ." C. Naranjo and R. Ornstein, *On the Psychology of Meditation.* New York: Viking, 1971.

Page 202: Joseph Epes Brown, "The Wisdom of the Contrary," *Parabola* (February 1979), 4(1): 54–66.

Page 204: "Roshi Philip Kapleau tells the story . . ." Philip Kapleau, ed., *The Three Pillars of Zen: Teaching, Practice and Enlightenment.* Boston: Beacon Press, 1965.

Page 205: ". . . one of the great spiritual masters, Nicephorus the Solitary, writes on this very subject . . ." E. Kadloubovsky and G. E. H. Palmer, eds., *Writings from the Philokalia on Prayer of the Heart.* London: Faber & Faber, 1951, p. 32.

Page 205: ". . . the *Spiritual Exercises* of St. Ignatius Loyola . . ." See Anthony Motolla, trans., *Spiritual Exercises of St. Ignatius.* New York: Doubleday, 1964.

Page 206: See Brother Lawrence, *The Practice of the Presence of God,* previously cited, p. 18.

Page 207: For more on the Japanese tea ceremony, see D. Suzuki, *Zen and Japanese Culture.* London: Routledge & Kegan Paul, 1959.

Page 208: "A. Kasumatsu and T. Hirai, performed EEGs . . ." A. Kasamatsu and T. Hirai, "Science of Zazen," *Psychologia* (1963), 6: 86–91. See also Y. A. Akishige, "A Historical Survey of the Psychological Studies on Zen," *Kyushu Psychological Studies* (1968), 5: 1–56.

Page 214: Christopher Lasch, *The Culture of Narcissism.* New York: Norton, 1979.

Page 214: For the seminal article on life review, see Robert Butler, "The Life Review: An Interpretation of Reminiscence in the Aged," *Psychiatry* (1963), 26: 65–76.

Page 219: ". . . 1940s motion picture *It's a Wonderful Life.*" See Donald C. Willis, *The Films of Frank Capra.* Metuchen, NJ: Scarecrow Press, 1974. Also Leland A. Pague, *The Cinema of Frank Capra.* Cranbury, NJ: A. S. Barnes, 1975.

Page 221: For more on regret and counterfactual thinking, see Janet Landman, *Regret: The Persistence of the Possible.* New York: Oxford University Press, 1993. See also Mary K. DeGenova, "If You Had Your Life to Live Over Again: What Would You Do Differently?" *International Journal of Aging and Human Development* (1992), 34(2): 135–43.

Page 222: See G. Gallup, "Fifty Years of Gallup Surveys on Religion," *The Gallup Report,* No. 236, 1985.

Chapter 6

Page 235: See Roger Gould, *Transformations.* New York: Touchstone, 1979.

Page 235: See Gordon Allport, *The Individual and His Religion: A Psychological Interpretation.* New York: Macmillan, 1950.

Page 237: "I had to pay the price of admission." What Marjorie Stoner discovered during her Search and Struggle is sometimes referred to in psychotherapeutic literature as "transitional faith." For more on this subject, see Vicky Genia, "Transitional Faith: A Developmental Step Toward Religious Maturity," *Counseling and Values* (October 1992), 37(1): 15–24.

Page 238: ". . . ninety-two terminal cancer patients . . ." Clifford H. Swenson, Steffen Fuller, and Richard Clements, "Stages of Religious Faith and Reactions to Terminal Cancer," *Journal of Psychology and Theology,* (Fall 1993), 21(3): 238–45.

Page 242: For more on helping and service, see Ram Dass and Paul Gorman, *How Can I Help?* New York: Knopf, 1985.

Page 242: ". . . sixty-five men and women between the ages of thirty and ninety." Kathleen Stetz, "The Relationship among Background Characteristics, Purpose in Life, and Caregiving Demands on Perceived Health of Spouse Caregivers." *Scholarly Inquiry for Nursing Practice* (Summer 1989), 3(2): 133–53.

Page 250: "That was the really big thing: I could forgive her." On the importance of forgiveness in psycho-spiritual development, see John Gartner, "The Capacity to Forgive: An Object Relations Perspective," in Mark Finn and John Gartner, eds., *Object Relations Theory and Religion: Clinical Applications.* Westport, CT: Praeger, 1992. See also Charlotte M. Rosenak and Mark G. Harnden, "Forgiveness in the Psychotherapeutic Process: Clinical Applications, *Journal of Psychology and Christianity* (1992), 11(2): 188–97.

Page 256: "Meditation, in a nutshell, is a means of stilling the mind by focusing attention . . ." See M. West, ed., *The Psychology of Meditation.* Oxford: Clarendon Press, 1987. D. Shapiro, Jr., and R. Walsh, eds., *Meditation: Classic and Contemporary Perspectives.* New York: Aldine, 1984.

Page 256: For further information on the process of meditation and spiritual development, see Daniel Goleman, *The Meditative Mind: The Varieties of Meditative Experience.* Los Angeles: Jeremy Tarcher, 1988.

Page 257: "A statement from American Zen Buddhist master Bernard Glassman . . ." Quoted in Peter Occhiogrosso, *Through the Labyrinth: Stories of the Search for Spiritual Transformation in Everyday Life.* New York: Viking, 1991, p. 162.

Page 260: "There were times when prayer itself brought up uncomfortable, distressing thoughts and feelings . . ." Dan Wakefield, *Returning: A Spiritual Journey.* New York: Doubleday, 1988.

Page 261: ". . . shaking your fist at God." See Pierre Wolf, *May I Hate God?* Paulist Press, 1979.

Page 263: "The passage I was searching for was folded down." See Sören Kierkegaard, *The Journals of Kierkegaard* (Alexander Dru, trans.). New York: Harper, 1959, p. 201.

Chapter 7

Page 269: " 'Go deeper,' the Zen Buddhist roshi said." Philip Kapleau, ed., *The Three Pillars of Zen.* Boston: Beacon Press, 1965, p. 253.

Page 270: "Then all at once I was struck . . ." Philip Kapleau, ed., *The Three Pillars of Zen,* previously cited, p. 205.

Page 270: "The Italian psychiatrist Roberto Assagioli characterizes . . ." See Assagioli's essay "Self-realization and Psychological Disturbances," previously cited, p. 37.

Page 271: ". . . sought after in all spiritual traditions . . ." For the idea of Breakthrough in the Christian mystical tradition, see Matthew Fox, *Breakthrough: Meister Eckhart's Creation Spirituality.* Garden City, NY: Doubleday, 1980.

Page 272: "St. Paul refers to . . . 'the peace that passeth understanding.' " See John White, ed., *The Highest State of Consciousness.* New York: Doubleday, 1972.

Page 274: "This search was an integral part of life for primordial people across the globe . . ." See M. Harner, *The Way of the Shaman: A Guide to Power and Healing.* San Francisco: Harper, 1980. Also John Hallifax, *Shaman: The Wounded Healer.* New York: Crossroad, 1981.

Page 274: "Bronislaw Malinowski writes . . ." Bronislaw Malinowski, *Magic, Science and Religion and Other Essays.* New York: Free Press, 1948, p. 56.

Page 274: "the great malady of the twentieth century," writes Thomas Moore . . ." Thomas Moore, *Care of the Soul.* New York: HarperCollins, 1992.

Page 275: "But where, one asks, is mention made of altered states of consciousness . . . ?" See Charles Tart, ed., *Altered States of Consciousness.* 3rd ed.; New York: HarperCollins, 1990.

Page 275: For William James's most condensed and specific writings on mysticism, see William James, *The Varieties of Religious Experience,* previously cited, Lectures 16 and

17. See also E. Taylor, *William James on Exceptional Mental States: The 1896 Lowell Lectures*. Amherst: University of Massachusetts Press, 1984.

Page 276: For more information on transpersonal psychology, see Charles Tart, *Open Mind, Discriminating Mind: Reflections on Human Possibilities*. San Francisco: Harper, 1986. Ken Wilber, J. Engler, and D. Brown, *Transformations of Consciousness: Conventional and Contemplative Perspectives on Development*. Boston: Shambhala, 1986. Robert Ornstein, *The Psychology of Consciousness*. San Francisco: W. H. Freeman, 1972.

Page 276: "In a 1988 Gallup survey titled 'The Unchurched American' . . ." See George Gallup, Jr., and Jim Castelli, *The People's Religion: American Faith in the 90's*. New York: Macmillan, 1989.

Page 278: "A peak experience is, to a degree, absolute." Katinka Matson, *The Psychology Today Omnibook of Personal Development*. New York: Morrow, 1977, p. 310. See also Abraham Maslow, *Toward a Psychology of Being*. Princeton, NJ: Van Nostrand Reinhold, 1968. Also Gordon L. Flett, Kirk R. Blankstein, and Paul L. Hewitt, "Factor Structure of the Short Index of Self-actualization," *Journal of Social Behavior and Personality* (1991), 6(5): 321–29.

Page 279: "Arthur Koestler describes an experience . . ." Quoted in Colin Wilson, *The Occult*. New York: Vintage, 1971, pp. 561–62.

Page 280: Jack Kornfield, *A Path with a Heart*, New York: Bantam, 1993, p. 109.

Page 280: "For someone living an uptight, head-restricted experience, a hot bath can feel extraordinary." See Jacob Needleman, *The Heart of Philosophy*. San Francisco: Harper, 1986.

Page 281: "In the spring of 1967 I was living in New York's East Village . . ." On the impact of psychedelics in the 1960s, see Jay Stevens, *Storming Heaven: LSD and the American Dream*. New York: Perennial Library, 1987. See also Robert S. Ellwood, *The Sixties Spiritual Awakening*. New Brunswick, NJ: Rutgers University Press, 1994. Walter Truett Anderson, *The Upstart Spring: Esalen and the American Awakening*. Reading, MA: Addison-Wesley, 1983.

Page 284: "Wilson quotes Aldous Huxley . . ." Quoted in Colin Wilson, *The Outsider*. New York: Delta, 1956, p. 299.

Page 285: "It was just then that I had my Experience." J. D. Salinger, *Nine Stories*. Boston: Little, Brown, 1953, p. 250.

Page 286: ". . . the following narrative from a British schoolboy . . ." Quoted in F. C. Happold, *Mysticism: A Study and an Anthology*. Harmondsworth: Penguin, 1971, p. 130.

Page 286: "Another fragmentary Breakthrough moment is described by Pamela Gordon . . ." Dan Wakefield, *Expect a Miracle: When Miraculous Things Happen to Ordinary People*. New York: Walker, 1996.

Page 287: Psychologist James Fowler tells of a poignant Breakthrough moment. See James Fowler, *Stages of Faith*. San Francisco: Harper, 1981. On death as the teacher, see Ernest Becker, *The Denial of Death*. New York: Free Press, 1973. Stanislov Grof and Joan Hallifax, *The Human Encounter with Death*. New York: Dutton, 1977.

Page 288: "One tells of a British armored car officer hit . . ." Colin Wilson, *The Occult,* previously cited, p. 345.

Page 289: "The British officer's story brings to mind another testimony." Richard Wilhelm, trans., *The I Ching,* previously cited, pp. xxv–xxvi.

Page 289: Tolstoy's great novelette *The Death of Ivan Ilyich.* Count Tolstoy's great novelette has been translated and anthologized in numerous short story collections. See, for instance, Maynard Mack et al., eds., *World Masterpieces,* vol. II. New York: Norton, 1956.

Page 292: "The Indian poet Rabindranath Tagore underwent . . ." *Values.* London: Unwin Brothers Ltd, Printed for Private Circulation, 1951, p. 35.

Page 292: "Bernard Glassman, a contemporary American Zen master, tells of his Breakthrough . . ." Peter Ochiogrosso, *Through the Labyrinth,* previously cited, p. 99.

Page 293: "A firsthand account of transfiguration has come down to us from a disciple . . ." See Kenneth Leech, *True Prayer: An Invitation to True Christian Spirituality.* Harrisburg, PA: Morehouse, 1995.

Page 295: "Richard Jefferies . . . *The Story of My Heart* . . ." Quoted in Happold, *Mysticism: A Study and an Anthology,* previously cited, pp. 385–88.

Page 296: "In his famous book *Cosmic Consciousness* . . ." See R. M. Bucke, *Cosmic Consciousness: A Study in the Evolution of the Human Mind.* New Hyde Park, NY: University Books, 1961.

Page 297: "Such a moment is described by an anonymous woman known only by her initials, C.M.C." As collected by Dr. R. M. Bucke, *Cosmic Consciousness;* see entry above.

Page 297: "The Roman Catholic monk Bede Griffiths in his autobiography . . ." Bede Griffiths, *The Golden String,* New York: P. J. Kennedy & Sons, 1954.

Page 303: Thornton Wilder, *Our Town.* New York: Coward-McCann, 1938. See the end of Act III.

Page 308: ". . . the concluding lines of the poem *The Conference of the Birds.*" See Farid Ud-Din Attar, *The Conference of the Birds* (C. S. Nott, trans.). London: Routledge & Kegan Paul, 1954, pp. 131–33.

Page 309: "To walk, we have to lean forward . . ." Skynner's words were cited by the British actor Patrick Stewart, *Star Trek*'s famous Captain Picard, at the memorial service for Gene Roddenberry, creator of the *Star Trek* series. See *Entertainment Weekly,* May 6, 1994, p. 25.

Chapter 8

Page 311: "This must be like what the early Christians experienced . . ." An important vehicle used today by a number of Christians is the method known as "contemplative prayer." One of the principal expounders of this method is Thomas Keating. See his *Invitation to Love: The Way of Christian Contemplation.* Shaftesbury, Dorset:

Element Books, 1992. See also M. Basil Pennington, *Centering Prayer: Renewing an Ancient Christian Prayer Form.* New York: Image Books, 1982.

Page 311: ". . . the autobiography of Edwin 'Buzz' Aldrin . . ." Edwin Aldrin, *Return to Earth.* New York: Random House, 1973.

Page 312: "We do not understand that life is paradise . . ." Fyodor Dostoevsky, *The Brothers Karamazov* (Ralph Matlow and Constance Garnett, trans.). New York: Norton, 1976, p. 273.

Page 312: "The unitive life is not lived apart from humanity." Frances Vaughan, *The Inward Arc.* Boston: Shambhala, 1986, pp. 95–96.

Page 312: Somerset Maugham, *The Razor's Edge.* Garden City, NY: Doubleday, 1944.

Page 313: "When Freud looked at mysticism . . ." Sigmund Freud, *Civilization and Its Discontents.* New York: Norton, 1961. See also Freud, *The Future of an Illusion.* On Freud's reductionist confusion of mature religious experience with regressive infantile narcissism, see Ken Wilber, "The Pre-Trans Fallacy," in R. Walsh and Frances Vaughan, eds., *Paths Beyond Ego: The Transpersonal Vision.* Los Angeles: Jeremy Tarcher, 1993. See also Mark Epstein, *Thoughts Without a Thinker.* New York: Basic Books, 1995.

Page 314: "Dag Hammarskjöld, to take a contemporary figure . . ." For the source of the quotes included here, see Dag Hammarskjöld, *Markings.* New York: Knopf, 1964. On the inner life of Dag Hammarskjöld, see Sven Stolpe, *Dag Hammarskjöld: A Spiritual Portrait* (Naomi Walford, trans.). New York: Scribner's, 1966.

Page 315: "A classic example is the story of Theseus and the Minotaur." For a thorough discussion of labyrinths and the spiritual quest, see Penelope Reed Doob, *The Idea of the Labyrinth from Classical Antiquity Through the Middle Ages.* Ithaca, NY: Cornell University Press, 1990. For information on ways the labyrinth is used in spiritual practice today, see Lauren Artress, *Walking a Sacred Path: Rediscovering the Labyrinth as a Spiritual Tool.* New York: Riverhead Books, 1995.

Page 319: "I use the term inflation . . ," Edward Eddinger, *Ego and Archetype.* Baltimore: Penguin, 1973, p. 7.

Page 320: "Christianity also practically equates sin with inflation . . ." Edward Eddinger, *Ego and Archetype,* previously cited, p. 63.

Page 322: See Hans Selye, *Stress, Not Distress.* Philadelphia: Lippincott, 1974. See also Hans Selye, *The Stress of Life.* Rev. ed.; New York: McGraw-Hill, 1976.

Page 323: "Joseph Campbell dedicates a section of his book . . ." Joseph Campbell, *The Hero with a Thousand Faces,* previously cited, pp. 193–96.

Page 325: "Consider the story of American Zen Master Charlotte Beck." Lenore Friedman, *Meetings with Remarkable Women,* previously cited.

Page 326: "How to live more meaningfully with those we love . . ." Rick Fields et al., *Chop Wood, Carry Water.* Los Angeles: J. P. Tarcher, 1984.

Page 326: "I think the biggest koan study is the study of our life." Lenore Friedman, *Meetings with Remarkable Women,* previously cited, p. 89.

Page 326: "Writer Emilie Griffin reached the same conclusion . . ." Emilie Griffin, *Turning: Reflections on the Experience of Conversion.* Garden City, NY: Doubleday, 1980. For a psychological perspective on conversion experience, see C. Christensen, "Religious Conversion," *Archives of General Psychiatry* (1963), 9: 207–16. Lewis R. Rambo, *The Psychology of Conversion.* Birmingham, AL: Religious Education Press, 1992.

Page 327: "Merton himself tells the story   ." see Edward Rice, *The Man in the Sycamore Tree. The Good Life and Hard Times of Thomas Merton,* New York: Harcourt Brace, 1985.

Page 328: "We are not converted only once . . ." Thomas Merton, letter appearing in *Informations Catholiques Internationales* (April 1973), cited by J. Pasquier, "Experience and Conversion," *The Way* (1977), 17: 121.

Page 328: "In an interview McClelland talked about . . ." Joan Borysenko, "Healing Motives: An Interview with David C. McClelland, *Advances* (Spring 1985), 2(2): 35–37. See also Allan Luks, with Peggy Payne, *The Helping Power of Doing Good.* New York: Fawcett Columbine, 1991. Pitirim Sorokin, ed., *Forms and Techniques of Altruistic and Spiritual Growth.* Boston: Beacon Press, 1971.

Page 331: ". . . the mystical side of Judaism as embodied in the Kabbalah." For studies of the Kabbalah, see Charles Poncé, *Kabbalah: An Introduction.* San Francisco: Straight Arrow Press, 1973. Also Adolphe Frank: *The Kabbalah.* N.p.: University Books, 1967.

Page 334: Bernadette Roberts, *The Path to No-Self: Life at the Center.* Albany: SUNY Press, 1994. See also Bernadette Roberts, *The Experience of No-Self: A Contemplative Journey.* Rev. ed.; Albany: SUNY Press, 1994.

Page 334: "One reservation is needed . . ." Thomas Merton, *Zen and the Birds of Appetite.* New York: New Directions, 1968, p. 114

Page 334: "Somewhere in the back of the contemplative mind . . ." Bernadette Roberts, *The Path to No-Self,* previously cited, p. 45.

Page 337: "For Rachel the bas mitzvah represented an essential rite of passage . . ." On midlife rituals in the Jewish tradition, see Irene Fine, *Midlife and Its Rite of Passage Ceremony.* San Diego: Women's Institute for Continuing Jewish Education, 1983.

Page 339: "According to both ancient Egyptian and Buddhist doctrine . . ." See E. A. Wallis Budge, *The Book of the Dead: The Hieroglyphic Transcript of the Papyrus of Abi.* New Hyde Park, NY: University Books, n.d. See also W. Y. Evans-Wentz, *The Tibetan Book of the Dead.* New York: Oxford University Press, 1972.

Page 340: "In the process he becomes what the Bible terms the 'New Man.' " For more on the concept of *metanoia* and spiritual self-change from both a psychological and a biblical perspective, see Maurice Nicoll, *The New Man: An Interpretation of Some Parables and Miracles of Christ.* London: Vincent Stuart, 1950.

Page 346: "Hearing Jacob talk about his strange dream . . ." Jacob's dream, like Jung's experience on the operating table, presents imagery that is strangely consistent with popularly reported near-death experiences: moving through a dark tunnel, an encounter with judgment or life review, wise beings of light, and a reluctant return to the harsh material world. Recent studies of near-death phenomena, however, suggest that such imagery differs from person to person. See William J. Serdahely, "Variations from the Protypic Near-Death Experience: The 'Individually Tailored' Hypothesis," *Journal of Near Death Studies* (Spring 1995), 13(3): 185–96.

Page 346: For a complete description of Jung's near-death experience, see Jung, *Memories, Dreams, Reflections,* previously cited, Chapter 10. On near-death experiences, see also K. Ring, *Heading Toward Omega: In Search of the Meaning of Near-Death Experience.* New York: Morrow, 1984.

Page 349: This retelling of Narada's dream is based on a version presented by Heinrich Zimmer. See Heinrich Zimmer, *Myths and Symbols in Indian Art and Civilization.* New York: Harper Torchbooks, 1965, pp. 27–34.

Index

ABOUT THE AUTHORS

Harry R. Moody, Ph.D., is the cofounder and executive director of the Brook-dale Center on Aging at Hunter College. A graduate of Yale with a doctorate in philosophy from Columbia University, he has been a leading researcher in the field of aging for the past two decades. He lives in Westchester, New York. *David Carroll* has written several books on spirituality and self-help and is the author of an Emmy award-winning television production. He also lives in Westchester, New York.